SINGING THE GLORY OF LORD KRISHNA

American Academy of Religion
Classics in Religious Studies

Number 5
Baṛu Caṇḍīdāsa
SINGING THE GLORY OF LORD KRISHNA
The *Śrīkṛṣṇakīrtana*
translated and annotated by
M. H. Klaiman

Baṛu Caṇḍīdāsa

SINGING THE GLORY OF LORD KRISHNA

The *Śrīkṛṣṇakīrtana*
translated and annotated by
M. H. Klaiman

Scholars Press
Chico, California

SINGING THE GLORY OF LORD KRISHNA

by

Baṛu Caṇḍīdāsa

The *Śrīkṛṣṇakīrtana*
translated and annotated by
M. H. Klaiman

Library of Congress Cataloging in Publication Data

Baṛu Caṇḍīdāsa.
Singing the glory of Lord Krishna.

(Classics in religious studies / Scholars Press and the American Academy of Religion ; no. 5)
Translation of: Śrīkṛṣṇakīrtana.
Bibliography: p.
1. Krishna (Hindu deity)—Poetry. I. Klaiman, M. H. II. Title. III. Series: Classics in religious studies ; no. 5.
PK1718.B353S613 1984 891'.4412 84–3905
ISBN 0–89130–736-2
ISBN 0–89130–737–0 (pbk.)

Printed in the United States of America
on acid-free paper

This work is the richer for the interest and guidance
of SUKUMAR SEN—
a scholar—a teacher—
a great mind.

Contents

Preface

Apart from my own limitations, there have been obstacles in the production of this work, obstacles which would not have been overcome without the timely intervention of various parties. To acknowledge the latter, and in the hope of saying something instructive about the former, I am burdening this already lengthy manuscript with a preface.

Śrīkṛṣṇakīrtana (SKK) first came to my attention as the most important of Middle Bengali literary texts in 1976. I was at that time a Fulbright scholar in Calcutta, India, making a preliminary search of materials for a doctoral dissertation in linguistics. From 1978 to 1980, under the sponsorship of the American Institute of Indian Studies, I returned to Calcutta to write a dissertation on Bengali semantics and historical syntax. I had, in the interim, read the whole of SKK and excerpted the portions needed for the dissertation.

It had also occurred to me in the interim that the text had value for extralinguistic purposes and ought to be translated into English. At the outset I did not know that the same idea had already occurred to several capable scholars, none of whom succeeded in producing the desired translation. Over the years I have come to appreciate why not.

The first difficulty in studying Middle Bengali, let along translating the literature of that period, is finding a teacher both competent and willing to assist. The University of Calcutta scholar with whom I first read SKK in 1976 pushed away the text after a few sessions with a grimace and the comment, “It's too vulgar.” Subsequently I read SKK for a year with Dr. Edward Dimock at my home institution, the University of Chicago. Upon returning to Calcutta in 1978, for want of immediate assistance with SKK, I studied it independently for a time in the library of the Bangiya Sahitya Parisat or Bengal Academy of Literature. This is the institution which holds the original manuscript and publishes the text. Later in 1978 I was permitted to embark on what turned into two years' study of SKK with a legendary expert on Indian linguistics and the Bengali language.

I do not pretend, incidentally, that dedicating this work to that person has appreciably lessened the debt he is owed. Simply stated, were it not for his interest, genius and generosity, no English translation of SKK would exist today.

By this time, translating SKK had become my objective in studying it.

The need then arose for a photocopy of the original manuscript. This led to unanticipated complications. The Bangiya Sahitya Parisat, repository of the SKK manuscript, was no longer providing scholars with microfilmed and photocopied reproductions at a few hundred rupees' cost. My efforts to persuade them to reinstate the service were unavailing.

I had nearly given up hope on the matter when an unexpected ally materialized in the person of Nilratan Sen, a Bengali specialist at Kalyani University, West Bengal. Over a year's time, Dr. Sen arranged to obtain a photocopy of the manuscript at nominal cost from a source outside Calcutta, a source that had much earlier secured a duplicate microfilm of the SKK manuscript from the Bangiya Sahitya Parisat. Arriving in good condition a few months prior to my departure from the field, the photocopy has served well in clearing up doubtful and conflicting readings in published editions of SKK. For this I owe Dr. Sen, his family and associates my warm gratitude.

I am also in debt to Dr. Pabitra Sarkar, a member of the Bengali department at Jadavpur University, Calcutta, for going over a highly preliminary form of the translation before my departure from the field in 1980.

Following the fieldwork stage of the project, two obstacles to completing it had to be addressed. The first problem was finding a source of sponsorship for the project, which was up till that point unsponsored. The second was finding a publisher willing to bring the material to light. Sponsors and publishers are both difficult to obtain for translations of little-known Indian texts. Moreover, as I gradually learned, the chances for success further decrease when the text in question is neither old enough to shine in the prestige of Sanskrit culture, nor young enough to be regarded as contemporary writing.

In recent years, applications for academic projects involving translations of Asian texts have been entertained by a few scholarly organizations in the US. These include the American Institute of Indian Studies, the Translations Program of the National Endowment for the Humanities, and the Translations Project Group of the Association for Asian Studies. These as well as several less likely funding sources were approached, but none could be persuaded to lend assistance to SKK. Similary, publishers in India and Great Britain to whom SKK was proposed all declined it, invariably in the express fear that its publication would prove a financial liability.

The project made no progress for about a year owing to these problems and, even more so, to their effect on morale. However, a series of events beginning in early 1982 conspired to revitalize the endeavor.

I was fortunate, first of all, to receive valuable and practical advice through discussions with Dr. Anoop Chandola of the University of Arizona; later, with his colleague, Dr. Richard Eaton; and still later, with

Dr. James Foard of Arizona State University.

A second factor was the award—for the purpose of translating SKK—of a Visiting Scholarship in the Center for Asian Studies at Arizona State University for 1982–1983.

Finally, a major impetus to the completion of this work has been the interest taken in it by Scholars Press and by representatives of the American Academy of Religion, which has sponsored this publication.

I am, accordingly, indebted to a number of individuals for having mediated in the crucial last stages of the birth of this translation: to Dr. Sheldon Simon, Director of the Center for Asian Studies at Arizona State University; to Betty Parker, the Center secretary, who assisted in proofreading the manuscript; to the former Editor and Production Manager of Scholars Press, Dr. Davis Perkins, who responded promptly and enthusiastically in 1982 to my publication proposal; to Drs. James O. Duke and William A. Clebsch of the American Academy of Religion, who helped steer my manuscript through the AAR publications process; and to the Scholars Press staff directed by Dr. Conrad Cherry.

There is, in addition, one person to be acknowledged, a person who has been with the translator almost from the conception of this project, and who has remained nearby to the end of the labor. As the spirit of *madana*, enmaddening love, manifestly guides and sustains the poetic momentum of *Śrīkṛṣṇakīrtana* so, for me too, there is one Madan who sustains, supports, loves and inspires, and who has tangibly and intangibly contributed to *Śrīkṛṣṇakīrtana* through an unfailing interest in its translator.

Introduction

For more than half a century, a translation of Baṛu Caṇḍīdāsa's *Śrīkṛṣṇakīrtana* (SKK) has been needed by persons who lack Middle Bengali language skills, since without a consideration of the actual text it is impossible to choose among conflicting scholarly evaluations of SKK's content and significance. This is the first of two motives for bringing the work out in translation. The other motive—and the point of this introduction—is to suggest a reexamination of the intellectual and social origins of the religious movement to which SKK pertains, the Bengal Vaishnava movement.

Since its discovery in 1910, SKK has received almost simultaneously the richest scholarly praise and the most damning criticism. According to one scholar, "The 'Śrī-Kṛṣṇa-Kīrttana' belongs to what may be called . . . *Early Middle Bengali* . . . and its importance in the study of Bengali, in the absence of other genuine texts, is as great as that of the works of Layamon, Orm and Chaucer in English."[1] Another scholar states, "It will be acknowledged by connoisseurs of poetry that the advent of Baṛu Caṇḍīdāsa at the outset of the true medieval [period of] Bengali literature is an event worthy of note from various standpoints, and that his *Śrīkṛṣṇakīrtana* is a work of unprecedented choiceness, not only for the middle ages, but for the whole of Bengali literature."[2]

On the other hand, the scholar Majumdar dismisses the poet and his masterwork, remarking, ". . . the gross nature of this work leads us to believe that the poet was incapable of writing any good lyric."[3] In the same vein Sukumar Sen attributes to SKK a quality of "coarseness," stating that the tone of the work is "jarred at times by obscenity."[4] He also disagrees with the earliness of the date assigned to the work by certain scholars; the substance of his objections will be examined below.

Unfortunately, the question of SKK's "choiceness" or "coarseness" goes beyond differences in literary taste. What is at stake is the dating of

[1] Suniti Kumar Chatterji, *The Origin and Development of the Bengali Language*, 3 vols. (London: Allen & Unwin, 1970), 1:129.

[2] Asitkumar Bandyopadhyay, *Bāṃlā sāhityera itibṛtta*, 3d ed. (Calcutta: Modern Book Agency, 1970–), 1:348 [in Bengali]. For convenience I have translated the cited passage from the original Bengali.

[3] A. K. Majumdar, *Caitanya: His Life and Doctrine* (Bombay: Bharatiya Vidya Bhavan, 1969), p. 79, n. 16.

[4] Sukumar Sen, *Chandidas* (Delhi: Sahitya Akademi, 1971), p. 52.

the text and its authenticity as a Vaishnava composition.

It is significant that SKK's detractors usually disavow SKK's connection to Caitanya, the medieval Vaishnava saint of Bengal. Majumdar, for instance, precedes his remark on SKK's "gross nature" by saying, "Most probably Caitanya had not read the *Śrī-Kṛṣṇa-kīrtana*. . . . It is difficult to subscribe to the view that the Caṇḍīdāsa whose songs Caitanya enjoyed was the author of the *Śrī-Kṛṣṇa-kīrtana*."[5] Sen for his part comments, "the main note of the poem running through the whole of it is frankly erotic, so much so that it is really hard to believe that these songs had obtained approval from Chaitanya."[6] The logic of these views seems to be this: SKK could not have been liked by Caitanya; if it were not liked by Caitanya, in all likelihood it was not known of, or given any attention, by Caitanya; if Caitanya were ignorant of it, it cannot be an authentic pre-Caitanya work.

However, as Bandyopadhyay points out,[7] Caitanya's presumed lack of acquaintance with SKK does not entail that the work postdates his life. There is evidence internal to the text that it considerably predates the age of Caitanya. Furthermore, there are indications that his contemporaries knew the text,[8] and there is even some evidence that Caitanya listened approvingly to recitations of portions of SKK.[9] Details will be given later.

Scholarly reluctance to accept evidence of SKK's historical status reflects the current state of research on early Bengal Vaishnavism. In all humility I must point out that what I shall have to say on the subject conflicts with the views of many better established scholars in the field, including my own teachers. I would nevertheless suggest that the current confusion in scholarly opinion about SKK—the earliest extant Bengali language Vaishnava text—is due to certain mistaken tendencies in the analysis of Bengal Vaishnavism itself. These are, first, the tendency to equate Bengal Vaishnavism with Caitanyaism and, second, the tendency to adopt a sanitized view of the social milieu and intellectual origins of the early Bengal Vaishnava faith. Moreover, the latter tendency (in my opinion) stems from a common willingness of scholars both Western and Eastern to accept uncritically the image which the Vaishnava movement presents of itself, an image deliberately cultivated through the movement's liturgical writings and through Vaishnava biographies of Caitanya. There is, consequently, an unmet need to assess the origins of Bengal Vaishnavism in light of facts about the social history and human

[5] Majumdar, *Caitanya*, pp. 78–79.

[6] Sen, *Chandidas*, p. 13.

[7] Bandyopadhyay, *Itibṛtta*, p. 314.

[8] *Ibid.*, pp. 304 ff.

[9] S. K. De, *Early History of the Vaiṣṇava Faith and Movement in Bengal* (Calcutta: General Printers & Publishers, 1942), p. 84.

geography of Bengal. The next section is intended to address this need.

* * *

Originating in central India just prior to the first Christian millennium, the cult of Viṣṇu-Krishna spread over the following centuries to the north and south extremes of the Indian subcontinent. In the fourth through sixth centuries A.D., the cult made steady progress eastward.[10] There an intense artistic development of Vaishnava themes gave rise to the twelfth-century Sanskrit work *Gītagovinda* by the Bengali poet Jayadeva. A sect of Bengali Vaishnavas arose in the sixteenth century attributing its leadership to the charismatic and saintly Caitanya. In time, this movement developed the philosophical and theological apparatus of a distinct religion. Recently, with the emergence of a Western subsect of Bengal Vaishnavism—the Hare Krishnas (ISKCON)[11]—the cult of Krishna may even be said to have evolved into a world religion.

Studies of Bengal Vaishnavism assign Caitanya a position as the movement's founder, catalyst and central figure—not less than a saint in the dispassionate view of the scholarly, and in the minds of believers, Radha and Krishna come to earth in a single body. The major events of his life are without doubt of paramount importance for the study of the movement's origins.

He was born Viśvambhara Miśra in Navadvīpa (modern West Bengal) in 1486, the last child of Brahman parents. Of their ten offspring only Viśvambhara and an older brother survived.[12] He was given an education appropriate to his caste and to the modest circumstances of his family. After completing his studies, he became a teacher. For pecuniary reasons he not only followed this profession locally but also, for several months, in eastern Bengal. The tour is said to have been a financial success.

In his youth he had a reputation as a merciless critic and teaser of the local Vaishnavas. It was therefore a matter of joy and consternation for them when the twenty-four-year-old Viśvambhara, sent to Gayā to perform funeral rituals for his newly deceased father, returned home suddenly and ecstatically converted to the faith. In time he would take the monastic name Śrīkṛṣṇa Caitanya (He who has Consciousness of

[10] Suvira Jaiswal, *The Origin and Development of Vaiṣṇavism* (Delhi: Munshiram Manoharlal, 1967), chap. 6 ("Extent of Influence").

[11] The Hare Krishna (ISKCON) organization was founded in New York in the mid-sixties by an adherent of Caitanyite Vaishnavism. This individual, most commonly known as A. C. Bhaktivedanta Swami, was originally named Abhay Charan De and was born in Calcutta on September 1, 1896.

[12] Majumdar, *Caitanya*, p. 108, states that the first eight children of the family did not survive and that all of these were girls. Causes of their deaths are unreported. For a study of the status of female children in rural Indian families see Barbara D. Miller, *The Endangered Sex* (Ithaca, NY: Cornell University Press, 1981).

Krishna).[13] In Navadvīpa, he propagated a style of religious practice involving public celebration of Krishna's worship (*saṃkīrtana*) complete with song, dance and processions. Not only did he succeed in inculcating this new practice among numerous followers, but he also dramatically neutralized local opposition to his fledgling movement. The opposition arose from two quarters: orthodox Hindus, largely followers of the Śākta sect; and the kazi or Muslim magistrate, the local representative of the Muslim rulers of the country. When this magistrate issued a prohibitive order against *saṃkīrtana*, Caitanya promptly led a procession of followers en masse to the magisterial residence. Following negotiations, the Navadvīpa Vaishnavas received carte blanche to carry out religious practices as they saw fit.

Caitanya, then, organized his followers and legitimized their community standing within a year of his own conversion. Thereafter, as if to reconfirm his accomplishment, he abruptly withdrew from the community. In early 1510 he renounced his home and journeyed to various places under the traditional regimen of an itinerant ascetic. He went first to southern India, accompanied by at most one or two disciples and staying strictly with fellow Brahmans along the route. During his travels he welcomed into the fellowship of Vaishnavism many of the rejected of orthodox Hindu society: untouchables, degraded Hindus, and even occasional recanting Muslims. In personal conduct, however, Caitanya was obedient to the rules of his caste and station, touching no food not prepared by Brahmans and scrupulously shielding himself and his disciples from contact with women.

After his southern tour Caitanya journeyed to the sacred Vaishnava shrines of Vṛndāvana in northern India. On the return journey he met two brothers, Rūpa and Sanātana, men destined to become important figures in the Bengal Vaishnava movement. At the time of meeting the saint they were, however, degraded Hindus—Brahmans who had lost caste on account of having served in the court of Husein Shah, the Muslim ruler of Bengal.

Caitanya had a genius for choosing lieutenants of loyalty and distinguished ability. He gave the two brothers instruction and dispatched them to Vṛndāvana. Eventually they and their nephew Jīva would be reckoned among the six Vṛndāvana goswāmins, or masters of the faith, hand-selected by Caitanya to provide the movement's theological and liturgical basis.

For his part Caitanya wrote virtually nothing. At the age of thirty he

[13] Norvin J. Hein, "Caitanya's Ecstasies and the Theology of the Name," in *Hinduism: New Essays in the History of Religions*, ed. Bardwell L. Smith (Leiden: E. J. Brill, 1976), pp. 15–32.

gave up all direct activity in the Vaishnava movement, evidently preferring to remain in a constant state of ecstatic communion with the sublime. He settled in the company of some disciples at Puri, where he remained until his death in 1533.

Majumdar evaluates Caitanya as "the founder of the last great Vaiṣṇava sect."[14] De, in a more cautious tone, states that "Although the term Bengal Vaiṣṇavism is not co-extensive with the religious system associated with the name of Caitanya and his adherents . . . Caitanyaism . . . is Vaiṣṇavism *par excellence* in Bengal."[15] A few pages later he asserts, "It is difficult to say in what particular form Vaiṣṇavism existed in Bengal before Caitanya."[16] Mukherji characterizes the time of Caitanya as an era of "lamentable decadence of religious life and ideals in Bengal."[17] Vaishnavism there was "in a wretched and degenerated condition. . . . At this time Caitanyadeva appeared as a *Messiah*."[18] Dimock credits "the intense and unprecedented revival of the Vaiṣṇava faith in Bengal" of the sixteenth century to "the leadership and inspiration of Caitanya."[19]

Such are scholarly estimations of Caitanya's place in the socio-religious milieu of medieval Bengal. In light of them it is well to bear in mind Caitanya's life story, since it reveals some information about the dilemma of the orthodox Hindu community of western Bengal in Caitanya's time. Caitanya's early and, we are told, financially lucrative foray into eastern Bengal; his quasi-allegorical meeting with the kazi; his choice of the fallen Brahman brothers as accomplices in his mission; his selective ambivalence toward orthodox social practices—all this is suggestive of pressures for a restructuring of the local Hindu social order. The conditions for this restructuring were independent of Caitanya since—as will now be discussed—they had been in the making for centuries.

Between approximately the twelfth and sixteenth centuries A.D. there occurred an event of inestimable significance for the future pattern of human settlements in Bengal: a major eastward shift in the course of the Ganges River.[20] Agriculture and civilization prior to that shift tended to be concentrated in a narrow strip of territory running north

[14] Majumdar, *Caitanya*, p. 1.
[15] De, *Early History*, p. i.
[16] *Ibid.*, p. 6.
[17] S. C. Mukherji, *A Study of Vaiṣṇavism in Ancient and Medieval Bengal* (Calcutta: Punthi Pustak, 1966), p. 162.
[18] *Ibid.*, p. 161.
[19] Edward C. Dimock, Jr., *The Place of the Hidden Moon* (Chicago: University of Chicago Press, 1966), p. 25.
[20] N. D. Bhattacharya, "Changing Courses of the Padma and Human Settlements," *National Geographic J. of India* 24.1–2 (March–June 1978), pp. 63–65.

and south in western Bengal. This was the Ganges' original course, presently the course of the Bhāgīrathī-Hooghley. About the twelfth century, after silting up that original course, the Ganges embarked on a gradual "Eastward March"[21] which brought the eastern territories and tribes into first-time contact with Hindu and Islamic civilization.[22]

Coincident to the Ganges' movement toward and eventual convergence with the Padmā River system came the onset of Islamic rule in Bengal. This process began with the conquest of the Hindu seat of power at Nadīyā, in western Bengal, in 1204.[23] The Ganges' gradual eastward shift and attendant alteration in the rich reparial plain worked hand in glove with Islamic designs for the material exploitation of Bengal's underdeveloped eastern tracts. The culmination of these intertwined processes may be seen in the establishment of the seat of Moghal rule in eastern Bengal, at Dacca, in 1610.

During this time the locus of Hinduism, culturally and socially, did not shift substantially from its position along the Ganges' original course. However, the developments just outlined imposed certain pressures upon and within the Hindu community. Mukherji writes that Bengal in the fifteenth century "was under the occupation of the Muhammedan rulers, who were alien both in race and religion . . . it can be easily surmised that the politico-religious life of the Hindus was not at all safe and secure during the Muslim rule in Bengal in the medieval times. But this was not all. The tyranny of the foreign ruler was also accompanied by the greater oppression of dominant Brāhmanism with its conservative outlook and despotic spirit."[24] Moreover, "Minute rules and restrictions of an unchanging and stringent code of religious and social duties were prescribed, and the effort is best exemplified by the great, but narrowly conservative, work of Raghunandana who was probably an older contemporary of Caitanya."[25] Contrary to what one might suppose, the rigidification of the norms of conduct was probably not a response to the threat of conversion; for, as Eaton points out, the target of Islamic conversion was not the Hindu mainstream in the west but the indigenous population of the east "which had but the lightest contact with the Hindu religious or caste structure."[26] The Hindu tightening of ritual procedures and caste rules actually represented a mechanism

21 *Ibid.*

22 Richard M. Eaton, "Approaches to the Study of Conversion to Islam in India," in *Islam and the History of Religions*, ed. Richard C. Martin (Berkeley: University of California Press, 1983).

23 For a concise treatment of Islamization and its cultural and material repercussions in Bengal see Richard M. Eaton, "Islam in Bengal," in *Bengal: The Islamic Heritage*, ed. George Michell (London: Art and Archaelogy Research Papers, 1983).

24 Mukherji, *Study of Vaiṣṇavism*, p. 162.

25 De, *Early History*, p. 22.

26 Eaton, "Approaches," prepublication copy, p. 7.

for holding intact a society no longer endowed with the political devices for reaffirming its legitimacy. In its effects the tightening mechanism, however, only tended to further erode the integrity of the Hindu community.

One need look no further for a clear illustration of this point than the case of the brothers Rūpa and Sanātana. Were there not certain evidence of its historicity, one might be tempted to treat their story as social allegory. These were men of scholarly acumen and refined Brahman upbringing who, notwithstanding, had consorted with Muslims. Consequently they were denied the privileges to which they had been born; yet they succeeded in winning rehabilitation and distinction in the highest echelons of a new social movement, Caitanyite Vaishnavism.

The allegorical quality of the Rūpa and Sanātana story arises from the fact that their situation was widely shared. In their time, the best educated men of the Bengali soil were usually of high caste and generally Brahmans. Practical necessity obliged many of them to seek employment outside their community. The Muslim court, for its part, had a demand for servants of this caliber. It grew increasingly dependent over time on the efficiency and skills of Hindu entrepreneurs and administrators, who could be utilized to further the economic and political objectives of Islamic rule. A number of high caste Hindus acceded to this need.

The reactionary position of orthodox Hinduism could not but be uncompromising, for the purity of Bengali Brahmans, already clouded since the Islamic conquest, was regarded as irretrievably lost through deliberate association with Muslims. Accordingly, men like Rūpa and Sanātana were relegated to a burgeoning class of degraded Brahmans, the members of which were reckoned on a par with untouchables. In a sense their position was even more precarious than that of untouchables; their caste status was not changed (i.e., lowered) but lost; that is, they had become declassified. In this way the Hindu society increasingly glutted itself with the waste of its human debris.

Obviously, the disintegration of Hindu society, by the tossing out of the most elite and industrious members, was a process which could not continue indefinitely. It could end only in one of two ways: with the extinction of brahmanical Hinduism itself, or with a massive restructuring of brahmanical religious doctrine and social ethic.

In religious doctrine and practice, the revolution which Caitanyite Vaishnavism brought about is too well known to require comment. Here I shall amplify only on the changes it inspired in Hindu social ethic. Caitanya's movement did not only accept the outcaste and outcasted; it also tended to provide adherents with a definite place within a newly integrated social order.

As Nicholas comments, "Social order is a serious problem in frontier society everywhere. . . . For centuries, in the lower delta, authority was poorly organized; centers of officialdom were few and widely scattered.

It seems likely that Islām and Vaiṣṇavism functioned to provide authority in anarchic frontier society, and that they did so through loosely constituted religious organizations. The Vaiṣṇava form of this organization is called a maṇḍalī (circle, congregation); it is organized around a particular guru, who may be called a gosvā̃i by his followers, and is frequently constituted by persons from more than one village."[27]

An instance of how Vaishnava village organization serves to maintain community order is the institution of widow-Vaishnavism. Nicholas cites a case of a caste Hindu woman who, after widowhood, became pregnant and bore a son.[28] Orthodox Hindu society holds no place either for a child begotten in this way or for its mother. In this particular case, however, neither was ostracized. Rather, at the instance of the local gosvā̃i, the mother was put through a Vaishnava conversion ceremony and the child was assigned to the widow-Vaishnava (bedo baiṣṭam) caste. As Nicholas remarks, "Vaiṣṇavism legitimates the illegitimate in the microcosm of the village."[29]

According to Vaishnava religious doctrine, neither personal background nor social circumstances are bars to spiritual attainment. Moreover, persons of extremely varied background have embraced the faith. This does not mean, however, that they are admitted into the Vaishnava community on precisely the same basis. Only a limited amount is known so far about the demographics of Bengal Vaishnavism from the sixteenth through eighteenth centuries, but there is enough to suggest a definite outline of the movement's social makeup.[30]

Geographically, Vaishnavism acquired the bulk of its adherents in an area where Islam was also highly successful, the lower Gangetic delta of eastern Bengal.[31] This would suggest that, after Caitanya, Vaishnavism broke with the Hindu tradition centered on the old course of the Ganges, adapting its expansion as the demographic, cultural and economic epicenter of Bengal shifted to the east. One might even be tempted to conclude that Islamic expansion provided the Vaishnava movement with an impetus and a model for popular conversion, although too little is known about Vaishnava conversion mechanisms at this point to argue for this with certainty.

Sociologically, Vaishnavism again followed the general pattern of

27 Ralph W. Nicholas, "Vaiṣṇavism and Islām in Rural Bengal," in *Bengal Regional Identity*, ed. David Kopf (East Lansing: Asian Studies Center, Michigan State University, 1969), p. 44.

28 *Ibid.*, p. 42.

29 *Ibid.*, p. 43.

30 For one of the most detailed existing treatments of the demographics and internal organization of the Caitanyite Vaishnava movement see Joseph Thomas O'Connell, "Social Implications of the Gauḍīya Vaiṣṇava Movement" (Ph.D. diss., Harvard University, 1970).

31 Nicholas, "Vaiṣṇavism and Islām," pp. 39–40.

Islam, though some particulars must be noted. Like Islam, Vaishnavism acquired its numerical base in Bengal among agriculturalists, artisans and service castes.[32] It is underrepresented, however, at the two extremes of the caste continuum. The lowest ranking menial and laboring classes have remained virtually untouched by Vaishnavism. Also relatively few in number are Vaishnavas from the highest Hindu castes.[33]

Notwithstanding, the Brahman element unquestionably comprises the apex of the Bengal Vaishnava movement. Caitanya, the founder of the new Vaishnava religion, was a Brahman. He adhered to rules of his own caste and did little to sway others from obedience to theirs.[34] Five of the six goswāmins he deputed to Vṛndāvana had been born into the Brahman caste. The same held of many leading figures of the early Vaishnava movement who remained in Bengal; e.g., Nityānanda, who seems to have been originally named Kuvera Paṇḍita;[35] Kamalākṣa Bhaṭṭācārya, better known as Advaita Ācārya;[36] Śrīvāsa Paṇḍita and his grandnephew Vṛndāvana-dāsa;[37] Gadādhara Paṇḍita; and Śrīnivāsa, who received the title Ācārya after Caitanya's death.[38] Several of these figures founded descent lines through which the structure of authority in the Vaishnava community has been perpetuated for generations.[39] Bengal Vaishnavas to this day exhibit a strong affinity for brahmanical social standards and also enjoy a certain degree of identification with Brahman social ranking in the public consciousness.[40] This even applies to the movement's recent spinoff, the Hare Krishna organization. Its most adept participants receive initiation as Brahmans, and it is only from their ranks that cooks are recruited for the feeding of the entire membership.[41] It follows, then, that however hostile Caitanya and his

32 *Ibid.*, p. 40.
33 *Ibid.*
34 De, *Early History*, pp. 81–82.
35 *Ibid.*, p. 58.
36 *Ibid.*, p. 24.
37 *Ibid.*, pp. 59, 38.
38 *Ibid.*, p. 108.
39 *Ibid.*, p. 63; Dimock, *Place*, pp. 88ff. Śrīnivāsa's line holds a special significance in the present context; one of his descendants, Rādhāmohana Ṭhākura, was a great champion of parakīya-vāda, or the doctrine—popular in some schools of Vaishnavism—that societally and religiously unsanctioned affairs of spirit and body reflect truer love than exists in conventional unions. Moreover, others among Śrīnivāsa's descendants, to be discussed below, have helped preserve the historical ties between the Caitanyite movement and that quintessential parakīya-vādin text, the *Śrīkṛṣṇakīrtana*.
40 Surajit Sinha, "Vaiṣṇava Influence on a Tribal Culture," in *Krishna: Myths, Rites, and Attitudes*, ed. Milton Singer (Chicago: University of Chicago Press, Phoenix Books, 1971), pp. 64–89.
41 Faye Levine, *The Strange World of the Hare Krishnas* (Greenwich, CT: Fawcett, 1974).

companions might have been to the orthodox component of Hindu society, the Caitanyite movement is not and has never been an antibrahmanical movement. Rather, it has merely brought about a revision in brahmanical standards of religious doctrine and social ethic.

According to Jaiswal, Vaishnavism in the immediate pre-Christian era arose in response to a crisis within brahmanical Hinduism. In brahmanical society "The period between 200 B.C.–[200] A.D. was one of the great social upheavals. The old order of varṇa was considerably weakened by the advent of the foreign hordes in considerable numbers and . . . an improvement in the conditions of the lower varṇas, especially the śūdras, and necessitated the removal of at least some of the disabilities imposed upon them in the earlier scheme of things. The door of Vedic rites and worship was closed to the śūdras; so the progressives among the brāhmaṇas, took hold of the non-Vedic, popular cults and preached brāhmaṇical rules of social ethics through them. Of these, the cult of Vāsudeva-Kṛṣṇa was one of the most powerful, and the brāhmaṇisation of this god was effected with his recognition as an incarnation of the brāhmaṇical god Nārāyaṇa-Viṣṇu."[42] There are powerful parallels between the situation just outlined and the condition of the Hindu orthodoxy in sixteenth-century Bengal. Foreigners had entered the country in force. The assimilation of the tribal hordes was impending; they would obtain some place in the life of the country with or without the cooperation of the brahmanical Hindus. The question of greatest import was: what would be the status of the latter community and its traditions in the new order of things? As survival was of the essence, it seems inevitable that some effort toward that end would have ultimately taken place, no matter whether Caitanya personally had trod the soil of Bengal or not.

Perhaps inevitable, too, was the Bengali Brahmans' choice of Vaishnavism as the vehicle of social revision, much in the fashion of the Brahmans of nearly two millennia earlier. The difficulty of evaluating the precise relationship of historical Bengali Vaishnava belief to the Caitanyite movement arises from the fact that sources of evidence about the former are inadequately exploited. Jayadeva's *Gītagovinda*, to be sure, constitutes vital evidence as to the milieu of Vaishnava religion and its intellectual background in early medieval Bengal. But there is another source of evidence that, though still inadequately considered, exceeds *Gītagovinda* in value, both because of its greater temporal proximity to the Caitanya age and its closer affinity to the folk dimension of Vaishnavism in Bengal; and that source is *Śrīkṛṣṇakīrtana*.

* * *

[42] Jaiswal, *Origin and Development*, p. 11.

SKK is the only surviving pre-Caitanya Vaishnava text in the Bengali language. In the view of some it is also the most grossly erotic text in the Bengali language. To be sure, eroticism per se is not unusual in an Indian work, least of all in Vaishnava poetry; witness *Gītagovinda*. But the eroticism in SKK goes beyond mere description of characters' physical charms or suggestion of their psychological scenarios. SKK contains detailed accounts of the sexual intercourse of Radha and Krishna. The dialog, moreover, includes lurid teasing, suggestive banter and swapping of the coarsest insults. (Specifics of SKK's content will be gone into in the next section.) Therefore SKK's potential for the investigation and reconstruction of the milieu of pre-Caitanya Bengal Vaishnavism has been suppressed under the weight of scholarly conviction that the text can have nothing to do with the Caitanyite movement—that it is so inimical to the standards of piety and taste propounded by Caitanya that its very authenticity must be questioned. Yet there is evidence from within the Caitanyite movement itself to suggest otherwise.

According to De,[43] a number of Caitanya's contemporaries and followers composed literary pieces for entertainment on the Radha-Krishna theme. For instance, Rūpa and Sanātana, together with their nephew Jīva, contributed to this body of writing (notwithstanding their extensive pursuit of more scholarly areas such as grammar, theology, philosophy, etc.). Other Vaishnavas who contributed works of this class include Kṛṣṇadāsa Kavirāja (*Govinda-līlāmṛta*) and Raghunātha-dāsa (*Dāna-keli-cintāmaṇi*). It may be accordingly assumed that these works were written for the approbation of others in the movement and were not considered inconsistent with Vaishnava piety. However, De provides summaries of many of these pieces that make clear their comic and erotic content; they include episodes such as Krishna demanding tax from Radha and her friends, Radha stealing Krishna's flute, Krishna replicating himself at Radha's suggestion to make love to her friends, etc. Though some of these works have been published, practically none have been translated into any Western language and hardly any are available or accessible at the present time.

However, there exists a recent critical edition of one important work of this class containing running translations of the original Sanskrit-Prakrit text into Hindi and English. This work is a playlet (bhāṇikā) by the Vṛndāvana goswāmin, Rūpa, entitled *Dāna-keli-kaumudī* ("Moonlight on the Game of Tax-Collecting").[44] A synopsis of the content may be given as follows:

Radha and some of her girlfriends are on a journey carrying dairy

[43] De, *Early History*, chap. 7 ("The Literary Works").

[44] Rūpa Goswāmī, *Dāna-keli-kamudī*, ed., trans., and with commentary by S. N. Shastri (Indore, India: Bharati Research Institute, 1976). Page numbers in the present text refer to this edition.

goods. As they go along, one of Radha's friends points out a nearby spot where Krishna has painted figures of musk on Radha's breasts (pp. 45–46). Presently Krishna approaches in person, accompanied by some cowherd friends and by an older woman, Nandīmukhī. Pretending to be a revenue official, he blocks the dairymaidens' path demanding taxes. First he requests revenues on their dairy goods (p. 118), but changes his mind and decides the young women should be taxed for their physical charms (p. 123). When Radha refuses to pay, Krishna proposes that she turn herself over to him in lieu of tax (pp. 132–33). Radha comments on Krishna's boldness and lack of modesty, but he replies that he is only anxious to perform a great service to her (urusevā, a pun for "attendance on the thighs"). The elderly Nandīmukhī suggests that Radha raise her garment a bit and satisfy Krishna with a glimpse of her breasts (p. 159). All the cowmaids in irritation denounce Nandīmukhī as a dirty minded woman (dubbuddhie) (p. 160). The good natured squabbling, humorous repartee and erotic double entendre continue at length. Ultimately a senior cowherd woman named Paurṇamāsī enters (p. 272) and assures Krishna that, if he will forebear for the moment, she will see that the object he desires will be available to him that very evening (p. 287). Thus Krishna's goal of a tryst with Radha is accomplished; the matter is resolved to everyone's satisfaction; and the *Dāna-keli-kaumudī* comes to an end.

In SKK there is a tax episode (see synopsis below) that parallels *Dāna-keli-kaumudī* in a number of respects. Certain themes and literary conventions are clearly common to both. However, the similarities are not so close as to indicate that either work directly inspired the other. This suggests that there was an early medieval genre of Vaishnava writing to which SKK belonged and on which the Caitanyite composers of Radha-Krishna pieces also drew. From this it does not follow that SKK itself was known to members of the early Caitanyite community, although there is some independent evidence pertinent to this possibility.

The Bengali biography *Caitanya-caritāmṛta*, completed approximately in 1615 by Kṛṣṇadāsa Kavirāja, contains three passages indicating that Caitanya was acquainted with the verses of a poet Caṇḍīdāsa. These passages are cited by De.[45] They state that (1) Caṇḍīdāsa verses were among those recited when Caitanya was with a South Indian Vaishnava, Rāmānanda Rāya; (2) songs by Caṇḍīdāsa, along with others of Vidyāpati and the *Gītagovinda*, greatly pleased Caitanya; (3) toward the end of his life, in his frequent deliriums, Caitanya was soothed by the recitation of songs by Caṇḍīdāsa, again together with verses of Vidyāpati and *Gītagovinda*.

These passages are significant in that the author of SKK is the only poet

[45] De, *Early History*, p. 84.

Caṇḍīdāsa for whom a pre-Caitanya dating has been definitely proposed. However, it is not specifically mentioned that the Caṇḍīdāsa whose verses so enthralled Caitanya was SKK's author. Even if Kṛṣṇadāsa had stated this, it could be objected that he did not have direct knowledge of Caitanya's life and could have mistakenly credited the saint with a knowledge of SKK materials. Therefore the biography by Kṛṣṇadāsa provides no certain proof that Caitanya knew the work of SKK's author. There is, however, evidence that his trusted contemporaries did.

A commentary on the *Bhāgavatapurāṇa* entitled *Vaiṣṇava-toṣaṇī* is attributed to Rūpa's brother Sanātana.[46] In this work, the name Caṇḍīdāsa is linked with the names of two episodes which are actually part of SKK. These are the dāna (tax) and naukā (boat) episodes.[47] This is extremely significant evidence for SKK's Caitanya connection since, among the various Bengali poets who have styled themselves Caṇḍīdāsa, only one is known to have composed a work containing such episodes—and that poet is the poet of SKK.

Assuming that the work Sanātana alludes to is indeed the SKK, it is highly likely that it was the same poet whom Kṛṣṇadāsa was referring to in *Caitanya-caritāmṛta*; for if a person as influential in the Caitanyite community as Sanātana knew that artist's work, then with virtual certainty it would also have been known to Sanātana's colleagues and contemporaries, including Caitanya himself.

The *Vaiṣṇava-toṣaṇī* evidence for SKK's Caitanya connection is not undisputed. It has been claimed that the poet mentioned by Sanātana is not to be identified with the author of SKK, and that the dāna and naukā episodes mentioned in the commentary really represent excerpts from some Sanskrit composition by a different poet Caṇḍīdāsa.[48]

Notwithstanding, there is only one known work authored by a poet Caṇḍīdāsa containing "tax" and "boat" episodes. That work is SKK. There is no evidence for the existence of any work in Sanskrit by a poet of the same name containing episodes on the same themes. Nor is there any motivation for proposing its existence—other than for the purpose of distinguishing the Caṇḍīdāsa mentioned in *Vaiṣṇava-toṣaṇī* from the author of SKK, a work widely regarded as unworthy of Caitanyite prestige.

This is why note deserves to be taken of Rūpa's *Dāna-keli-kaumudī*. The synopsis of it above is intended to demonstrate that raciness and eroticism in themselves constitute no reason for excluding a writing from the Bengal Vaishnava tradition. Nor does the subjective factor of taste, for *Dāna-keli-kaumudī* suffers from a shortness of this quality. SKK is

46 *Ibid.*, pp. 25, 110. This work, dated 1578, is also known as *Daśama-tippaṇī*.

47 Sen, *Chandidas*, p. 17; Bandyopadhyay, *Itibṛtta*, pp. 304–5.

48 Mukherji, *Study of Vaiṣṇavism*, p. 127. Also see Sukumar Sen, *Bāṅgālā sāhityera itihāsa*, vol. 1, pt. 1, 6th ed. (Calcutta: Eastern Publishers), p. 143 [in Bengali].

composed in the vernacular, an idiom that, if not always elegant, carries with it a quality of vivacious honesty. *Dāna-keli-kaumudī*, on the other hand, is composed in the sacred language, Sanskrit—an idiom ill suited to the content of the work, which reads pedantically in consequence. If the two pieces are objectively judged and compared for tastefulness of composition and literary excellence, SKK should emerge as the clear superior.

* * *

It is estimated that SKK is the second oldest piece of literature in Bengali which survives nearly intact to the present.[49] The extant version of the text contains some 412 songs. These vary among themselves in format, but more than half (226 songs) share a common length: seventeen lines, plus the obligatory bhaṇitā or signature line. The signature lines identify the poet, Baṛu Caṇḍīdāsa,[50] and dedicate the songs to his patron deity, Bāsalī or Vāsalī. Each song closes with a bhaṇitā. Each begins with an assignment of its rāga and tāla, indicating that oral recital was intended.

The poet's objective was evidently to create a work of narrative momentum sufficient to hold an audience's attention through the several evenings that a complete performance would last. At the same time, the frequency of bhaṇitā lines indicates an expectation that the songs could be individually recited. The work seems to have been aimed for general Bengali audiences of the period. Those educated in Sanskritic sources of the Krishna legend would have taken satisfaction in the text's close conformity to that tradition; while the poet's use of the simple vernacular idiom must have made SKK accessible to the most ordinary villager. That the Krishna theme is fundamental to the work indicates the already considerable local appeal of the god and his legendary adventures. Moreover, the poet's estimation of audience taste is apparent from his having concentrated upon the divinity's youthful and amorous exploits. There is no way to say with certainty whether the poet was right in this estimation, other than to examine his masterwork for oneself and gauge one's own reactions.

SKK is divided into thirteen sections (khaṇḍas) of varying length, from a few to as many as 110 songs. In synopsis the sections are as follows:

Janmakhaṇḍa (Episode of His Birth) introduces the three principal characters of the story. These are the adolescent Krishna, the Lord

[49] The earliest literature in the language, said to be composed in Old Bengali, is the *Caryāpadas* or Buddhist sahajiyā songs. See Nilratan Sen, ed., *Caryāgītikoṣa* (Simla, India: Indian Institute of Advanced Study, 1977).

[50] In some signature lines he is identified simply as Caṇḍīdāsa; in a few cases he is identified as Ananta or Ānanta Baṛu Caṇḍīdāsa.

Supreme, who has been incarnated on earth as a cowherd's son; an exquisite cowmaid of some eleven years named Radha, who we are told is an incarnation of the goddess Lakṣmī, and who serves as chief object of Krishna's amorous interests; and Radha's great-aunt Baṛāyi (Granny), a kind of caricature of the *sakhi* character of *Gītagovinda*—an aged woman of grotesque demeanor who seems to be a seasoned procuress.

Tāmbūlakhaṇḍa (Episode of the Betel Quids) portrays Krishna's unsuccessful first attempts to woo Radha in the conventional way by having Granny take her flowers and quids of betel leaf. When Radha reacts adversely, Granny and Krishna plot to humiliate her until her spirit is broken.

Dānakhaṇḍa (Episode of the Tax) reveals Krishna posing as a contentious revenue official. He detains Radha on her way to market, demanding that she either pay taxes or offer her favors. After a protracted dispute, he impels her to submit to his amorous advances.

In Naukāhaṇḍa (Episode of the Boat), the ever-scheming Krishna adopts a new guise, that of a ferryman. On her way to market, Radha contracts with the disguised Krishna to take her across the Yamunā River; once underway, Krishna succeeds in making love with her.

Bhārakhaṇḍa (Episode of the Load) finds a rapidly maturing Radha turning the tables on Krishna. When he shows up in the forest in the garb of a porter, she arranges for him to carry her wares of dairy goods to market. In return, she offers assurances of erotic gratification. These ultimately prove worthless as she manages to give him the slip after marketing.

In Chatrakhaṇḍa (Episode of the Umbrella), Krishna is enraged by Radha's treachery in the previous episode. He confronts her on the homeward path, but Radha craftily succeeds in beguiling him once more. This time she persuades him to accompany her carrying an umbrella over her head in the afternoon sun.

Vṛndāvanakhaṇḍa (Episode of the Vṛndāvana Gardens) takes place in a kind of fabulous park built by Krishna, filled with every variety of flowering and fruiting plant. Luring the cowmaids there through Granny, Krishna dazzles them with the contents of his springtime pleasure garden. He then replicates himself, takes each cowmaid into a separate arbor and—much to Radha's chagrin—makes love with every one of them. A jealous quarrel ensues, but ultimately Radha and Krishna patch up their differences.

Kāliyadamanakhaṇḍa (The Vanquishing of Kāliya Episode) tells of Krishna's struggle to eject a formidable serpent from a whirlpool in the Yamunā River. This episode provides an occasion for the poet to bring out Radha's growing affection for the god, an affection that surfaces in her plaintive mourning when Krishna appears to perish in the course of the adventure.

Yamunākhaṇḍa (Episode of the Yamunā River) takes place in the same spot. Having vanquished the serpent, Krishna entertains himself and the cowmaids with water sports and horseplay. This section reaches a climax with Krishna's theft of the clothing and jewelry of the bathing cowmaids.

Hārakhaṇḍa (Episode of the Necklace) finds Radha complaining to Krishna's family because, in returning her clothing at the end of the preceding episode, he has withheld her necklace.

Krishna's revenge for this act of treachery is the subject of the Bāṇakhaṇḍa (Episode of the Arrows) section. Impersonating the god of love, Krishna shoots Radha with arrows made of flowers. In this way he wins her total submission.

Vaṃśīkhaṇḍa (Episode of the Flute) foreshadows Krishna's ultimate desertion of Radha. Smarting under his indifference, Radha manages with Granny's connivance to steal a flute much played and treasured by him. The tearful Krishna creates a hilarious spectacle by begging and badgering Radha and the other cowmaids for the whereabouts of his instrument. Ultimately, after much wrangling, Radha does return Krishna's flute, but does not succeed in winning a renewal of his love.

The last section, Rādhāviraha (Radha's Isolation) represents the concluding blow for Radha. Desperately lovesick, she attempts to win Krishna back. He will have none of it. SKK concludes with Krishna's departure from the pasturelands for the fulfillment of his divine mission to destroy tyrannical forces upon earth.

* * *

Little is definitely known of the circumstances of SKK's composition apart from that which can be deduced through evidence internal to the text itself. It is the only known work of the poet Baṛu Caṇḍīdāsa, about whom nothing is known independently. His title, Baṛu, indicates that he was a temple Brahman. His erudition in Sanskrit is apparent from his having composed introductory Sanskrit verses for some of the songs in SKK, as well as from his frequent allusions in the text to classical puranic legends and to *Gītagovinda*. His familiarity with the erotic, quasi-tantric *sahajiyā* tradition of the medieval period in eastern India (a tradition that also influenced Caitanya) is apparent from his portrayal of Krishna, late in SKK, as a sahajiyā yogi (Rādhāviraha, song 29).[51] His devotion to the mother goddess is evidenced by his choice of the sobriquet Caṇḍīdāsa 'Slave of Caṇḍī' and by his dedication of the songs of the text to Bāsalī or Vāsalī. Caṇḍī is a name of the mother goddess; Bāsalī or Vāsalī

[51] For one of the more substantial existing treatments of the sahajiyā tradition, see Sasibhusan Dasgupta, *Obscure Religious Cults*, 3d ed. (Calcutta: Firma K. L. Mukhopadhyay, 1969), chaps. 1, 3, 4, 5, 6.

is a form in which she is worshipped in western Bengal, particularly Birbhum and Bankura districts. However, an examination of Bāsalī temples in the village of Nānur (Birbhum) and the town of Chātnā (Bankura) suggests that this form of the goddess lacks a fixed iconographic representation.[52] It is interesting that her worship and that of the poet's namesake Caṇḍī was strongly condemned by early leaders of Caitanyite Vaishnavism.[53]

Baṛu Caṇḍidāsa's SKK is known from only one manuscript, or properly speaking, from about 200 intact pages of a single handwritten, cotton paper manuscript. The numbering of the intact pages indicates that the manuscript is lacking two full pages at the beginning; scattered losses also occur in the middle, and an unknown number of leaves are missing at the end.[54] It was in this condition that the manuscript was discovered in a West Bengal village in 1910. SKK's discoverer had taken hospitality for the night in Kā̃kilyā village, near Bisnupur (Bankura District, West Bengal). In his host's cowshed he found a basket among some debris on a shelf; within the basket he discovered some old manuscripts in a neglected condition, including the one we now know as SKK.[55] Significantly, the owner of the household and its cowshed, Debendranath Mukhopadhyay, was a descendant of the daughter of Śrīnivāsa Ācārya; this Ācārya had been active in the local propagation of the Bengal Vaishnava movement after Caitanya's death.[56]

SKK has been repeatedly published since 1916 by the Bangiya Sahitya Parisat or Bengal Academy of Literature at Calcutta, where the manuscript is still housed. Its discoverer, the late scholar Basanta Ranjan Ray, a collector of manuscripts for the Parisat, was the first to edit the text. It was also Ray who assigned the name SKK to the manuscript, as it lacks the leaves that might have provided its title page and a concluding collophon.

Issue has been taken with Ray's naming of the work because, it is contended, the actual title is separately recorded. Bandyopadhyay[57] points out that the manuscript was discovered with a slip of paper that, in his estimation, constitutes a library record. He believes it is from the

52 This observation is based on the translator's field investigations of December, 1978. One temple was visited at Nānur (near the town of Bolpur) and two were visited at Chātnā, where one temple is in the main part of town and the other on the estate of a local nobleman, Triguṇa Rāy.

53 Dimock, *Place*, p. 112.

54 Basanta Ranjan Ray, "Introduction (*bhūmikā*)" (section *puthi*) in *Śrīkṛṣṇakīrtana*, 9th ed. (Calcutta: Bangiya Sahitya Parisat, 1973) [in Bengali].

55 Madanmohan Coomar, "Introduction to the Ninth Edition (*nabama saṃskaraṇera bhūmikā*)," *ibid.*

56 See above, n. 39.

57 Bandyopadhyay, *Itibṛtta*, pp. 288 ff.

'gā̃thāghara' or royal manuscript library of Bisnupur. Members of the line descended from Śrīnivāsa Ācārya's daughter's son, according to Bandyopadhyay, were closely associated with the Bisnupur royal house during the seventeenth century. The slip of paper discovered with the SKK manuscript, reproduced in Bandyopadhyay's book, is dated in the year A.D. 1682 (that is, Bengali 1089). It states that one Śrīkṛṣṇapañcānana borrowed pages 95 through 110 of the manuscript on the 26th of Āśvin (September–October) and returned them on the 21st of Agrahāyaṇa (November–December).[58]

Bandyopadhyay's point in all this is to argue that Basanta Ray ought to have inferred the correct name of the manuscript from the library slip, which attributes the borrowed pages to a work it names as 'Śrīkṛṣṇa Sandarbba' and, again, as 'Kṛṣṇasandarbba'. To Bandyopadhyay, Ray committed a surprising lapse in not taking the name of the manuscript from this slip.

Unfortunately, interesting though the issues may be concerning the work's nomenclature, they are perhaps among the smallest of the many controversies that have accrued to SKK since its discovery a scant three-quarters of a century ago. The question of SKK's dating, for instance, is far more controversial and much more serious.

As should be clear from the preceding, the total external evidence bearing on the circumstances of SKK's composition is meager. Therefore its dating is mainly to be determined by evidence internal to the text; particularly, the language in which it is composed. The dating of the physical manuscript will be excluded from the following discussion. Even though it has been widely discussed, it seems to me to be a side issue not directly relevant to the dating of the text; clearly the manuscript is of later provenance, but only an assessment of its contents can determine the work's actual dating.

In the first few years after SKK's discovery, certain scholars proposed a relatively early dating, owing to the archaism of this text's language in comparison with that of other known Middle Bengali works. These scholars included two distinguished linguists and Bengali specialists, Muhammad Shahidullah and Suniti Kumar Chatterji. The latter has assigned the text to the last quarter of the fourteenth century.[59] The evidence for this date is integral to Chatterji's general thesis on the linguistic development of Bengali, and cannot be refuted without the collapse of the entire dissertation. Although Chatterji at no one place in his work presents all

[58] If the slip refers to the manuscript that Ray named SKK, then the pages referenced would correspond to the last seven songs of the Bhārakhaṇḍa section, and probably to the whole of the Chatrakhaṇḍa section. The latter cannot be said with certainty because the concluding part of Chatrakhaṇḍa is missing from the manuscript which Ray discovered.

[59] Chatterji, *Origin and Development*, p. 118.

his arguments for the early dating of SKK, some portions of the total evidence are given in summary form in the section on phonology (pp. 132–33) and the section on prosody (pp. 273–300).

Sukumar Sen has, however, set forth some linguistic evidence against a very early dating of SKK. In his estimation the work cannot be older than A.D. 1600,[60] although, as Bandyopadhyay points out, Sen fails to suggest some definite period in which the work might have been composed.[61] Sen's linguistic arguments against the text's pre-1600 dating may be summarized as follows:[62]

(a) Some phonetic processes regarded as evidence for SKK's antiquity are observed to take place even in modern dialects of Bengali; therefore they are inadmissible as evidence for an early dating of the work. The processes include the derivation of aspirate stops from stop + aspirate combinations (tohmākho from tohmāk[a] + ho); occurrence of nasal aspirates (samhe for same or sabe); and certain peculiar verbal formatives (rahilache for rahiche).
(b) SKK contains a number of words in forms which typify later historical stages of Bengali. Some are Brajabuli forms (jāṇala, bhaila, punamī); some are typical of the modern colloquial speech (ekhuni, curaṇī).
(c) Some words in SKK occur in alternate forms, the one older and the other more modern (cumba/cuma, duiṭi/duṭi). Some such alternates reflect vocalic coalescences which are historically unattested outside SKK until the modern stage of the language (dauṛī/daṛī, baiśe/base).
(d) One word, rāga, is found in the text conveying a semantic sense it did not acquire before the seventeenth century.
(e) The copyist, at one point in the manuscript, wrote and then scratched out a word which is a modern idiom (ḍombacaṇḍālī).

Herewith I respond to these points. As regards (a), it may be observed that the fact of a given phonetic process being current in some present-day dialects does not mean an identical process could not have been taking place in the language half a millennium ago.

Some of the forms on which arguments (b)–(c) are based may arise from occasional errors in the copyist or copyists' rendering of the manuscript. In the event of a mistake, a copyist's natural inclination would be to err in favor of forms of the current speech. This could give rise to alternate forms of the same word within the manuscript.

60 Sen, *Itihāsa*, pp. 136ff.
61 Bandyopadhyay, *Itibṛtta*, p. 302.
62 Sen, *Itihāsa*, pp. 140–43.

The usage alluded to in (d) could have come about by the copyist's mistaken substitution of a contemporary word for an older word with the same sense.

Argument (e) evokes an explanation along the same lines; the very fact that the copyist caught and scratched out the purportedly modern expression is sufficient to suggest that the expression did not belong to the original text, and had been written into the manuscript by error.

Moreover, assuming for the moment that (a)–(e) are all valid arguments, their combined weight is nevertheless small against the cumulative linguistic evidence for SKK's earlier dating. As has been mentioned, in presenting arguments (a)–(e) Sen has not proposed, much less defended, a definite alternative dating of the work.

Sen does, however, provide one more argument for SKK's late dating; in fact, it is the first of his arguments. It is observed that SKK contains some Perso-Arabic loan words, of which Sen lists about a dozen examples.[63] These include two words (majurī and majuriā) which have a common base of Perso-Arabic provenance (majur-) to which Bengali affixes have been added. Sen contends that borrowing of Perso-Arabic lexical items and the operation of processes of native word formation upon borrowed lexical bases could not have taken place in the Bengali language as early as the end of the fourteenth century. This, he argues, is evidence that SKK cannot be dated to that period.

The obvious comparison this invites with English loan phenomena in Bengali has been noted by Bandyopadhyay[64] and may be elaborated upon. The British dominated Bengal from 1757 until India's independence in 1947, a period of 190 years. Due to this period of foreign occupation, as students and speakers of Bengali may be aware, the language has become literally unspeakable without the use of English loan vocabulary.[65] Going backwards in history, the Muslim conquest of Bengal began in 1204, while SKK is assigned a hypothetical dating in the late fourteenth century; this is a nearly comparable timespan. However, Sukumar Sen—who is an authority on Bengali linguistics—contends that the timespan would not have sufficed for the borrowing into Bengali of about a dozen Perso-Arabic lexical items and the beginnings of word formation upon borrowed bases.

In this writer's view, Sen's position at best provides a good illustration of how irrelevant the principles of scientific linguistics can be when it comes to what is evidently an ethnically and culturally laden issue.

[63] *Ibid.*, pp. 139–40.

[64] Bandyopadhyay, *Itibṛtta*, p. 304.

[65] According to Chatterji, *Origin and Development*, p. 218, Jnanendra Mohan Das' dictionary of Bengali, 1916 edition, lists some 75,000 Bengali words and compounds of which 700 are English borrowings. This would place the English component of the Bengali vocabulary in 1916 at nearly one percent.

* * *

To this point the discussion has not gone beyond the value of SKK for historical interpretation and reconstruction and the linguistic niceties involved in the question of its dating. In order not to leave the impression that the text has nothing further to offer I hasten to direct attention to that which is just ahead—a translation that, I hope, may convey some suggestion of the literary quality of the original.

This translation is based primarily on the 1935 edition of SKK, the second edition of Basanta Ranjan Ray published by the Bangiya Sahitya Parisat. This particular one of the Parisat's editions was selected because of the greater accuracy attributed to it by Calcutta scholars. It was, however, compared line for line with the Parisat's ninth (1973) edition, the latest edition at the time of my research in Calcutta. Where discrepancies between editions or doubts arose, final authority was given to a photocopy of the original manuscript which I obtained during the research period in Calcutta.

Like all translators I have tried for literal accuracy without transgressing naturalness in the target idiom, which in this case is my native American English. In order to reproduce or evoke the original to the fullest possible extent I have also attempted, in all but a few songs, to achieve a rhythmical effect suggestive of the meters of the original.

Each section of the translation is followed by annotations. These are supplied liberally—perhaps at times even redundantly—in keeping with the poet's evident intention that the work be accessible to the widest possible audience.

The end matter includes an appendix of plant names aimed at explicating the poet's copious references to Indian flora. More than a hundred separate plant species are mentioned in SKK. Each horticultural allusion, moreover, reflects a certain expressive intention on the poet's part. It is hoped that, with the help of the Appendix, the nuances which the poet intended may be reconstructed.

Finally, there is a bibliography of some of the works consulted in the translating and annotating of SKK.

The standard style of romanization has been followed in reproducing material from Indian languages, with a few exceptions. In the annotations to the translation, I have deviated from standard transcription when reproducing modern Bengali, so as to follow a system more faithful to current pronunciation. Thus in these transcriptions all sibilants are represented by [s]; vowels represented in orthography but not pronounced are omitted; the distinction between long and short [i] is omitted, as is the distinction between long and short [u]; the character [a] represents the vowel sound in das 'ten'; [aa] represents the vowel sound in aami 'I'; and [ae] represents the vowel sound in aek 'one'.

Throughout this work, moreover, some words are consistently given in anglicized spelling for convenience; e.g., Krishna (kṛṣṇa); Radha (rādhā); Vaishnava (vaiṣṇava); Brahman (brāhmaṇa); Ganges (gaṅgā); Nanda Ghosh (ghoṣa); Benares (vārāṇasī); and the like.

Finally, Indian names pertaining to publishers and to authors of modern works are reproduced without diacritics and generally with silent vowels omitted.

Janmakhaṇḍa*

Song 1

The Earth[1] told the never-aging gods of the heavy strain of her burdens.
Thereupon they urgently resolved to destroy Kaṃsa.[2]

The gods all met and held a council in heaven.
The creation was being destroyed because of Kaṃsa!
By what means could his death be brought about?
They deliberated together and spoke with Brahmā.[3]
Brahmā went with all the gods to the ocean.
They pleased Hari[4] in the water with their praise:
"In your various forms, you have wreaked destruction upon demons;[5]
By your pleasure, you may also bring about the assassination of Kaṃsa."[6]
Hearing this, Nārāyaṇa[7] chuckled and immediately
Presented them with two hairs—a white one and a black.
"These two hairs are to be in the house of Vasudeva.[8]
In Devakī's womb they will become Halī[9] and Vanamālī.[10]

* *Janmakhaṇḍa* 'Episode of His Birth', name of the opening section of the narrative song collection *Śrīkṛṣṇakīrtana*. According to Hindu legend, the deity Viṣṇu was persuaded to incarnate himself as Krishna for the destruction of malevolent forces in the world. Krishna has a long and varied terrestrial career of which *Śrīkṛṣṇakīrtana* covers only the childhood and adolescent stages. The *Janmakhaṇḍa* section of *Śrīkṛṣṇakīrtana* explains the circumstances of Krishna's birth among rural herdsmen. The opening song of this section is preceded by an introductory Sanskrit verse.

1 Pṛthvī, a name of the earth or earth goddess.

2 Kaṃsa, name of the usurper of the throne of Mathurā, a kingdom in north-central India. According to some accounts Kaṃsa's birth in the royal house took place due to the rape of a queen by a demon. His tyrannical extremes provoked the indignation of the gods and they plotted his downfall.

3 Brahmā, name of the creator deity of the universe. In the Vaishnava tradition this god is subordinated to Viṣṇu.

4 Hari, a name of Viṣṇu-Krishna. He is said to recline in the primordial sea.

5 Viṣṇu takes ten legendary incarnations for ridding the earth of demonic forces.

6 The eighth incarnation of Viṣṇu is Krishna, whose mission includes the overthrow of Kaṃsa.

7 Nārāyaṇa, name of an archaic cult deity of India, popularly identified with Viṣṇu-Krishna.

8 Basula or Vasudeva, name of an important member of the herdsmen's community and husband of Devakī, who gives birth to Krishna.

9 Halī or Haladhara, a name of Krishna's brother and companion in many adventures.

10 Vanamālī 'Wearer of Forest Garlands', an epithet of Krishna.

The demon Kaṃsa will be destroyed by their hand."
After obtaining this boon, all the gods went to their dwellings.
The gods bided their time.
—A song of Baṛu Caṇḍīdāsa, attendant of Bāsalī.[11]

Song 2

Hearing the good counsel of the gods,
The sage Nārada[12] went before Kaṃsa.
He was gray of beard and gray of head—
A dwarfish figure in simian garb.
With twisted face and mad demeanor
Nārada danced in like a frog.
He laughed intermittently for no reason,
Playing lame for a moment, then blind.
Everyone present was intrigued
To observe his motley contortions.
He sprang up one moment and reached for the sky;
The next moment he was sprawled on the ground.
He arose and spoke nothing but raving;
He waggled his head outlandishly.
Then out, out he stuck his tongue
And bleated like a stupid goat.
Kaṃsa, watching, was seized with mirth.

Song 3

"What is this glee, Kaṃsa, which brings a smile to your lips?
Don't you know your own destruction is at hand?
The eighth child that Devakī bears
Will have awesome powers. It's he who will kill you![13]
I have told you everything.
Contrive now to save your life!"
On hearing all this, Kaṃsa was shaken.
He took counsel with all his ministers and courtiers.[14]

[11] Each song of *Śrīkṛṣṇakīrtana* ends with a conventional signature line. The signature lines identify the poet, Baṛu Caṇḍīdāsa. In many instances (such as this one), they also mention his patron deity, Bāsalī—one of the forms of the mother goddess. Translations of the signature lines are omitted hereafter.

[12] Nārada, name of a sage, said to have been born in one of his lives as a monkey. Nārada is mentioned in many puranic stories, often in episodes from the life of Krishna. At this point in *Śrīkṛṣṇakīrtana*, he resorts to bizarre tactics to gain the king's attention.

[13] Sesi tohmāra yama, 'It's he who will be your Yama (god of death).'

[14] Cinti rahīta 'pondered, took counsel' should be substituted for cintira hīta which appears in some editions of *Śrīkṛṣṇakīrtana*.

From then on, men were engaged
To murder Devakī's children.
Then Nārada personally hastened forth
And told Vasudeva the whole story.
"Any children Devakī bears hereafter
Kaṃsa will brutally destroy;
But her eighth child shall be Nārāyaṇa, the Lord.
He will guide you from that time on.
By his direction, all will be saved."

Song 4

After Nārada's speech, the resolute Kaṃsa
Destroyed Devakī's first six children.[15]
At that juncture, all the gods met
And placed the two hairs in Devakī's womb.
Recalling how Kaṃsa had slain her six infants,
Devakī trembled with apprehension.
The white hair which was put into Devakī's womb
Became the mighty one named Balabhadra.[16]
Pretending to miscarry, he went on his own
And developed in Rohiṇī's[17] womb.
The dark one remained in Devakī's womb—
Wielder of the conch, the discus, the mace and the bow.[18]
Knowing this to be Devakī's eighth pregnancy,
Kaṃsa imperiously hired watchmen.
Devakī conceived a handsome child, a fine male;
Day by day her lovely person burgeoned.
Eventually Devakī was ten months' pregnant.

Song 5

In the month Bhādra, at the time named Vijaya,[19]
The night was dark and the clouds showered rain.
At this auspicious time divine Hari, who is Jagannātha,[20]

[15] According to *Bhāgavatapurāṇa* 10.85 (Tagare 1978), in adulthood Krishna was prevailed upon by Devakī to restore these six sons to life.

[16] Balabhadra 'Honored for Prowess', one of the names of Krishna's elder brother (also see n. 9).

[17] Rohiṇī, name of one of Vasudeva's wives. For safety, she is sent away to the pasture community, where she gives birth.

[18] Viṣṇu is depicted with four arms, each of which holds one of the symbols named here.

[19] Bhādra, name of a month in the Indian calendar year corresponding to August–September. It falls in the rainy season. Vijaya literally means 'triumph'.

[20] Jagannātha 'Lord of the World', an epithet of Viṣṇu-Krishna.

Wielder of the conch, the discus, the mace and the bow,
Attained birth as Krishna on the eighth lunar day[21]
While the moon was in the house of Rohiṇī.[22]
At once Vasudeva was alerted thanks to the gods,
Though the people of Gokula[23] were in slumber.
At that same time, Yaśodā bore a daughter
Unawares, for she too was sleeping.
Then Vasudeva set out with Krishna in his arms.
Kaṃsa's watchmen, lost in sleep, failed to detect them.
Seeing Krishna, the river Yamunā gave way for a path;
Vasudeva went across to Nanda's house.[24]
Placing the infant Vanamālī on Yaśodā's bosom,
Vasudeva brought home Yaśodā's baby girl.
Her cries awakened Kaṃsa's watchmen;
They informed Kaṃsa of Devakī's delivery.
Kaṃsa dashed the girl to death on a stone slab,
But from heaven she addressed Kaṃsa:
"A child will yet rise up in Nanda's house to kill you!"
When he heard this, Kaṃsa schemed to murder Krishna.
First, Kaṃsa engaged Pūtanā;[25]
She pretended to nurse Krishna. He slew her.
After that he sent the twin arjuna trees;[26]
Krishna destroyed them in one blow.
One after another he sent Keśī[27] and other demons.
Krishna trounced them all in moral combat.
In this way, Dāmodara grew up in Gokula.

21 The day of Krishna's birth is called janmāṣṭamī from janma 'birth' + aṣṭamī 'eighth day of a lunar fortnight'. It is traditionally celebrated on the eighth day of the dark fortnight of the lunar month Bhādra (see n. 19).

22 Rohiṇī, name of a constellation, not related to Rohiṇī the wife of Vasudeva (n. 17).

23 Gokula, name of the pastoral community outside Mathurā, separated from the latter by the Yamunā River, a great tributary of the Ganges.

24 Nanda Ghosh, name of a cowherd and the husband of Krishna's foster mother, Yaśodā.

25 Pūtanā, name of a female demon. In an attempt to poison Krishna she offers her services as a wet nurse, only to have the life sucked out of her.

26 Ārjuna, the arjuna plant; see Appendix. The twin trees are uprooted by Krishna who, tethered to a mortar, nonetheless manages to crawl away so that the mortar catches between the trees and fells them. In other treatments of this incident the deed is said to release twin celestial brothers who had been embodied as the trees owing to a curse. The arjuna incident accounts for Krishna's epithet Dāmodara 'Tethered at the Waist'.

27 Keśī, name of a demon who terrorizes the pasturelands in the form of a monstrous horse. According to *Bhāgavatapurāṇa* 10.37 (Tagare 1978) and *Harivaṃśa* 80 (Bose 1940), Krishna thrusts his arm into the beast's mouth, whereupon it gags and dies.

Song 6

Hari was born at the bidding of all the gods
And took his pleasure on the earth as Vanamālī.
His long, wavy hair was dark, thick and soft;
A peacock's feather adorned it.[28]
His forehead with its splendid sandalpaste markings
Was delicate at the temples, broad and prominent at the brow.
His nose was straight and finely nostriled. His eyes were blooming lotus.
His eyebrows bristled like a pair of bows.
His lips were made, as it were, of twin corals
And the nets of Varuṇa embellished both his ears.[29]
His arms, like a pair of elephant trunks, reached to his knees.[30]
His hands were lotuses with ruby-studded fingertips.[31]
His chest seemed to be a slab of emerald
And his shanks, a pair of tree trunks.[32] His waist was slender.
His nails were like an array of gem-encrusted moons.
His body, by its splendor, overshadowed a brimming raincloud's luster.
This extraordinary hero was to effect Kaṃsa's downfall;
His person bore the portents of royalty.[33]
With jeweled ornaments twinkling on every limb,
Splendidly garbed in yellow, and holding his flute,[34]
He went on his rounds and looked after the calves.

[28] The peacock's feather is a rustic adornment associated with Krishna in art and iconography.

[29] Baruṇera jāla 'the nets of Varuṇa.' The poet compares Krishna's splendid ear ornaments with the nets of Varuṇa, a marine deity. Nets of a design similar to dangling earrings are still used in India. They consist of a circular wooden frame with a meshed interior, raised and lowered in and out of water by means of a series of ropes attached to the perimeter of the frame at one end and grasped together in the hand at the other. The passage implies that, as Varuṇa binds and paralyzes men by his existential nets, so Krishna binds by his immense charm.

[30] Long arms are a traditional feature of masculine beauty in India. See n. 33 below.

[31] Māla in the original text should be substituted by maṇi as proposed by Mukherji 1971:40–42; thus: kurubinda maṇi nirmmita 'embellished by ruby-gem (fingernails).'

[32] Literally 'his two thighs are fine (rāma) rambhā' (banana plants; see Appendix).

[33] Highborn men are said to be distinguished at birth by thirty-two marks, listed by Ray 1973:178 as follows: long nose, arms, eyes, jawbone and knees; fine skin, hair, body hair, teeth and forefingers; ruddy eyelids, soles, palms, palate, lips, tongue and nails; upraised chest, shoulders, nails, nose, pelvis, and face; short neck, loins and penis; broad pelvis, forehead and chest; deep navel, voice and intelligence.

[34] The sylvan flute, like the peacock's feather (see n. 28), is closely associated with Krishna.

Song 7

For the sake of Krishna's enjoyment,
The gods said to Lakṣmī:[35]
"Be born on earth as Radha!
Let all the world be heartened!"
That's why, through Padmā's womb,
In Sāgara's house, she was born:
Enchantress of all the beings of the universe,
Desire's milkmaid to passion's fluid.[36]
She was marvelous, a golden doll,
Delicate as the parrot tree blossom.[37]
Day by day the charms of her person grew,
Increasing like the waxing moon.
With Krishna in mind, the gods made her
The wife of impotent Abhimanyu.[38]
Observing Radha's youthful charms,
Abhimanyu said to his mother:
"Have her Granny stay beside her."

Song 8

Abhimanyu's mother thought this over
And hastened to Padmā's household.
She asked about Radha's Granny,
The elderly sister of Padmā's father.
This Granny had command of many tactics
To protect Radha on the way to market.[39]
Her hair was as white as yaktail.
Her forehead was sunken on both sides.
Her eyebrows looked like streaks of lime.
Her eyes were two pebbles in sockets.
She had large nostrils and no bridge in her nose.
Her cheekbones were raised, but her cheeks, nonexistent.
Her teeth were large and her word was unreliable.
Her lips were more prominent than a camel's.
Her arms were like a pair of sticks

[35] Lakṣmī, name of a goddess and consort of Viṣṇu. In *Śrīkṛṣṇakīrtana* Radha is treated as an incarnation of Lakṣmī.

[36] Ratirasakāmadohanī 'woman who milks (arouses and satisfies) the desires for passion's juices (pleasures)'.

[37] Śiriṣa 'parrot tree'; see Appendix.

[38] Āihana or Abhimanyu, name of Radha's husband, and brother of Devakī.

[39] Young women of the community are assigned to carry dairy produce for sale in the market at Mathurā.

And her two breasts dangled all the way to her navel.
Her gait was crooked; her voice thick with rheum.

> "I've been engaged by Abhimanyu's mother to chaperone you;
> Be pleased to travel to Mathurā with me."
> "Granny, I'm fortunate an experienced lady has been chosen.
> Come then, I'll go to Mathurā."

Tāmbūlakhaṇḍa*

Song 1

The dairymaids prepared milk and milk goods for sale,
Covering their wares with fine cloths.
They gathered together all in high spirits,
Careful to stay close to Granny.
Radha, in her unstinted beauty, as usual
Went along on the forest trail to Mathurā.
This day, in lively spirits
And high humor, all the maids
Stepped ahead briskly,
Unheedful of Granny.
Radha paused under a medlar[1]
And watched for Granny's approach.
She squatted there with head in hand.
Granny must have strayed.
Radha wondered,
"Why is Granny late?"
It frightened her to be alone in the forest.

Song 2

After losing Radha, Granny wandered about.
With her eyes she could not make out the path.
Perplexed over her grandniece, Granny fretted to herself:
"What should I do? Where shall I go?"
Granny had lost her way in the thick of Vṛndāvana;[2]
God alone could tell what was in store!
In her feelings and thoughts Granny was uncertain.
"Where shall I go to find Radha?
I'm all alone in this dark forest;
I've lost Radha, now how will I manage?"

* *Tāmbūlakhaṇḍa* 'Episode of the Betel Quids', name of the second section of *Śrīkṛṣṇa-kīrtana*. In India, betel quids are traditionally offered by friend to friend or lover to sweetheart. In this section, hoping to inspire Radha's favor, Krishna makes this and other offerings to her through Granny.

[1] Bakula, a tall tree, the Indian medlar; see Appendix.

[2] Vṛndāvana, name of a forested area within the Gokula pasturelands.

Going some distance, Granny observed
Many cows which were grazing in Vṛndāvana.
Seeing them, the old lady was encouraged.
"I shall ask the cowherd for news of Radha,"
Granny thought. She approached and beheld,
Holding a staff, her grandson[3] Krishna.
Granny happily joined him.

Song 3

Seeing the old lady unexpectedly in Vṛndāvana,
The king of gods[4] asked politely,
"Where do you come from? What is your business?
Why do you wander alone in Vṛndāvana?"
"I've come from the dairylands. I'm an old dairywoman.
My darling grandniece got ahead of me.
While trailing her, I missed the path.
Sonny, give me directions to Mathurā."
"Why do you wander with your little grandniece?
Give me the details, where'd you lose her?
What's the name of the girl? What does she look like?
Old lady, you must explain things properly."
"As we traveled to Mathurā for selling our milk goods
I lost that precious beauty in Vṛndāvana.[5]
It's my grandniece that's missing. Her name is Candrāvalī.[6]
Listen, the girl is slim and delicate, Vanamālī!"
"I'll tell you precisely the way to Mathurā;
But first you do just as I say.
I'm making a condition; if you accept it,
Then I'll bring you together with Radha."[7]

[3] Granny and Krishna have a fictive relationship owing to Krishna's purported birth in Nanda's house. Radha is married to a brother of Krishna's fictive mother and Granny is Radha's mother's father's sister (Janmakhaṇḍa, song 8). Thus Krishna is fictively Granny's great-grandnephew.

[4] Devarāja 'King of Gods', here an epithet of Krishna. At this point he gives the appearance of not recognizing Granny. See n. 7 below.

[5] Trailokyasundarī 'the most beautiful woman in the universe (literally "three worlds")'. The three worlds are heaven, the mortal world and the underworld.

[6] Candrāvalī 'Moonbeam', another name for Radha in this text; however, in popular tradition Radha and Candrāvalī are separate characters who vie for Krishna's affection.

[7] By now it is clear that Krishna recognizes Granny and knows the girl she is speaking of. Yet a few lines hence he requests a description of her. This provides the poet with a ground for the glowing description of Radha in the following song. However, the total context is curious; for while Krishna has already laid eyes on Radha, he swears in song 5 (below) that Granny's description has sufficed to excite his ardor for her. Overall this suggests a prior connivance between Granny and Krishna.

"You are my great-grandnephew, you're like my second self.
I will do exactly as you say.
I swear to it, I'll do your bidding;
I'd rather commit murder than fail you."[8]
"Since I am to go in search of Radha,
You must describe her in detail."
Granny welcomed Krishna's request.

Song 4

Colorful vermilion embellishes the part of her hair[9]
Like a dawning sun arising through a raincloud.
Seeing the flawless splendor of her golden lotus face,
The moon has gone a million miles away in embarrassment.[10]
The lady is incomparable, she is capable of seducing an ascetic.
My grandniece, Radha by name, is an unsurpassed beauty.[11]
Seeing the loveliness of her rippling unbound tresses,
Clusters of mangosteen[12] buds stay in the forest for shame.
Seeing her sloe eyes gleaming in mascara,
Dark waterlotuses immersed in water smolder.[13]
Seeing the whiteness and smoothness of her throat, the conch is
mortified;
It dives without delay into the waters of the ocean.
Seeing her two exquisite breasts,
Ripe pomegranates split open from humiliation.[14]
Her waist is slender, her hips are ample;
She moves languidly, more sensuously than a swan.
Day by day her fresh youthful charms are developing.

8 Literally 'I should kill a Brahman if I were to do otherwise.' According to *Manusmṛti* (Bühler 1886) the killing of a Brahman is a serious offense calling for at least four times the penance required in the case of other murders.

9 Radha wears a mark of vermilion in her hair as a token of married status. It is more an attraction than a warning to a would-be lover, for—like many adolescent brides in this society—Radha is still innocent of physical love (as she confesses in Dānakhaṇḍa, song 54 below).

10 Lāje gelā cānda duī lākha yojane 'the moon has retreated in shame two hundred thousand yojanas (200,000 x 5 miles = 1 million miles).' The moon is said to have retreated from the earth because of the supposed superiority of Radha's flawless face to its own flawed face.

11 Paduminī (= padminī), a term applied in Indian erotics to the most desirable class of women; for discussion see Siegel 1978:112 (and references therein). For a pictorial rendering see Randhawa 1962:148–49.

12 Tamāla 'mangosteen', a tree noted for dark attractive bark; see Appendix.

13 Tapa kare 'they smolder,' i.e., with the heat of penance.

14 The tendency of ripened pomegranates to split is attributed here to jealousy inspired by Radha's ruddy, ample breasts.

Song 5

After hearing from your lips this tale of Radha's beauty,
Granny, I cannot restrain my feelings.
The cruel god of love with unfaltering aim,
Granny, has pricked my heart sorely.
You are more to me than life. I tell you, Granny,
It's you who must make Radha accept me.
The trees are wearing the flowers of spring;
The bees are drinking their nectar.
Cuckoos with voices of honey are calling.[15]
For all these reasons I feel restless.
Lovesickness grows to excess in me;
You must do something about it.
Your coming here is my good fortune.
I entrust my purpose to you.
This is one time you must assist me,
The lord and quintessence of the universe.
Fulfill my hopes, Granny; make Radha want me!

Song 6

My great-grandnephew, I am your Granny.
Your good is my urgent concern.
I shall prevail upon her for your sake,
And I'll spare no argument to convince her.
My dear Krishna, tell me Radha's location.
I'll gladly go and seek your interests.
I know all the techniques of this business;
They'll serve to unite your heart with hers.
I'll make every effort to meet your needs;
On your bidding I could give up my life!
I can unite what doesn't match—
Even if she were chaste like Sītā.[16]
Hand me some flowers and betel-leaf quids;
I'm taking them to Radha.
Don't delay, Krishna, tell me Radha's location,
And give me something special to say to her.
I'll go at once in search of Radha.

[15] Pañcama śara gāe 'they sing major fifth intervals,' a reference to the bitonal call of the cuckoo.

[16] Sītā, name of the wife of the legendary king Rāma (n. 21), a paragon of wifely and feminine virtue.

Song 7

I'll tell you Radha's location; let it come to me.[17]
Granny, you should bear my words in mind:
My heart's in flames over Radha. Let me know
Where she stays and all the places that she visits.
As my trusted messenger, take these betel quids;
That lovely innocent waits beneath a medlar.
Take her a basket brimming with these quids
And with magnolia, rose chestnut and jasmine.[18]
She'll try on the flowers, she'll sample the betel;
Then you tell her all from start to finish.
Speak with folded hands.[19] Use these words:
"Nanda's son, Radha, has sent me.
Radha, try this camphor-scented betel.
Be gracious to Krishna's entreaties.
Hearing from my lips of your darting eyes,
Of the vermilion and bracelets that grace your head and arms,
Of the anklets on your feet that jingle as you walk,
He, the king of gods, is enmaddened.
I'm your Granny, your fondest well-wisher.
Radha, pay heed to my counsel:
Smile upon him and accept him, Radha."

Song 8

The hour was right, the day was auspicious.[20]
Granny, in most happy spirits,
Paid her respects to all the gods
And bowed at the feet of Lord Rāma.[21]
Bearing Krishna's request in mind,
She went in search of Radha.
She fashioned strings of magnolia blooms,
Rose chestnut, and several kinds of jasmine.
She arranged the blossoms with utmost care,

17 Literally 'I'll meditate and tell you Radha's location.' Krishna uses his supernatural powers to divine Radha's whereabouts.

18 Cāmpā 'Michelia (a relative of magnolia)', nāgeśara 'rose chestnut', neālī 'double flowered Arabian jasmine', māhlī 'single flowered Arabian jasmine'. For details about all these blossoms see Appendix.

19 Folding or pressing together the upraised palms is a gesture of supplication.

20 Śubha tithi bāra subhakṣaṇe 'on an auspicious day of the (lunar) month, on an auspicious day of the week, and at an auspicious instant.'

21 Rāma or Rāmacandra, name of a legendary hero, husband of Sītā (n. 16 above), and seventh avatāra or descent of Viṣṇu, widely worshipped in India.

Topping them with camphorated betel.
All around Vṛndāvana she looked
Till she caught sight of Radha.
With great affection they kissed each other
And clung together closely.
Asking Radha's story—
"Are you well, Grandniece?"—
She seated herself beside Radha.

Song 9

"You are my Granny, I am your grandniece.
How did you manage without me?"
"It was torment, Radha, not to see you.
By grace and good fortune now I've found you."
"Granny, why were you so delayed?
Tell me the truth, what happened?"
"I'll tell you the truth if you'll be gentle.
You should give me this assurance."
"You should relax and tell your story, Granny.
From my side you need have no worry."
Cheered by this, Granny began to speak.

Song 10

Radha,
Krishna has filled this basket with flowers
And betel. He sends them to you.
Do what I say, cowmaid; do nothing else.
Fill your cheeks with camphor-scented betel
And with musk . . .[22]

* * *

"Radha, if you won't love him,
Your life may be in danger!"
I said as much, but I could not gain her trust.

Song 11

Since I heard from your lips of Radha's youthful beauty,
Day and night my being smolders. My heart is restless.

[22] A leaf of the extant *Śrīkṛṣṇakīrtana* manuscript is missing at this point; the text resumes with Granny addressing Krishna.

I tell you humbly, Granny, nothing gives me comfort.[23]
My reason's gone. Language fails me. You're my refuge.
Don't deny my hopes, Granny; you must find some solution.
If Radha's consent isn't won, Granny, I—Krishna—will perish!
Take my pleadings to heart, Granny; you should not disdain them.
You must be for me a raft in the cruel sea of longing.
From now on Granny, I, the divine Vanamālī, am your servant.
Realize this and persist, Granny. Go and plead with Radha.
At your age, what you have heard and seen must be enormous.
This way you've learned each fine technique of carrying out these matters.
Cajole Radha, Granny; tell her any sort of story.
Just one time indulge me. Radha has to be persuaded.
Dear Granny, one time more take a basket filled with betel.
Go to her, entreat her, coax her. Bring Candrāvalī here.
Speak to Radha as I tell you: She must gladden Krishna.

Song 12

Again Granny gave Radha betel quids and accessories
With fine cloth proffered by the lovesick Krishna.

Seated by Radha, Granny turned her face away and giggled.
She offered her the camphored quids and spoke her piece by stages.
"Where's this scented betel from, Granny? And the fancy muslin?
The jasmines and the other flowers—who has sent these presents?"
"Come now, Radha; let me tell you, Krishna's almost dying.[24]
He sends you to know he's stifling in the torment of your absence."
Radha shuddered in every limb when she heard this message.
The strings of blooms and camphored betel—she flung them on the ground.
Granny rose, rebuking Radha: "You mustn't do such a thing!
The son of Nanda, praised by all, will die if you won't see him!"
"At home I have a handsome husband. He has highborn features.[25]
Is some cowpoke from Nanda's house fit to be my lover?"
"If you give your love to the god recalling whom all sins vanish,
And seeing whom one gains deliverance, you'll dwell in Viṣṇu's heaven."
"Damn the woman, damn her life, and may her husband perish[26]

23 Eṛilõ gharera āśa 'I've given up hope of home,' i.e., I've become a distracted homeless wanderer with no comforts.

24 Pā̃ca ābathā 'five elements' are those into which a corpse dissolves (fire, water, air, space and earth). The text literally says 'it's pā̃ca ābathā for Krishna,' suggesting his death or extreme distress.

25 Literally 'His body has auspicious tokens,' congenital marks that bode well.

26 Literally 'Damn the life of a woman and let her husband fall into a whirlpool. . . .'

Who has a place in God's abode by taking on a lover!"
In misjudgment she disdained the dashing son of Nanda.[27]

Song 13

My body, messenger, is unhardened.
I don't know a lover's advances.
I'm telling you the truth;
Look now, I swear to it.
Messenger, don't argue; keep quiet.
I'm hardly more than a child.
Radha's a small girl, unripe for love.
You're foolish to bring me his betel;
You've only earned my displeasure.
That Krishna has fantastic schemes.
He should feel repentant.
Let him heed my words; if not,
He'll perish because of Radha.[28]
I don't follow his teasing talk;
I don't know the sports of love.
Go back; discourage Vanamālī.
Let me learn of what love is;
Then I'll summon Krishna.
We'll spend all night embracing.
You look foolish to me,
Exhausting yourself to oblige him.
That's why you forget I'm a child.
Go to Krishna; tell him
To quit hoping for my love.

Song 14

> Receiving Radha's message, the glib old lady
> Promptly went and addressed Madhusūdana:[29]

"My body is tender like gooseberry blossoms.[30]
It's not yet ripe for love.
Rebuff him, Granny; refuse Nanda's son.

[27] Nāgaraśekhara nāndera sundara 'Nanda's darling, the pinnacle of urbanity.'

[28] Yabẽ nā maribe rādhāra salira kāraṇe 'if he's not to die because of Radha's stake.' Śali 'stake' loosely means any sharp and tormenting thing; more strictly it means a shaft used for impaling petty criminals. In Bhārakhaṇḍa, song 17, Radha specifically threatens to have Krishna punished by impalement.

[29] Madhusūdana, a name of Viṣṇu-Krishna.

[30] Labalī, the country gooseberry or its blossom (see Appendix).

My youth isn't ready for him."
You see, Radha is very resistant.
This is how she answers.
Now what should I tell her, Cakrapāṇi?[31]
"The gifts you've been bringing are pointless, Granny.
Who risks nose and ears for adultery?[32]
Krishna has sent you out of delusion.
Why mention to me what he says?
Granny, when I learn about love, I'll dispatch you;
I'll summon Dāmodara[33] to Vṛndāvana.
At that time I'll meet with him;
My ripened youth will sate him.
Don't plead, Granny, and don't invite insults;
Just make stupid Vanamālī understand this."
What Radha says is not hopeful for you.

Song 15

Last night, Granny, I had a dream.
Radha came and sat on my bed.
Right then the love god punctured my heart.
I made pleasant talk. Oh, Granny,
I can't live, can't manage without seeing Radha.
What I say is the truth.
Her hair is glossy, like a dark cloud.
Her face is the full moon.
Her lilting words are a stream of nectar.
I covet her completely.
Put your hand upon me, Granny;
See how my fever's mounting.
Granny, I can't endure this anguish;
In Radha's absence, I'm dying.
If you permit me to see her once,
Then my life will be saved.
Realize this and hasten to Radha.

Song 16

> Assiduously the old lady went and conveyed
> The earnest words of Krishna, rapt in thoughts of Radha.

[31] Cakrapāṇi 'Discus Wielder', an epithet of Viṣṇu-Krishna.

[32] Disfigurement by cutting off the ears and/or tip of the nose is a traditional punishment. Typically, it is applied to adulterous women.

[33] Dāmodara 'Tethered at the Waist', an epithet of Krishna; see Janmakhaṇḍa, n. 26, above.

Jagannātha had a dream in the night:
Candrāvalī, listen, he touched your bosom!
Your breasts were like two golden lotus buds;
Their touch overwhelmed him with passion.
Sorely afflicted, Krishna has sent me—
I've no interest, I'm only informing you—[34]
Being a dairymaid, you're a bit simple, Radha.
Would you have on your conscience a murder?
For want of you, Krishna's out of his senses.
Your love is all that can save him.
Consider this, Radha. See your own profit.
Just once you must make Krishna happy.
After all, Radha, why squander your youth?
Use it to give Krishna pleasure.
Just once, Radha, spare his life
And cleanse yourself of wrongdoing.[35]
Radha, give him just one word of hope.

Song 17

"How can a woman your age think such things?
Hearing this, who would speak well of you?
Nothing you say, top to bottom, is seemly.
My man would flay you alive if I told him.
You awful old woman, you've no sense of shame.[36]
That's why you tell me this business.
Don't keep repeating the same things to me.
My husband's strict. I respect him.
I wouldn't have come to this place with you
If I had known you were so crooked.
You're my great-aunt, I'm your grandniece!
To think I'd hear such talk from you.
If ever again you jest with me so,
I'll certainly put a stop to you.
Eat these betel-leaf quids yourself.
Take stock of yourself. Go to Krishna!"
She said this in rage and gave Granny a slap.

[34] Mare bhāla jīe bhāla jāṇāilō tore 'He lives, fine; he dies, fine—I'm just informing you (of his condition).'

[35] Literally 'cleanse your own sins in the ocean.' That is, propitiating the god confers monumental spiritual advantages not to be passed up for the petty dictates of conventional morality.

[36] Literally 'you have no shame from your fathers'; i.e., you have grown up utterly without a sense of decorum.

Song 18

Receiving Radha's message, the glib old lady
Promptly went and addressed Madhusūdana:

My husband never touched me in anger,
Nor did my in-laws abuse me.
Now that I'm old, Krishna, on your account
I've been punished. I want to take poison!
I'm angry, Krishna. I won't stay. I'm leaving.
It's all your fault, Krishna, what I've suffered.
I thought in every way of your interests.
But Radha said things so unpleasant;
When I recall them I smolder inside.
Krishna, don't you feel indignant?
I've gone many places in many men's service.
All women have shown me esteem.
For your sake, I approached Radha;
She flung your betel at my feet.
And such stinging words Radha uttered—!
If you won't take vengeance yourself,
Then when people hear of this you'll be despised!

Song 19

If the messenger did wrong,
Why didn't she tell me?
What did hitting Granny accomplish?
On the strength of Granny's account,
I must make good my honor.
Whoever hits my go-between
Must suffer in full for the grievance.
As Hanumān was in the service of Rāma[37]
So is my spokesman to me.
She can renew a broken love.
She can dangle ropes
Where needles can't enter!
On any mission, should a spokesman of mine
Be slapped? Then why should I send her?
I'd do better to swallow poison.
At her age, my spokesman's been beaten!
Wherever my representative goes
She is offered tributes.

[37] Lord Rāma (n. 21) is said to have been assisted in his legendary adventures by a devout companion, the monkey chieftain Hanumān.

She can unite what doesn't match.
I'll have the herdsmen organize
To contribute milk for Granny.
I'll keep Granny at my home. I'll please her
By serving her
And make good my error.

Song 20

Krishna, I labored for your sake.
I told her all kinds of things.
But Radha threw your betel at my feet.
The foolish girl wouldn't listen. Krishna,
Radha slapped me—see for yourself!
What soul can bear such an insult?
I smolder all the more to recall
The threats she made against you;
She didn't even spare your parents.
She hissed in rage like a cobra.
No woman's this bold in all the world
Nor in all our family.[38]
Because of you, she made me suffer.
I wish I no longer had to see her.
She goes frequently to sell milk in Mathurā.
Think of some way to trouble her!
Only then will my heart find comfort.

Song 21

Granny,
I'll sit under the kadamba[39] beside the Yamunā. I'll detain Radha by claiming taxes.
Granny,
I'll loot all her wares and eat up her dairy goods; I'll confiscate her jewelry.[40]
Granny,
I'll disgrace Radha by claiming these taxes; your honor and mine will be salvaged.

38 Hāṇe kule ekho nāhĩ pāṭābukī tiri 'Not one (such) incorrigible woman (as Radha) has been among our forebears or is to follow in our posterity.'

39 Kadama or kadamba, a shade tree (see Appendix). In *Śrīkṛṣṇakīrtana* there is frequent mention of a particular kadamba tree on the embankment of the Yamunā.

40 Sātesarī hāre 'multistranded (literally, seven-stranded) necklace.'

Granny,
Accept my plan. Accompany Radha; take her to Mathurā market.
I'll block her way; you sop her feelings by speaking to me roughly.
I'll scatter her milk. I'll rip her top apart and touch her bosom.
I'll take her by force, if you approve, into the thick of Vṛndāvana.
When her spirits are spiked with love's arrows, I'll act like an ascetic.
You'll sit beside her and make a joke of it!

Song 22

Carefully keeping Dāmodara's intentions in mind,
The sly old lady sweetly addressed Radha.

Granny informed Radha deceptively:
"I've rebuffed Krishna as you wished.
Krishna gave up and went back home.
Come on, let's dash to town for selling.
Let's ask all the dairymaids, Radha.
We'll go to Mathurā without worries."
Hearing Granny's proposal, Radha gladly
Made plans with all the dairymaids.
She departed for Mathurā with Granny,
Talking with her friends of many matters.
After selling the milk and milk goods at market,
Granny hurried home with Radha.
With little smiles and honeyed words,
Granny contrived to keep Abhimanyu happy.
Radha regularly went to Mathurā in this way;
She sold milk and milk products and came home.
She fetched the earnings for her mother-in-law.

Song 23

Impatient with delays, the lovestricken Mādhava,[41]
With Radha in his heart, approached Granny and spoke:

It's been a long time since you gave your assurance, Granny.
I can't sleep for thinking of Radha.
Why do you promise, then disappoint me?
You still haven't had me meet Radha.
Head for Mathurā market with Radha;
I'll wait on the path, posing as a tax collector.

[41] Mādhava, a name of Krishna. The original reading śuci rādhāmādhāya mādhavaḥ seems to be mistaken; in this translation hṛdi has been substituted for the less plausible śuci.

I'll set out, Granny, at dawn tomorrow.
Don't forget my instructions:
Go sleep tonight in Abhimanyu's house;
When dawn breaks, leave at once.
The urge within me grows acute.
I can't bear not to see Radha.
You yourself know every trick,
So what instructions need I give you?
When I see Radha, I'll demand taxes;
Both hot words and cold I'll be speaking.
You may chide me, Granny, without fear.

Song 24

After receiving Krishna's instructions, the sly old lady
Spoke to Abhimanyu's mother about Radha's going to Mathurā.

At dusk, Granny went to Abhimanyu's house
And advised Abhimanyu's mother:
"Milk and dairy goods are wasting in the house.
It's time to go marketing in Mathurā.
My friend, admonish Radha with care
So that early tomorrow she'll be ready.
Think this over and see for yourself—
Without selling, how can a cowherd have profits?
My friend, I look out for your good day and night;
That's why I want to take Radha with me.
I myself will go as her chaperone;
No one can find fault with that.
I'll be taking many cowherds' wives and daughters—
You may send Radha among them."
This way, Granny obtained for Radha
The approval of Abhimanyu's mother;
So Radha was persuaded to travel to Mathurā.

Song 25

Ghee,[42] yogurt, buttermilk and milk
Radha readied and covered with fine cloths.
She took the leave of her mother-in-law
And got dressed before it was morning.
With Granny and her friends, Radha set out
And merrily headed for Mathurā.

[42] Ghṛta 'clarified butter (ghee)', a traditional cooking medium.

Her face was like lotus, her eyes like a doe's.
Her brow's arc eclipsed the half moon.
Her cheeks were a pair of butter tree blossoms;[43]
Her lips were like flame of the forest.
Her nose surpassed the sesame flower;[44]
Her porcelain throat shamed the conch.
Her arms were twin garlands of golden jasmine.
Her budding breasts were like lotus.
Her waist was a drum;[45] her navel was deep.
Her hips and her buttocks were full.
Her feet were two blushing hibiscus.[46]
Her thighs resembled elephants' trunks,
But she moved with a gait far more stately.

43 Mahula or madhuka, the butter tree or its blossom (see Appendix).

44 Tilaphula jiṇi nāsā '(her) nose defeats tila (sesame or sesamum),' a plant with a small, compact flower. See Appendix.

45 Ḍamaru, a small hourglass-shaped drum.

46 Thalakamala 'changeable hibiscus', a plant whose blossom is nearly white on first opening and turns red by night. See Appendix.

Dānakhaṇḍa*

Song 1

At this juncture Krishna was seated
Near the Yamunā[1] embankment.
Thirsting for Radha's nectar-sweet lips,
He addressed Granny.

"Granny, where are you going with all these cowherds' wives?"
From near the Yamunā embankment Krishna had emerged to block the path.
"It's little Krishna! Why do you block the pathway, cattle tender?
Candrāvalī is going . . ."[2]

* * *

Why, Krishna, you're treating me roughly!
What will my husband say when he hears?
None of my friends would be loath to inform him.
I'll be punished; you'll be put to death.
I bow before you, Krishna. I beg you,
Release me this once to go home.
Krishna, my youth is not suited for you.

Song 2

I've the power to levy taxes;
Don't mistake me, Radha.
Don't you recognize me—Krishna,
Gladdener of dairymaids?
On your head the vermilion is fetching;
Your hair is beautifully arranged.

* *Dānakhaṇḍa* 'Episode of the Tax', name of the third section of *Śrīkṛṣṇakīrtana*. In this section Krishna poses as a tax collector in order to accost Radha. The tax theme in Vaishnava literature and art antedates the present text by at least several centuries. On its antiquity in literature see Majumdar 1969:199; for evidence of it in sculpture see Coomaraswamy 1972:69.

1 See Janmakhaṇḍa above, n. 23.

2 One and one-half leaves of the extant *Śrīkṛṣṇakīrtana* manuscript are missing at this point. In the missing portion Krishna evidently manhandles Radha and smashes some of her containers of dairy produce. The text resumes with Radha addressing Krishna.

You travel with your milk and ghee;[3]
You avoid me and hasten to Mathurā.
But now I've caught you in my grasp;
What way can you escape me?
Your waist is so thin[4] it sways in the breeze.
The sight makes the coolest mind[5] waver.
Your breasts are two plump pomegranates;
They tantalize Nanda's son Krishna.
Render all my taxes, then go;
Or pay me with your caresses.
You shall not disappoint me, Radha!

Song 3

Radha's slender body trembled when she heard Krishna's answer. She spoke in distress to Granny as follows:

A girl of only eleven years
Is delicate, Granny, like lotus petals.
A man whose lust is roused to see her
Should perish for his baseness. Granny,
Krishna asked for my embrace.
I'll die if he should touch me.
My friends are leaving one by one,
But Krishna blocks and teases me,
Pretending that he's taking tax;
He wants to unfasten my bodice, Granny.[6]
Why does Vanamālī trouble
Me and not the other cowmaids?
Sometimes he demands a tax, and
Other times he blurts out nonsense.
Granny, do as I request:
Try to discourage Madhusūdana.[7]
He must renounce his hopes for me.

[3] See Tāmbūlakhaṇḍa above, n. 42.
[4] Muṭhi eka mājhā bāe hāle 'Your waist is one handspan, it sways in the wind.'
[5] Munimana 'the mind of a wise ascetic'.
[6] Kāñculī, a woman's short blouse or bodice.
[7] See Tāmbūlakhaṇḍa above, n. 29.

Song 4

Hearing Radha's message as conveyed by Granny,
The crafty Krishna thirstily addressed Radha:

"Face me, fair Radha; listen to Hṛṣīkeśa,[8] who requests you
To tell where you live. Where is your home? And, Radha, where are you going?"
"I live in Gokula. I'm from the cowherd community. Why are you asking?
Lots of us cowmaids[9] are carrying wares; we're off to the city to sell them."
"Set the basket down from your head. Let's take a look at your wares.
Give an accounting of the goods you're taking to town with you, Radha."
"Buttermilk, yogurt, milk and ghee. This is the lot; they're my wares.
What's the reason you're demanding to know the contents, Krishna?"
"Don't you know I'm the revenue officer? I take all the taxes.
You can travel to Mathurā city after you make your donation."[10]
"The longer I live, the more I hear! What double talk this is.
There's never been a tax on dairy products bound for market!"
"Tut-tut, Radha, you're very childish. See here, this account book is proof.
Save your honor, watch out for yourself. Make good all your taxes, then vanish."
"It's been said that there was justice[11] in the realm of Kaṃsa . . .[12]

* * *

To think this late in life I'd hear such fables, Tax Collector!
Listen, Master Cakrapāṇi, you're innately shameless!"[13]
Krishna snatched at Radha's clothes; his anger masked his glee.

[8] Hṛṣīkeśa 'Bristle-Haired', an epithet of Viṣṇu-Krishna.

[9] Ṣola śata gopī, literally 'sixteen hundred cowmaids,' i.e., all of the numerous dairymaids. Sixteen hundred or sixteen thousand is the traditional number of Krishna's amours.

[10] Bhāṇḍe ṣola paṇa diā̃ māhādāna cala mathurā nagare 'Go to Mathurā city after depositing into the coffers sixteen paṇas.' The term paṇa or pana signifies a unity of eighty. Sixteen of anything suggests a round or all-inclusive figure; see preceding note. The requested tax would be paid in cowrie shells, the traditional currency.

[11] Rāma rājya 'a Rāma's kingdom,' i.e., a just kingdom; see Tāmbūlakhaṇḍa above, nn. 21 and 37.

[12] Half a leaf of the extant manuscript is missing at this point; the text resumes with Radha addressing Krishna.

[13] Tora bāpa māe lāja nāhĩ, literally 'You have no sense of shame from your mother and father,' i.e., you failed to learn modesty in earliest childhood. Cf. Tāmbūlakhaṇḍa above, n. 36.

Song 5

Radha's slender body trembled when she received Krishna's answer.
She spoke in distress to Granny as follows:

"I told you earlier I'd not go to market, Granny; there's bad people.
You reassured me, you brought me here. It's you I must contend with.
Krishna forced me to put down my wares. He spoiled my ghee and yogurt.
He broke my necklace and ripped my bodice; he has defiled my person.[14]
How much penance has fate ordained?[15] What am I fated to suffer?
My time all goes in drudgery. I don't enjoy a bit of gladness.
In former lives, did I do harm to elder folk or Brahmans?[16]
Is this the reason fate prescribed a lifetime filled with sorrows?[17]
Or did I not keep a former life's vow? Is that the reason I suffer?[18]
Nanda's son will not relent. The workings of fate can't be thwarted.[19]
My life must end at dark Krishna's hands; then my misdeeds will be canceled.[20]
I'll wear no more baubles. I'll smash this tiara; my head I'll wipe clean of vermilion.
What is the reason that Krishna detains me? I can't understand his intentions.
Kaṃsa, our ruler, is fierce like a demon. Suppose he should hear of what's happened!
Stop this, Dāmodara! You must release me; I have to reach home in a hurry.

[14] Tana bigutila 'He molested my bosom.'

[15] Koṇa bidhātāe moka gaṛhileka kata likhi dukhabhāre 'What providence has fashioned me, writing how much burden of sorrows?' See n. 17 below.

[16] Mistreating respectable older persons, Brahmans, or others of high rank is believed a possible cause of suffering in one's later existence.

[17] Tekāraṇe bidhi dukhagaṇa lekhila sāṭhīhāre 'Is that the reason fate inscribed sorrows in my sāṭhīhāra?' Providence is believed to inscribe the fate of a child on its forehead six nights after its birth. This event is referred to as sāṭhīhāra.

[18] Failing to observe a vow one has sworn to a deity is believed to bring retribution in one's later existence.

[19] Lalāṭa likhita khaṇḍana nā jāe 'The writing on the forehead can't be disobeyed.' See n. 17 above. Radha attributes her encounter with Krishna to her inauspicious fate. See following note.

[20] Here and in other remarks (see n. 30 below) Radha suggests a latent belief in Krishna's powers and in the inevitability of her own submission to him. Nonetheless she struggles desperately against his advances to the end of Dānakhaṇḍa, unwilling to acknowledge his divinity and abandon conventional standards of belief and behavior. Radha's eventual submission to the god seems to foreshadow the theme of devotional submission in subsequent Bengali maṅgalkāvya literature, on which see Clark 1955.

If our King Kaṃsa should hear of this later, you'll suffer the blame,
Cakrapāṇi!"
Turning aside with a langorous sigh, lovely Radha sank down to the
ground.

Song 6

Hearing Radha's message as conveyed by Granny,
Krishna relinquished her wrap[21] but addressed her thirstily:

Radha, you're turning your back on me, and you haven't accepted my
offer.
My glances descend on the charming summits which sit on the orbs of
your bosom.
Looking from one to the other, my mind is enraptured. Consent and
you'll save me.
I long to drink from these lips of your sweetness. Your face is the moon
at its fullest.[22]
Give up your fear, indignation and anger. Oh Radha, it's me that men
speak of
As Gadādhara in Gayā and Mādhava in Prayāga.[23] I'm asking for your
acceptance.
Radha, you won't even cast me a glance, so resentful are you in your
spirits.
Such youthful beauty you have, yet you stare at the bauble that gleams
on your finger.
None of the charms of your youth will remain for all time, dairymaid.
Think this over.
Taste love with me and you'll reap their rewards. You must gratify your
Vanamālī.
Ponder on this in your heart, lotus lady; I'm lotus-naveled Viṣṇu.[24]
I'm senior in age to you, peerless in breeding; why don't you accept me,
your Krishna?

[21] Añcala, literally the end of a garment. Here it probably refers to a thin wrap thrown over a woman's upper torso, covering her bodice.

[22] The full moon, to which Krishna repeatedly compares Radha's face, is said to contain nectar.

[23] Gadādhara 'Macewielder', an epithet of Viṣṇu-Krishna (see Janmakhaṇḍa above, n. 18); Mādhava, a name of Krishna (see Tāmbūlakhaṇḍa above, n. 41); Gayā, a city in Bihar; Prayāga, the modern Allahabad (a city in Uttar Pradesh). Both Gayā and Prayāga are traditional pilgrimage centers for the worshippers of Viṣṇu-Krishna.

[24] Tohme padumini āhme padmanābha 'You are a padminī (see Tāmbūlakhaṇḍa above, n. 11), I am Padmanābha (lotus-naveled).' In the Vaishnava tradition Viṣṇu is depicted in a reclining position with a lotus emerging from his navel, from which arises the creator deity Brahmā. See Bhandarkar 1965:30–31, 45.

You will gain nothing if you disappoint me; and, later on, you'll be sorry.
This youthful beauty will not last forever. Look up, look at me, see my face!
Red waterlotuses hide in their ponds out of shame after seeing your feet.
Even the regal swan slinks to the water whenever it sees you in motion.
Krishna is thwarted not even by gods; nor by demons, and least of all mortals!

Song 7

Radha's slender body trembled when she heard Krishna's answer.
She spoke in distress to Granny as follows:

Nothing good is spoken by that shameless Cakrapāṇi.
Hoping for my love, he's taking taxes on this pathway.
I'm detained while other dairymaids—my many girlfriends—
Are free to go their way. My past misconduct will not spare me.[25]
Dearest Granny, for my sake I beg you to oppose him.
By your grace, this once, I might be able to go homeward.
How does Krishna dare to make remarks about my bosom?
By his childish lust he brings disgrace upon his household.[26]
Abhimanyu is my husband. May he live forever!
He's profound in wisdom and in valor he's unequaled.
Krishna always thinks about the wives of other cowherds;
This belies his boasts about his birth and noble background.
Granny, what is there for me to talk with him about?
He did not have grounds to spoil my buttermilk and ghee.
Make him stop his tax collecting schemes and other mischief.
How can he abuse me as he's done for no good reason?
Youthful as I am, I'm hardly suitable for Krishna.

Song 8

Hearing Radha's message as conveyed by Granny,
The crafty Krishna thirstily addressed Radha:

I've the king's concession to take road and market taxes;
That is why I'm posted near the Yamunā embankment.
You are going often to the market in the city;
You must pay in full the revenues that you're incurring.

[25] Dāruṇa karama doṣe āhmāke rahāe 'He detains me because of the fault of my harsh karma.' See n. 20 above.

[26] Tāra gota muṇḍileka āhmāra yaubane, literally 'His family is headshaven because of my young breasts,' i.e., Krishna's family will fall into disgrace (symbolized by the shaving of the head, a public stigma) because of his improper interest in Radha's physical beauty.

Listen, dairymaid, you must pay taxes on your produce.
I collect the royal duties in the realm of Kaṃsa.
Pay your tax in ghee and yogurt to the stated figures;
You may go when every item in your wares is paid for.
Don't be skeptical of this; I'm telling you sincerely,
It was all because of you I took up tax collecting.
I'll make you an offer, Moonface; listen. Since I like you,
I'll reduce your total tax by fifty or a hundred.
Understand? Let's have a squeeze in payment of those taxes!
It's a point of honor, Radha. You must keep your standards.
I, your Krishna, figured up your tax for you in person.[27]
It's nine hundred thousand cowries you are in arrears for![28]
Figure for yourself if this is so or isn't, Radha.[29]

Song 9

(Long ago, at the advice of wise Nārada,
Vasudeva took you and left you with Nanda.
Whom can I speak to about all these matters?
Krishna, you'll really take power in Mathurā!)[30]
I'm going to issue a protest advising
That Krishna, the tax taker, started a quarrel.
Many times I've paid respects to King Kaṃsa;
So, when he hears of this, he will come armored.
And when the news reaches bold Abhimanyu,
He'll take his weapon and slice you to pieces.
Listen now, Krishna, to what I am saying;
In your own heart, why, consider the matter.
I'll pay no tribute; you must not expect it.

Song 10

"I have twelve years' taxes coming. Listen to me, Radha,
Proof of what I say is written here in my account book."
"I go all the time to town for selling dairy produce;
You've no right to block me on my way to market, Krishna."
"Radha, in your silken garments, you are most exquisite.
Sandalpaste shines through the wispy ringlets on your forehead."
"I'm well bred. I'm married to a fine distinguished person.

27 Khaṛī pāṛī 'using chalk,' i.e., with calculations.
28 Naba lakṣa kaṛī 'nine hundred thousand cowrie shells.'
29 This is a subtle jibe at Radha, whom Krishna knows to be an unschooled dairymaid incapable of checking his figures.
30 The poet reveals that Radha is aware at some level of Krishna's transcendent nature, as she demonstrates in this aside. See n. 20 above.

I don't owe you anything. I trespass against no one."[31]
"Listen, foolish girl, there's twelve years' taxes you must pay me.
Fate has brought you here so I can carry out my duty."[32]
"You're a cowherd, Krishna, and you have a cowherd's thinking.
You've caught me alone and unprotected in the forest."
"I may be a cowherd but I'm God to your King Kaṃsa!
In this universe there's not a hero who can match me."
"Go and show to whom you will the manly pride you're flaunting.
You'll be dead if Kaṃsa gives your head a good sound bashing."
"No, I won't. Your Kaṃsa couldn't do a thing to me.
There is just one thing that could unmake me. It's your beauty!"
"Shut up, Krishna, don't you speak. Don't make such wicked comments.
You are well aware that Abhimanyu is my husband."
"You won't leave until you pay in full your twelve years' taxes!"

Song 11

How can you not pay the taxes, how will you reach market?
Tell me, clever Radha, why should I give up the pathway?
I take taxes, Radha, at each tollway near the river.
You may see if this is so or not from my account book.
Dairymaid, you must surrender twelve years' worth of taxes.
This alluring youth of yours enraptures Vanamālī.
I protect the underworld and heavens, cunning Radha.
I keep contacts on the earth. What will your schemes accomplish?
All throughout the universe I gather tributes, Radha.
Is there any soul who has the power to evade me?[33]
I'm Yaśodā's son; I hold a flute in hand. And, Radha,
I have been observing that you're stunningly attractive.
That's the reason why my heart is drawn to you, oh Radha.
I'll rescind your taxes if you'll heed my proposition.
On the other hand, if you continue not to heed it,
Then I'll have to capture you and force you to embrace me.
Radha, you must realize this and offer your approval.

[31] Kāra kā̃ca ālite nā deõ moẽ pāe, literally 'I don't set foot on anyone's unhardened mud wall.' The wall in question is a type of ridge put up in rural areas to separate fields of standing crops, especially rice.

[32] Or as a reward for good behavior in the past. The original passage is: mohora karamẽ tohmā āṇi dila bidhī.

[33] A stylistic feature of this poet is the sudden punctuation of mundane passages with lines of sobering import. This section is an example.

Song 12

My age is all of eleven years.
How can you ask me for twelve years' taxes?
I'm aware of your intentions.
People will hear of this; then they'll despise you.
Give way, Krishna, and don't obstruct me.
You'll be safe if I get to the city.
You, Vanamālī, are well matured.
I'm a baby compared to you.
Though a bee may suffer from hunger,
A lotus bud can't yield him nectar.
I'm the daughter and wife of respectable men.
What's my fresh beauty to you?
Though he may spot a ripe quince[34] on a tree,
A crow who desires it still cannot eat it.
I haven't even heard about love.
Krishna, this once spare my honor.
My lord Nārāyaṇa, I beg this of you.

Song 13

Seeing this budding youth of yours,
My heart is swept away.
As I observe now how lovely you are,
My longing for you increases.
Offer me an agreeable answer;
Let my ears drink of that nectar.
Raise up this moon of your face, look at me.
You're Radha, I'm Vanamālī.
You and I are now acquainted.
Abandon your apprehensions.
The tax you owe me is so substantial
You don't have the means to provide it.
Think this over to yourself
And carry out my wishes.
You are in the prime of life;
Your figure is fully ripened.
It's my object in taking taxes.

[34] Bela, a fruit with a hard shell. See Appendix.

Song 14

Radha's slender body trembled when she heard Krishna's answer.
She spoke in distress to Granny as follows:

A flower bud,[35] Granny, is pleasing to see
Though it wears no perfume till its season;
But when in blossom, a bud of a girl
Has an air that confounds a man's reason.[36]
What a disaster I have to contend with.
A revenue agent's in Gokula.
I'm taking merchandise worth many cowries
But can't get to market to sell it.
I shall send notice to Kaṃsa, the king,
Making sure that he apprehends Krishna.
I'm going often to sell dairy products;
No word about taxes has reached me.
Is the king presently anxious for cash?
We could pay him a tax on our produce.
Some of my girlfriends and I got together;
We're dashing to market for selling.
What right has Krishna to tease me like this?

Song 15

Hearing Radha's message as conveyed by Granny,
The crafty Krishna thirstily addressed Radha:

The moment I noticed your face like a lotus—
From then I surrendered my heart to you, Radha.
The charms of your youth overwhelm divine Krishna.
You're the moon in full measure. Relinquish your nectar![37]
I noticed your nose, Radha, straight as an eagle's;
Your ears are so tiny, they look like two nestlings.[38]
The eyes of a deer cannot charm like your glances.
Your cheeks and your lips are like flame of the forest.[39]
Your teeth are more dazzling than gems in a series.

[35] Cā̃pā, a relative of magnolia; see Appendix.

[36] Tāta nāhī̃ gandhera parase / bikasilẽ mohe munimaṇe / hena saba nārīra yaubane 'It hasn't a trace of fragrance; when it blooms it can charm the mind of a wise ascetic; such is every woman in youth.'

[37] See n. 22 above.

[38] Gidhinī sadṛśa tora dekhõ duī kāna 'Your two ears look to me like those of a female vulture.' The intent of the simile is unclear.

[39] Ādhara bandhulī gaṇḍa madhuka samāne 'Your cheeks are like butter tree (blossoms) (madhuka) and your lips, flame of the forest (bandhulī).' See Appendix.

Your body outshines burnished gold by its luster.
The fruit of the fanpalm is shamed by your bosom.[40]
Your waist is as taut as the waist of a lion.
There sit in devotion three folds near your navel.[41]
Your thighs look like excellent tree trunks inverted.[42]
With your feet, you surpass blushing blooms of hibiscus.
With your gait, you have made regal swans to look clumsy.
With these charms of yours I, Nanda's son, feel enchanted.

Song 16

"When I see your loveliness, my thoughts begin to waver.
I am sure my heart will burst! My chest is splitting open."
"If one's heart is bursting and his chest cannot withstand it,
Let him weight his neck[43] and die by plunging in a whirlpool!"
"Do you know you're Ganges and Benares in one body?
You are holy ground to me, a sacred place of worship."
"Krishna, don't you feel ashamed to blabber all this nonsense?
Listen to me, king of gods, I'm married to your uncle!"
"That's a lie you're telling. You're not married to my uncle.
I'm the monarch of the gods; I claim you for my consort."
"What a mighty thrill you must be feeling as you say this!
Could a hardened thief be pleased so much to rob his neighbor?"
"You have said that very well, Candrāvalī, my princess.
What you have yourself remarked is strictly my intention!"[44]
"You're not in your senses, Krishna. You're as hot with craving
As a wasted person who observes a tasty dinner!"[45]
"Dairymaid, you might as well forget about escaping!"

40 Tāla, a plant with round, coconut-sized fruits; see Appendix.

41 Lobhẽ nābhītale base tīna rūpa balī 'At the base of your navel there eagerly sit three lovely folds (balī).' Bali 'fold, wrinkle' is a pun on the name of a legendary demon, Bali, said in puranic accounts to have usurped the gods' domains only to be cheated of them by Viṣṇu as follows: Viṣṇu approached in his dwarf descent and asked for as much territory as he could span in three strides. On receiving Bali's consent Viṣṇu took two strides which respectively encompassed the earth and the heavens. Bali was converted and requested Viṣṇu to place his third foot on his head and send him to the underworld. Since the third foot is said to have emerged from Viṣṇu's navel, Bali ended up sitting devotedly under the navel of the god and it is to this image that the present passage alludes.

42 See Janmakhaṇḍa above, n. 32.

43 Galāta pāthara bāndhī dahe pasī mare 'Let him tie a stone to his neck, enter a whirlpool and die.'

44 Krishna is, as it were, an amorous thief who intends to violate the house of Abhimanyu by seducing his wife.

45 Jaruā dekhiā̃ yehna rucaka āmbala 'Like a feverish person who sees a tasty sour curry.' In Bengal, a feverish person is subjected to a bland diet of items like milk, sago and barley water, no matter how he may crave a dish of sour or otherwise strongly seasoned food.

Song 17

I made a yoke from Brahmā's staff
And put the first plow to the earth.[46]
I used a mountain for churning the sea;
The rope I attached was a serpent.[47]
Dairymaid, how can you hope to escape?
Krishna takes tax, girl, for you!
Stationed in Vṛndāvana,
I play my songs on a flute.
Have no doubt about it:
I am Krishna, scourge of demons.
My fortress stands on Sumeru peak;[48]
I live upon its summit.
Kāliya will be trounced with ease[49]
By the one named Vanamālī.
You belong to the cowherding folk;
Why don't you give me some pleasure?[50]
You've no hope to get away.

Song 18

Near the house of Nanda he and I were raised together.
Now I find that Krishna acts as rudely as a savage.[51]

[46] The passage seems to allude to some myth, which I have not succeeded in tracing, concerning the first plowing of the earth. The reference to Brahmā's staff is also obscure. Plowing, in any case, is associated with Krishna's brother Haladhara 'Plow-Wielder' (see Janmakhaṇḍa above, n. 9). According to *Bhāgavatapurāṇa* 10.65 (Tagare 1978), this brother used his plow to alter the course of the Yamunā River.

[47] Bāndhilõ bāsukī daṛā 'I fastened Vāsuki as the rope.' According to puranic accounts Viṣṇu and the gods competed against the race of demons to churn up amṛta, the nectar of immortality, from the primordial ocean of milk. To this end the gods used the legendary mountain, Mandara, as the churning rod and Vāsuki, a celestial serpent, as the rope for churning. For illustrations of the churning apparatus traditionally used in India, see Randhawa 1971:55 and Archer 1957, Plate 4.

[48] Meru or Sumeru is the Indian Olympus, a fabled mountain upon which dwell the chief deities.

[49] Kāliya, name of a malevolent serpent banished by the youthful Krishna from the Yamunā River; for a complete account see below, Kāliyadamanakhaṇḍa, the eighth section of *Śrīkṛṣṇakīrtana*.

[50] Krishna claims to be of noble descent while Radha comes from the humble cowherd community. Krishna's remark implies that it is the duty of Radha, as a female of lower status, to gratify him.

[51] Caṇḍāla kāhnāñi 'Krishna the caṇḍāla.' Caṇḍāla is the name of a Bengali caste group having a low position in the Hindu social hierarchy; according to Sukumar Sen (personal consultation), the members of this caste have been traditionally employed by royalty as executioners. On their recent history and status in Bengali society see Sekhar Bandyopadhyay 1981.

Even tigers feel uneasy when they know they're stared at;
Look, though, how my nephew acts! You're very shameless, Krishna.
You are just a cowherd, Krishna. Don't you feel embarrassed?
I'm your aunt, your uncle's wife. How dare you ask for taxes?
Tax man, don't you have a better way to earn your living?
Picking on your aunt—will mountains sway before this youngster?[52]
You've been overtaken by an awful curse in childhood.
Krishna, I go all the time to sell our dairy produce.
You have not been bilked by me of any rightful payments.
Krishna, what excuse have you this time for being nasty?
When your dad and mother hear of this, they'll scold you badly!
You should read our sacred texts, our holy lore, the Vedas—[53]
There you'll find I'm justified in everything I'm saying.
See how great a sin you'll earn for troubling married ladies.

Song 19

All of Nanda's household knows my father's Vasudeva.
Radha, why do you insist you're married to my uncle?
Devakī's my mother and my uncle is King Kaṃsa.
You go far afield in saying you and I are kinsmen.
Radha, you could be my brother's wife, but not my uncle's.[54]
I, your Vanamālī, tell you this in jest to tease you.
"Uncle's wife," you mutter, "uncle's wife!" you keep on saying.
If I had my wish, it's you my darkest sins would land on.[55]
If you dare to say this one more time, so help me, Radha,
You will have your earthen vessels smashed by cowherd Krishna.
Why do you scorn rapture, Radha? You're not simple-minded.
Raise your face and look at me, away with all my sadness!
Press me to your upraised bosom, Radha. Hold me closely.
Then I may have respite from the sting of your aloofness.

[52] Poera mukhe parabata ṭale 'Do mountains quake before a child?'

[53] Purāṇa āgama beda 'purāṇas, āgamas and the Vedas.' The term purāṇa usually refers to eighteen major compendiums of legends and philosophy composed in Sanskrit from the early centuries A.D. to the first part of the Middle Ages. For discussion of the puranic genre see Wilson 1972, Publisher's Note and Introduction. Āgama may be said loosely to refer to Saivite and tantric lore. The Vedas—Ṛg, Yajur, Sāma and Atharva—are the most ancient extant Sanskritic compositions, incorporating the foundations of Hindu religion and philosophy.

[54] An Indian woman living in her father-in-law's house typically enjoys an affectionate relationship with her husband's younger, unmarried brothers. It is not unheard of for such a relationship to build into a full fledged love affair; see the anthropological study of middle class Bengali women by Roy 1975.

[55] Mora mahāpātaka paṛu tora muṇḍe '(The consequences of) my capital sins should descend on your head.'

Who's the fool who told you you were married to my uncle?
He should have both eyes put out. He ought to be beheaded.
The way to treat Nārāyaṇa is like a husband's brother.

Song 20

Radha was stricken with horror when she heard Krishna's answer.
She addressed herself partly to Granny and partly to Madhusūdana:

His aunt's swelling bosom disturbs Krishna's thoughts.
Being moonfaced, he speaks words of honey.[56]
The shameless boy calls me a sister-in-law.
He doesn't respect his relations.
What have the fates prearranged for me, Granny?
My nephew accosts me for taxes.
A nephew's too closely related to sleep with;
This arbor's no place to dispute it.[57]
A nephew is just like a god to me, Granny.[58]
He's punishing me with his teasing.[59]
Revenue's not what he has on his mind;
Krishna ought to speak only of taxes.
Combined with his teasing, he makes awful threats;
He's provoking his aunt in this manner.
I am betrayed by these tokens of youth;
Krishna's losing his shame since he saw them.
Nanda's son wants to exploit me for love.

Song 21

Hearing Radha's message as conveyed by Granny,
The crafty Krishna thirstily addressed Radha:

Time and again you are telling me, Radha, "I am the wife of your uncle."
Kaṃsa the king is my enemy. What if he hears we're related? He'll kill you.

[56] See n. 22 above. Radha's grudging expression of admiration for Krishna's attractiveness suggests a motivation for her eventual submission.

[57] Kike kāhnāni̅ bala kare e kun̄ja mayāṇe 'What does Krishna pressure (me) for at this arbored clearing,' i.e., why must this discussion take place near the entrance to a forest glade, the conventional rendezvous place of lovers.

[58] It is ironic that Radha professes to accord Krishna the respect due a divinity while rejecting his claim to divine status.

[59] Mora karmmadoṣe kāhnāni̅ hena paṛihāse 'It's due to my unfortunate karma that Krishna teases me like this.' See n. 20 above.

One who looks out for her interests—she is the type of girl people call clever.
Realize this, Radha, and do not reject me. I am your lord Cakrapāṇi.
As Nanda's son, Radha, I'm overwhelmed at the sight of your breasts. Come embrace me.
In this, the succulence of your first youth, it appears that your figure's in blossom.
Ripe marmelos[60] offer no competition against these two fruits of your bosom.
I cannot think about anything else; I've gone out of my mind since I saw them.
Let me survive by a touch of them; give your consent to your debonair Krishna.
You're speaking falsely to claim we're related; you're just playing coy with me, Radha.
Lend your attention, take heed of my warning; nothing's accomplished through diffidence.
The woman who foolishly squanders her season, rejecting the bliss she is offered,
And keeping the charms of her youth to herself, makes a fool of herself in most cases.
But she is a good and experienced lady whose youth is enjoyed by a lover.
She's like a jasmine whose bloom looks its best when a bumblebee hovers about it.[61]
Don't disregard this. Display your good sense, Radha; don't disappoint me, your Krishna.

Song 22

Why call me "sister-in-law", Vanamālī?
Aren't you aware of your kinsmen?
Calling your aunt by such terms isn't proper.
You're young, yet your actions are shameless.[62]
Even the Ganges would travel upstream
Before what you've asked would be granted.
I have a husband, he stays in my house.
Aren't you afraid of him, Krishna?
Are you so wayward already you don't

[60] Śrīphala or bela, the marmelo or Bengal quince. See Appendix.

[61] Māhlī, the single flowered Arabian jasmine (see Appendix); bhramara 'bumblebee'. The flower referred to is pure white in contrast to the type of bee referred to, which is large and black.

[62] Ālapa baese khāili lāje 'You've done away with your shame at a small age.'

Have some sense of yourself? Go back home.
Chaste is the term we bestow on a lady
Who's only enjoyed by her husband.
She finds no rapture with somebody else
For whose pleasure her household could suffer.
You should consider your family's honor
And banish these schemes from your thinking.
Don't go on hoping to win my affection.

Song 23

> "Radha, your remarks on chastity have been noted;
> Speak no more. Pay attention now to my calculations."

Come on, it's Krishna who's holding the chalk;
Radha, let's figure the tax that you owe.
Three and a half is your full height in cubits.
Tax on it costs twenty million as follows.[63]
Gracing your head is a circlet of flowers;
One hundred thousand's my figure for that.
The hair on your head is more glossy than yaktail;
I fix its tax at two hundred thousand.
With its vermilion, your head charms the world;
Three hundred thousand's the figure for that.
Your face resembles a flawless full moon;
Four hundred thousand's the figure I'll write.
Dark waterlotuses serve you for eyes;
There I am charging you five hundred thousand.
You have a nose better shaped than an eagle's;
For that my tax comes to six hundred thousand.
On your ears glisten your gem-studded earrings;
I expect seven hundred thousand for that.
Precious gems cannot outtwinkle your teeth;
That adds no fewer than eight hundred thousand.
And you have lips red as balsam apples;[64]
Nine hundred thousand's my figure for them.
Your porcelain throat is as white as the conch;
I set a tax of one million for it.
Your hands are lotus; your arms, lotus stems;
I set their tax at eleven hundred thousand.
Moonbeams in series are shamed by your nails;

63 The figure of twenty million is arrived at by adding the separate figures given in the balance of the song.

64 Bimba 'balsam apple', a plant with edible red berries; see Appendix.

Twelve hundred thousand's the figure for them.
Twin Bengal quinces resemble your bosom;
I must assess them at thirteen hundred thousand.
Your waist with three folds in it sways in the breeze;
That calls for payment of fourteen hundred thousand.
Your thighs bear a likeness to fine plantain trunks;
They shall be taxed at fifteen hundred thousand.
These feet of yours look like two blushing hibiscus;
For them I'm charging you sixteen hundred thousand.
Your lower trunk outdoes a solid gold slab;
For that I'll take sixty-four hundred thousand.[65]
There's no way out without paying the tax;
What I, Dāmodara, say is the truth!

Song 24

What's the tax for, Krishna? How is this a customs station?
Why do you obstruct me on the pathway, nephew Krishna?
You've put on a false display of calculations, Krishna.
You'll get into trouble when this news is heard by Kaṃsa.
What a fight I'm faced with on the pathway to the city.
Let me get my hands on your account book, I'll destroy it.[66]
You are just a cowherd. Does the way you talk befit you?
As a proper housewife, I'm embarrassed for you, Krishna.
Thanks to all this mischief, you've no prospects, past or future.[67]
What fool would have let you levy taxes on this pathway?
Krishna, why do you go round in circles with these stories?
No one ever heard of taking tax on someone's body!
I have wares of milk and yogurt, buttermilk and ghee;
Only on these things are you permitted to claim taxes.
Everyone is well aware of Abhimanyu's valor.
Don't you have the sense to recognize that he's my husband?
Or are you so greedy now you disregard that, Krishna?

65 The extraordinary value placed on Radha's lower abdomen rounds out Krishna's sum. See n. 63 above.

66 Pā̃ji puthī tohmāra ciribõ bāma hāthe 'With my left hand I'll tear up your account sheaf.' The left hand is considered inauspicious in contrast to the right and is reserved for toilet functions.

67 Literally 'you've destroyed two worlds,' i.e., past merits and future prospects. The spiritual merits Krishna has earned or will earn are negated by the demerits produced through his acts.

Song 25

Your lotus face is the revelation of the autumn moon;
Your eyes surpass a pair of wagtail birds.[68]
Your lips, beloved, shimmer like flame of the forest.
With such beauty, why do you reject Krishna?
Listen, adorable one, embrace me; then you may go.
I cannot control my thoughts, they are absorbed in you.
Jeweled earrings adorn your ears.
Your breasts resemble twin Bengal quinces;
Upon them sparkles a necklace of filigree blooms.[69]
Seeing it, Radha, I cannot restrain my feelings.
I, Yaśodā's son, Govinda by name,[70]
Am unable to sleep after seeing your beauty.
Unfasten your bodice, Radha, and give me an embrace;
Let me feel the undulations of your milky bosom.
Radha, my love is won through great merit.
By union with me, one goes to heaven.[71]
Realize this, Radha, and fulfill my aspirations.

Song 26

My youth is a treasure; it's sealed in my heart.
There's a bodice beneath my pearl necklace.[72]
Krishna, take all these adornments of mine;
Just let me go home once. Release me.
Krishna, I don't know what love's about, nor
Owe you taxes. You'll kill me for nothing.
I'm still eleven, I haven't reached twelve. Krishna,
Why does it please you to hurt me?
I can die once but not twice; I'll complain
To our demonish ruler, King Kaṃsa.[73]
Why leave your conch and your wheel, mace and bow
To take tax, Krishna, blocking the pathway?
Give way just once, Krishna, let me go home.

[68] Khañjana 'wagtail bird', a restless and darting creature.

[69] Hāra mañjarī, a necklace of flower shapes made in filigree.

[70] Govinda, a Prakritized form of Gopendra 'Lord of Cows', an epithet of Krishna.

[71] Surapura, the abode of the gods.

[72] Gajamukutā 'elephant pearls', the finest and costliest type of pearl, popularly said to be obtained from the headlobes of elephants.

[73] Radha has several risks to confront in approaching the king. She is a simple village girl and, even if allowed access to the king, can be put to death if her complaint is dismissed. Compounding the danger is Krishna's claim that he is the king's officer.

Song 27

Radha, your face is a lotus in blossom;
Lily-pad blooms[74] are your eyes.
Your teeth are more splendid than gems; they're like sumptuous
Pearls dipped and rolled in vermilion.[75]
Radha, my dear one, my heart has been lost to you.
Look, I can't manage my feelings.
Your bosom is shaped like a couple of mounds.[76]
My thoughts are held captive between them.
I've had no peace from the time that I saw them.
Give your consent and I'll touch them.
Your waist is more sculptured than that of a lion.
Your thighs are more shapely than tree trunks.
Your feet are hibiscus; your movements are languid.
Your clothing is made of fine muslin.
I, Nanda's boy, am enraptured to look on
The burnished gold sheen of your figure.
Hoping for love, I've been asking for taxes.

Song 28

I've been going quite a while to market in the city.
On this trail I've never seen a tax collector, Krishna.
You've become a roadside bandit, Krishna, on this pathway;
That's why you're not sorry for the shameful things you're saying.
Give up that unwholesome talk! You're very shameless, Krishna.
I don't understand your talk of love, I'm just a baby.
Don't be so intrigued, Murāri,[77] when you see my beauty.
Just by seeing others' things, a beggar cannot claim them.
Why do you keep talking like a madman? Do you realize
How absurd you're sounding? Why don't you contain your feelings?
If you've jurisdiction on this forest trail for taxes,
How, then, can you be so overwhelmed with lustful feelings?
In my heart there's not the slightest germ of crude desire.
Why don't you release me and consort with other women?
Why are you creating so much trouble for me, Krishna?
How I wish I didn't have to see your face before me.
You must give up hoping for me right this minute, Krishna!

74 Nīla utapale 'dark waterlotus'; see Appendix (utapale).

75 Krishna likens Radha's teeth, attractively coated in red dye from chewing betel, to pearls rolled in vermilion powder.

76 Śambhu 'Beneficent', an epithet of Śiva, the deity of dissolution; also a term applied to mounds consecrated to Śiva. Krishna compares Radha's bosom to them.

77 Murāri 'Foe of the demon Mura', an epithet of Krishna.

Song 29

You say you've readied your yogurt and milk and are going to market to sell them;
Why do you wear this fine costume? Your fresh budding youth in itself is attractive.
Seeing such beauty, your cowherds act sheep-like; they fasten their eyes on some corner.
Your looks charm the gods—what to speak of mere mortals!—they even enrapture ascetics.
Smile at me, Radha, your lover. It's Krishna who blocks you; what use is your temper?
Winking with jewels of all colors, the earrings astride both your cheeks are most splendid;
They're like two suns which arise from both sides of that moon of your face, full and beaming.
Hearing your delicate voice, which is sweeter than droplets of succulent nectar,
I, Nanda's son, feel enchanted. Allow me to enter your arms; please embrace me.
Colorful silks are your garments; they wave as you gracefully go on the pathway;
And on your forehead, Candrāvalī, I see a wonderful sun of vermilion.
Anklets resound on your feet every time as you carry your produce for selling.
Now that you're in Krishna's grasp, by his hands all your finery's going to be ruined.
You're a young lady. You're twelve years of age, and your bodice is bright with its colors;
And, on your throat, there's a necklace of pearls. I feel tantalized as I observe this.
Radha, I'll give up the tax on your dairy goods; kiss me and let me embrace you.

Song 30

Radha's slender body trembled when she heard Krishna's answer. She spoke in distress to Granny as follows:

Granny, I'm melting away like a figure of butter left out in the sun.
How can I offer what Krishna's demanding? I'm terrified out of my senses.

Lost am I, lost![78] What has fate prearranged for me? Why did I travel here, Granny?
No longer will I wear muslin or silk. I won't brighten my head with vermilion.
I'll give up adorning my feet and my arms; I'll stop wearing my anklets and bracelets.
Granny, I won't venture out of my house; I will stay in the care of my husband.[79]
I'm just an underaged dairymaid, caught in the pitiless clutches of Krishna.
Granny, aren't some of the other girls trying to eavesdrop on what Radha's saying?

Song 31

Hearing Radha's message as conveyed by Granny,
The crafty Krishna thirstily addressed Radha:

I want to say just one thing, Radha; listen.
Give me your love. Leave your worries and anger.
Your hair falls in ringlets; your dark tresses glisten.
The sun seems to dawn in your mark of vermilion.[80]
Your brow is the bow of the love god, your eyes
Are his arrows. Your nose is a reed.[81]
Your face is a wonderful lotus; your lips
Are more splendid than flame of the forest.
Jewels can't outsparkle your glistening teeth; why, the
Pomegranate bursts when it sees them![82]
Your throat is as lustrous as conchshell; and, Radha,
Your breasts are a couple of quinces.
Your hands are like lotus. Your arms are their stems; and
Your fingers are buds of magnolia.[83]
Your waist shames the lion; three creases adorn it.

78 Hari hari, a cry of despair related to the Sanskrit root hṛ 'be lost'. The expression is sometimes translated as a summoning of the god Hari (Krishna) himself. This seems unlikely in the present context, where Radha's concern is not to call upon Krishna but to send him away. Moreover, the expression 'hari hari' is put into the mouth of Krishna himself in *Gītagovinda* 3.3 (song 7) (Miller 1978), not a context where the god appears to be summoning himself.

79 Gharata bāhira nahõ baṛāyi go sāmīra baṛai dulālī 'I won't be out of my house, Granny; (I'll be) my husband's pampered pet.'

80 See Tāmbūlakhaṇḍa above, n. 9.

81 Ṇālika yantra samāne 'like a tube instrument,' i.e., straight and slender.

82 See Tāmbūlakhaṇḍa above, n. 14.

83 Campaka, a relative of magnolia; see Appendix.

Your thighs are a pair of fine tree trunks.[84]
Your feet are a couple of red waterlotus;
Your grace far surpasses the swan's.
What is your reason for letting these opulent
Charms of your youthfulness languish?
Offer a smile and express your approval.

Song 32

Radha's slender body trembled when she heard Krishna's answer.
She spoke in distress to Granny as follows:

All of the cowherds do honor to Krishna;
Why does he covet their women?
I've my own husband at home; later on
Krishna's certain to die at his clutches.
Stop Vanamālī. You must try to stop him,
Or don't put the blame on me later.
Let Cakrapāṇi protest as he will,
I won't pay him a bit of attention.
That taker of tributes has ruined his life;[85]
He's defying the wife of his uncle.
I cross the Yamunā River for selling
My wares, stocked with milk goods and ghee.
He's much too big to do similar service;
He'll use his aunt for his profits.
I don't rely for my pleasures on others,[86]
Nor venture to them and accost them.
Krishna must not go on hoping for me.

Song 33

Hearing Radha's message as conveyed by Granny,
The crafty Krishna thirstily addressed Radha:

Adorable Radha, hear my request:
Make love in your blossoming youth.
Radha, your youth is the wealth of a miser;
Your freshness is stored in a bundle.
Radha, pay heed to me. Give of your freshness
Before it begins to decay.

84 Rāmakadalī, equivalent to rāmarambhā; see Janmakhaṇḍa above, n. 32.

85 Tina loka khāā̃ māhādāṇī, literally 'a revenue official who has spoiled three worlds,' i.e., who has canceled out the merits earned in his past, present and future existences. See n. 67 above.

86 Kāra pāna cuna nāhī̃ khāõ, literally 'I don't eat anyone (else's) betel quids with lime.'

Mangos and trees of black plum are in blossom;
Their laden branches are bowing.
How long will you hoard your blossoming youth?
Some divine artisan fashioned this bosom;[87]
Why, even the old can't resist it.
Radha, this beauty will not last forever;
In time, both your breasts will be gourds.
Youth is a bubble of water, Radha;
Regret will outlast it to haunt you.
Out of the universe, I've chosen you.
Consider this; give me your love.
Cling to me during your blossoming youth.

Song 34

Kaṃsa is a fearsome king.
You know this. Don't be stubborn.
Who's prepared to shelter you
If he resolves to kill you?
Don't mix me up in a criminal scheme
For which you could forfeit your life.
I belong to Abhimanyu.
If you use force, Vanamālī,
I shall protest it in front of the king.
I'll see to it that he arrests you.
Krishna, though you're a gentleman's son,
Your behavior just doesn't become you.
You do unwisely in pressuring me;
You'll be sentenced to pay for your actions.
You haven't listened to scripture; you don't know
The rules that concern proper conduct.[88]
You want a lover, that's why you take taxes.

Song 35

Once a mighty sage by name Parāśara existed,
Whom the world regarded as the purest of ascetics.
He had congress in a river with a fishing maiden;
Thus was born a gifted sage, the author of the Vedas.[89]

[87] Viśvakarmā, name of the legendary artisan of the gods.

[88] Purāṇa kathā 'the stories of the purāṇas' (hence scripture; see n. 53 above); dharama bebathā 'code of conduct.'

[89] Tāta upajilā bedabyāsa tapodhana 'Thence was born Vedavyāsa, rich in austerities.' Legend has it that Parāśara, a hermit, encountered the fishing girl Satyavatī one day while crossing the Ganges River. The girl's mother is said to have been a fish. Her union

Radha, all the things you've said are sheer exaggeration.
Wise men share the viewpoint that adultery's not sinful.
There were once five Pāṇḍavas, the sons of Lady Kuntī.
Whose five husbands they became is known to everybody.[90]
With the gods so many courtesans cavort, like Rambhā—[91]
How are all these girls allowed to make their home in heaven?
On the head of Śiva rests the Gaṅgā's triple courses;
With a man named Śāntana that Gaṅgā once consorted.[92]
Radha, if it's wrong to find enjoyment with a woman,
How can that same Gaṅgā touch the universe around us?
No harm comes of loving one's own wife or someone else's.
Be aware that all displays of chastity are pointless.
Recognize this, then fulfill my hopes without misgivings.

Song 36

Radha's slender body trembled when she heard Krishna's answer. She spoke in distress to Granny as follows:

Tārā, wife of Guru, was abducted by the moon;
To this very day he bears the stigma of his mischief.[93]
Indra used deceit to take his pleasure with Ahalyā;
On his body there sprang up a thousand female organs.[94]
This is really striking talk. You ought to hear it, Granny.
Krishna says adultery is not a sinful practice!
Sunda and his brother Upasunda were companions.
Owing to Tilottamā, they lost their lives together.[95]

---

with Parāśara is said to have produced Vyāsa or Vedavyāsa, legendary author of the Vedas, the epics and the purāṇas (see n. 53 above).

90 According to the epic *Mahābhārata*, Kuntī was the mother of five sons known by the patronymic Pāṇḍava. Draupadī was the common wife of all five.

91 Rambhā ādi beśyāka ramanti tridaśe 'The (celestial) courtesans, Rambhā and so forth, cavort with the thirty.' Rambhā is the name of one of the ladies of pleasure said to reside in the paradise of Indra, the king of the gods. The thirty referred to represent the traditional number of major divinities in Indra's heaven.

92 Gaṅgā, the Ganges River, sometimes called tripathagāminī 'three-coursed' (because it is said to flow through heaven, the mortal world and the underworld); Śāntana, name of a legendary king and husband of Gaṅgā. Their union is said to have produced Bhīṣma, an important character of the *Mahābhārata* epic.

93 Tārā 'Star', the legendary wife of Bṛhaspati 'Jupiter', tutor and priest of the gods, had a liaison with one of her husband's pupils, Candra 'Moon'. The moon is said to be blemished with its dark spots as a result.

94 Ahalyā, name of the wife of the legendary sage Gautama. Falling in love with Ahalyā's beauty, Indra disguised himself as her husband and made love to her. Gautama caught them in the act and cursed them both.

95 Tilottamā, name of an enchanting maiden supposedly created by Viśvakarmā (see n. 87 above) at the instance of Brahmā in order to thwart the demon brothers Sunda and Upasunda. In legend the brothers quarrel over the girl and destroy one another.

There was once a pair of demons, Śumbha and Niśumbha;
On account of Pārvatī, the two of them expired.[96]
Rāvaṇa of Laṅkā had a very lengthy lifespan;[97]
Ultimately he, too, had to perish due to Sītā.[98]
Granny, since you know these things, you must discourage Krishna.
Why does he persist in telling me such made-up stories?
Granny, say to him, "You'd better think it over, Krishna.
Realize for yourself what's best for you and go back homeward."
See to it that he does not continue to provoke me.

Song 37

Hearing Radha's message as conveyed by Granny,
The crafty Krishna thirstily addressed Radha:

A splendid magnolia chaplet encircles
Your hair, like a ponderous cloud wreathed in lightning.
Adorning your head, your enticing vermilion
Resembles the sun at the moment of rising.
A crescent shaped moon, as it were, marks your forehead.
Your ears, which are brightened by earrings, look splendid.
Your nose is a sesame flower; it's matchless.
Your cheeks look as gorgeous as lotus-bloom petals.
Your eyes are a couple of flickering wagtails;[99]
Your mere sidelong glance could enchant an ascetic.
Your teeth are so gleaming, they outshine your baubles,
With crescents for lips that eclipse balsam apple.
Your throat is like conchshell, your breasts like two sheldrakes.[100]
Your arms are the stems of your lily-bloom hands, and
Your figure reminds me of golden magnolia.[101]

[96] Śumbha and Niśumbha, names of two demon brothers who supposedly defeated the gods in battle and jointly proposed marriage to the goddess Pārvatī. She responded by challenging them to a contest in which they and their forces were defeated. Details are given in the Devī-Māhātmya section of *Mārkaṇḍeyapurāṇa* (Pargiter 1969).

[97] Cauda cau yuga āyu laṅkāra rābaṇa 'Laṅkā's Rāvaṇa had a lifespan of four times fourteen (i.e., fifty-six) eons.' Rāvaṇa, name of the legendary demonic ruler of Laṅkā (Ceylon) and adversary of King Rāma (Tāmbūlakhaṇḍa, n. 21).

[98] See Tāmbūlakhaṇḍa above, n. 16. Rāvaṇa abducted Sītā and was assassinated subsequently by Rāma.

[99] See n. 68 above.

[100] Koka 'ruddy goose' (Monier-Williams 1976), an aquatic bird often compared to a woman's breast in Indian literature due to its plumpness and its tendency to be seen in pairs.

[101] Kanaka campaka 'golden campaka.' The campaka is a yellow blossom related to magnolia. See Appendix.

Your navel's as deep as the Ganges,[102] while lions
Withdraw to their caves at the sight of your waistline.
Both of your thighs look like finely shaped tree trunks.
The elephant takes to the forest in shame on
Observing your movements so graceful, so fragile.
Even in paradise you have no equal—
Heaven has set a gold image in motion.
The demons and gods churned the sea to create you![103]

Song 38

Filled to perfection, your face is the moon, and
Your speech is so sweet, it's ambrosia embodied.
Untempered gold is the sheen of your body;
Glistening jewels are your teeth, while your throat
Is like conchshell. Please tell me the truth, dearest Radha;
Didn't we churn up the sea to create you?[104]
Clusters of luminous suns form your earrings.
Your gait is majestic and, with your sweet fragrance,[105]
You capture the gods—there's no help for mere mortals!
Your glances are stunning, like venomous serpents.[106]
Your bosom resembles an elephant's headlobes.[107]
Your navel's a chalice of liquid enchantment.[108]
Your gem-studded anklets resound with your movements;
The universe quivers in rapture to hear them.
Candrāvalī, you are replete in all virtues.

[102] Nābhi gabhīra tora preyāga upāmā 'Your navel is deep, comparable to Prayāga.' Prayāga, the former name of Allahabad (see n. 23 above), is the point of confluence for the Ganges and Yamunā Rivers; the depth of the water there is considerable.

[103] See n. 47 above. Krishna likens Radha to the divine nectar for which the gods churned the primordial sea. On the comparison of Radha to nectar see also n. 22.

[104] Debāsura mahodadhi mathila ki tore 'Did the gods and demons churn the ocean of milk for you?' See preceding note.

[105] Gajarājagati parimala pārijāta '(You have) a gait like a regal elephant and a fragrance like the coral tree blossom.' On the coral tree (pārijāta) see Appendix.

[106] Kālakūṭa viṣahari jāṇala kaṭākṣa 'Your glances are known to be (like those of) venomous Viṣahari.' Sukumar Sen in private discussions has suggested an alternative reading, kālakūṭa viṣaharija āṇala kaṭākṣa '(Your) glances are the fire that springs from the poisonous Viṣahari('s glances).' According to Sen 1971:671 Viṣahari is a name of the snake goddess Manasā, a sister of Vāsuki (see n. 47). She is said to store poison in her left eye.

[107] Surarājagajakumbha kucayugala 'Your pair of breasts are the headlobes of the king of gods' elephant.' Elephants are the mounts of royalty; the king of gods, Indra, rides a fabled pachyderm named Airāvata. Elephants have two round prominences on either side of their heads which swell during the rutting season. It is to these lobes on Airāvata's head that Radha's breasts are compared.

[108] Telānī gabhīra nābhi lābaṇya jala 'Your navel is a deep oil-vessel, charm is the liquid (within it).'

I, Vanamālī, am stunned by your beauty.
With jokes, smiles and pleasantries, gladden your Krishna.

Song 39

You're collecting revenues to earn a living, Krishna.
Why do you neglect your tax to court some married woman?
How you're acting seems to me entirely perplexing.
Did you have some older person teach you this behavior?
Krishna, show some reason. Pay some heed to what I'm saying.
All my ghee, my buttermilk and yogurt have been ruined.
Yesterday itself Yaśodā fed you from her bosom;
Now, as customs agent, you are asking me for tributes.
Is there any realm in which one hears such far fetched stories?
Isn't there the slightest sense of shame within you, Krishna?
I am barely twelve years old, I'm still not in my teens.[109]
See this for yourself and keep your thinking free from passion.
Though my body looks attractive, it can't give you service;
Like a blossom filled with pollen,[110] it contains no sweetness.
I'm a dairymaid, I go for selling dairy produce.
Why are you detaining me? It serves no purpose, Krishna.
Trouble me no longer, Krishna; don't expect to win me.

Song 40

Radha, it's fitting that we should share love. I'm Murāri, your lord, you enchantress.
I am absorbed in you, Radha. The gods know it well; there's no question about this.
Do not reject me; I'm Krishna, your love. Radha, you are perfection unstinted.[111]
You are Candrāvalī. I'm Vanamālī by name. We'd look splendid together.
You shall possess Krishna thanks to your merits. Consider. Why forfeit a treasure?
Under the kadamba tree we'll make love. All the gods are aware of this fully.

[109] According to Sen 1971:100, the reading e bāra of the text as published should be changed to ebāra 'eleven'.
[110] Ketakī kusuma yena dhulīẽ sāja 'It's like a screwpine blossom, decorated with pollen,' i.e., fine to behold but devoid of nectar inside. On the screwpine plant (ketakī) and its flower see Appendix.
[111] Saba kalā saṃpunī, a pun; 'full of all charms' (kalā 'charm, artfulness, finesse') or 'complete (as a moon) in all digits' (kalā 'digit of the moon'); see again n. 22 above.

Right now you spurn my request without cause. You'll be sorry for this in the future.
You are an unsurpassed beauty.[112] Your husband's the impotent servant of Kaṃsa.
You've no relations with your Abhimanyu. Partake of those pleasures with Krishna!

Song 41

The king cuts off the head of any petty rogue he catches.
Haven't you been listening? He's extremely unrelenting.
I'll protest with such effect the matter will be famous.
I am, after all, your aunt and you're my nephew, Krishna.
I'm a dairymaiden both ingenious and intrepid.[113]
Why don't you respect me as the wife of Abhimanyu?
Have you taken up the golden flute you carry, Krishna,
After finding me to be unusually attractive?
I am to be looked at, Krishna, not to be enjoyed with.
You could earn a beating, taste the lash, or be imprisoned.
Don't try, handsome Krishna, to divert me any longer;
I must take my wares to Mathurā, the royal city.
Have some sense of who you are. Stop longing for me, Krishna.

Song 42

> "I'm at your mercy. My parched heart is stifling
> In flames fierce as snakebite from fires of passion,
> So quickly decant me your lips' nectar, Radha.
> My comfort depends on the bliss you'll accord in desiring to vanquish my sorrow."

"Radha, here are camphor-scented betel quids for eating.
Banish passion's torment! Let me kiss you and embrace you."
"Krishna, is there any lore[114] where tales like this are heard of?
You're my nephew, Krishna. I am married to your uncle!"
"'Married to your uncle! Uncle's wife,' you keep repeating.
Passion's painful arrows should descend upon you, Radha."[115]

112 Padumini = padminī; see Tāmbūlakhaṇḍa above, n. 11; and cf. n. 24 above.

113 Āhme nāgari goālī baṛāyi cauhālinī 'I'm a sophisticated (nāgari) cowmaid, a great cauhālinī.' According to Bandyopadhyay 1978:1.888, the word cauhālinī derives from cuhāna, name of the Rajput dynasty to which the twelfth-century figure Pṛthvīrāja, last Hindu emperor of Delhi, belonged. The implication is that Radha is an aggressive or amazon-like woman.

114 Purāṇe; see n. 53 above.

115 Mora pā̃ca śara tāpa paṛu tora muṇḍe 'The torment of my five arrows should fall on your head.' The love god carries five arrows made from flowers. On the identification of

"Tell me where your home is, Krishna. Where have you been living?
Kaṃsa is His Majesty our ruler. Don't you fear him?"
"His Majesty your ruler Kaṃsa cannot do a thing.
No one frightens me, the son of Devakī named Krishna."
"Like a monkey with a shriveled coconut in hand,[116]
If you try to force me, you will not achieve your purpose."
"I can smash your earthenware and spoil the contents, Radha.
I can pull your clothes off. You know nothing of my nature."
"Don't go pawing at my clothes, you stupid fellow! Listen.
You'll receive the proper outcome if my milk goes rancid!"
"Take me in your arms and, with your heart enmaddened, Radha,
Bite me with your teeth and let me have my proper outcome."[117]
"That's enough of spicy talk. Control your feelings, Krishna."

Song 43

"Granny, Radha wrongly makes refusals which cut me to the quick.
But what is her anger to me, for I delight in coquettish shows of fury!
Arrange so that, overcome with passion, she makes me a fixture
Of the golden jugs of her breasts, which hold her ambrosial essence."

Her face is resplendent; it glows like a lotus. Her eyes are a couple of wagtails.
The eyebrows above are arresting; they look like a couple of motionless cobras.[118]
One should not only gain many rewards, but be king after seeing such portents.[119]
But for me, Granny, there's no guarantee of survival, how much less of kingship.
Folding my hands, I'm imploring you, Granny; you have to restore my existence.
Only if Radha accepts Krishna's love can he live; this is what you must tell her.

Krishna with this god see below, Bāṇakhaṇḍa, the eleventh section of *Śrīkṛṣṇakīrtana*.

116 Mākaṛera hāthe yehna jhunā nārīkala '(I am) like a shriveled coconut in the hands of a monkey,' i.e., Krishna tries in vain to violate Radha. In private discussions Edward Dimock has suggested that nārīkala 'coconut' is a pun on nārī kola 'woman's lap' or 'woman's bosom.'

117 This couplet is reminiscent of *Gītagovinda* 10.11 (song 19) (Miller 1978).

118 Sukumar Sen has suggested in private discussions that cobras are in constant motion except when mating, which is considered an auspicious event; hence Krishna's observation. For an alternative interpretation of this line see Ray 1973:214.

119 Observing several auspicious omens (see preceding note) in sequence is interpreted as a sign that one will soon acquire possessions or gain in status.

Her throat wears a necklace of multiple strands, while her teeth are more brilliant than gemstones.
Her hands look like lotus. Her arms are their stems; and her breasts look like twin golden flagons.
Her navel's a river; the creases above are its banks; her broad hips are its beaches.
Upon them her waistband of gold is creating appropriate waterfowl noises.[120]
The hairline beneath Radha's navel resembles a dagger. Her buttocks are shields.
How strange; without even directing a blow she's already disabled my spirits.
Outside one may not observe it, but inside I smolder in flames of desire.
Let me advise you most humbly, I don't find a moment's relief from this torment.
Her feet are like blushing hibiscus; her thighs are the trunks of two finely shaped plantains.
The consummate delicacy of her movements surpasses the swan's regal graces.
I have descended to earth in the hope of partaking of pleasure with Radha.

Song 44

Hearing Krishna's message as conveyed by Granny,
Radha, who was losing ground, addressed Granny as follows:

Hearing from your very lips the things that Krishna's saying,
I've been trembling in my heart. I feel extremely anxious.
If he had the right to levy taxes on this pathway,
Why would Krishna set aside his work to praise my beauty?
What a wicked soul is Vanamāli! Look now, Granny,
I present my hands before you, clasped in supplication.
Why have you listening to what Krishna says? Moreover,
Why do you approach me to repeat the things he's saying?
It was to protect me that my husband's mother called you.
Is it proper, then, for you to act in such a manner?
Krishna is a cowherd boy. He's very hard to manage.
Why are you at all concerned about the things he blabbers?
If, on his behalf, you're so romantically inspired,
You can go yourself and do some visiting with Krishna.
But if you are still concerned about my welfare, Granny,

120 The jingling of Radha's metallic waistband is compared with bird calls appropriate to the riverside scenario alluded to in the preceding line.

Pay no more attention to the things that Krishna's saying.
Let us both keep quiet and remain apart from Krishna.

Song 45

So saying, Radha turned silent and lowered her face.
With Granny she remained aloof for some minutes.
Then, interpreting Radha's silence as assent,
The lovestricken Krishna impetuously addressed her:

I summoned the parrots from cages, the ducks from the lakes and the birds from the forest.
One by one all those good creatures responded, yet you still won't give me an answer.
Girl, will you spurn me and vanish away?
Seeing your youth, I've no wish to release you.
Your chest is of gold; it is filled by two jewels.
You keep them concealed in your muslin apparel.
You cheat me by taking the treasures away.
Let me examine them. Take off your bodice!
Your face is the perfect round orb of the moon.
Your color resembles raw turmeric, Radha.[121]
Seeing your delicate waist and your hairdo,
I, king of gods, feel entranced with your beauty.
Radha, your face casts the hint of a smile; I see
Moonlight exposed as your teeth show their luster.
Don't keep resisting me, Radha. Embrace me.

Song 46

"Oh, why don't you go tumble down Bhairavaghāṭī's slopes?[122]
Tie a pitcher to your neck and plunge inside the Ganges.
If you keep on making propositions to me, Krishna,
It will take an ocean to wash off your evil doings.
Check our lore and legends,[123] Krishna. There you will discover
How much sin a person earns who lusts for married ladies."
"Radha, your two thighs comprise Bhairavaghāṭī's slopes.
Why should I go far from here when they are so convenient?
Your two breasts I'll fasten like twin pitchers to my neck;

[121] The golden color of turmeric is considered auspicious, while processed turmeric is believed to have medicinal and cosmetic properties. A bride's complexion is commonly treated with turmeric paste for a beautifying effect prior to her wedding.

[122] Bhairavaghāṭī or Bhairavapatane 'Awesome Slopes' or 'Śiva's Slopes', name of a spot on the Ganges in the Himalayas where a legendary sage, Jahnu, is said to have had a hermitage. See Ray 1973:215 for details.

[123] Āgama purāṇe; see n. 53 above.

Give the word and I shall plunge within your charming Ganges.
Listen to me, sweet-faced Radha, wife of Abhimanyu,
I have expert knowledge of the means for sin removal!"
"Krishna, you know nothing when it comes to proper conduct.
You just say the opposite of everything I tell you.
Krishna, I have figured out exactly what you're thinking.
No one in this world is as impertinent as you are.
Don't obstruct me, Krishna. Give me leave to travel homeward.
Now it's afternoon, while it was early when I came here."
"Radha, pay attention to me. Here's my ultimatum:
If I, Krishna, don't obtain your love, I won't release you.
Knowing this, my Radha, come and seat yourself beside me.
Hurry, Radha, don't delay! Come hasten to be near me.
Otherwise I'll keep you bound until you pay your taxes."

Song 47

"Has that mighty king become so desperate for money
That he lets this rascal levy taxes on the pathway?"
"Listen to my message, Radha. You are just a cowmaid.
I am Vanamāli, lord supreme; there's no one higher."
"How can you demand a tax from me on ghee and yogurt?
Krishna, I am married to your uncle. You're my nephew."
"I take taxes at the shore, at market and on roadways.
What you have is worth not less than several hundred cowries."[124]
"Several hundred cowries for these wares of milk and yogurt?[125]
Krishna, what you're claiming is absurd, you crooked tyrant!"[126]
"I churned up the ocean in a former lifetime, Lakṣmī.[127]
I was Hari. I am Krishna now and you are Radha."
"You're inventing falsely all these tales of former lifetimes.
How could you be Hari, Krishna? How could I be Lakṣmī?"
"Radha, you don't know that I have existential powers.
All is of my body—heaven, hell, the world of mortals."
"You who are a cowherd call yourself the cosmic refuge.[128]
You will be a laughingstock when people come to hear this."
"I won't let you go today unless I get my taxes!"

[124] Ṣola pana 'sixteen paṇas'; see n. 10 above.

[125] Sukumar Sen has suggested in private discussion that dudha dadhira 'of milk and yogurt' be substituted for the original text reading deha dadhira 'of (my) body and yogurt.' The translation reflects this substitution.

[126] Goāre (goāra) has the original sense 'rural constable', hence it takes on the derived meaning of a crooked and/or overbearing rustic.

[127] See Janmakhaṇḍa above, song 7, line 2.

[128] Jagata nibāsa 'refuge of the world.'

Song 48

Oh, Krishna, you've made my buttermilk rancid.
You've ruined my ghee and my yogurt.
The sun which was rising now stands in the west.
My dairymaid friends all forsake me.
You wouldn't let me proceed to the market;
You falsely detain me for taxes.
Always I've gone as I wished with the cowmaids;
We'd visit the market for selling.
How could I know you're a toll agent, Krishna?
Disaster has struck on this highway.
Krishna, collecting the tax is your duty.
Why shirk it as you have been doing?
Like a wild doe, whom the world seeks to harm
For her flesh, I look round, seeking freedom.[129]
Even my earrings now seem like a hindrance;
My clothes and my jewelry betray me.

Song 49

Close to the Yamunā River I romp
With my snake-headed anklets and hair in cascades.[130]
At Nanda's house I play games. All the while
Due to fear of me, Kaṃsa the king gets no sleep.
What will you go to the town for at present?
Here in Vṛndāvana you can taste pleasure.
Radha, your figure reminds me of gold; you
Resemble a swan in the grace of your movements.
Your breasts are quite firm and your waistline is slender.
Your youth is exquisite. Extend your affection!
Don't go on, beautiful Radha, resisting.
Your eyes are enormous, they're swimming in nectar.
A garland-bloom[131] chaplet cascades from your hair;
This shows that your season has come to make love.
The glow of your lips puts to shame balsam apple;
Your glistening teeth look exactly like pearls.
My thoughts are all steeped in your blossoming freshness.

[129] Compare the Old Bengali *Caryāpadas* 6.3 apaṇā māṃsẽ hariṇā bairī 'the deer is betrayed by its own flesh'; see also Rādhāviraha below, n. 89.
[130] Paera magara khāṛu māthe ghoṛā cule '(I have) magara anklets on my feet and a mane of hair on my head.' Magara refers to a mythical aquatic serpentine beast whose head is often depicted on anklets and armlets. Long or manelike hair (ghoṛā cule, literally 'horse hair') suggests early childhood in a boy.
[131] Dolaṅga 'garland flower'; see Appendix.

Song 50

Radha's slender body trembled when she received Krishna's answer.
She spoke in distress to Granny as follows:

"Wares of ghee, yogurt and milk I prepared, then I put on a sari of silk.
All round my hair bees are murmuring. These are the reasons why Krishna detains me."
In her distraction the dairymaid wept, saying, "What will remain to take homeward?
Krishna is levying taxes on dairy goods; he's not afraid of King Kaṃsa.
Under the kadamba tree Krishna sits; on his flute he's incessantly playing.[132]
Wanting to clasp me by force, Krishna ruined my milk goods and smashed the containers.
Krishna has pilfered my cream; at the base of a fig tree he squatted and ate it.
I feel afraid in my heart when I look at black Krishna; my thoughts are unsteady.
Krishna's a scamp with his heart set on evil, a threat to the households of cowherds."

Song 51

Hearing Radha's message as conveyed by Granny,
The crafty Krishna thirstily addressed Radha:

I feel disturbed in your absence. I can't keep the cows strapped and fastened securely.
There's not a sign of the calves, they're astray; and the tethering ropes are all missing.
Footloose, your Krishna meanders the pasture. He's thinking of you every moment.
Some who have houses where cows have been straying say, Beat him! while others say, Catch him! . . .[133]

Song 52

Radha's slender body trembled when she heard Krishna's answer.
She spoke in distress to Granny as follows:

Granny, I would fly to such a place, had I been born a bird,
Where I would never see the face of Krishna.
How I long to leave this world! I feel like taking poison. Let the

[132] Literally, plays on the flute with mouth and nose.
[133] A complete leaf of the extant manuscript is missing at this point.

Earth make room inside, I want to hide there.
Listen to me, Granny. It is certain I will perish
If young Krishna overcomes me on this pathway.
Shattering the pots, he spoiled the dairy goods; he thinned the milk.
He doesn't care that we are aunt and nephew.
Everyone considers him my nephew Vanamālī; yet
He called me "dairymaid" and spoiled his prospects.[134]
Krishna acts mature while in appearance he's a youngster;
If one says, "Let go! Let go!" he holds on tighter.
It's hurting me like poison to discuss that son of Nanda
And Yaśodā. He's an awful roadway nuisance.
He's abused me on the trail, demanding twelve years' payments; make him
Set aside his hopes for taking duties.

Song 53

"Listen, my enticing Radha, I've blocked off this pathway. You have me, a youthful cowherd, to contend with.
I'll subdue your insolence at once; I hold a mace in hand.[135] So pay your taxes, don't prolong the matter."
"I'm the wife of Abhimanyu, pinnacle of virtues. Does a mountain move, confronted by a youngster?
Let me warn you, you'll be scolded by your parents, Vanamālī. Time is passing, don't obstruct the pathway."
"Radha, gorgeous darling, don't regard me as a youngster. Listen, I am really monarch of the gods.
Hear the truth, my darling: when a thunderbolt descends it has such power it can even break a mountain."
"You're a cowherd; you control the cattle with your flute in hand. But still you block the path and levy taxes.
Why should you detain me? How much power do you have? You won't be able to withstand the pressure, Krishna!"
"This is all unbearable, the things you say, you scabby slut![136] You're very hard to deal with for a woman.
You're not acting nicely. Who will tolerate this kind of thing? I'll hold you by your clothes and take my taxes!"
"Abhimanyu's fiercer than a blade. The king is very stringent. Why do you prolong the matter, Krishna?

134 Tina loka khāā̃. See n. 85 above.

135 Monā̃ gadā hāthe dharõ 'I hold a mace in hand'; see n. 23 above.

136 Pāmarī chenāri nārī 'scabby sluttish woman.' Pāmara refers to skin disease. The word chenāri seems to derive from chī (an injection of disgust) + nārī 'woman'.

You will be regarded with contempt when I inform on you at home. You mustn't blame me once that happens."
"I'd give you a beating if you weren't a woman, sweetheart. Listen, Radha, I won't drop my highway taxes.
I'll stamp out the might of your demonic ruler Kaṃsa; I can challenge him or any man of valor."
"Don't let's fight here on the pathway. Look, with folded hands I am requesting you take my tax correctly.
Let me go, be gracious. I've had neither food nor water. It was morning when I came here, now it's evening."
"I will not accept your taxes! You must let me touch your bosom. That's my final offer to you, Radha."

Song 54

Krishna, don't be crazy. Keep your feelings in control.
Manly though he is, my Abhimanyu doesn't chase me.
If you leave your toothmarks after forcing me to kiss you,
How can I go home and make excuses, Gopīnātha?[137]
Lord Gadādhara, I bow before you and request you,
You must show some pity toward me. Just this once release me.
You're of cowherd birth. How can you say the things you're saying?
Why should someone else's wife arouse your interest, Krishna?
What salvation is there if the cowherd Nanda hears this?
Think it over in your heart; and, Krishna, stop insisting.
Krishna, take my string of pearls to satisfy your taxes.
Never more will I set out for visiting the city.
All my milk and ghee and other merchandise are ruined.
I've my husband's mother, plus his sisters, to contend with.
I am just a dairymaid, a tiny girl named Radha. Listen,
I don't even know what passion feels like, Vanamālī.
Don't obstruct me, Krishna; give me leave to travel homeward.

Song 55

Look Radha, if you were seeking me, you wouldn't
Find me; I'm Krishna, the chief of the gods.
Driven by longing, I've come to you. Who would
Discover a trove and mishandle the treasure?
Just this one time you must spare my existence;
I'll pay you back with invaluable baubles.
Youth is the time for enjoying love's pleasures.
Let me find joy as your lotus face blossoms.

[137] Gopīnātha 'Master of Dairymaids', an epithet of Krishna.

Cast your eyes sidelong and look at me. What is my crime,
That you go from me, turning your back?
I'm Lord Gadādhara. Now join your Krishna
And reach the far side of the sea of desire.
We can amuse ourselves here in Vṛndāvana
Once you present me your word of approval.
Don't let your Krishna become disappointed.

Song 56

"Some call you Gadādhara while others call you Krishna.
You're the one who blocks the road and makes demands for taxes."
"You're a simple dairymaid, that's why you do not know me.
I'm the holder of the conch, the mace, the bow and discus."
"You're a cowherd, Krishna, yet you call yourself Lord Hari.
Don't you know you'll die at once when Kaṃsa hears about you?"
"It will be no feat for me to slay the demon Kaṃsa.
I can capture you by force as well and take my taxes."
"Many cowmaids go with me for selling goods at market;
On the path we girls will use our fists to thrash you soundly."
"Charging at you headlong, I could simply bash your brains in.[138]
I may have long hair,[139] but don't regard me as a youngster."
"You apply your manly force intimidating women.
This must be how you've attained your vast importance, Krishna!"
"Don't prolong your fussing, Radha. Hand the taxes over.
I, your Krishna, won't release you now without the taxes."
"You must not obstruct the path, for you're the son of Nanda.
Look, I touch your feet. Will you not show some mercy toward me?"[140]
"You can venture home when you've agreed to love me, Radha."

Song 57

> Radha's slender body trembled when she heard Krishna's answer.
> She spoke in distress to Granny as follows:

The mother and the sisters of my husband rule our household.
I can't disobey them. What excuse will I go home with?
Look, my very breasts, which he calls marmelos, betray me.
Tell me, Granny, isn't there some plan that I can follow?
Don't you hear me, Granny? It's my life that's being toyed with!
Krishna wants those favors which are only for one's husband.

138 Muṇḍẽ muṇḍẽ ḍusāā̃ māribõ tohmā hele 'Bashing head against head, I'll kill you with ease.'

139 Māthe ghoṛā cule. See n. 130 above.

140 Touching a person's feet is a gesture of deference and humility.

He's about to kill me with the sudden tugs he gives me,
Pawing at my necklace, at my wristlets and my bodice.
Saying that my absence pains him, Krishna asks to hold me;
Then he seeks to kiss my face, comparing it to lotus.
Granny, I can't comprehend what Krishna calls affection!
I don't understand him. Krishna's talking very strangely.
How can I outwit him, Granny? I am just a baby.
What will my most flawless[141] husband say if he should hear this?
Swearing I'm a priceless jewel, he takes my hand, demanding
Love in place of tax. I have to hide my face, embarrassed.[142]
Granny, put a stop to Madhusūdana.[143] Rebuff him.

Song 58

I am god of gods, the lord supreme; I'm Vanamālī.
Listen, dairymaid, I've wasted too much time in doldrums.
Now my heart is set at last on tasting some enjoyments.
Let's dismiss life's sorrows. You must offer your caresses.
Radha, don't you recognize me? Don't you hear my message?
The master of the world[144] has come to Gokula for tributes!
I'm the one who holds the conch, the mace, the bow and discus.
You don't know me, Radha; you're a simple cowherd woman.
When the angry king of gods[145] sent rain in flowing torrents,
I protected Gokula by holding up a mountain.
You arrange your hair like Śiva's;[146] you wear silks; and, cowmaid,
When you go for marketing you dress extremely finely.
Radha, these two breasts must be the handiwork of heaven;
I, Janārdana,[147] feel stupified when I behold them.
You are going often, dairymaid, to sell your produce;
You evade the tax and always manage to escape me.
If you will embrace me, Radha, I'll rescind the taxes.

141 Sāmī guṇanidhī 'my husband, a trove of virtues.'

142 Sāna dei māthe, literally 'I give sāna on my head.' Saan de- or saan kaaṛh- in dialects of modern Bengali refers to the act of pulling the border of one's sari over the face to exhibit shame or reluctance.

143 Madhusūdana, see Tāmbūlakhaṇḍa above, n. 29.

144 Jagannātha, see Janmakhaṇḍa, n. 20, and see n. 33 above.

145 Śacīpati 'Husband of Śacī', an epithet of Indra, the traditional king of the gods (a status which is arrogated by Krishna in the Vaishnava tradition). According to *Bhāgavatapurāṇa* 10.24–25 (Tagare 1978), Krishna advised the herdsmen to abandon their worship of Indra, controller of clouds and rains. In response Indra unleashed heavy storms on the Gokula pasturelands for seven days and nights. Krishna, however, raised Govardhana mountain on one finger to shield the cowherds and in this way humbled Indra.

146 Śambhu, see n. 76 above. Śiva is depicted with a massive topknot of hair.

147 Janārdana 'Mover (Agitator) of Men', an epithet of Viṣṇu-Krishna.

Song 59

Radha's slender body trembled when she heard Krishna's answer.
She spoke in distress to Granny as follows:

Call a skillful barber,[148] Granny; see to it he comes here.
I will have him trim away my fancy hairdo,[149] Granny.
After Krishna saw this hairdo, Granny, and my bosom,
From that moment onward he's been laboring to win me.
God, what have you done, what have you done in making woman!
She is like the doe, whose flesh incites the world to harm her.
On my eyes I wear mascara; on my forehead, Granny, marks of
Sandalpaste. The sight of these has Nanda's son distracted.
No more will I dress in silks of brilliant colors, Granny.
Since he saw them, Krishna has been seeking my caresses.
Also, Granny, I must clean my head of its vermilion;
And I'll have to pound my conchshell bangles into powder.[150]
Lastly, I must rip apart my multistranded necklace.
Krishna has been asking me for love since he observed it.
I think I should drown myself inside a whirlpool, Granny.
I don't act improperly with other women's husbands;
Don't encourage Krishna to annoy me with his teasing.

Song 60

Hearing Radha's message as conveyed by Granny,
The crafty Krishna thirstily addressed Radha:

"Radha, you go very often for selling.
Why do you cheat me of revenue payments?"
"You're very shameless, you cowtender. Krishna,
Which of my items is subject to taxes?"
"Yogurt, that milk and your ghee are the items.
Why do you cheat on your revenue payments?"
"The longer I'm living, the more I am hearing!

148 Nāpitera po, literally 'a son of a barber'; i.e., a person whose skill runs in the family, a thorough professional.

149 Kānaṛī khõpā 'a hairbun (khõpā) in kānaṛī style.' For speculations on the meaning of kānaṛī see Sen 1971:137 and Ray 1973:219. Cutting off the hair is a disfigurement a woman may choose to fulfill a vow, avoid an undesired marriage, demonstrate protest or the like.

150 In Bengal the conchshell bangle is a mark of married status. Smashing the bangles on one's wrist is a feminine gesture of protest or despair, suggesting that the woman's marriage is finished.

Tax isn't taken on milk, ghee and yogurt!"
"It's for your sake I'm a revenue agent.
Why don't you ask Balabhadra, my brother?"
"Why should I ask Balabhadra about it?
Is he more impudent even than Krishna?"
"You have foul thoughts for a girl of good breeding.[151]
I have a mind to subdue you this moment."[152]
"Only a man with no care for his prospects[153]
Would claim on this path he's a revenue agent."
"You have to pay me a full twelve years' taxes.
Otherwise I can arrest and destroy you."
"Make hollow threats to whomever you'll make them—
Even your daddy could never arrest me!"[154]
"Beautiful Radha, give heed to my offer.
I'll drop your taxes if you will embrace me."
"I don't know why, Krishna, you should resort to
Such ludicrous pranks out of amorous longing."
"What an unmasculine race are the cowherds;
The women, compared with the men, are more bullish!"[155]
Krishna continued to block Radha's progress.

Song 61

Radha, you head is embellished with blooms and your hair is most finely arranged.
The Master of Night[156] is your face; while your earrings are studded with glistening gemstones.
Your head with its streak of vermilion looks splendid, and so does the gleam of your teeth.
Your throat is adorned with great pearls,[157] while your lips shimmer brigher than flame of the forest.
Make good the tax, Radha. You can't evade it. Your goods will be seized when you're captured.

[151] Baṛāra jhi tora bhāla nahe matī 'You, a gentleman's daughter, do not have a good mentality.'

[152] Āji karȭ tora pañca saṅgatī 'Just today I'll do your pañca saṅgatī.' Pañca saṅgatī = pā̃ca ābathā; see Tāmbūlakhaṇḍa above, n. 24.

[153] E loka o loka se jana khāe, literally 'the person who destroys this world and that world. . . .' See n. 67 above.

[154] Dekhāha e kāṭha dāpe 'you show these wooden (i.e., hollow) powers.' The casual reference to the father represents a personalized insult.

[155] Puruṣe ādhika tirī āṇḍiā, literally 'The women are more ballsy than the males,' i.e., the men are like castrated bulls (bullocks).

[156] Niśānāthe 'Master of Night', the moon.

[157] Gajamutī 'elephant pearls'; see n. 72 above.

Time and again, when you carry your wares, you escape me by changing your pathway.
This time it was a coincidence, Radha, you came and fell right in my clutches.
I shall collect all your tax on the spot; what is more, I'll destroy all your produce.
You're not aware of my powers. It's I who am lord of the gods, Jagannātha.[158]
Your arms are a couple of golden stems. Your breasts are two goblets inverted.
Your waist is one handspan in width, while your hips are stupendous; they rouse my desire.
Your feet look like blushing hibiscus. Your thighs are the trunks of two finely shaped plantains.
I should get hundreds of thousands in taxes for each of these parts of your body!
You must surrender the payment on them; then proceed as you wish to the city.
But, Radha, if you can't make good the taxes, then listen to this proposition:
Smile just a little and seat yourself here at my side. You'll fulfill all my longing.

Song 62

Mother-in-law gave me warning: "Small daughter,
Don't go for selling your milk goods tomorrow.
That's not the time you should travel to Mathurā market.
Krishna is likely to shatter your vessels.
He's the king's nephew, your foe;[159] he'll lay waste to
Your dairy goods. You will be troubled by him on the pathway."
You'd better leave me alone, Vanamālī.
She's very strict. When I'm home, she'll rebuke me.
Brave Abhimanyu is also at home; he's my husband.
Don't you attempt to use force, Vanamālī.
Once Kaṃsa learns of this, you could be banished.
I'll tell my mother-in-law; I'll be crying.
I shall denounce you by name to her, Krishna.
Later I know you will say little Radha's the culprit.
I shall no longer eat food from black pots;

158 Āhme jagannātha tridaśa īśara 'I am Jagannātha (the master of the world), lord of the thirty (gods).' See nn. 91 and 145 above.

159 Dadhī khāiba tora āne / rājabhāginā bala kariba tore bāṭe 'He will ruin your dairy goods antagonistically; the king's nephew will use force against you on the road.'

I'll keep away from the shade of black clouds.
I'll burn a candle to get through the shadowy night.
I won't drink milk from a cow that is black,
Nor use mascara that's black on my eyes.
I'm simply terrified when I observe you, black Krishna.
You are a boy only twelve years of age,
Still wearing babyish curls on your head.[160]
You'd better realize this, Krishna, and leave me alone.
Don't keep on asking for tax you're not owed.
Go to your home with your honor intact.

Song 63

Everywhere writing is done in black ink.
Everyone thrives thanks to rain from black clouds.
Milk from black cows can be very nutritious;
The king of the gods wears a black gemstone necklace.[161]
Radha, you're wrong to find fault with black Krishna,
The excellent child of Yaśodā and Nanda.
Tresses adorning one's head may be black;
A lotus-like face with black brows may look splendid.
Black bumblebees make a lotus grove charming.
A lady entrances the world with mascara.
The blemishes on the moon's bosom are black;
The ringlets your cheeks are festooned with are black.
Your eyes, dairymaid, are entrancing black lotus.
Your dear Vanamālī is black but most handsome.
The full moon may shine from the fringe of black clouds;[162]
Radha, accept this and don't feel disheartened.
Heed the appeal of your black darling, Krishna.

Song 64

You black creature! Don't you try to trifle with me, Krishna.
You are blind with passion. You can't see where this is leading.
You are black of body, and your heart is black too, Krishna;
Blocking me, you falsely claim to be a tax official.
Krishna, you're a stupid youngster, asking me for taxes.
I'll have Abhimanyu come. Your life will be in danger.

160 Tora māthe śobhe ghoṛā culā 'A mane of hair embellishes your head'; see n. 130 above.

161 On the king of the gods see n. 145 above. I have not been able to discover the significance of the necklace of black gems alluded to in this line.

162 The imagery suggests Krishna's desire to cover Radha's fair body with his own shadowy form in lovemaking.

You have ripped my bodice and you've pulled apart my necklace;
Then you rifled through my wares for no good reason, Krishna.
You have spoiled my yogurt, milk and ghee. You smashed the vessels.
How could such a bull in rut be from a herdsman's household?[163]
You destroyed my buttermilk and milk, my ghee and yogurt,
Then you turned your face away and cackled peals of laughter.
Krishna, you are shameless! Even now you ask for taxes.
You and I will be the butt of lots of gossip, Krishna!
Show some sense of who you are and go back homeward, Krishna.
You do very rashly to claim tax without permission.
Krishna, give up hoping for my love; don't block the pathway.

Song 65

"Listen, I'll explain accounts to you, my darling Radha.
Sixteen hundred[164] is the toll I take at customs stations."
"It would seem the king is very anxious now for money.
On this path he's placed a rascal as a tax official."
"I'm no rascal, Radha; I'm a man of firm conviction.
No one in the universe defeats my resolution."
"You should feel ashamed for making such a statement, Krishna.
On your lips there lingers still your mother's milk's aroma!"
"Radha, I'm no child. I'm God to you and Abhimanyu.
You don't seem to recognize me, Radha. I'm Lord Krishna."
"I would like to take my milk and ghee to town for selling.
Let me go my way; just move aside a little, Krishna."
"It's because of you I have become a madman, Radha.
That is why I must beset you, Radha, on this pathway."
"If you're such a madman, you should go consult a clinic!"

Song 66

In my first years I claimed Pūtanā's life.[165]
It was with ease I destroyed the Cart-Monster.[166]
Twin demons, Radha, were haunting two trees;[167]
I took their lives and dispatched them to Hades.[168]

163 Goāla kule ki tohme upajilā sāṇḍa 'Are you a bull born into a cowherd family?' For upajilā, Ray 1935 and Ray 1973 give the reading upajila.
164 Ṣola śata 'sixteen hundred,' i.e., a round sum; see n. 10 above.
165 See Janmakhaṇḍa above, song 5 and n. 25.
166 Sakaṭa āsura 'Śakaṭa (Cart) the demon.' Śakaṭa is the name of a mythical demon engaged by Kaṃsa. According to *Bhāgavatapurāṇa* 10.7 (Tagare 1978), the demon approaches Krishna in the form of a cart only to be kicked to pieces by the child.
167 See Janmakhaṇḍa above, song 5 and n. 26.
168 Tāhāro parāṇa laā̃ nilō̃ yamapūra 'I took their lives also and carried them to the abode of Yama (death).'

Dairymaid, do not accuse me of boasting;
Everyone knows of my potency, Radha.
Radha, the winds[169] had us tightly encircled;
Storms raged one week, day and night, in the pastures.[170]
Hailstones rained down in a hammering torrent.
I saved the cowherds by lifting the mountain.[171]
Once, with the stout Hanumān as companion,
I built the causeway between here and Laṅkā.[172]
My brother, Lakṣmaṇa, killed Indrajit.[173]
"Victory!" clamored the gods, "Victory!"
Radha, you have to pay heed to my stories;
All the world knows about Krishna's great valor.
Krishna's a trove in your hands; you might lose him![174]

Song 67

Radha's slender body trembled when she heard Krishna's answer. She spoke in distress to Granny as follows:

It was my pathetic mother who first named me Radha;
No one was concerned that it might carry evil omens.[175]
Yet I'm such a wretched woman, cursed with meager fortunes.[176]
I've approached this place and must contend with Krishna's teasing.
Granny, why did I set out for town? I'm lost, I'm lost now![177]
I'm a wretched woman, overtaken by disaster.
I have traveled twelve years, Granny, selling dairy products;
Never was I challenged by an actual tax collector.[178]

169 Literally 'the forty-nine winds,' a reference to the traditional number of Maruts, a class of deities in the Vedas. They make up Indra's retinue. See Macdonell 1974:78 and Mani 1975:489–90.

170 The original text reads 'It stormed in Gokula seven days and nine nights.' This is apparently in error.

171 On the miraculous raising of Govardhana mountain see n. 145 above.

172 Hanumāna māhābira hailā sārathi / tabẽ kailõ setubandha āhme dāśarathi '(When) the stalwart Hanumān was my lieutenant, then I, Dāśarathi ("Son of Daśaratha", i.e., Rāma), made the setubandha (legendary bridge between the southern tip of India and Śrī Laṅkā).' See n. 97 and Tāmbūlakhaṇḍa above, n. 37.

173 Indrajit 'Defeater of Indra', name of a son of Rāvaṇa who once defeated Indra in battle; slain in the battle at Laṅkā by Rāma's brother Lakṣmaṇa (see preceding note).

174 Pāche hārāyibi kolera nidhī kāhne 'Later you could lose the treasure in your lap (or: of your bosom) who is Krishna.'

175 Hāchi jiṭhī keho tāta nā dila birodhā 'No hāchi jiṭhī lent opposition to that.' Hāchi jiṭhī is literally 'sneezes and lizards'; here it is used in the general sense of evil omens.

176 Āhme dukhamatī nārī āṭhakapālī 'I'm a wretched woman, narrow-fated (literally, narrow-foreheaded).' See n. 17 above.

177 Hari hari; see n. 78 above.

178 Dānīra poẽ 'the son of a tax collector,' i.e., a real or professional tax collector; see n. 148 above.

Now a very unrelenting Krishna has opposed me;
I will have to make this known so Kaṃsa will take notice.
I am just a little girl, the daughter of a cowherd.
Wicked Vanamālī must give up his urge to have me.
Just for once let Krishna show that he upholds my honor;
Krishna ought to show some mercy, sparing my existence.
It's with tears and trembling that I ask you very humbly,
Just this once within your heart take pity on me, Granny.
Find a way to fend off Krishna; do this on my bidding.

Song 68

Hearing Radha's message as conveyed by Granny,
The crafty Krishna thirstily addressed Radha:

"You're so alluring, a natural seductress.[179] My heart quickens pace when I see you.
With your aloofness, my thoughts are untranquil. Oh, how can I go on surviving?"
"Krishna, don't say things like this. You don't have any modesty. Where are your parents?[180]
You've merely spotted a juicy affair; you're entranced by the wife of your uncle."
"Why must you say, 'I'm your aunt, I'm your aunt'? I've been driven insane by love's goading.
Radha, you're trying to use unfair means to elude me; I know all about it."
"You're a child, Krishna; you can't understand what I'm saying. I see your intentions.
I am just Radha, a dairymaid; I'm very small. I know nothing of passion."
"I'm dashing Krishna, your cowherd pursuer, and you are a twelve year old lady.
This is most lovely, your blossoming youth; you should gladly bestow it upon me."
"My blooming youth is a treasure that's sealed. There's no possible way you could rob it.
I have a poisonous snake in this youth; if you touch and are bitten, you'll perish!"
"I am your Krishna and you're my Candrāvalī. Till I am dead I can't leave you.

[179] Paduminī = padminī; refer to n. 112 above.
[180] Literally, 'you have no shame from your parents'; see n. 13 above.

You say your youth is a poisonous snake—I'm an excellent venomist, Radha!"
"There is no end to these intricate arguments! Krishna's too smart, he unnerves me.
What sort of folly induced that cruel Granny to have me approach by this pathway?"
"Look at your lover, bestow an embrace on me. Why are you overexcited?
How is your Granny at fault? It's because of my merits that you have been brought here."
"Milk that is hot can't be drunk through a straw; when it's cooled, it is tasty for drinking.
Breasts which are starting to bud are like marmelos; no one enjoys them unripened!"
"When someone's hungry for something, he couldn't care less if it's ripe or it isn't.
He'll eat it as he encounters it till all his hunger is gone, clever Radha!"
"Krishna, I'm looking you square in the eye and I'm warning you: better avoid me.
Even a tiger will not eat a creature he meets face to face in the forest."
"Beautiful Radha, discard your misgivings. Be pleased to agree to my wishes."

Song 69

Sharing laughter feels so sweet; it's sweet exchanging glances.
Oh my Radha, this is what impelled me to approach you.
Don't allow the thought of this to trouble you. Embrace me.
I am Jagannātha;[181] it's for you I feel impassioned.
Why have you been giving me these sidelong glances, Radha?
At the very sight of you, my feelings start to flutter.
Like the wagtail bird, your eyes are fidgeting and darting;
Even so, their aim outscores the arrows of Arjuna.[182]
Anything you say I will deliver to you, Radha.
I can fetch the moon down from the sky if you request it.
Fire of the forest is your lips;[183] your face is lotus.
With your gleaming teeth, you cast a pall on precious gemstones.
Offer me your love this once, don't leave me disappointed.
Someday, if you try, you will not find Lord Hṛṣīkeśa.[184]

181 Refer to n. 144 above.

182 Arjuna, name of the third of the five Pāṇḍava brothers in the *Mahābhārata* epic (see n. 90 above), characterized as an outstanding archer.

183 Ādhara bandhulī 'Your lips are flame of the forest (bandhulī).' See Appendix.

184 See n. 8 above.

No one pair of lips would serve to praise your beauty fully.
Radha, you are flawless. You've enchanted me, Murāri.[185]
Gratify me, Nanda's son, by letting me embrace you.

Song 70

Radha's slender body trembled when she heard Krishna's answer.
She spoke in distress to Granny as follows:

Damn to blazes, Granny, the existence of a woman!
I have been betrayed by my alluring youthful beauty.
I shall not be able to endure this torture, Granny.
I am like the doe, whose very flesh is her unmaking.
Lost, I'm lost![186] There isn't any way to go to market.
Listen, that black Krishna is my adversary, Granny.
What was that unlucky time when I began my journey?[187]
There were no ill omens to prevent me from proceeding.[188]
He's demanding love, my very husband's nephew, Granny!
I shall have to end my life by suicide to stop him.
In my golden basket, Granny, there were silver pitchers;
I had draped them all with cloths of muslin to protect them.
Now the milk and buttermilk have spoiled. The ghee is ruined.
All the other dairymaids go on and leave me stranded.
I shall go in tears and bring this news to Kaṃsa's notice.
Krishna won't have any right to blame me for this later.
Talk to him again; no more let Krishna seek to win me.

Song 71

Hearing Radha's message as conveyed by Granny,
The crafty Krishna thirstily addressed Radha:

"I drew the scriptures,[189] like toys, from the ocean; I play in the role of Murāri.
I've destroyed demons and trounced evil spirits. The conch, wheel and mace are my emblems."

[185] See n. 77 above.

[186] Refer to n. 177 above.

[187] Kamaṇa āsubhakṣaṇe bāṛhāyilõ pā 'At what inauspicious moment did I extend my foot?'

[188] Hā̃chi jiṭhi tāta keho nāhī̃ dila bādhā, literally 'No sneeze or lizard forbade me from that.' See n. 175 above.

[189] Veda 'scriptures'; see n. 53 above. According to puranic accounts Viṣṇu made his first descent upon earth in the form of a fish so as to rescue the Vedas from the bottom of the ocean.

"You make a show of things, Krishna. Your thinking is cunning—what schemes you resort to!
Not on your soul could you go to the lowest of realms[190] and recover our scriptures!"
"I posed as Rāma and massacred Rāvaṇa; I reduced Laṅkā to ashes.
With the assistance of Lakṣmaṇa, I rescued Sītā and made good my honor."[191]
"The ramparts of Laṅkā were tall as the sky; by his spirit alone one might reach them.
Keep to your pasture, you cowtending boy! You're a liar and so is your brother!"
"I'm Vanamālī! I'm Krishna! Lord Hari! I'm tending the cows as a pastime.
I do not lie to you. Both of us brothers earn tributes because of our powers."
"Impudent Krishna, you don't understand. With my lips I could blast you like lightning.
You could be dead for your own sinful actions if Kaṃsa should hear what you're up to."
"I held the earth on the tip of my tusk on assuming my boar incarnation.[192]
I tore a demon apart[193] in my man-lion guise. Don't you know of this, Radha?"
"Krishna, I know what a hero you are. You are boasting for nothing, please stop it.
You've told enough of your stories. Your daddy himself couldn't do what you speak of."[194]
"Dairymaid, you're not aware of my forebears. You don't understand, you're too simple.
I have been born in a warrior house,[195] and my father's the brave Vasudeva."
"Don't go on arguing. I must proceed to the city. Don't hope to attain me."

190 Sapata pātāla giā 'by going to the seventh hell.' Indian cosmology has it that there are seven regions below the earth, successively atala, vitala, sutala, talātala, rasātala, mahātala and pātāla, the lowest of realms.

191 Refer to n. 173 above.

192 In his third descent Viṣṇu is said to have taken the form of a boar and to have retrieved the earth from the underworld by raising it on the tip of his tusk.

193 In his fourth descent Viṣṇu took a form partly human and partly lion. In this guise he attacked and destroyed the demon Hiraṇyakaśipu.

194 See n. 154 above.

195 Kṣatriya kūle jarama āhmāra 'My birth is in the kṣatriya clan.' The kṣatriyas represent the group of castes traditionally occupied in the political and military affairs of society. Krishna's affiliation with this group arises from his birth ties to the local ruler.

Song 72

Underneath a tree[196] beside the Yamunā's embankment—
That is Krishna's central station, Radha.
You cannot evade me, Radha, using tricks or speeches.
Offer me your love in place of payment.
I am Krishna. I collect the taxes on this pathway.
Why don't you make good your taxes, Radha?
I'm the one who holds the conch, the mace, the bow and discus.
I'm the highest god, Lord Vanamālī.
You are Abhimanyu's wife, replete in all perfection;[197]
You are called Candrāvalī, my Radha.
There was once a time you were the wife of Cakrapāṇi.[198]
How have you been able to forget this?
It's because of you I have descended from the heavens;
Go when you've embraced me for the taxes.
Moonfaced one, my Radha, you must listen to my message.
All my hopes for love are placed in you.
Inbetween these breasts, you're holding captive my attentions.

Song 73

You're the leader of the gods, according to your statement.
How, then, can you let your thoughts be drawn to married women?
In these woods you circulate, attending to the cattle;
Now, for no good purpose, you attempt to levy tributes.
Krishna, you must give up your unwholesome propositions.
Abhimanyu's bound to take your life if he should hear this.
I must purify my ears, I'm feeling so embarrassed![199]
Won't you, even now, come to your senses, cowherd Krishna?
Don't continue struggling so intently for me, Krishna.
I will never heed the propositions you are making.
Why do you continue to belabor matters, Krishna?
I have closed my ears to all the things that you are saying.
You should realize this and keep your thoughts away from mischief.
Turn around, go home again the way that you have come here.
Why are you resorting to a scheme like this one, Krishna?
For you I'm a very close relation.
Since you know this, you must give up hoping to possess me.

196 Kadamera tale 'under the kadamba (tree).'

197 Saba kalā saṃpunī, see n. 111 above. Also see Tāmbūlakhaṇḍa above, n. 6.

198 See Tāmbūlakhaṇḍa above, n. 31.

199 Bhūmi chuiā̃ hātha parasaõ duī kāne 'I touch the earth and apply my hands on my two ears.' Since the earth is considered to be pure, touching the ground and applying the hands to the body is a gesture of self-purification—in this case, for having heard improper talk.

Song 74

On your hair I notice there's a medlar-blossom garland.
A hundred thousand cowries is the tax for your vermilion.
Your nose, a bloom of sesamum,[200] has all the world enchanted.
Pay a hundred thousand and no less for your mascara!
Dairymaid, don't go! Don't go! You must set down your produce.
I'm an agent for the customs house. I shall assess you.
Buttermilk and ghee are there with you; there's milk and yogurt.
For the vessels on your head my tax is sixteen hundred.[201]
Now, my pretty Radha, how do you propose to manage?
Dairymaid, you're not allowed to travel any further.
You can't pay a cowrie of the revenues I'm asking;
So, oh Radha, give me your embrace in place of taxes.
Why do you disdain Lord Madhusūdana,[202] my Radha?

Song 75

Though you may be god of gods[203] and master of the cosmos,
You have seized me by the clothes and disarranged my hairdo.
You have pried inside my blouse to violate my bosom.
I don't know how Nanda's son could act as you are doing.
Who will I report to with these never heard-of stories?
Krishna, you have brought about my total devastation.[204]
You have tried to take away my necklace and my bracelets.
You mistreat me, hoping for my kisses and my favors.
Krishna, you've disdained the law and turned your thoughts to mischief.
Your descent to death's abode[205] will happen any instant.
Thinning down my milk, you smashed the pots and spoiled the produce.
Krishna, you deny that I'm your aunt and you're my nephew.
Calling me a dairymaid, you've undermined your prospects.[206]
Everyone's aware that you're my nephew, Vanamālī.
If I do not give you the results you merit, Krishna,

200 Tilaphula 'sesame flower', the small blossom of the sesame plant; see Appendix.

201 Refer to n. 164 above.

202 Refer to n. 143 above.

203 In private discussion it has been suggested by Sukumar Sen that the reading dehera debatā 'god of the body' of the original text be replaced by debera debatā 'god of gods.' The translation reflects the replacement.

204 Pañca saṅgati; refer to n. 152 above.

205 Niyaṛa haila tora yamera karaṇa 'For you Yama's (death's) intervention has become imminent.'

206 Dui loka khāã bola āhmāra goālī 'destroying two worlds, you call me dairymaid'; see n. 67.

Then, just as before, you'll go on menacing this pathway.
I must quickly summon Abhimanyu and King Kaṃsa.

Song 76

"Come on, dairymaid; beneath this tree, the kadamba, be seated. I'll explain the facts to you completely.
I, your Krishna, take my tax on roadways and my tolls at river stations.[207] What design, what scheme can help you?"
"Listen, you are shameless, Krishna! Why are you demanding taxes? How can there be taxes on my produce?
If you have no way to earn a living, what you ought to do is go from house to house and beg for handouts!"
"Are the cowherds pressed for money? Abhimanyu shouldn't live for sending such a woman out for hawking!
When he has this woman in his house, why should he lack for riches? He should put you in my house on binder."
"With no husband, there's no refuge.[208] I'm a cowherd woman from my birth; with milk and ghee I stock my produce.
You are just a cattle tender, thinking you are lord almighty; yet your fortune comes to just four cowries."
"You don't know my existential powers. You're a simple cowmaid. All this world comes under my dominion.
I have only taken on a cowherd's guise. If I desired, I could not just bond you, I could buy you!"
"Thoughts like this would not occur to any truly wealthy person. What you say is clear, I understand you.
You've discarded decency and steeped your thoughts in mischief. You take taxes while insisting you are wealthy!"
"I've been on this path in hopes of you. My tax exists through all the ages, in this world, in hell and heaven.
If you're still determined to preserve your youth's attractions, then I'll have to fetter both your hands together."
"Krishna, you're depraved, you prankster. Listen to me, why should you insult me as you're doing on this pathway?
Am I living in your house? Are you obliged to feed me? Don't you recognize the power of King Kaṃsa?"

[207] Sukumar Sen has suggested in private discussions that kulaā̃ in the original text, which is uninterpretable, be replaced by kuta laā̃ 'taking ferry tolls.' This yields the reading kara kuta laā̃ ghāṭe kāhna māhādānī bāṭe 'Taking tax and crossing tolls at the embankment, Krishna is (also) the official tax collector on the road.'
[208] Pati chāṛī nāhi gatī 'There's no recourse after losing one's husband.'

"I'm Dāmodara,[209] the god who's vanquished demon armies. You're displaying such temerity before me!
I shall kill the demon Kaṃsa, then I'll make your courage crumble. Let us see if anyone will shield you."
"You are just a cowherd boy. The stories you've been telling are fantastic.[210] Who'll believe them when he hears them?
On this pathway you take taxes. I am Abhimanyu's wife. If you use force, the king will come to know this."
"If I wish to, I'll use force and shatter all your earthen vessels, ruining your dairy produce, Radha."

Song 77

With your charming flute and with your head of lavish ringlets,
All the men of wisdom pay their homage to you, Krishna.
How could that same Krishna smash my pots and spoil my produce?
Who can I inform of what you've done? There's no one present.
I must go at once to find Yaśodā and inform her,
"Seeing I was unprotected, Krishna tried to harm me!"
You have tried to get inside my blouse and touch my bosom.
If your head were taken off, I think you would deserve it!
I am now aware that you're a roadway menace, Krishna.
I can have your head cut off by telling this to Kaṃsa.
As a dairymaid, I've come and gone this way for ages;
No one up till now has ever said a word to tease me.
Vanamāli, offspring of Yaśodā, you should perish!
That alone might take away the torment of your teasing.
What is this that's happened to me on the way to market?
Nanda's son has smashed my pots and ruined all my produce.
Krishna, don't prevent me any more from going homeward.

Song 78

Earlier, under the kadamba, Radha, I viciously damaged your produce.
What sort of spell have you cast on me, Radha? I can't comprehend how you've done it.
This is the reason my thoughts are disturbed, for besides you, I know nothing other.
Come on, let's go to Vṛndāvana forest; take care of me, Gokula's Krishna.[211]

[209] Refer to Tāmbūlakhaṇḍa above, n. 33.
[210] Bola ākāśa pātāla, literally 'you talk heaven and hell.'
[211] Rākha gokulera kāhna 'Take care of Krishna of Gokula' or alternatively, 'Tend to the pastureland's black (bull).'

What have you used to enmadden me, Radha?
A woman should not kill a man. Just this once you must comfort your Krishna, my Radha.
Hungry or thirsty, I can't eat or drink. In your absence my thoughts are unsteady.
Nighttime and daytime my mind has been reeling. The sight of you, Radha, revives me.
I have no wish to go home, though my dad, Nanda Ghosh, has been trying to find me.
Yaśodā, my mother, is crying. She frets; but at home I don't find any comfort.
Like a flash flood in a river, or dreams in the night, so is youth in a woman.
You should yourself give your favors[212] to one who deserves them; it's you who will profit.[213]
Various trees bring forth fruit, but within themselves they have no way to enjoy it.
Worldly things carry no substance, esteem comes from offering service to others.[214]
You are a full-fledged young woman of cowherd descent. You go often to market.
All are enchanted to look on your loveliness; even dried timber sprouts blossoms!
I, your Dāmodara, feel overwhelmed as I long for your love in your absence.

Song 79

Radha writhed on the ground and cried out,
"To blazes with blossoming youth!
Krishna would not let me travel to market.
My tears fall like rainstorms in summer.[215]
Granny, you're heartless. Suggest some solution!
This Krishna is bound to destroy me.
Where has he been up to now with his trickery?
Why does he dwell on my beauty?

212 Hāthe tuliā̃ deha dāne 'Raising it in your hand, bestow your gift (or: tax). . . .'

213 Āpaṇa pune uttama jane hāthe tuliā̃ deha dāne 'Hand over your gift, for your own merit, to a deserving person.' Personal merit is thought to accrue by the performance of laudable acts.

214 Saṃsāra āsāra para upakāra karilẽ kirīti thāke 'The world (or: one's family) is insubstantial, there is (real) glory by doing service to another.'

215 Mora dui ākhi dhārā śrābaṇe 'My two eyes are the cloudbursts in Śrāvaṇa.' The month of Śrāvaṇa falls in midsummer during the full force of the monsoon.

He wants to take me by force in some forested
Arbor[216] where he can enjoy me.
He says, 'I can't eat in spite of my hunger;
In spite of my thirst I can't drink.
All of my body feels pained in your absence.'
He lusts for his aunt. Shameless Krishna!
I had my ghee and my milk products ready
But couldn't reach market to sell them.
Now you should give me instructions to follow."

Song 80

Hearing Radha's message as conveyed by Granny,
The crafty Krishna thirstily addressed Radha:

Your hair is entwined with perfumed blossoms, Radha,
And yet, you begrudge me a fitting reception.[217]
I'll spoil your produce by smashing your vessels—
Where's Abhimanyu? Let him come and shield you.
Give me the taxes, then go, darling Radha.
Otherwise, go after pledging your favors.
I crushed proud Rāvaṇa, ruler of Laṅkā.[218]
It will be easy to trounce your King Kaṃsa.
I'll go kill Bāṇa in Śonitapura.[219]
Just for now, I'm taking tax by the river.
I don't tell lies. It's the truth absolutely:
I've levied hundreds and hundreds in taxes.[220]
So, Radha, do not prolong the discussion.
If you can't pay, pledge your charms and then vanish.
See here, your blossoming youth's just beginning.
Radha, you're wearing fine clothes made of muslin.
Sit at my side and I'll cancel your taxes.

Song 81

Radha's slender body trembled when she heard Krishna's answer.
She spoke in distress to Granny as follows:

216 Kuñjatale 'into the arbored area', i.e., into a likely trysting place (see n. 57 above).

217 Āhmāta nā pāta rādhā nāgarībeśa 'Radha, you don't extend to me your amorous hospitality.' Beśa (here 'house, hospitality') is a pun having the alternate meaning 'dress, adornment' (compare the preceding line of the text).

218 Refer to nn. 97 and 173 above.

219 Bāṇa, name of a legendary thousand-armed demon and ruler of the city of Śoṇitapura, defeated by Krishna after the latter's departure from the pasturelands.

220 Literally, 'I've collected official taxes by (units of) one hundred twenty.'

Krishna sat under the kadamba waiting;
He abused me for tax I don't owe.
I'll plunge right into the Yamunā's current
If Krishna breaks down my resistance.
Tell Abhimanyu about this at home;
Tell him Krishna has Radha entrapped.
I am the sister-in-law of his mother;
All are aware we're related.
Only himself does he hurt by his teasing.
Krishna disdains his relations.
He pulled the bracelets I wore from my arms
And, relieving my ears of their earrings,
He gave a tug at the bodice I'm wearing.
Who would be able to stand this?
Listen to what I'm instructing you: tell
Abhimanyu, my husband. Get going.
I won't give Krishna encouragement, Granny.

Song 82

Hearing Radha's message as conveyed by Granny,
The crafty Krishna thirstily addressed Radha:

"You've been going often to the city market, Radha.
That's why I'm demanding that you make good all your taxes."
"Where's your home and who commissioned you to take these taxes?
Be completely truthful as you tell your answer, Krishna."
"I live in my pasture home with Nanda and Yaśodā.
It's for your commission that I've started taking taxes!"
"I'll present my case before our fearsome ruler Kaṃsa;
After that, Murāri, you won't stay alive much longer."
"I shall kill your fearsome ruler Kaṃsa. When that's over,
I'll stay on beside the Yamunā, collecting taxes."
"You're my husband's nephew, yet you've turned your thoughts to mischief.
You will face your utter devastation any moment!"[221]
"Don't attempt to use your woman's guile upon me, Radha.
You will not proceed until you've reconciled with Krishna."
"Listen, now, Murāri, don't create a confrontation.
I have nothing taxable—just visiting the city."
"You have wares of dairy goods; you've milk as white as camphor.
On such items I collect substantial taxes, Radha."
"I had yogurt, buttermilk and milk; the water in them

[221] Refer to n. 152 above.

Separated out. Now let me go, Lord Cakrapāṇi!"
"You are not to go unless you offer your caresses!"

Song 83

Planting yourself at the base of the kadamba
Next to the Yamunā, you're taking taxes.
You've been mistreating a number of dairymaids;
When Kaṃsa hears of this, you'll simply perish.
Who are you, asking for taxes, Murāri?
I am the wife of the brave Abhimanyu.
You've picked a fight, asking falsely for taxes.
You're not aware of yourself, cattle tender.
Don't be excessively difficult, Krishna.
Give up your squabbling. I'm going to market.
If you intimidate me on this pathway,
Then the results will land squarely on you;
I will become what the world calls a killer.
Give up at last on those wicked intentions.
Contemplate this to yourself from the start
To the end; give me leave to be going.
Don't hope to win a concession from me.

Song 84

I'm taking tax on this path, having thought
Matters through; for my mind's on your youthfulness, Radha.
You're quite audacious, of this I'm aware; using
Speeches or tricks, dear, you want to reach market.
How can you say that my tax is a fraud, Radha?
Everyone knows I take tax on this pathway.
Radha, you don't know my innermost being.
Knowing my duty, I sheltered the herdsmen.[222]
Now, for your sake, I'm collecting the taxes.
Realize I'm truly the lord Cakrapāṇi.
If you have qualms about killing a person,
Then, with one kiss, you may spare my existence.
Do not do other than this; I'll reward you
With fitting esteem, my adorable Radha.
Over you, daytime and night, I'm perplexed; why,
My heart has been lost to your youthful attractions.
Give me some hope for your love, don't refuse me!

222 Refer to nn. 171 and 145.

Song 85

Though you lack a livelihood, you claim to levy taxes.
No one ever hears of men indulging in such conduct.[223]
There are many other dairymaids; you overlook them,
Picking out that very girl who's married to your uncle.
How could I have known that you took taxes on this pathway?
Krishna, just this once you must be gracious and excuse me.
You've been taking care of cows because it is your duty.
How, then, can you spend your thoughts on women who are married?
If it is the truth that you're divine, oh Vanamālī,
Why are you engaging in the kinds of things you're doing?
You're a prankster, Krishna, and your wits are like a cowherd's.
I can just imagine what a family you come from.
All my girlfriends have departed, leaving me abandoned;
Here I am, alone and unprotected in the forest.
Krishna, let me go. Don't keep extending the discussion.
Look, look, over there my husband Abhimanyu's coming!
Now that you're aware of this, you'd better leave me quickly.

Song 86

When he crossed the Yamunā, my father Vasudeva
Put me in a cowherd household due to lack of judgment.
It was from the womb of Devakī that I was born here;
Kaṃsa is so terrified of me that sleep eludes him.
Radha, don't try starting a commotion over nothing.
How could he, your husband Abhimanyu, dare to come here?
You've been pointing out your girlfriends when I ask for taxes;
"I'm not in arrears!" you keep insisting to me, Radha.
You should not be swearing falsely, Radha, in my presence.
Give me an embrace and then go anywhere you fancy.
You've been taking dairy goods and milk with you to market.
Now your path is occupied by Nanda's offspring Krishna.
Don't attempt to reason with me, Radha, on the subject.
You must simply pay me back for twelve years' unpaid taxes.
Time and time again you cheat me, Radha, and escape me.
Look at this, I've caught you by the clothes; how will you leave me?
I, your Krishna, long for your embrace. I'll drop the taxes.

223 Loka dharama nāhī́ śuṇi 'This is not heard of as (part of) the world's code of conduct.' Cf. n. 88 above.

Song 87

When I started from my home, I saw a woman selling oil.[224] Upon the withered branches of a tree, black crows were cawing.[225]
Just in front, a woman with an empty pot was going.[226] Yet I made my way, not heeding these dark omens; now I'm punished.
Krishna, let me go. Don't hold me back by tugging at my clothing, Krishna; I must go to Mathurā and reach the market.
Look, a hundred thousand people travel by this road to market; after I've succumbed, will you elude them all and vanish?
You yourself don't plan to marry; why are you amassing riches? You won't use them for yourself nor offer them to others.
I am married to your uncle. Everyone knows you're my nephew. If you overpower me, the world will be upended.
You're a cowherd from your birth; you mustn't be so stubborn. Go back home and ask your mother to explain your kinfolk, Krishna.
I'm a tiny girl, as soft as country berry blossoms.[227] Krishna, knowing this, you mustn't try to linger here beside me.
In a bud of jasmine, why, a bumblebee will find no nectar, Krishna, till it blossoms as a flower.

Song 88

Since I, Gadādhara, noticed your beauty,
My soul has been rent with desire.
You have achieved Vanamālī's submission,
Candrāvali; give up resisting.
Why do you harbor ill thoughts in your heart?
Give me your gracious approval.
You cannot justify making a waste
Of your flourishing, upstanding youth.[228]
You must accept this yourself with conviction.
It simply won't do to refuse me.
While I remain in possession of life
To release you is out of the question.

224 Oil pressers, who extract oil from mustard seeds for cooking and other purposes, belong to a lowly caste; the sight of them is thought inauspicious.

225 The crow is regarded as the messenger of Yama (death). A dried or withered tree branch, like the crow, symbolizes death.

226 When one is beginning a journey, the sight of someone carrying an empty pot is thought to suggest that the purpose of one's mission will not be fulfilled.

227 Labalīdala kõyali 'tender as petals of country gooseberry (labalī) (blossoms)'; see Appendix.

228 E tora unnata yaubane 'with this, your advanced yaubana.' Yaubana refers both to youthfulness and to the incipient youthful breasts of a girl.

All my sensations are steeped in your being;
What soul could attempt to dissuade me?
Hoping for love, I've caught hold of your clothes.
What impels you to keep me despairing?
You should be cheerfully seated beside me.

Song 89

Don't you hold my clothes. My body shakes in terror, Krishna.
I don't know what love's about; I'm just a tiny baby.
I myself can see I'm very much a youngster, Krishna.
If one opens fruit before it's ripe, no juice is found there.
Just one time release me, Krishna, I must go to market.
A boat that's made of flowers, Krishna, can't withstand a burden.
There's no scent to be enjoyed within a bud of jasmine.
You must understand this and stop clinging to me, Krishna.
Though it may be large, a pomegranate has no liquid
Till the core has ripened very thoroughly within it.
Listen to me, ignoramus, let me tell you something.
Milk that's heated tastes refreshing only after cooling.
Krishna, through a straw, one can't partake of milk that's heated.
Even if you're hungry, you can't use both hands for eating.
I'm a little girl. I do not know a thing, my Krishna.
Please withdraw your hopes for me at once, Lord Vanamālī.
You should go back home, my Lord Gadādhara; excuse me.

Song 90

"Listen carefully to what I have to tell you, Radha.
You should feel attracted to me. Kiss me and embrace me."
"Please don't speak, don't tell me things like this, Lord Cakrapāṇi.
I have shut my ears to the improper words you're saying."
"Radha, I have not suggested anything improper.
You belong to me; you're not the wife of Abhimanyu."
"Krishna, I cannot endure the kinds of things you're saying.
Was there any time when I was married to you, Krishna?"
"Radha, I've described to you the saga of King Rāma.[229]
Can't you recognize me even now, my foolish Radha?"
"What a lot of lies you tell, my handsome Vanamālī!
But Candrāvalī is not deceived by what you're saying."
"Dairymaid, you're too naive to understand the matter.
Satisfy me with a taste of love. Give up your coyness."

229 Rāmāyanakathā rādhā kahila tohmāre 'Radha, I've told you the rāmāyaṇa story.' *Rāmāyaṇa* is the name of the epic recounting the adventures of Rāma; refer to n. 173.

"Lord Dāmodara, I have no knowledge of love's savor.
Have some pity on me. Just one time you must release me."
"Radha, while your Krishna lives, he never will forsake you!"

Song 91

Radha's slender body trembled when she heard Krishna's answer. She spoke in distress to Granny as follows:

Listen to me, Granny, Krishna's an actor; he's very persuasive in speaking.
Listen to me, Granny, there's no solution by which I can make my way homeward.
Listen to me, Granny, Krishna is very unyielding. Take measures against him!
Listen to me, Granny, since I fell into his hands, I am losing my reason!
Listen to me, Granny, think to yourself of some scheme so I'll regain my freedom.
Listen to me, Granny, don't speak to Krishna about it; then I won't be frightened.
Listen to me, Granny, if Krishna hears of it he will be heartened, the rascal.
Listen to me, Granny, let's link our wits, yours and mine, and let's make some arrangement.

Song 92

"You are not to reach the town of Mathurā, my Radha;
On this road is unrelenting Krishna, son of Nanda."
"Let that Krishna mingle with the dirt on this one roadway;
We'll go by some other road to market for our selling."
"Krishna will pursue you, spoiling all your ghee and yogurt,
On whatever pathway you may take to go to market."
"On that path if Krishna uses force against me, Granny,
You and I will join and give him just what he has coming."
"He can spoil your milk and dairy goods and smash your vessels.
He can fragment, bit by bit, the bodice on your bosom."
"Granny, are you feeling fearful when you look at Krishna?
If he's harsh, we girls will promptly use our fists to thrash him."
"Straightaway you're making hollow boasts, my darling Radha.
When we get there, you'll be like a serpent-charmer's serpent!"
"Granny, with the things you're saying, I feel apprehensive.
Tell me some solution now. What scheme should we be using?"
"Krishna will not budge, and his intentions are misguided.
Come on, Radha, leave this pathway; let's flee through the forest."

"Granny, if that Krishna finds us going through the forest,
Then what strategy should we resort to? Tell me, Granny."
"If relentless Krishna overtakes us in the forest,
Then we will directly hand the taxes to him, Radha."
"Krishna's tricky. What if he will not accept the taxes?
Think this over to yourself. What shall we do then, Granny?"
"I'll come up with such a plan by which we can escape him.
Once we reach our home, I'll make no good or adverse comment."
"Granny, why, take care; you have to think of some solution
So that I can be delivered this one time from Krishna!"
"Krishna won't withdraw without receiving your affection!"

Song 93

Krishna has still not put childhood behind him.
Why, then, is he so intent upon passion?
I have tried so many plans to elude him;
Krishna has shown not a sign of frustration.
It's not befitting for Krishna to love me;
No one believes common gems can scratch diamonds.
Krishna should not be the source of my ruin;[230]
How can he think of committing such actions?
None of his conduct makes sense to me, Granny;
Everything Krishna is saying is twisted.
He neither knows for himself, nor asks others.
There's no relief in the cosmos from Krishna![231]
Everyone says he is "little boy Krishna";
Nobody knows of his methods or doings.[232]
Krishna is teasing me so. Can you even
Suppose that the offspring of Nanda deserves me?
Sumptuous pearls[233] never flatter a monkey!

Song 94

> Hearing Radha's message as conveyed by Granny,
> The crafty Krishna thirstily addressed Radha:

Dairymaid, in your confusion, you fool, you don't

[230] Hotita, the original reading of the text, is replaced by haite 'from' following a suggestion made by Sukumar Sen in private discussions. Tāhāra haite nahe āhmāra maraṇa 'My death is not (to be) from him.' 'Death' seems to refer indirectly to loss of chastity.
[231] E tīna bhubane, literally, 'in these three worlds' (heaven, the mortal world and the underworld); cf. Tāmbūlakhaṇḍa above, n. 5. Also see n. 33 above.
[232] See n. 33 above.
[233] Gajamutī, cf. n. 157 above.

Know how upset Krishna feels in your absence.
I go around in a stupor; I plead for you.
It's for your sake I take tax on this pathway.
By your consent, common gems can scratch diamonds!
Thinking of you, I, your Krishna, can't eat
Nor put on my fine clothes. I'm distracted without you;
And all through the night even slumber evades me.
Come, dairymaid, let me say something. Listen:
Kiss and embrace me. Revive me, your Krishna.
Radha, your gem-laden earrings are brilliant;
Your armlets are gleaming, your head wears vermilion.
Give your consent; do not squander that body, for
Nowhere does one see a truly chaste lady.
Krishna's love, Radha, is won through great merit;
At death you'll gain freedom or journey to heaven.[234]
Now, darling Radha, fulfill my desires.

Song 95

Radha's slender body trembled when she heard Krishna's answer. She spoke in distress to Granny as follows:

When you can repeat his words to me so freely, Granny,
Then there must be no escape for me from this disaster.
I shall be thrown out by Abhimanyu when he hears this.
You will take the other side; the blame will be on Radha.
Only since you've had me wander through this dreadful forest
Have I figured out that your intentions are not seemly.
What will I do, Granny? You'll get by with words or ruses.
Using force, he's bound to break my multistranded necklace;
Back at home, what will my husband say when he observes that?
There was no excuse for you to bring me by this pathway.
Now, through false designs,[235] I must get home by fooling Krishna.
After I escape this time by fooling Krishna, Granny,
We must never go again to Mathurā hereafter.
Having such a granny close to me, I'm feeling frightened.
This, in turn, is shameful for you, you yourself must realize.
Now that you're aware of this, be true to what is proper.

234 Mailẽ mukuti kibā surapura jāie 'When one dies one (gains) emancipation (of the soul) or else one goes to the abode of the gods (heaven).'

235 Michẽ chācẽ, literally 'by false design-molds.' Chāca refers to a wooden block on which a design is cut, used to mold or impress a design upon pottery or other objects. One is reminded of the English phrase 'false impression.'

Song 96

> "Radha, these good observations of yours appeal to my thinking.
> Now flee the vexations of love, for this entire incident is
> disastrous!"[236]

As Radha went fleeing through the wilderness,
Krishna overtook her and stopped her in her tracks.
Granny turned back instantly on seeing what had happened;
Great cheat that she was, upon the main path she dawdled.
Observing Radha alone, Krishna figured to himself,
"Granny has complied with my earlier instructions."
Calling, "Granny, Granny!" Radha wept, her eyes flowing.
She found herself forsaken in the middle of the forest.
With his own garment Krishna wiped her tears away.
He said, "Don't be afraid, Radha;
Raise your eyes now, look at my face.
Radha, no witnesses are here in the deep forest.
You and I, Radha, are in the prime of our youth;
Let's make our lives worthwhile by enjoying love.
I'll relieve your firm round breasts of this necklace
And I'll loosen the wristlets from your arms.
Now, Radha, tease me in a lively frame of mind."

Song 97

"You've removed the necklace I had on; you took my wristlets.
I had not imagined, Krishna, owing you such riches.
How could I foresee that I would find myself alone here?
Let me go; I'll travel to the town, then homeward, Krishna."
"You may take your yogurt and your ghee to market, Radha;
Still, I shall not let you have the road unless you'll love me.
Thanks to my good fortune, fate has made you all alone here;
Now you must set fear aside and gratify your Krishna!"
"I have stringent in-laws and my husband, too, is fearsome.
Leave me, Krishna, I have far to go. The sun is setting."
"Do not stall me, Radha. Set aside your apprehensions.
Radha, let's not give up our acquaintance; come embrace me!"
"We've a dauntless ruler on the throne; he's very ruthless.
I'm completely terrified of him. This once release me."
"You need not fear anyone if you'll submit to Krishna.

236 Duḥsvanaṃ, which occurs in the original text, is obscure. Sukumar Sen in private discussion has suggested substituting ducchunaṃ (duḥ + śunaṃ), yielding the sense 'disastrous' as given in the translation. Ray 1973:228, however, suggests interpreting the original reading as 'unspeakable', i.e., 'this entire incident is unspeakable.'

I'm divine Gadādhara, the master of the cosmos."
"This time, Krishna, since you're Nanda's son, you must release me.
When some time has passed[237] I shall accept your proposition."
"Radha, when a treasure's in one's grasp, who can renounce it?"

Song 98

Alone in the woods, the abashed Radha, that exemplary cowherd woman,[238]
Pondered at length now as she contemplated Hari before her.

I had neither seen nor heard that, in these arbored forests, there were trailside bandits such as I'm now seeing.
Here for twelve years I've been going to the town of Mathurā and no one's ever said a word about it.
Krishna wants to clasp me tightly; I'm aware of his intentions. This is why Nārāyaṇa[239] mistreats me.
I may break my bracelets, my pearl necklace I may tear asunder; even then I won't heed Krishna's pleading.
Yet, if I approach the royal gates and make this known to Kaṃsa, I might be the one whom people censure.
Abhimanyu's fiercer than a blade; the king is very ruthless. Why must Krishna tease me in this manner?

Song 99

"Radha, why be fearful of either Kaṃsa or of Abhimanyu?
Listen to me, you agile evoker of streaming passions!"[240]

I deceived Bali and sent him to Hades.[241]
I shielded Gokula, lifting a mountain.[242]
Playing the fish, I recovered the scriptures,[243]
Haunting the lowest of hells[244] to uplift them.
Radha, you arrogant girl, you don't know me.[245]

[237] Literally, 'when some days have gone. . . .'
[238] Abhīrakautukā, literally 'the cynosure of the Abhīras.' Abhīra refers to a pastoral tribe with which certain versions of the Krishna legend associate the god's origins. See Jaiswal 1967:80–85.
[239] See Janmakhaṇḍa above, n. 7.
[240] Rasasandohasādhike 'Oh woman expert in the exhaustive milking of (passion's) juices!'
[241] Dātā bali chaliā̃ mo nilō̃ pātāle 'I deceived generous Bali and took him to the lowest realm.' See nn. 41 and 190.
[242] See n. 145.
[243] Beda uddhāritẽ kailō̃ mīna abatāra 'I made the fish descent to rescue the Vedas.' See nn. 53 and 189.
[244] Pātāla giā̃ tāra karilō̃ uddhāra 'Going to the lowest realm, I rescued them.' See n. 190.
[245] Yaubanagarabẽ rādhā na cihnasi more 'In your youthful arrogance, Radha, you don't

Posing as Śrīdhara, I shall possess you![246]
Playing a boar, when I lived in the wilderness,
I raised the earth on the tip of my tusk.[247]
I murdered Rāvaṇa, posing as Rāma.[248]
No one exceeds my invincible powers!
I'll dismiss Granny[249] and take you to Gokula;
As we are making our way, I'll molest you.
I'll overthrow your imperial Kaṃsa;
Why are you having misgivings, my Radha?[250]
I am named Hari; I've trounced demon armies.
Now it's for you I've descended as Krishna.
Please Nanda's offspring deliciously, Radha!

Song 100

I shall not fulfill your hopes for amorous amusement.
Krishna, see this for yourself; consider:
You'll commit an error by submitting to your passions;
You will cast a stain upon your people.[251]
Krishna, in your heart you ought to contemplate the matter.
Making love with me would not be proper.
From a bud like mine,[252] a bumblebee would never get his fill
Of honey; he like lotuses in season.
As, from eating shrimp, you might break out in rashes, Krishna, your
Physique could bear the taint of ghastly evils.[253]
Hunger for a solid meal will not be quenched by fruit. It isn't
Right to love the wives of others, Krishna.
Krishna, raging fires aren't put out with butter; after you

---

recognize me.' For evidence of Radha's arrogance consider the closing line of song 93 above.

246 Śrīdhara 'Possessor of Śrī (Lakṣmī)', an epithet of Viṣṇu-Krishna.

247 Tanuta barāharūpẽ thāki banabhāge / medanī dharila āhme daśanera āge 'Living in the wilderness with my body in the shape of a boar, I held the earth on the tip of my tusk.' See n. 192.

248 Śrīrāmarūpẽ 'in the form of Lord Rāma'.

249 Literally, 'I'll send my emissary (away).'

250 Guṇasi pā̃nca sāta, literally 'you are thinking five and seven'; i.e., different things are in your mind at the same time.

251 Jaramaka tarẽ kule kalaṅka thuibẽ 'You will place a stigma on (the members of) your lineage for life (i.e., for as long as they live).'

252 Āhmāra mukule nāhĩ pāe madhubhare 'He (the bumblebee) doesn't get his fill of nectar in my bud,' an indirect reference to the female organ.

253 Iñcalā khāā̃ kāhna bāra pāṛibe / āghora pāpẽ toẽ gāya beāpibẽ 'By eating shrimp, Krishna, you may cause rash to occur (on your body, and in a similar way) you might spread your person with dreadful (evidence of) sins.' As many people get rashes from eating shrimp, so Radha warns Krishna that one may bear the physical stigma of one's misdeeds. See n. 93 above.

Make love just once, your lustful thoughts will burgeon.
Ponder what I've said; you are a gentleman[254] and must maintain
Priorities.[255] My youth won't suit you, Krishna.

Song 101

> "Your wits which are wizened from selling buttermilk, Radha,
> Have been cheating you out of intimacy with me.
> I am a raging fire—no cowherd youngster indeed!—
> A raging fire in the wilderness of Kaṃsa's dynasty!"

"I'm well acquainted with love, so, my Radha, you mustn't regard me as childish.
You should bestow your consent on me, Radha; see here, I am holding your clothing."
"Listen to what I am telling you, Krishna; why, you mustn't dare to abuse me.
Contemplate this in your heart: will divine moral justice excuse what you're doing?"
"I'd fear divine moral justice, my Radha, why, if I stole wives from another;
You, though, are Lakṣmī; you're part of eternal Murāri. Why don't you concede this?"
"In some existence of long ago, Krishna, why, let us say you were my husband;
In this existence, who'd ever believe it, Murāri? You might yourself see this."
"Women are wayward, contemptible creatures.[256] My Radha, why, you ought to trust me.
No divine being is greater than I am;[257] of whom are you so apprehensive?"
"I've my own husband at home, nephew Krishna. Why, listen to me, Vanamālī:
Previous, present and future, you've spoiled you whole life.[258] Do you know who you're teasing?"
"Show me a cheerful expression, my Radha. Why, look, I've caught hold of your clothing.

[254] Māhājana 'great person'.
[255] Āga pācha kari kāja kara 'Do first things (first) and last things (last).'
[256] Chāra tiri bāmā jāti 'Women are dirt, a sinister (literally: left-side) race.' See Rādhāviraha below, n. 187.
[257] For deha 'body' in the original text substitute deba 'god'. Cf. n. 203.
[258] Tīna loka khāā̃; see n. 85.

Any time swans in their ponds find a lotus, of course they uproot and enjoy it!"[259]
"If you and I should make love someday, Krishna, why, it should be good for us jointly.
But there arise only troubles in love affairs; there are no benefits, Krishna."
"I cannot wait any longer, my Radha; why, you must give heed to my offer.
When I behold you alone in this forest, the shafts of the love god bombard me!"[260]
"After observing your character, Krishna, why, words fail to come to my lips."

Song 102

As she observed the likes of Hari's behavior there in the woods,
Radha thought about Granny angrily at length.

"Damn her and blast her, that fool of a Granny; I'd like to ignite her with fire.[261]
She had me trek through the midst of this wilderness; now she has purposely vanished.
How can she stand for a man who is not Abhimanyu to bother his woman?
Krishna, her grandnephew, straddles the pathway and stalls to his heart's satisfaction.
Nanda has got a belligerent son who mistreats me; he will not release me.
This is the kind of a road on which terrible Granny has seen fit to lead me!
Grabbing my clothes, he's impeded me. What sort of scheme can I use to elude him?
Granny has started a fire in kindling and stood to one side while it blazes!
I left the path when I came here. My yogurt's gone bad and my buttermilk's ruined.
Krishna's corrupted my Granny; my utter destruction[262] is right in his clutches.

[259] In private discussions Sukumar Sen has remarked that the fact that waterfowl are prolific breeders may be the reason they are so often used to connote fecundity or sexuality in this text. For a similar passage see song 110 below.
[260] See n. 115.
[261] Anala bulāō̃ gāe 'I'll pass fire all over her body.'
[262] Pā̃ca ābathā; see Tāmbūlakhaṇḍa above, n. 24.

In this deep wilderness he's going to murder a woman. He's shredded my bodice;
He's raked my breasts with his fingernail scratches; with all of his yanking, he'll kill me.
He's entwined jasmine and clove blooms which laden his hair; it is wound very tightly.[263]
Though Krishna's come from the womb of Yaśodā, he's failing to honor his elders.
Mother-in-law and her daughters are sharp just like blades, while my husband's quite stringent.
If I go home in a physical state such as this, what will be my salvation?"
Pondering this, Radha cast her eyes sidelong and peered for a moment at Krishna.

Song 103

Ah, my chest is entered by the woodmites of your sidelong glances; they have bored inside me and, within my heart, are lodging.
Now bestow a kiss upon me, let me drink your nectar. Make my spirits happy just one time by letting me embrace you.
Listen, sweet-faced Radha, save young Krishna's life just once. Since I beheld your fair complexion, your two doe-like eyes, your beauty . . .[264]
In this mundane sphere, you sparkle brilliantly, like lightning streaks against a cloud. To me your face looks like a fulsome moon.
These two breasts of yours resemble crucibles of gold; while, on the top of them, a necklace made of giant pearls is dangling,
Gleaming like the river Ganges coursing down the slopes of Meru mountain.[265] Since I noticed this, my feet refuse to travel.
Answer me by smiling, lovely, dashing Radha; for, since I—the god of gods—beheld you, I have come to earth to mingle.[266]

Song 104

Oh my Krishna, as I went toward market in the city,
You were staring at me as, from path to path, you followed;

[263] The description of Krishna's dandyish dress is made in ironic comparison to his unmannerly conduct, and to Radha's presently disheveled state.

[264] Due to apparent scribal error, part of a line is missing at this point; in the translation, the remaining fragment of the line has been merged with the preceding line.

[265] Yehna śobha kare sumeru gaṅgāra dhāre 'sparkles as does the stream of the Ganges (on) Sumeru.' As it makes its way toward the mortal world, the Ganges is thought to spill down the slopes of the fabled Meru (Sumeru). See nn. 48 and 92.

[266] Kalāyilõ āsiā̃, literally 'I've come and sullied myself (by contact with the earth; i.e., earthly affairs).'

Only then I realized that what's happened was predestined.
You, the son of Nanda, will not ever let me leave you.
Handsome Krishna, I'll entrust myself to your embraces
If at all times you agree to honor my conditions:
Krishna, the tiara on my head must not be broken;
Folding hands, I'm kneeling at your feet as I beseech this.
Krishna, you must not unstring my multistranded necklace;
Nor must you dishevel any finery I'm wearing.
Furthermore, upon my lips don't press your teeth to excess;
For, if they observe the toothmarks, all my friends will gossip.
You must not leave fingernail impressions on my bosom;
There'll be no release for me if Abhimanyu sees them.
I'm Candrāvalī, a soft and slender little maiden;
In my fear I'm shaking like a frond of tender plantain.
Have some pity for me in your heart as you embrace me.

Song 105

On gaining Radha's consent, with a heart incited by love's goading,
The high-stepping Mādhava[267] whizzed through the maneuvers of love[268] in spectacular sequence.

Krishna embraced Radha in various ways.
Then he pulled the necklace from her bosom and removed it.
With his hands he fondled her stupendous breasts and hips;
Radha squirmed and struggled in fear of his fingernail scratches.
Winning Radha's consent, Krishna exultantly
Made love to her upon a bed of foliage.
He kissed her cheeks, her throat, her lips, her eyes;
He joined his face to hers and drank her sweetness.
Disregarding Radha's conditions, he carelessly
Bit Radha's lips with his teeth.
He touched her buttocks and put his hands on her thighs.
Jagannātha was highly impassioned;
All the desires which he had cherished for so long
Were fulfilled in that amorous endeavor.
Krishna was gratified; he heaved a deep sigh.
In hopes of making love again, he took away her jewelry.
When that act of love concluded, Radha was dismayed.

267 Mādhavaḥ . . . udāravikramo, literally 'high-stepping Mādhava.' See Tāmbūlakhaṇḍa above, n. 41.

268 Ripukramaṃ 'enemy maneuvers', here denoting the maneuvers associated with love, which has long resisted Krishna. Ripu also refers to any of several human passions including physical love.

Song 106

"First you took my necklace off, the one with several strands.
From my head you lifted my tiara; from my ears
You took my earrings; and my throat you have divested of its beads.
At this tender age, you have already done great mischief.
You have taken forcibly whatever jewels were on me;
Now give me instructions; what excuse can I go home with?
You've removed the bracelets and the armlets from my arms.
You have snatched my rings and golden wristlets; from my ankles you
Removed my anklets and my golden, bell-embellished anklets.[269]
You are glib in speech, while in your conduct you are callous!
I'm as fragile as the blooms of parrot trees[270] in springtime;
When you took my toe-ring off,[271] I suffered great discomfort.
Now you've stripped my body, not a jewel remains upon it.
In this first encounter,[272] you have acted most unseemly."
Radha, in disgruntlement, abandoned all her jewelry;
As she headed back once more, she came across her Granny.
Granny chuckled secretly upon observing Radha.

Song 107

Granny asked the following of Radha, smiling gently:
"All this time, since running off from me, where have you been to?
Your entire figure seems to be in disarray;
I cannot make proper sense at all of your behavior.
Darling grandniece, you must not reply to me with falsehoods;
You must tell your story to me accurately, Radha.
Who on earth has taken all the baubles you were wearing?
How is it I'm finding you like this, so out of humor?
From your lips the coloring of betel quids has vanished;[273]
Judging by this, Krishna must have caught you in the forest.
Why is it you look as though you're utterly exhausted?
I can't understand what inclinations you have, Radha.
When I saw how late you were, I felt extremely anxious."

269 Kanakakiṅkinī nilĕ pāera nūpura 'You took my foot's anklet (nūpura) and golden (kanaka) kiṅkinī.' A kiṅkinī is an ornament with small hanging bells.

270 Śirīṣa 'parrot tree'; see Appendix.

271 Pāsalī, a toe-ring connected by a chain to an anklet.

272 Prathama sanehe 'in our first love.'

273 The characteristic red stain acquired by frequent chewing of betel quids has been worn off by kissing.

Song 108

Granny, it's a lucky thing that, once more, I have met you.
In my husband's absence, do you see the state I've come to?
I have had an awful fright alone there in the forest;
Fortune has consigned me to a life with many sorrows.
Come on, Granny, take me back with you, we'll travel homeward.
I've been devastated;[274] it is all because of Krishna.
In the middle of Vṛndāvana, with great insistence,
Krishna struggled hard with me, demanding my affection;
Since I was alone, I snugly wrapped my clothes around me
And, at peril to my very life, stood up to Krishna.
In his fury, he divested me of all my baubles;
In addition, Krishna also disarrayed my person.
Many ugly things were likewise said to me by Krishna.
Granny, what I've told you is the truth with no evasions.
Who knows where you were, though, Granny, or what was your motive
When you left me stranded in the middle of the forest.
It is you whose inclinations, Granny, aren't apparent.

Song 109

I'm very old and my vision is poor.
I cannot move along quickly.
There in Vṛndāvana, I lost my way;
That was the reason I left you.
Don't harbor feelings of anger against me;
It was bad luck you were stranded.
You had proceeded ahead of me; it was
By chance you were picked up by Krishna.
Don't think adversely of me in your heart;
One must look out for herself.
Look, darling Radha, I'm kissing your face;
You're like my duplicate spirit.
Only by finding you now am I living
At all; I've been rescued by heaven.
Later on, what shall I tell Abhimanyu
If he should approach me with questions
When he observes that your jewelry is gone?

274 Bhaila pāñjara śeṣa, literally 'I've been reduced to a ribcage.'

Song 110

Underneath the kadamba beside the river Yamunā is where my blouse got soaking wet from sweating.
Granny, in the way that waterfowl disturb a pond, that was precisely how I got disturbed by Krishna.[275]
Tell them, tell them, Granny, at the house of Abhimanyu, Krishna blocked me and was falsely claiming taxes.
All the ornaments I had—my necklaces, my armlets and the rest of it—he roughly confiscated.
In an arbor, any grievances that Krishna might have had against me, he avenged himself for fully.
Krishna wrenched my arms and shattered all my bracelets; likewise, too, he tore apart the bodice on my bosom.
I was in the empty wilderness when Krishna got ahold of me; he overcame me and embraced me.
I did not encourage him no matter how he badgered me for love. I've told the truth; let's now head homeward.

[275] See n. 259 above.

Naukākhaṇḍa*

"Being the more intelligent, Radha has somehow managed by her superior wit
To win release from Krishna's eager grasp. The doe-eyed girl has come home with me."
Abhimanyu's mother accepted Granny's account and enjoined Radha
From going to Mathurā for selling yogurt, buttermilk and ghee.
Granny heeded the order not to sell dairy goods. Thereafter she avoided
Visiting Mathurā with Radha.[1] For a long time they remained at home.

Song 1

Then, his heart set on the amorous enjoyment of Radha,
Krishna contrived an opportunity and eventually managed to speak someplace with Granny:

"Not seeing Radha, my heart is uneasy.
Sleep doesn't come day or night for this reason.
Granny, I'm troubled by Radha's aloofness.
I'll never survive if I don't get to see her."
"Radha is the wife of Abhimanyu. She's most stubborn.
I can't make her come to you by arguments or efforts.
You yourself must offer me some strategy, some tactic;
Just as you determine it, I'll carry out your service."
"Take milk for selling at Mathurā market.
Lie for my sake, telling Radha as follows:
'This time, the path I shall take will be different;
Then you'll be free from the clutches of Krishna!'"
"Krishna, your suggestion is attractive to my thinking.
Take a look, the season of the monsoon is approaching.[2]

* *Naukākhaṇḍa* 'Episode of the Boat', name of the fourth section of *Śrīkṛṣṇakīrtana*. In this episode Krishna accosts Radha at the Yamunā River, posing as a ferryman. The episode is introduced by three verses in Sanskrit.

[1] The reading sa rādhikā of the text as published should be replaced by sarādhikā 'with Radha'.

[2] Upasanna haila hera bariṣā samae 'See, the time of rains approaches.' The monsoon

I shall go to Mathurā for marketing with Radha;
Take a boat and wait beside the Yamunā embankment."[3]
"I am delighted by what you're suggesting.
Let me go pick out some wood in Vṛndāvana.[4]
I'll try my hand at constructing a dinghy."

Song 2

Krishna went away; he cut the timber with precision.[5]
He figured an auspicious time to fabricate the keel.[6]
He hewed four boards of equal size[7] to give the boat its body.
Sitting-planks he put inside, attaching raising covers.[8]
He filled the chinks between the planks throughout the boat with fiber.[9]
Then he took it to the river Yamunā and launched it.
While the boat was being crafted, Krishna had been thinking:
"Two at most, not three, is all the riders it should carry."[10]
Thinking out his strategy in greater detail, Krishna
Gleefully constructed one more vessel, which was larger.
Deep inside the river he immersed the second vessel;
Later, with the first one, he set out for the embankment.
There he stayed, observing whether Radha was approaching.

---

lasts through the greater part of India from the latter part of June through September.

3 See Janmakhaṇḍa above, n. 23. Like many Indian rivers, the Yamunā near the pasturelands is reduced to a dry bed each year until the onset of monsoon. Accordingly the route taken by the dairymaids to Mathurā market varies with the seasons.

4 See Tāmbūlakhaṇḍa above, n. 2.

5 Kāṭha kāṭila giā̃ bibidha bidhāne 'He went and cut the wood by many procedures,' i.e., meticulously.

6 Śubhakṣaṇa bujhi kaila dāṇḍāra pātane 'Figuring out the auspicious moment, he did the fabricating of the keel (daṇḍa).' The keel is the backbone, the most fundamental part of a watercraft.

7 Cāri pāṭa cirī nāa dila yokha māpe, literally, 'Splitting four planks, he gave the boat yokha māpe.' Yokha māpe (modern Bengali maap-jop) refers to the act of measuring objects up against one another. See Turner 1962–1966, entry 10525. In other words, Krishna split four planks, measured them against one another and constructed the main part of the boat from them.

8 Tāta guṛhā yoṛi dila taulajhā̃pe 'In it he put sitting-planks (guṛhā, modern Bengali guṛaa) with raisable (taula) covers (jhā̃pe, modern Bengali jhããp "shutter, lid").'

9 Ghalā pāṛi suraguṭhi dila saba nāe 'All throughout the boat, the chinks (ghalā, modern Bengali ghaal "wound") he stopped up with suraguṭhi (sura = suṇḍa "tube" + guṭhi = guṭikā "stopper, solid thing"; hence suraguṭhi "tubular insulation").'

10 Duī chāṛī tīna jana jāta nāhī̃ jāe 'Beyond two passengers, it is not to be ridden by three.'

Song 3

With her acumen for deception, Granny addressed Radha thus
To lure the charming girl to Mathurā as Krishna had requested.

Do not do anything, Radha, which doesn't conform to the plan I'm suggesting.
I wouldn't tell you advice which is not in your interest; you know this sincerely.
You haven't traveled to Mathurā lately. Why let your dairy goods spoil here?
Listen to me, we are cowherds by birth. We're producers of dairy and milk goods.
Why are you suddenly paying no heed to this? What is the folly you're seized with?
Get all your girlfriends to follow along. We shall gather and plan this together.
After we've come to a single accord, we shall travel to Mathurā, Radha.
Let's get our dairy goods ready, since that is the only career which sustains us.

Song 4

Krishna attacked me in highwayman fashion
Before, when I headed for Mathurā market;
Just like a bull trampling crops on a rampage
He ruined my milk goods and smashed the containers.
Don't you suggest such a thing to me, Granny;
While going, that scamp of a Krishna would catch me.
That time, besides using terrible language
He watered my milk, and my buttermilk also.
He made my elaborate hairdo disheveled
And even tore open the blouse on my bosom.
Breaking my bangles, he snatched off my necklace
And then he took off both my earrings and bracelets.
After I witnessed such conduct in him
I could only survive by your graciousness, Granny.
Now you advise me to visit the city.
What sort of blunder is this that you're making?
I feel dismayed by the very suggestion.

Song 5

"This time I shall take you on a different pathway, Radha.
Give up your suspicions, go to Mathurā for selling."
"Granny, by what pathway will you take me when we travel?

Let me know the answer to this, speak to me sincerely."
"There are two approaches to the Yamunā embankment.
We won't go upon the path where Krishna levies taxes."
"How shall we arrive across the Yamunā? It's swollen.
Be completely truthful with me, tell me the solution."
"Lately by the Yamunā the king has stationed dinghies.
In them people cross conveniently and go to market."
"If he should accost me when I've reached the other landing,
How would I release myself again from Krishna's clutches?"
"Krishna isn't ever seen across the river, Radha.
He does not have jurisdiction there for taking taxes."
"Through his mother, Abhimanyu's barred my trips to market.
How am I to make my way there, lacking his permission?"
"That's well stated. What you've said impresses me as valid.
Come then, Radha, let's approach your husband and his mother."
Then, proceeding hastily, they went to them and told them:
"Why do you keep dairy goods and milk at home, decaying?
With such folly, we shall end up begging for our living!
Knowing this, send Radha off to Mathurā for selling."
Exercising use of different tactics in this fashion,
Granny took consent from them and offered it to Radha.
Having gained permission, Radha cheerfully departed.

Song 6

Radha made ready her merchandise—dairy goods white as the screwpine in blossom.[11]
The she draped fine muslin cloths on her basket of gold and her pitchers of silver.
Letting her girlfriends, the dairymaids, know of the plans she had made, Radha called them.
Then they set out, those young daughters of cowherds. Observing them as they departed,
Who would not turn for a second appraisal of Radha, the fairest among them?
Late in the night, with the morning approaching, the cuckoos had started their chorus.
Even with that, she had not felt at all like arising from slumber this morning.
Still, with the lateness of hour, she couldn't remain in her bed any longer;

[11] Sundhi ketakī sama sājāiā̃ dahī 'Preparing her dairy goods which were like white waterlotus (sundhi) or screwpine (ketakī). . . .' Both plants produce white blossoms. See Appendix.

She was to travel to Mathurā city this morning for selling her produce.
Radha made ready her merchandise: buttermilk, yogurt and milk,
cheese and ghee.[12]
Putting on delicate armlets of gold, she appeared most exceedingly
lovely.
Anklets attached to her feet jingled restlessly, pealing in time with her
movements.
Radha proceeded toward Mathurā city for selling her produce at market.
When she'd decided a program together with all of her dairymaid
girlfriends,
Radha set out; in a mood of unbounded delight she commenced on her
journey.
Both by her husband and mother-in-law she'd been given permission to
travel.

Song 7

In the lead was Granny; with her staff in hand, she plodded.
After her the cowmaids bore their dairy wares in baskets.
Slowly Granny traveled toward the Yamunā embankment,
Keeping off a certain path where Krishna'd asked for taxes.
Making great frivolity with teasing, dance and laughter,
All the cowmaids went along, accompanied by Granny.
Quite a hubbub they stirred up, those many dairymaidens,[13]
Singing joyous tunes[14] in cheerful spirits as they traveled.
All the friendly dairymaids were looking up to Granny;
She in turn went lumbering toward Mathurā, their leader.
When they'd walked awhile, they reached the Yamunā embankment.
All set down their produce near the landing of the river.
When they had conferred together, they requested Granny,
"Tell us, where's the boatman who will take us toward the city?"[15]
Granny then responded, "You must listen to me, grandniece.
Look, you'll see a boatman over there, he has a dinghy.
Just you give a cheerful call, Candrāvalī, to rouse him!"

12 Ghṛta dadhi dudhe sājiā̃ mila cukā (text as published reads: milacukā) 'Readying ghee (ghṛta), yogurt (dadhi), milk (dudhe), mila and cukā. . . .' Mila (see Turner 1962–1966, entry 10134) is a soft cheese made from milk solids (widely known in India as panīr). Cukā (Sanskrit cukra 'sour'; see Turner, entry 4850) is buttermilk, which is also called ghola in the present text.

13 Ṣola śata gopījana 'sixteen hundred dairymaids.' See Dānakhaṇḍa above, nn. 9 and 10.

14 Gāyitẽ maṅgala 'while singing maṅgalas.' Maṅgala is a type of song sung on the theme of some particular deity whose propitiation elicits domestic happiness.

15 Pārakara mathūrāka ghāṭoāla kahī 'Where's the boatman who does the ferrying for Mathurā?'

Song 8

Lowering her basket of wares on the Yamunā's bank,
The dairymaid looked all around and exclaimed,
"We left at dawn; it is getting so late.
How long till we reach the Mathurā side?
Where has the ferryman gone from the crossing,
The one who must ferry our baskets of produce?"
Radha Candrāvalī went for the boatman;
All her companions, the dairymaids, followed.
When some distance had been gone, a tiny boat was spotted.
Radha made her way ahead and hastened up beside it.
After going close to it, the dairymaid lamented,
"How are we to get across inside this tiny dinghy?
One by one to Mathurā is how we must cross over.
It will not withstand the load if all climb on together.
Listen, boatman, pull your dinghy up beside the landing.
All of us must get to town for market. Take us over!"
As he heard what Radha had to say, the boatman chuckled.

Song 9

Pulling the boat up to shore, Krishna shouted,
"Come, all you dairymaids, climb aboard ship!"
Seeing the Yamunā, Radha felt fearful.
"Before me," she answered, "take all of my girlfriends."
"My boat is made of just five wooden planks.
I'll cross your friends over one at a time."
"We're taking milk goods to Mathurā city.
Get all my friends over safely at once."
Krishna exulted at Radha's decision.
Quickly he took all her girlfriends across.
Then, pulling Granny beside her, the dairymaid
Said, "Take us quickly, the waves are terrific!"
"Three people's weight is too much for my dinghy.
How can you get over, Radha, with Granny?"[16]
Radha, on hearing this, took a decision:
"Boatman," she said, "first you ferry my Granny."
Granny climbed into the boat unescorted;
Krishna rejoiced as he ferried her over.
Waiting her turn to cross last, Radha fretted.

[16] Krishna gives himself away by addressing the dairymaid by name, but she seems not to notice.

Song 10

"Radha, don't be anxious about the boat's capsizing
Because you see it heavily filled with Yamunā water; do as I say!"

Look, I am Krishna! Because of you, I am the ferryman at this embankment.
Radha, before you can cross in my dinghy, you'll have to take care of my payment.
Don't be afraid of this watercraft, Radha. You might as well climb on the dinghy;
As you can see, it is I who am captain—Gadādhara, lord of the cosmos!
It was because of my longing for you that I ferried the rest of them over.
That's why you ought to present me a smile and be seated beside me, my Radha!
It is for your sake alone I've constructed this dinghy and launched it here, Radha.
You should reward me, your Krishna, with compliments; then you can travel to market.
Anyway, what do you hope to accomplish by visiting Mathurā, Radha?

Song 11

Terrified on taking in Krishna's message, Radha[17]
Wailed a bit and said the following to Madhusūdana:

If I'd known Krishna took tolls at this crossing,
Would I have stayed by myself without Granny?
Why did I have all my friends cross before me?
Youth is to blame for my fate; it's betrayed me.
What's come to pass at this Yamunā landing?
Why did I want to reach Mathurā market?
That Jagannātha who troubled me earlier—
I have again fallen into his clutches.
I was insane to embark on this journey.
Heaven protect me, a cowmaid unguarded!
I have been born in a cowherding household
Because of my actions in earlier lifetimes.
Now, as I go to sell milk goods at market
He waylays my desolate path, nasty Krishna!

[17] Rādhā darabhayāturā (the text of the 1973 edition mistakenly reads darabhayātuyā) 'Radha who was distressed (āturā) with the timidity (bhaya) of fear (dara).' The same compound occurs in Sanskrit verses preceding several songs in *Śrīkṛṣṇakīrtana*, including song 25 of this section; Bhārakhaṇḍa, song 4; Hārakhaṇḍa, song 2. In the present context the compound darabhayāturā may be a pun since dara has a second meaning 'stream' (i.e., 'distressed with timidity of the stream').

Listen, I'm asking you humbly, Dāmodara,
Ferry me quickly, I must go with Granny.
Krishna, my friends will be leaving without me.

Song 12

I've this boat of five wood planks.
I myself control the helm.
Loading it with dairy goods,
You intend to cross the stream.
Look, pay heed to my demands.
I won't budge until you pay.
I took all your girlfriends over
Safely, just as you had asked.
If I am to ferry you,
Give your necklace on deposit.[18]
Since I saw your moonlike face,
I've staked out the Yamunā.
If you'll now give your consent,
I'll take you across at once.
I've immersed my thoughts in you.
Hold me tight, make good the tolls.
That is what I crave completely.

Song 13

"While, in our boat, we go plying the flowing expanse of the Yamunā River,
Give your consent, promise we will make love. You should not disregard my entreaties."
"Don't be impertinent. You are a ferryman, why do you try to provoke me?
What kind of conduct is this, talking sin by the shores of a river that's sacred![19]
Aren't you aware of the rules of right conduct?[20] The woman you're teasing is married!

[18] Bāndha deha sātesarī hāra 'give your multistranded necklace (as) security.' See Tāmbūlakhaṇḍa above, n. 40.

[19] Punya nadī 'auspicious river.' According to Mani 1975:894, the Yamunā River is worshipped as a goddess of black complexion carrying a water pot in her hand and mounted on a tortoise. Legend has it that heaven can be attained by bathing in the Yamunā. For Vaishnavas, of course, it is revered as the scene of Krishna's dalliances. Cf. Dānakhaṇḍa above, n. 102.

[20] Nā jāṇa dharmma bicāra 'you don't know the judgment (bicāra "conception, codification") of right conduct (dharma).' Cf. Dānakhaṇḍa above, n. 88.

Just take my dairy wares over the Yamunā. I must reach Mathurā quickly."
"What are the shores of the holiest river to me, I'm consumed with love's prickings.
Bearing in mind neither goodness nor evil, I'll ravish you forcibly, Radha!"
"Take me by force, will you? I'll simply perish by throwing myself in the river.
Sun, wind and water[21] will lend me their witness; I'll see that you're charged with my murder!"
"What king of conduct is this, you desire to die when I playfully tease you?
I'll take you over the Yamunā, Radha; just render the tolls you girls owe me."[22]
"You've taken money from each of my friends as you ferried them over the river.
Now you're requesting that I should again pay those tolls. Oh, your folks must be shameless!"[23]
"I've held you hostage for all of the others. You'd better comply with my wishes!"

Song 14

All through adolescence I've been coddled by my husband.[24]
Krishna, I'm a treasure which is sealed and can't be plundered.
Ferry me across the Yamunā. Observe your duty.
My fresh youthfulness is hardly suited for you, Krishna.
Shameless Vanamālī, don't mistreat me on this pathway.
I don't know a thing, I'm just a tiny baby cowmaid.
You must take me over quickly. All my dairy produce—
Yogurt, milk, my buttermilk and ghee—are spoiling. Krishna,
Don't you recognize me? I'm the wife of Abhimanyu.
Yesterday a cowherd boy, today you're customs agent!
On that side is Mathurā; the Yamunā divides us.
I would like to cross this ford[25] and sell my dairy produce.
You're the boatman at this crossing; take me over quickly.

[21] Sun or Sūrya, wind or Vāyu (also called Pavana), and water (Varuṇa) are all divinities.

[22] The reading dāna ghāṭa in the original text should be reversed, i.e., ghāṭa dāna 'crossing tolls.'

[23] Nilaja bāpa tohmāra 'you have shameless fathers'; i.e., your immodesty is deeply ingrained. Refer to and cf. Dānakhaṇḍa above, nn.13 and 180.

[24] Prathama yaubana sāmī gelā tule dharī 'My early youth went placed in cotton (tule) (by my) husband.' Tule dharī 'placing in cotton,' i.e., handling as something fragile.

[25] O āritẽ in the text as published should, according to Sen 1971:102, be read as oāritẽ '(over) the ford' (from Sanskrit avatārika 'incline').

Yaśodā is your mother; she's the sister of my husband.
I am married to your uncle; that makes you my nephew.
Cakrapāṇi, how can you make wicked propositions?
Give up being headstrong, take control of your emotions.

Song 15

Hearing your message, I find it peculiar;
How does your youth have a seal on it, Radha?
When I encountered you once in Vṛndāvana,
We enjoyed love. Can it be you've forgotten?
Dairymaid, how can you say, "I know nothing"?
Granny knows well Vanamālī's your lover!
I'll ferry over your ghee, milk and yogurt
And, for your baubles, I'll make restitution.
Everyone's learned of our getting together;
Moonfaced one, why are you snubbing me lately?
Don't tell me, Radha, that we are related!
You've had the luck to be courted by Krishna!
It's for your sake I take tolls at this ferry.
Why are you wasting your youthfulness, Radha?[26]
Come aboard ship, Radha; give up your folly.
You and I ought to make love on the river.
I've spent so long here awaiting you, Radha.

Song 16

What, do you oppose me at the Yamunā embankment?
I must quickly get to town for market.
You're transgressing reason by your teasing of me, Krishna;
You'll receive a scolding from your parents.
You have learned no manners in your childhood, shameless Krishna.
Toward your uncle's wife you make such comments!
Krishna, you've been spending all your life in tending cattle;
This accounts for how you've been behaving.
Now you say you're charging payment at this river crossing.
On this pretext, you're proposing mischief.
You've already taken all my friends across the river;
Now you want to force me into staying.
I shall have you branded as the killer of a woman
After I go plunging in the river.
Ferry me across; give up your wicked notions, Krishna.

26 Kisere bañcaha rādhā prathama yaubane, literally, 'Why do you pass (live [fruitlessly] through) your early youth, Radha?'

Very close at hand are my companions.
Stop this, Krishna. You must not provoke me any longer.

Song 17

“Smile, if only slightly, as you come aboard the vessel.
Do so of your own free will; don’t have misgivings, Radha.
In the dinghy’s hold, you may set down your produce, Radha.
After I have ferried you across, I’ll take your money.
Radha, don’t do anything except what I advise you;
I myself, the Lord Supreme, control the helm. I’m Krishna!”
“Five planks three and one-half cubits long make up your dinghy.
You have pulled it up along this landing with great effort.
Very circumspectly I’ve approached the vessel, Krishna;
Mutely[27] I’ve observed that, through the joints, it’s taking water.
All my body’s trembling out of agitation, Krishna.
I don’t want to go across in such a damaged dinghy!”
“You’re not understanding matters, dairymaid; you’re silly.
Why, I take all royal people over in this dinghy!
Lower down your merchandise. The hold’s the place to stow it.
Bail the water out that’s leaking inward, don’t be bashful.
I shall row this dinghy, taking hold of both the paddles;
On the other shore I’ll moor it; that won’t take a twinkling.”[28]
“Listen, Krishna, here’s my frank opinion. You’re a prankster.
In that boat there’s not the smallest space to stow my produce.
In my heart I flinch to see the breakers in the river.
Who the hell, besides, can bail out half a boat of water?[29]
Is this how you operate as boatman at this landing?
Don’t you feel ashamed to use this damaged boat for crossing?”
“Dairymaid, you fool, you haven’t understood the matter.
Never in your lifetime have you traveled on a ferry.[30]
Why, it’s all because of you I’ve built and launched this dinghy.
Radha, make my charges good. Award me your affection;
Then you can go home again if you won’t cross the river.”

Song 18

Building this boat with great care, at this landing
You’ve launched it, you say, for the sake of your living.

[27] Nihuṛiā̃, according to a suggestion made by Sukumar Sen during personal consultations, derives from Sanskrit nibhṛta ‘surreptitiously’.

[28] Nimiṣeka nahibeka cāpāyibō̃ kūle ‘It will not be one eye-blink (before) I shall moor it on the (other) shore.’

[29] Kāra bāpē̃, literally ‘by whose father?’ See Dānakhaṇḍa above, n. 154.

[30] Literally, ‘In no lifetime have you ever crossed in a boat.’

You hold the Yamunā River concession;
Everyone, so you insist, takes your ferry.
Why do you tell me these ludicrous stories?
I was your object in building this dinghy!
Why are you talking like this now that my turn
Has come? You were willing to ferry the others.
Your boat was seaworthy up till this instant;
How is it suddenly out of commission?
Your inclinations defy comprehension.
With your proposals, I'm inwardly reeling.
Speak if you'll tell me the truth, Vanamālī;
That's when this cowmaid might enter your dinghy.
Look, since you don't have a seaworthy vessel,
Why did you ever accept your position?
Don't you feel any embarrassment, Krishna?

Song 19

Musky darkness fills, between your breasts, the astral spaces.[31]
Giant pearls are strung across, like stars they hover over.[32]
Scratches from my nails, resembling crescent moons, appear there;
Seeing those enticing sights, my thoughts are overpowered.
After I observed this youthful beauty you're possessed of,
Near the river Yamunā I've taken my position.
As my river crossing tolls, I'm claiming many cowries,
Since you are the foremost of the many dairymaidens.[33]
Listen, darling, you can ascertain what I am saying;
Learn from common knowledge, Radha, if it's true or isn't.
Here's my ledger, lovely Radha. Listen to the figures.
Look, your wares of yogurt, ghee and buttermilk are listed.
For the vessels on your head, a tidy sum's outstanding;[34]
Pay, or I will take your layered necklace[35] and your bracelets.
Contemplate, Candrāvalī, the benefit you're gaining;

[31] Mṛdamada kucayuga gagana mājhāra 'The middle (space between) your two breasts, darkened with musk paste, is the sky.' Musk is rubbed on the forehead and chest for color and fragrance.

[32] Tahita nakṣatragaṇa gajamutīhāra 'The stars thereon are (your) elephant-pearl necklace.' Refer to Dānakhaṇḍa above, n. 233.

[33] Ṣola śata gopī mājhẽ tohme āguāna / ṣola śata kutaghāṭe mora māhādāna 'You are the foremost among the sixteen hundred dairymaids; at the river station my official tolls are sixteen hundred.' Refer to n. 13 above.

[34] Bhāṇḍa māthe ṣola pana dāna āhmāra 'the pots on your head are (worth) sixteen panas' tax to me.' See Dānakhaṇḍa above, n. 10.

[35] Sātesarī hāra 'multistranded necklace.' Cf. n. 18 above.

You have made the master of the universe your subject!
Radha, offer me—your lover Krishna—your embraces.

Song 20

Look, this is a gentlemen's society you live in.
Hearing of this, what will people say throughout the kingdom?
Good and evil differ, Krishna; show discrimination.
Do you find adultery in any sacred legend?[36]
I perceive what you intend; I understand. But, Krishna,
How can you commit adultery and foul your person?[37]
You yourself admit that you've displayed ungallant conduct
Killing off the kṣatriyas;[38] your very lips proclaim it.
As a toll collector, you've been menacing the landing;
Now your brutish scheming is directed at a woman.
Fiercer than an elephant, my Abhimanyu's dauntless;
Finding something wrong, he'll take one's ears and nose for vengeance.[39]
Disregarding that, you've let your heart be drawn to Radha.

Song 21

"Listen, I am warning you, Candrāvalī, my princess;
I'll convey you to the other landing of the river
Only while the Yamunā is not disturbed by tempests.
Come aboard and hoist your dairy wares inside the dinghy."
"All my friends, except for me, have gone across already.
Now it's growing late; the marketplace will be deserted."[40]
Thinking in this manner, Radha climbed aboard the dinghy.
In the hold she set the basket with her dairy produce.
"Calling you aboard, I did not know the boat's condition.
Such a damaged dinghy isn't suitable for boarding.
Still, my lovely Radha, you must come to some decision:
Will you stay on this side here or travel to the other?"
"Just like your assurances, this dinghy won't hold water.
Cakrapāṇi, like your word, the watercraft is leaking!
Now that I have come aboard alone and stowed my produce,

36 Komaṇa purāṇe 'in which purāṇa?' See Dānakhaṇḍa above, n. 53.

37 Literally, 'Why, with your unblemished body, do you commit adultery?'

38 Kṣatriya māriā̃ tohme nikṣatri kailẽ 'You've behaved unlike a warrior by killing the warriors.' In his sixth incarnation Viṣṇu descends upon earth as Paraśurāma, enemy of the warrior caste (kṣatriyas). See Dānakhaṇḍa above, n. 195, and see Wilson 1972:320–23.

39 See Tāmbūlakhaṇḍa above, n. 32.

40 Hāṭa ukhuṛibe 'They will be striking the market.' On ukhuṛ- 'pull up, strike' see Sen 1971:76. The market stalls are put into place in the early hours and the entire market is struck, like a set, in the afternoon.

Take me over, Krishna, but proceed with utmost caution."
"Wife of Abhimanyu, you must listen to my counsel.
Water's bubbling in; you'll have to bail out. Act quickly!
Hurry, Radha, move into the center of the dinghy;
I'll take you across at once, you have no need to worry."
At the river's midpoint, there arose a mighty tempest.
Waves which were the size of mountains smashed against the dinghy.
Radha then exclaimed to Krishna, "Row the dinghy! Paddle!
This one time you'll have to save my life from danger, Krishna!"
As the waves were reaching to the level of the heavens,
Krishna turned his eyes upon the face of Radha, grinning.
"Radha, what's the strategy or tactic I should follow?
I can't get my dinghy past the middle of the river."
"How should I know one way from another? I'm so frightened.
Krishna, I will have you charged with killing me, a woman.
I submit my plea to you in utter supplication:[41]
I will give you anything you want—just take me over!"
"Listen with attention to my proposition, Radha.
No one else is here, it's you and I alone together.
I will get you out of this catastrophe; don't worry.
Offer your delicious love to Krishna in this dinghy!"
Tears emerged from Radha's eyes in flowing streams and torrents.
Imperious Candrāvalī lamented loudly, "Mercy!"
Radha was in panic over Krishna's proposition.

Song 22

"Now that we are inundated with gushing waters aroused by the surging waves,[42]
Radha, do my bidding for the sake of preserving your life!"

Radha, I'm paddling. This boat won't reach shore.
To Yamunā offer some blooms and vermilion;[43]
To Hanumān, son of the wind, give your necklace;[44]

[41] Daśaneta tṛna kari bolõ mo tohmāre 'I say to you, taking grass between my teeth (i.e., adopting the pose of a dumb animal).'

[42] The manuscript reading atha rādhe pure payaḥ pūrodbhavakṛte dare, as the first line of this Sanskrit couplet, appears to be in error. I have adopted the following revised reading: atha rādhe pūre payaḥpūrodbhavakṛte dare.

[43] Flowers and vermilion are standard offerings to the mother goddess, here identified with Yamunā. Refer to n. 19 above.

[44] Hanumān (see Tāmbūlakhaṇḍa above, n. 37) is said to be the son of a she-monkey and of the deity Vāyu or Pavana 'Wind' (see again n. 21 above). In pāla 10, song 11 of the Vipradāsa *Manasāmaṅgala* (Sen 1953), the goddess Manasā calls on Pabanakumāra ('Wind-Offspring') Hanumān to sink the boats of the merchant Cāndo. As this suggests, Hanumān is thought to have the power to cause or withdraw a storm.

Present your delicious love, Radha, to Krishna!
My boat of five planks is upset by the wind.
You clambered on board in the face of my warning.
The wind's been aroused by your ill fortune, Radha.
The boat will not budge to one side or the other.
I've lost the power to paddle this dinghy.
You boarded ship through your own folly, Radha!
With your allurements you've charmed Jagannātha;
My arms are refusing to paddle the dinghy.
Besides, after taking your friends, I'm exhausted.
Allow me to drink your lips' nectar. Restore me!
Clasp me this once in your arms and embrace me.
Let Krishna feel joy as he ferries you over.
Drop your resistance, accept my proposal.

Song 23

Krishna, this dinghy is moving dead slowly.
You are yourself in command of the vessel.
Krishna, I boarded this boat on your promise.
Now that we're halfway across, don't mistreat me.
Take me for joining my Granny, Nārāyaṇa;
After we've made it across, I'll embrace you.
Hours are passing[45] and noon is approaching;
My husband's about to come home from the pasture.
Finding I'm not in the house, he'll berate me.
Have you no mercy or decency, Krishna?
Thinking of God, Krishna, row the boat quickly.
The river is stirred by a violent tempest.
The Yamunā current is pitching this dinghy;
The shaking and heaving is going to kill me!
The numerous dairymaids watch for my coming;
The boat's planks are shattering—that's my undoing.[46]
Krishna, just once you must spare my existence.

Song 24

By itself, your bosom is remarkably stupendous;
With your necklace, strung with giant pearls, the weight's tremendous.
In this world, existence isn't lightly come by, Radha.[47]

[45] Sāta ghaṭi gela 'seven hours have gone by.'

[46] Mohora karame nāe bhā̃gila pāṭe 'The boat's planks are splitting thanks to my (previous) deeds (karma).' Refer to Dānakhaṇḍa above, n. 25.

[47] It is thought that birth in human form is a hard-won reward for good conduct in

Cast the necklace overboard and let your breasts be lightened!
There's a mighty current, Radha; gales are strongly gusting.
For this reason, you must heed my proposition, Radha.
You are very massive in your hips and in your buttocks;
Furthermore, you've draped them with a golden waistband,[48] Radha.
Open up the clasp and, Radha, pitch that jewelry over.
Why think twice about it in a crisis situation?
Flowing lengths of fabric are encumbering your figure.
Tear that up, make pieces from it, cast it over promptly![49]
In addition, Radha, cast away your dairy produce.
Let the strain be just a little lightened on my dinghy.
Made of but five planks, this boat is hampered with our bodies.
Radha, toss the bodice from your bosom in the river!
Then you may cross over safely in this damaged dinghy.

Song 25

In terror, Radha discarded her jewelry and even the clothes on her body
Into the Yamunā River on receiving Krishna's instructions.

As Radha, the dairymaid, lightened her person,
He paddled the dinghy, intoning a chanty.[50]
The boat sped along like a comet in space, but
The gale winds revived when they'd gone half the river.
Radha said, "Krishna, be quick! Row us over!
My whole body trembles, observing the breakers!
Krishna, just once, get us past this disaster;
Whatever you ask I will do once we're over."
Dāmodara made the boat pitch even harder;
The fear Radha felt in her heart mounted double.
Krishna succumbed to the passion within him
By deftly upsetting the produce of Radha.
Buttermilk, yogurt and ghee then were scattered.
The terrified Radha sought Krishna's embraces.
"Hold me! But Granny must not learn this, Krishna,
For then so would Kaṃsa, as well as my husband."
When, much to his joy, Krishna heard these entreaties,

---

previous existences. Krishna advises Radha accordingly to take pains so as not to forfeit her life.

[48] Rasana, a belled metal waistband or girdle worn low on the hips; see Dānakhaṇḍa above, n. 120.

[49] Tīna bhāga cirī tāka pelāha ekhane 'Tear that into three pieces and fling it away right now!'

[50] Tabẽ hia hia bulī kāhna bāhe nāe 'Then Krishna rows the boat saying (singing) "Hee-oh, hee-oh."'

He capsized the boat; holding Radha, he floated.
Panicking, Radha clung tightly to Krishna.

Song 26

Krishna, you've ruined my milk and my dairy goods, causing my wares to be sunken.
Krishna, you've clasped me by force in the water; you're going to start a great scandal.
Krishna, my friends are all looking at us; you must not lift me up in the water.
Krishna, because of whatever desires you've nourished so long in your bosom,
You are now taking me, Krishna, along on the pathway of total destruction.
Krishna, whatever you do to me, do it entirely under the water.
Look, Krishna, all of my girlfriends are glancing about; this is making me nervous.
How about you, are you able to find any pleasure with me in the water?

Song 27

> Imbibing the words Radha spoke even as she was in the water,
> Hari clung to her at length in the throes of passion's intensity.

Krishna clasped Radha and embraced her tightly in his arms.
He kissed her face.
Her breasts resembled two buds of golden lotus;
Krishna fondled Radha there again and again.
Then Krishna attained such pleasure
It could not be described in a lifetime.
The handsome and dashing Krishna scratched her with his nails—
For a moment, Radha had mixed emotions.
Then love awoke in Radha's heart;
She held him tightly to her bosom.
Ever so slowly probing Radha's hips,
Krishna considered his life truly replete.
Krishna scoured Radha's buttocks with his nails;
Radha gave a start out of intense erotic rapture.
Because of the water, their lovemaking was prolonged;
From this, Jagannātha gained still greater gratification.
After that he took Radha over the Yamunā.

Song 28

Observing that Krishna had violated her in the water,
Granny now directed these questions to Radha:

The catechu[51] string on your hair is disheveled,
And how has the necklace come off from your bosom?
Grandniece, the sight of you gladdens my spirits.
Good fortune assisted you over the river.
Krishna disturbed you, it seems, in the water—
Your bracelets are broken, your finery's vanished,
Your lips are discolored, your breasts display scratches.
Your features, to me, look completely disordered.
Now you must tell me the true explanation!

Song 29

How could I go home without you, my Granny?
That's what I thought as I climbed on the dinghy.
When Cakrapāṇi propelled us some distance,
The boat leaked and water gushed in from all corners.
I had a fright in the Yamunā River,
But Krishna, the cowherd, transported me nicely.
"Radha," he told me, "heave over the jewelry
That's weighting your body! Now bail out the water!"
Abruptly the tempest blew harder than ever;
The dinghy went down in the depths of the river.
I would have drowned if it wasn't for Krishna;
He took hold of me and, by swimming, he saved me.
Krishna this time has performed a great service;
All of my life I can never repay him.
But, Granny, still I am feeling uneasy;
All of my merchandise sank in the water.
Is there a way for me now to go homeward?

Song 30

When she had heard Radha's tale, Granny asked all her dairymaid girlfriends this question:
"How will poor Radha go home? All the produce she had is submerged in the river."
All of her girlfriends consulted together until they had reached a decision;

[51] Khadira 'catechu', a type of plant or its flower; see Appendix.

Each gave a bit of her own milk or milk goods to Radha, replacing her
produce.
Radha proceeded to Mathurā town with her Granny as well as her
girlfriends.
Selling their buttermilk, ghee, milk and yogurt, they figured it time to
start homeward.
So, in due time, all the girlfriends assembled together with Radha and
Granny.
Reaching the Yamunā River embankment, they looked for a boat and
for Krishna.
Krishna had secretly kept in the water the second and roomier vessel;
Having the dairymaids clamber aboard, in one journey he ferried them
over.
Folding his hands, Krishna spoke before all of the dairymaids, saying
politely:
"Please don't withdraw the indulgence you've shown me. Forgive me for
any offenses."
Radha, on hearing the message of Krishna, clasped hold of his feet and
responded,[52]
"You took my ornaments earlier; so far, you've given back nothing,
Murāri."
Krishna was softened at heart; he returned all the baubles he'd taken
from Radha.
Then all the girlfriends of Radha returned to their homes in exuberant
spirits.
Krishna himself, after offering homage to Granny,[53] set out for his
household.

> Radha went home with Granny and apprised Abhimanyu
> Of having had hundreds of mishaps in crossing the Yamunā.
> The misinformed Abhimanyu thereupon forbade her to go to
> Mathurā;
> Throughout the monsoon season she sold dairy goods only at
> home.

52 See Dānakhaṇḍa above, n. 140.

53 Āpaṇa gharaka gelā kāhnāñī bandiā̃ baṛāyira pāe 'Krishna went to his own home after bowing at Granny's feet.'

Bhārakhaṇḍa*

Song 1

By now Hari's feelings were dominated by his passion for Radha.
At last, goaded by the urge to possess her, he spoke again with
Granny.

"Granny, it has been forever since my last meeting with Radha.
That is why my spirits have been very uncomfortable, Granny.
When I think of Radha, in my heart the attachment grows double.
Summon her without delay and you will have spared my existence."
"Abhimanyu's undertaken efforts to keep her protected.
All the time, his mother has been keeping an eye upon Radha.
I have not been able, consequently, to bring her before you.
You yourself must tell me, Hari, if you know any solution."
"Granny, it so happens that the season of autumn has started.
People travel overland these days on their Mathurā journeys.[1]
Say to Radha, 'At this moment, Krishna is not in command there.'
That way you can lure her to the opposite side of the river."
"I'll take Radha to the other side of the Yamunā River;
But, when we've arrived there, what technique should I make use of,
Krishna?
Offer me the answer. Be completely sincere with me, Krishna;
Once I understand it, I'll be happy to bring Radha over."
"I'll prepare a carrying device on my way to the river.
Then I'll wait along the trail, adopting the guise of a porter.
You must use your many skills and see to it Radha's persuaded
So that she'll entrust her load of produce to me for transporting."
"Krishna, you've expressed that well, and now you should move along
quickly.
I shall go with Radha and we'll travel to Mathurā market.
Through the gimmick you've devised, I'll satisfy all your desires."

* *Bhārakhaṇḍa* 'Episode of the Load', name of the fifth section of *Śrīkṛṣṇakīrtana*. Krishna adopts a new disguise, that of a porter, offering to carry Radha's goods to market in exchange for a consideration. Radha responds for the first time by turning the tables on Krishna.

[1] See Naukākhaṇḍa above, n. 3. By autumn, the river separating the pasturelands from Mathurā shrinks to a dry bed.

Song 2

Receiving Granny's advice, Mādhava hurriedly began
The preparation of an apparatus consisting of a carrier pole and
so on.

Krishna, the cowherd, set out for Vṛndāvana.
He selected and cut a branch from a hardwood tree.[2]
Making both ends pointed and the middle thick,
Divine Murāri shaped it well into a carrier pole.[3]
Krishna was smitten with love due to Radha;
He was bent on preparing a carrying device.
The device was to carry a double load. He scraped it smooth.[4]
On both ends he fashioned elaborate knobs.[5]
With burnt brick he polished it, making it shine.[6]
The carrier pole was most splendidly finished.
Cutting a jute plant, Krishna placed it in water;
After a day and a half, he removed it.[7]
He dried it, took its fibers and neatly arranged them;[8]
From these Dāmodara braided four strips of rope.
Tying stout knots, he constructed two hampers.[9]
He fastened a loop at the bottom of each.[10]
Attaching the hampers to the carrier pole,
Krishna crossed over the Yamunā River.

[2] Cāmaṛa gāchera bāchi kāṭileka ḍāla 'He picked out and cut off the branch of a hardwood (cāmaṛa, literally "leather") tree.'

[3] Bā̃hu (modern Bengali bā̃āk) 'a piece of long and bent pole borne on one's shoulder for carrying loads fastened to its ends' (Biswas and Sengupta 1976:878).

[4] Sucā̃che cā̃chila bhāra duī muṭhī 'He scraped smooth the carrier (bhāra) (which was designed for) two parcels (muṭhī "package, load" = modern Bengali moṭ [cf. modern Bengali muṭiyaa, muṭe "porter"]).'

[5] Guṭhī (modern Bengali guṭi) 'globule, blister'.

[6] Jhā̃oẽ ghasiā̃ tāka karila cikaṇa 'He made it shiny by polishing it with a piece of overburnt brick (jhā̃o, modern Bengali jhaamaa "piece of overburnt brick").'

[7] Nālicā 'jute'; see Appendix. Bāra pahara 'twelve praharas,' i.e., twelve three-hour periods, or thirty-six hours.

[8] Sukhāyiā̃ bāchiā̃ pāṭa karila susura 'He dried it and, selecting (strands of) jute, made them orderly.'

[9] Śikiā (modern Bengali sikaa, sike) 'a reticulated bag made of strings or wires, which is kept hanging usually from the wall' (Biswas and Sengupta 1976:1135); more generally, a hamper.

[10] Beṇḍuā (modern Bengali, bī̃ṛe, biṛaa) 'a coil of straw or cloth used as a pedestal for placing cooking-urns, pitchers, etc., and also for wearing as a headgear' (Biswas and Sengupta 1976:906). In a carrier device, the loop or beṇḍuā catches the pot at its rim. A rough illustration of the complete carrier device is given on the next page.

Bhāra or Carrier Device

Song 3

Then at daybreak, desirous of Padmanābha's[11] benefit,
Granny deceptively addressed Abhimanyu's mother:

"More than one time I have tried to urge Radha
To travel to town with her produce.
She has retorted she won't go to market.
Why, look at your son's wife's behavior:[12]
Radha's becoming a regular princess,[13]
Defiantly shirking her duties.[14]
Radha won't go to sell produce; the privileged
Descendant of herdsmen[15] sits idly.
Look, I'm informing you frankly: her meals
Aren't provided by providence, Mother![16]
Produce accumulates day after day. Let me
Call all her dairymaid girlfriends;
I'll take them all at one time. You yourself
Ask your son's wife to travel to market."

[11] See Dānakhaṇḍa above, n. 24.

[12] Dekha āihanera mā rādhāra carite 'Look, mother of Abhimanyu, at Radha's conduct!'

[13] Rājāra kõarī bhailī āihanera rāṇī 'Abhimanyu's wife (literally, "queen") has become a king's daughter.'

[14] Goālera kāma chāṛi kare biparīte 'She shows defiance, neglecting the work of a cow-herding person.'

[15] Goālera kule rādhā jarama labhiā̃ / dadhi bike nā jāe thākae basiā̃ 'Having won birth in a cowherd family, Radha does not go to sell dairy goods (but) sits around.'

[16] Bidhi nā likhita tāra kapālera bhāte / satyẽ āihanamāa kahilõ tohmāte 'Mother of Abhimanyu, I'm telling you frankly, fate hasn't inscribed her rice on her forehead!' See Dānakhaṇḍa above, n. 17.

Abhimanyu's mother considered the plan
And told Radha, "Get going with Granny.
What are you hoping to gain staying home?"

Song 4

> Taking the ample milk and yogurt provided by Abhimanyu's mother,[17]
> Radha apprehensively spoke with Granny.

Frightened when she heard her husband's mother's orders, Radha
Readied yogurt, buttermilk and ghee; she took this produce
And, on joining all her friends, Candrāvalī politely
Voiced what she was thinking of to Granny in this manner:
"Take me and proceed in such a way across the river
So that I should not be apprehended there by Krishna."
Radha went toward Mathurā for selling off the produce.
No one on the path this time attempted to obstruct her.
Radha reached the river's other shore; she felt delighted.
Then she set her wares down; she was growing quite exhausted.
"You must listen carefully to my instructions, Granny.
This is heavy merchandise, I cannot move it further.
Now that autumntime is here, I can't withstand the sunshine.
From this point to Mathurā there's still a lot of distance.
Fetch a porter, let him take this load of dairy produce.
He can split my merchandise in two and take both portions.[18]
Then it will be possible for me to reach the city."

Song 5

"If you lack the stamina for traveling to market,
Promise you will pay the porter fitting compensation.
You can give a call yourself for summoning a porter;
One of them will come along and meet us in a minute."
Radha showed approval of her Granny's plan by saying,

[17] According to the original text the reading of this line would be 'Taking the milk and yogurt which had been placed on the ground (bhuvi) by Abhimanyu's mother. . . .' In Ray 1973, the text is changed to read 'Taking the generous (bhūri) quantities of milk and yogurt dispensed by Abhimanyu's mother. . . .' The latter reading seems better suited to the context for, in later songs, it becomes clear that the dairy goods are indeed ample, so much so that Radha resorts to hiring a porter.

[18] Duī bhāga kari laū āhmāra pasāra 'He is to take my wares after splitting them into two parts.' See again the depicted carrier device (preceding page); half the load goes on either side.

"I'll give you my earnings when I've sold the milk and produce."[19]
Radha went alone along the pathway for a distance,
Calling out again and yet again, "Hey, porter! Porter!"
Then, in fresh disguise, and with the carrier contraption . . .[20]

* * *

"I shall not be able to accompany you further.
Understanding this, you should turn back and travel homeward."

Song 6

Let's go together. Why shrink from me, Radha?[21]
I shall reward you with bracelets and anklets.
Have you forgotten I did you a favor?
I took you over the Yamunā River.
Take me along with you, dairymaid Radha.
Radha, let's you and me travel together.
Look, I won't carry your burden. What will you
Accomplish by selling these dairy goods, Radha?
Cowherd girl, can't you make sense of the matter?
Do not be frightened to go with me, Radha; my
Home is none other than Mathurā city.
All through the town, I'm well known; I can offer you
Food when you're hungry and drink when you're thirsty.[22]
Don't be reluctant to go with me, Radha;
Building a bridge by the sea, I won Laṅkā.[23]
Now, seeking love, I would like to escort you.

Song 7

Do you wish death when your whole life awaits you?
Why stick your hand[24] in the mouth of a serpent?
Pining for love at a premature time
Is as galling as betel unseasoned with lime.[25]

19 By having Granny handle the money, Radha will lessen her chances of being overcharged by the porter. Her proposing this to Granny shows that she is unsuspecting of what is to follow.

20 One side of a leaf of the original manuscript is missing at this point. The text resumes as Radha, aware of Krishna's identity, addresses him.

21 Saṅge yāiū rādhā e dūre dūre 'Let's go together, Radha; (what's) this distance and distance?'

22 The implication is that Radha will be kept in town by Krishna as a mistress.

23 See Dānakhaṇḍa above, n. 172.

24 Sāpera mukhete kehne āṅgula desī 'Why do you put fingers in the mouth of a snake?'

25 Cūna bihane yehna tāmbūla titā / ālapa baese tehna birahera cintā 'Thinking of a lost

Don't you possess any sense of embarrassment,
Krishna? How dare you attempt to pursue me?
What's this frivolity? You are a porter,
A nobody; yet you want great people's company.
You want the moon to be placed in your clutches.
Why do you start such predicaments, Krishna?
You're of good birth; you're the offspring of Nanda.
Still, Krishna, being a male, you are lacking
In modesty, even when others are present.
Shirking the load, you propose other doings.
I'm not a coconut, you're not a monkey;[26]
Don't become flustered on seeing me, Krishna.
If you're to come with me, carry my produce.

Song 8

Radha, don't tell me such things. Don't suggest them.
The world will go under if Krishna bears burdens.
Indra will confiscate rains;[27] Brahmā, scriptures;[28]
Kapilā, milk;[29] Vasumatī, the harvests.[30]
Gentlemen won't keep their words of commitment
Nor hermits their penance nor scholars their judgments.
Ill-natured siblings will turn against brothers[31]
And powerful śūdras will turn against Brahmans[32]
And son against father and child against teacher.
Iniquitous men will prevail against goodness.
Serfs will cheat masters and housewives their husbands;
Women, betraying their vows, will lose virtue.
People will cheat those they offer protection,
While generous men who make gifts will withdraw them.
All will be jumbled because of your doing.
Besides that, the gods will be irked with you, Radha.
Honor my wishes. Don't load me with burdens!

---

love at an early age is as bitter as betel without lime.' In betel quids, lime is added as a seasoning in order to temper the abrasive taste of the betel.

26 See Dānakhaṇḍa above, n. 116.

27 The Vedic deity Indra is associated with such natural forces as rain. See Dānakhaṇḍa above, n. 145.

28 Brahmā beda haribeka 'Brahmā will withdraw the Vedas.'

29 Kapilā, name of a fabulous cow of lore and legend.

30 Vasumatī, a name of the earth goddess.

31 Kaniṣṭhe laṅghiba jeṣṭha haā̃ duṭhamane 'A younger (brother) will become wicked and defy an older (brother). . . .'

32 In the classical four-tier model of Indian society, the scholarly Brahman class occupies the highest tier and the laboring śūdra class, the lowest.

Song 9

You're the son of Nanda; you must hear what I am saying.
You do not have grounds on which to set aside the burden.
Settling on a wage, I have engaged you as my porter.
If you will not bear the burden now, I can't dismiss you.
Krishna, don't be stubborn. You will have to bear the burden.
Then I shall be happy to accompany you, Krishna.
You predict the cosmos would dissolve if you bear burdens—
Everyone, on hearing this, will ridicule you, Krishna.
One must not exaggerate about his own endeavors.
Krishna, take the load. I have to sell the goods at market.
All those born as cowherds carry loads of dairy produce;
No one feels the slightest bit of diffidence about it.
When it comes to you, why should you balk at bearing burdens?
This makes me suspect that you weren't born to be a cowherd.[33]
Think this over, Krishna. Take the produce on your shoulder.
I am being endlessly delayed in reaching market.
Come with me to Mathurā, let's reach the city quickly.

Song 10

I'm in control of the universe, Radha,
Yet you have singled me out as your porter.
It's not the load, but the shame, that's oppressive.
How shall I live in society, Radha?[34]
Don't say it, Radha, don't say it. What shame
It would be for Gadādhara, bearing a burden!
I killed the Cart-Monster, haven't you heard it?[35]
There were two arjuna trees I uprooted.[36]
I have descended to massacre Kaṃsa.
Now shall I carry your burden of produce?
Peddling these milk goods has addled your judgment;
You're not aware I am God in the highest.
You are extremely audacious, young cowmaid;
That's why you try to have Hari bear burdens.
This is your arrogant youthfulness speaking;
Anger arises in me as I listen.
Now, Radha, drop your unseemly proposals.

33 See Dānakhaṇḍa above, n. 33.
34 Kemane jāyiba rādhā sajanasamāja 'Radha, how will I go (in) genteel society?'
35 See Dānakhaṇḍa above, n. 166.
36 See Janmakhaṇḍa above, n. 26.

Song 11

We have spent three hours[37] near the Yamunā embankment.
How long must it take until I reach the city market?
Ghee and milk are spoiling, while the yogurt's turning sour.
Leaving me, my dairymaid companions are departing.
Will you take this load, Murāri dear, or won't you take it?
If you will not bear the load I'll find another porter.
All my many girlfriends have proceeded on before me;
I refrained from staying with the group on your persuasion.
How am I to manage, Krishna? Tell me the solution.
How should I respond to those to whom I furnish produce?
Krishna, if my friends all leave me, I will be abandoned.
I shall die of shame if we are seen by any person.
You don't have a sense of shame at all within you, Krishna;
This is why you never meet a single obligation.
I'll sell off my necklace and engage another porter;[38]
You can sit around and cool your heels, my dear Murāri![39]
Son of Nanda, turn around; be off with you, my Krishna!

Song 12

"Let me tell you something, dairymaiden. Listen, Radha,
I'm your Vanamālī. Let me bear your load of produce."
"Take that load of dairy goods. But listen, Vanamālī,
I'm a callow dairymaid, not suited for you, Krishna."
"This is no real labor, I can bear the load of produce;
But, as god of gods, I shall be terribly embarrassed."
"You will lose employment, Krishna, if you feel embarrassed.
King of gods, don't criticize me after that has happened."
"Radha, you have spoken well; that stimulates my thinking.
If you'll pledge your love, I shall be glad to bear the burden!"
"Fasten on the ropes and load the burden quickly, Krishna.
If the produce spoils, I'll take three times its price in cowries."
"Radha, your mentality is filled with endless gimmicks.
For this flaw, a eunuch has become your husband, Radha!"
"I do not know gimmicks, Krishna; I have clean intentions.
You're the one whose mind is filled with filth, a sea of mischief!"
"I shall not pick up your burden! Offer me your duties.

[37] Prahareka beli bhaila 'A prahara of time has passed . . . ,' i.e., a period of three hours has gone by.

[38] If Radha engages another porter, he will probably demand advance payment; all the more so, since Radha has already had a disagreement with her first porter.

[39] Basiā̃ thāka tohme sundara murārī 'You just remain here sitting, dear Murāri!'

Who'll take you to market when your taxes are outstanding?"
"Take the load of produce, don't prolong your pointless fussing.
If I'm satisfied, I shall accept your proposition."
Krishna was delighted in his heart to hear this promise.
Fumbling, he picked up the load; Candrāvalī was grinning.
"Even up the load so that the dairy goods won't scatter.
If the goods are harmed, why, with my girlish fists, I'll slug you!"
Then the son of Nanda rearranged the load and took it.

Song 13

He held at an angle the stout wooden carrier pole[40] after fixing the hampers.
Granny went first; Krishna trailed with the load; in the middle, for selling, went Radha.[41]
Taking the load on his shoulder, Janārdana[42] struggled toward Mathurā city.
Seeing the lord of lords laden with burdens, the gods were all bubbling with laughter.[43]
The ghee was apportioned in pitchers of silver, the milk goods in golden containers;
Such was the load borne by Lord Vanamālī. The dairymaid girl was exultant.
The merchandise slumped as he moved with the burden; some milk and some dairy goods scattered.
Radha, observing the golden and silver containers askew, struck her bosom.
Krishna, embarrassed, abandoned the load and escaped; Radha's friends looked and tittered.

[40] Cāmaṛa kāṭhera bā̃huka yoṛiā̃ teracha kaila sīkā 'Attaching the hampers to the pole of hard (literally, "leathery"; see n. 2 above) wood, he held it (the pole) at an angle.'

[41] Krishna adopts the rear position ostensibly as a sign of deference, though his probable motive is to obtain an unrestricted view of Radha's posterior. Notice his reference to her loins in song 20 below.

[42] Janārdana, see Dānakhaṇḍa above, n. 147.

[43] The original text reads: dekhi saba debāgana khalakhali hāse la bhābe majilā debarāje 'All the gods bubbled with laughter (but) the king of gods was immersed in thought.' In the translation, bhābe has been substituted by bhāre, i.e., bhāre majilā 'was engrossed with the burden'; the translation reflects this substitution.

Song 14

"Granny, on your advice he was made a porter[44] for the sake of
transporting the dairy goods.
Now he's ruined them! What shall we do?"

If I'd known that Krishna would allow the load to tumble,
Would I then have given him those heavy wares to carry?
He has made a shambles of my highly valued produce.
Granny, Krishna's brought about my total ruination!
Tell me, how can I proceed to market with this rubbish?
Every bit of merchandise is spoiled because of Krishna.
Neatly I prepared my ghee, my buttermilk and yogurt;
None among my dairymaid companions raised objections.
Granny, what's my plan? And what procedure should I follow?
How can I restore my wares of dairy produce, Granny?
At his own insistence, Krishna took the load of produce.
For this reason, I did not engage another porter.
Now let Krishna, on his own, reorganize the produce.
Out of self concern, he must once more pick up the burden.
Any yogurt, ghee or milk remaining in the vessels
Krishna should make use of for refurbishing the produce.
Granny, you yourself must make this clear to Nanda's darling.

Song 15

Urged again and again by Granny, at Radha's behest,
To carry the load, the angry Madhusūdana said:

Tell what I'm saying to Radha Candrāvalī:
Lord Vanamālī will bear no more burdens.
It is no use; she must make good my revenues.
She used her wiles to insult me severely.
That face of hers I'll no longer cast eyes on;[45]
Look, I am through with her dairy wares, Granny.[46]

* * *

44 Bhābikaḥ kutaḥ, the reading of the published text, should be substituted by: bhārikaḥ kṛtaḥ 'was made a porter.'

45 Āra śira tulī mukha nā dekhiba tāra 'I won't raise my head again (to) look at her face.'

46 Eṛila baṛāyi hera dadhira pasāra 'Look, Granny, I've forsaken her wares of dairy produce.' One side of a leaf of the manuscript is missing from this point.

Song 16

. . . ruining my merchandise completely.
So much of my yogurt, ghee and buttermilk he damaged—
Why don't you reply to him as follows:
He's made good, to that extent, the revenues I owed him!
Frankly, I must tell you something, Granny:
You had all to choose from, but you've fetched me one fine porter.
By his merest contact things are sullied.
Nowhere[47] have I ever seen a laborer so useless—
I can't even deal with such a porter.
Let him now go home, if he's concerned about his welfare.
Seeing such a porter, I feel nervous.
Order Krishna not to go on hoping to possess me.

Song 17

Taking in Radha's reply as conveyed by Granny,
Krishna thirstily addressed that consummate seductress:

"Gazing on your loveliness, I shouldered up your burden.
I'll take what I'm owed; I'll stand no opposition, Radha!"
"You're demanding taxes and the things you say are ugly.
You deserve to have your head cut off, that's my opinion."
"Even if I perish for the sake of you, my Radha,
I'll remain persistently beside you—I'm your Krishna."
"Since you are a laborer, you mustn't make such statements.
Stretching out your hand, will you obtain the moon, my Krishna?"
"I am not persuaded by the argument you're making.
In Vṛndāvana, I reached and held the moon, my Radha!"[48]
"Don't attempt to sow a bulb on which old leaves are growing.[49]
These days, when a criminal is caught, the king impales him."[50]
"I shall do away with your King Kaṃsa. Pay the taxes.
I'll remain your porter. Give consent for me to love you!"
"For my purpose, you are of no value as a porter.

[47] Kohno rāje nā, literally 'in no kingdom.'

[48] 'Moon' here as elsewhere is a metaphor for Radha herself.

[49] Purūba kālera pāte nā ruiha mūle 'Don't plant a tuber with earlier leaves.' Sukumar Sen has remarked in private consultations that old leaves on a tuber would indicate it is not a virgin plant; the line, accordingly, might imply that Krishna should not strive for an already married woman. For an alternative interpretation of this line, see Ray 1973:242.

[50] The original reading rājā dee tiriśūle means 'the king gives the trident.' The intended sense is probably rājā dee śūle 'the king gives (impales one on) the stake.' Possibly a pun is intended, since tiriśūle 'trident' can be analyzed as tirī 'woman' + śūle 'stake'. See Tāmbūlakhaṇḍa above, n. 28.

I'll engage another one, we'll travel to the city."
"Do not disappoint me; there's no reason for it, Radha!"

Song 18

Since I saw your loveliness, my heart has been about to burst. From all the world, it's you I have selected.
I'm your Krishna. Let me taste your ample youthful charms. Away with passion's burning pangs, however briefly!
I'll forgo your taxes and convey your load of dairy goods. The king of gods is charmed by you, dear Radha!
Listen, I shall grant you on the spot whatever fruits you may discover in Vṛndāvana; just keep them.[51]
Lotus blooms are blooming, while my heart's deranged from brooding. Spread a bed now at the Yamunā embankment!
Since I met you, I have lost my senses. Give permission; I'll present you a variety of baubles.
With your fresh alluring charms, you captivate my spirits. Now you must bestow the gift of your caresses.
Radha, you're Candrāvalī; while I, your Vanamālī, am the Lord. You disappoint me without reason.

Song 19

Though you might willfully plunder my cargo of produce in spite of my protests,
You can no more gain another man's wife than the moon in the heavens, my Krishna.
Why don't you give up the cargo of milk goods and beat a retreat, shameless Krishna?
Don't go on spoiling my ghee, milk and yogurt. I must go to Mathurā city.
Listen, my Krishna, to what I'm requesting: don't carry this cargo of produce.
I'd sooner carry the wares by myself; I will never submit to your cravings.
You have no right to take taxes; so how can you cancel my revenues, Krishna?
You're downright brazen-faced, scion of Nanda. Go home for the sake of your honor!
Nowhere does one observe dwarves reaching out with their hands to pluck fruit from palmyras![52]

[51] This foreshadows Vṛndāvanakhaṇḍa, the seventh section of *Śrīkṛṣṇakīrtana*. In that section (see text), Krishna creates a forested park stocked with fruiting and flowering plants, and invites the cowmaids to pluck what they wish.

[52] Kathā̃ nā dekhila bā̃ona hāthe tālataruphala pāe 'It is nowhere seen (that) a dwarf gets

Song 20

Taking in Radha's disagreeable[53] words, with a display of ponderousness
Hari lifted the load and addressed Granny as follows:

Why must Radha speak to me so cruelly when she answers?
What's the crime that I, Lord Madhusūdana, committed?
You should see the merchandise; it's extra heavy, Granny.
Just let Radha try to lift the load, she won't be able.
Radha should precede me; in the rear I'll take the burden.
You're an older person, Granny; you must go before her.
She has massive loins and buttocks, while her breasts are heavy;
God has showered all the charms of youth upon her person!
Look, it's autumn season. How the sun is burning, Granny!
Even Radha's father[54] couldn't take this load of produce.
Bearing burdens, all the other laborers have vanished;
Other than myself, there is no means to move this burden.
There's one message I want Radha, on her own, to tell me;
Then I'll gladly shoulder up her load of dairy produce.
I will do, in fact, whatever Radha should desire;
All the way to Mathurā I'll travel with her burden.
Only let her signal me assurance of some pleasure!

Song 21

Radha, lightheartedly savoring the humor of the situation,
Addressed Krishna on receiving his message as Granny conveyed it.

Never could my Granny walk the pathway all the distance.
Pick her wares up, Krishna; you must add them to the burden.
You can't win the wife of someone else by tricks or speeches;
Therefore, Krishna, I'm about to tell you my conditions.
Take the load of dairy goods to Mathurā. We'll go there;
Then I'll give my love to you upon returning, Krishna.
All the many dairymaids have traveled on before us.
Granny, for my sake, did not stick closely with the others.
When I look at Granny, I feel very sympathetic;
She can't keep that basket on her hip and make the journey.
Traveling to Mathurā, I must keep pace with Granny.

---

the fruit of the palmyra in hand.' The palmyra (tāla) is a tall, slender plant (see Appendix). Radha's breasts are repeatedly compared to its large, round fruits; cf. Dānakhaṇḍa above, song 15, line 11 (and n. 40).

53 Virasaṃ, literally 'unpalatable'.

54 See Dānakhaṇḍa above, n. 154; and cf. Naukākhaṇḍa above, n. 29.

She's extremely elderly and can't proceed there quickly.
If you should refuse to add her basket to your burden,
How can you in any way be offered my affection?
In your heart, you're covetous of winning me, my Krishna.
That explains your coming here and dogging me so closely.[55]
Now, Lord Madhusūdana, pick up the burden promptly!

Song 22

"I cannot do other than agree to take the burden;
But, in Granny's presence, you must give your word of honor."
"What will be accomplished by my swearing on it, Krishna?
When you've hauled the load I shall accept your proposition."
"Since I saw your bosom, my desire has been whetted.
That's the only reason I'm about to bear your burden."
"One should not appeal to any outside party, Krishna,
When one has such urges; one must keep these matters secret!"[56]
"These cakora birds, which are my eyes, feel fascination
Looking on the moon which is this face of yours, my Radha."[57]
"I cannot make any sense at all of your behavior.
Nowhere is there any such exasperating porter!"
"My behavior you already know about completely.
Hurry now, let's put your youthful charms in service, Radha!"
"I shall not accept your love unless you bear the burden!"

Song 23

"Fortune has been drawn for me by Fate in such a manner
So that the celestial bodies[58] cast their shadows on me.
Radha, you're the reason I've descended from the heavens.
Kaṃsa reigns contentedly and I must carry burdens!
Granny should go first and, Radha, you go in the middle;
In the rear let me, your lover Krishna, bear your burdens.
From this moment, Radha, I dismiss my inhibitions;[59]

55 Tekāraṇe āilā tohme āhmāra gahane 'That is why you have come (here) (keeping) in close contact with me.'

56 Lobha hayilẽ kāhnāñī ārati nā karī / gopata kājata kāhnāñī chaya ākhi bārī '(Even) if one has urges, Krishna, one does not make appeals; six eyes are barred from secret matters.' In other words, three cannot share a secret.

57 Cakora, name of an Indian bird about the size of a small chicken. It is celebrated for its habit of gazing at the moon (the latter is compared to Radha's face).

58 Candra dibākare 'the moon and the sun.'

59 Āji lājaka diā̃ tilāñjalī 'giving tilāñjalī to my modesty with immediate effect.' Tilāñjalī refers to an offering of sesamum in water, traditionally made in cupped hands to one's departed ancestors. See Bandyopadhyay 1978:1.1045.

I, your Vanamālī, take this burden on your orders.
It's at your behest alone that I perform such labor;
This is something you should firmly bear in mind, my Radha.
As we go the trail, let people, as they may, observe me;
I shall plod the pathways with your load of dairy produce.
What is this you've done? What have you done? I'm so embarrassed.
Why should I, the monarch of the gods, be bearing burdens?"
Setting down the load of produce just outside the city,
Krishna looked at Radha's face and spoke to her as follows:
"I have brought the load, now you must offer your embraces."

Song 24

Time and time again, with all her efforts, Radha urged him,
"Take the load of dairy produce, Krishna. Why refuse it?
Carry it with care so that no buttermilk will scatter.
When we come away, I'll give you kisses and embraces."
Speaking in this manner, that intrepid dairywoman[60]
Made the son of Nanda and Yaśodā bear the burden.
People laughed as Krishna bore the load of dairy produce;
Squatting, all of Radha's girlfriends had to turn their faces.
Throngs of gods, observing Radha's machinations, chortled:
"You have done an outrage, making Krishna carry burdens!"
Krishna took the load and walked toward market in the city.
Nārada was sitting by the pathway; he told Radha,
"Is this how you manage your affairs, you proper housewife?
Radha, you've forced Krishna, king of gods, to bear your burdens."
Krishna, with the load of dairy goods, approached the city.
Radha turned around from time to time to look at Krishna;
Thereupon he smiled a bit and cast her sidelong glances.

Song 25

> Impatient with delays, Krishna thirstily addressed Radha
> With a look which, though humble, divulged his desire.

Mathurā's a city of important people . . .[61]

* * *

What I promise won't go uncompleted;
Coming back, I'll give you my embraces.

[60] Cauhālinī goālinī 'intrepid dairywoman'; see Dānakhaṇḍa above, n. 113.

[61] One side of a leaf of the original manuscript is missing at this point. The text resumes with Radha addressing Krishna.

Don't be bashful, you must bear my burden.
Diffidence will gain you nothing, Krishna.[62]
You must take the load of produce quickly.
This is not a sully on you, Krishna.
Cowherds carry milk and dairy produce;
Who can say a word of disapproval?
You and I have come to an agreement;
I shall give you love upon returning.
Now you should be pleased to bear my burden.

Song 26

"I should carry burdens? There's no sense in what you're saying.
You have people making fun of me already, Radha."
"How could anyone be making fun of you, my Krishna?
Is there any dairyman who doesn't carry burdens?"
"By your many tricks, you've made me bear this burden, Radha.
I have aching shoulders from the strain; I've suffered greatly."
"There is never happiness devoid of sorrow, Krishna.
You yourself may see if that is so or not; ask Granny."
"I should question Granny? I know everything, my Radha.
Nowhere have I seen the likes of you, you daring woman!"[63]
"Do not say this. Don't speak so abrasively, my Krishna.
While returning, Cakrapāṇi, I'll fulfill your wishes."
"You have drenched my spirits in a flowing stream of sweetness!
Can you be sincere in what you're saying to me, Radha?"
"I have spoken truly, Krishna. Take the load of produce."

Song 27

> Imbibing her assurances, the impetuous Hari picked up the load
> And followed Radha, slackened by the sheer enormity of his exhilaration.

Krishna, attending to Radha's conditions,
Picked up and shouldered the burden of produce.
Trudging along at the rear, Vanamālī
Put his Candrāvalī Radha before him.[64]
Krishna Murāri began to cut capers
Without letting Granny catch sight of his doings.
Moving ahead in this way very slowly,
Krishna proceeded to enter the city.

[62] Cf. Dānakhaṇḍa above, song 21, line 11.
[63] Caũhāṇī = cauhālinī; refer to n. 60 above.
[64] See n. 41 above.

Physically he was unstable from passion;
He would do anything Radha requested.
When he reached market, he set down the burden.
After a time, all the produce was purchased.
Thinking that Radha would now head for Gokula,
Krishna grew exercised. Needing no longer
The carrier pole, Krishna dropped it at market
And traveled from pathway to pathway with Radha.
Hoping for love, he stayed closely beside her.

Chatrakhaṇḍa*

Song 1

Joining with her Granny, Radha merrily traveled the pathway.
Her buttermilk and yogurt, ghee and milk she had sold off completely
And she had escaped, besides, from Krishna in Mathurā city.
Now, as she proceeded home, Candrāvalī inwardly gloated.
Underneath a tree along the way, Radha paused for a moment,
Feeling rather badly frazzled due to the autumntime sunshine.
Supplicating Granny, Radha stated this message politely:
"Look at all my girlfriends, they're abandoning me and departing.
I don't know what Abhimanyu's mother might say when I reach there.
You're the only one who is my ally in all situations."
Seeking to explain herself, Candrāvalī said to her girlfriends,
"It must be apparent to you all that I'm terribly fragile.
I'll resume my homeward journey after the sun has descended.[1]
Give this explanation to my mother-in-law when you see her."
With the cooling breezes, her exhaustion was somewhat diminished.
All around her, Radha cast her darting and flickering glances.
Lurking to one side of her, she noticed a furious Krishna!

Song 2

Hari's feelings were wounded by his failure to gain Radha's
affection.
Now he swaggeringly addressed her in both gentle and harsh
terms.

I rule the gods, I am Lord Vanamālī.
How you've deceived me, you infantile cowmaid!
Radha, the council of gods made me leader;[2]
How can you fling such a god from your clutches?

* *Chatrakhaṇḍa* 'Episode of the Umbrella', name of the sixth section of *Śrīkṛṣṇakīrtana*. Angered by Radha's treachery, Krishna confronts her after her departure from the market. Radha, however, beguiles him into shielding her from the afternoon sun with his umbrella—an article which was not in common use in India's earlier times, and which was emblematic of royalty.

1 Rauda pāṛiā̃ āhme jāiba ghara, literally 'I'll go home after letting the sun go down.'

2 Tridaśagaṇe rādhā moke dhare māthe 'The thirty (gods), Radha, hold me at their head.' See Dānakhaṇḍa above, n. 91.

Promising rapture, you had me haul burdens;
This has made people disparage me greatly.
Over the universe I hold dominion;
Changing my forms, I annihilate demons.
Despite my divinity, I was deluded;
On your request, Radha, I bore your burdens.
I, Vanamālī, and Halī, my brother,
In Devakī's womb were conceived; she's our mother.[3]
I have descended here hoping to love you;
Why are you now disappointing me, Radha?
Still, dairymaid, you can heed my entreaties;
If you delay, you will lose Nanda's darling.[4]
Do not reject me. Bestow your embraces!

Song 3

Listen to sensible counsel, Murāri.
Just take your wages; you carried the burden.
I've no alternative way of proceeding;
This time you'll have to contain what you're feeling.
Krishna, my darling, you mustn't act rashly;
Have some concern this one time for my honor.
Look, all those girlfriends of mine are departing.
They'll all report to my mother-in-law. And then
How will I manage? That's why it's essential
For me to go home just as soon as I'm able.
Krishna, I wouldn't attempt to misguide you;
Why, figure this out for yourself, you can see it.
When and whatever condition arises
I do what conforms to the need of the moment.[5]
Now stop it, Dāmodara; I must go homeward.
I tremble within me for fear of my husband.
Beseeching me now will avail you no profit.

Song 4

"If you still won't act according to my wishes, Radha,
Then you must pay me a variety of tributes without delay!"

[3] Halī banamālī āhme e duyi bhāi / daibakī udare āhme labhila ṭhāi 'We two brothers, Halī and Vanamālī, were conceived in Devakī's womb.'

[4] Pāchē kaili nā pāibē nāndera nandane '(But) later you surely won't find Nanda's darling.'

[5] Yehena sambheda hae yakhane / tāra yoga kāma karī takhane '(Depending on) what sort of contingency occurs at any time, I act in accordance with it then.'

"Pay market taxes, pay tolls for the highway.
When you owe taxes, how dare you sell produce?"
"What a predicament I am confronting—
He's wrangling with me over tax he's invented!"
"I'll hold the main tax[6] no longer at issue;
Just pay me the surcharge[7] on produce, then vanish!"
"Now I am told there's a surcharge on produce!
Where have you been up till now, brazen tax man?"
"Very substantial indeed are my taxes.
I'll shatter your airs while I levy your tributes!"
"Must I pay separate tax on my milk goods
And separate tolls for the use of the roadway?"
"My written commission[8] and ledger confirm it;
Write down, if you will, all the separate charges."
"Krishna, you're brilliant, but don't be contentious;
Take from me regular roadway tolls only."
"Take this account[9] of your road tolls and taxes
And render the revenues you're to hand over!"
"What you demand are false revenues, Krishna.
Why bring distress on the path to a woman?"
"My tax for the pots on your head is one hundred.
Pay it and salvage your personal honor!"
"Right on the road, don't create a disturbance.
Your tax totals more than my assets and profits!"[10]
"I shall not ravish you. Give me affection!
If not, then I swear to it, I'll take your taxes!"
"Hold your umbrella for me and I'll love you.
If not, Krishna, drop those desires you're feeling!"
"I, Krishna, won't leave today without payment!"

Song 5

Radha's slender body trembled when she heard Krishna's answer.
She spoke in distress to Granny as follows:

He requests the roadway tolls apart from market taxes.
Handing me a bogus book, he says the proof's in writing.

[6] Dāṇa (= dāna) 'tax' here refers to the market tax.

[7] Bāje (modern Bengali byaaj) 'premium, bonus, surcharge' (as opposed to dāṇa '[basic] tax'; see preceding note).

[8] Likhana pāṭā 'written commission.'

[9] Hāṭa bāṭa dāna likhana neha 'Take this written (statement) of the market and road taxes.' See Dānakhaṇḍa above, n. 29.

[10] Lābhẽ mūlẽ bitta dānake nā̃ṭe 'The value (bitta) of my (combined) profits (lābhẽ) and capital (mūlẽ) don't extend to (the value of) the taxes.'

For the vessels on my head, he asks substantial payment.
Krishna is impertinent; he's fighting over nothing.
Krishna's tales are very puzzling, Granny. For a moment
He becomes a porter; in the next, a tax official.
I agreed with Krishna on a number of conditions;
He conveyed the burden for me only for that reason.
Krishna didn't haul my load of dairy produce nicely;
How am I obliged now to comply with what he's asking?
Shouldering the heavy load, despite my admonitions,
He allowed my wares to slump; my dairy goods were scattered.
At all stages, Hari has inflicted me with losses.
Still Murāri doesn't feel ashamed to ask for taxes.
Let him pay in cowries for the milk and goods he scattered.
Furthermore, he has to take the wages he has coming.
Speak to Krishna; say, "Give up your evil propositions!"

Song 6

Hearing Radha's message as conveyed by Granny,
The crafty Krishna thirstily addressed Radha:

Your charms are like water, your tresses are moss.
On your lotus-like face glisten bees, which are ringlets.
Your nose is a stem and your eyes, waterlotus.[11]
Your cheeks are like butter tree blooms in full blossom.[12]
Radha, you brim like a lake. I, your Krishna
Am feverish, dear, from your scathing indifference.
Your teeth are rose chestnut;[13] your smile is white lotus.[14]
Your lips represent blooming flame of the forest.
Your arms are like stems and your hands are pink lilies.[15]
Your breasts are a pair of unparalleled sheldrakes.[16]
Your navel's a lotus bud scantly in bloom.
On your waist, like a staircase of gold, lie three creases.[17]
Your buttocks are real slabs of ponderous stone, and
Your trunk is a gold plate attached to them, gleaming.[18]

[11] Netra ūtapala tora nāsā ṇāla daṇḍa 'Your eyes are waterlotuses, your nose is a tubular shaft.' On ūtapala (waterlotus) see Appendix.

[12] Madhuka, name of the butter tree or its blossom; see Appendix.

[13] Keśara 'rose chestnut', a tree with white blossoms; see Appendix.

[14] Kumuda, the white water lily; see Appendix.

[15] Bāhu tora mṛṇāla kara rātā utapala 'Your arms are lotus stems and your hands, red waterlotus (rātā utapala).' See Appendix.

[16] See Dānakhaṇḍa above, n. 100.

[17] The three folds in Radha's waist are compared to a staircase leading down to her 'water' (charm). See Dānakhaṇḍa above, n. 41.

[18] Radha is a metaphorical lake and her buttocks and lower abdomen are compared to a

Your thighs are great stalks and your feet, golden lotus.
Your anklets are bumblebees circling them, humming.
Nothing but you can extinguish my torment.

Song 7

Hearing Krishna's message, Radha's spirits were buoyant.
She pointedly conveyed her own fancies to Granny:

Ask him as I will to not keep making these advances,
Cakrapāṇi worries me with ceaseless importuning.
Let him hold, above my head, his very own umbrella;
Then I'll offer, Granny, my embrace to Jagannātha!
You yourself must say to Lord Gadādhara, my Granny,
That I'll heed his urgings if he'll carry the umbrella.
Granny, I prepared some wares of ghee and milk and yogurt.
Taking them to Mathurā, I sold them off at market.
At the mighty city, it was midday by that juncture;
In the burning sunshine, I've been frazzled to the marrow.
I'm extremely fragile, while the sun is overwhelming.
That's the reason I'm completely soaked in perspiration.[19]
Right down to the innards, my whole body has been roasting;
Honestly, I cannot budge a single step, my Granny!
Properly explain to Madhusūdana my offer
And convince him, Granny. I'll give Krishna my embraces;
Only let him come along and carry the umbrella.

Song 8

Receiving Radha's message, the glib old lady
Promptly went and addressed Madhusūdana:

After taking in your supplications, handsome Krishna,
Radha's mood has changed; her young and girlish heart has softened.
Radha is submitting to your love; that's your good fortune.
Be pleased, then, to hold above her head your own umbrella.
When you do this little task, you'll earn great compensation.
You should feel no qualms at all about the matter, Krishna.
Radha has expressed herself to me this time sincerely;
Therefore you should not consider further opposition.
Holding your umbrella over Radha's head, get moving.
You'll win love before you've gone much distance, Jagannātha.
Radha suffers in the sun; she cannot budge a muscle.

---

throne placed on its shores.

19 Tekāraṇe deha mora ghāme tolabale 'That's why my body is in a tolabala state from perspiration.' Tolabala (modern Bengali ṭal-mal) means 'an overflowing state'.

Now it's only fitting that you offer her a favor.
You may take her in the bushes for your own enjoyment[20]
After you have gladdened her by holding the umbrella.
Do not turn aside what I'm suggesting to you, Krishna;
You're sophisticated and can draw your own conclusions.
Quickly, over Radha's head go carry that umbrella!

Song 9

Hearing Radha's proposal as conveyed by Granny,
The crafty Krishna thirstily addressed Radha:

"Will it satisfy your pride to make me hold umbrellas?
I shall not be able to endure such great dishonor!"
"If it is romance that you're anticipating, Krishna,
Why don't you come close to me and carry the umbrella?"
"Give your love to me. Don't be unreasonable, my Radha;
Why are you attempting to entrap me with your gimmicks?"
"Have you no awareness of the universal doctrines?[21]
Does adultery occur in any lore or scripture?"[22]
"What is rule[23] or scripture to me? What is crime or justice?
I cannot endure the agony of your aloofness!"
"Why mooch off of someone else if you are so impassioned?
Take ascetic vows if getting married doesn't suit you!"[24]
"I am Hari, I am Hara; I'm the great ascetic.[25]
Joining palms, I'm begging for the alms of your affection!"
"Robbers die of torment seeing honest people's riches . . ."[26]

* * *

[20] Āpaṇāra sukhẽ tāka neha kuñjabane 'Take her for your own pleasure into a forest arbor. . . .' See Dānakhaṇḍa above, n. 57.

[21] Tīna bhubana bicāra 'the doctrines (bicāra) (applicable to) the universe (literally, "three worlds").' See Tāmbūlakhaṇḍa above, n. 5.

[22] Koṇa beda purāṇe āchae paradāra 'In which Veda or purāṇa does adultery occur?' See Dānakhaṇḍa above, n. 53.

[23] Śāstra 'rule, precept.' The term refers to a body of knowledge or any scientific system.

[24] Eteka ārati āche pare kehne māṅgī / bihā karitẽ nā juāe haa tohme yogī 'Why importune another (if) you have such desires? (If) it isn't fit (for you) to marry, become a yogi!'

[25] Āhme harī āhme hara āhme māhāyogī 'I am Hari, I am Hara; I am the ascetic supreme.' Hari is a name of Viṣṇu-Krishna and Hara a name of Śiva, a deity traditionally depicted as a mendicant ascetic (mahāyogī).

[26] Eight pages of the original manuscript are missing at this point. The balance of this section of *Śrīkṛṣṇakīrtana*, as well as the beginning of the subsequent section, are therefore lost.

Vṛndāvanakhaṇḍa*

Song 1[1]

". . . all the girls.
Summon them all, I'll look upon them;
Let my eyes be moistened with ambrosia!"
Fetching all the saplings for him,
Granny noticed that Radha was about[2]
And said to her abruptly,
"I'm taking a walk by myself with some water."[3]
On the insistence of Abhimanyu's mother,
Radha went along; she took the water.
Granny was elated to observe this.

Song 2[4]

These days, the gently blowing breeze
Of the Malabars[5] arouses love.
Sweet scented flowers are blossoming
To the bursting[6] of estranged lovers' hearts.
Radha, deprived of the sight of you,

* *Vṛndāvanakhaṇḍa* 'Episode of the Vṛndāvana Gardens', name of the seventh episode of *Śrikṛṣṇakīrtana*. Inspired by Jayadeva's *Gītagovinda*, the poet recounts the opulent charms of the forest in springtime. In this episode, Krishna constructs a pleasure garden named Vṛndāvana. Luring the dairymaids through Granny, he regales them with every variety of flowering and fruiting plant. The presence of the other young women eventually leads to jealous quarreling, but Radha assuages Krishna's feelings in one of the text's most beautiful passages (song 29).

[1] The missing leaves of the manuscript containing the last songs of the previous section also contain the first songs of Vṛndāvanakhaṇḍa. See Chatrakhaṇḍa above, n. 26. The text resumes about halfway into the first surviving song of the present section.

[2] Tāra saba biṭapa āṇiā̃ / tāra mājhẽ rādhāka dekhiā̃ 'As she fetched all his saplings, observing Radha in the middle of it . . . (i.e., in the middle of the woods).' The second line is omitted in Ray 1973.

[3] Water is the traditional stuff used by Indians for self-cleansing after toilet functions.

[4] This song is modeled on *Gītagovinda* 5, song 10 (Miller 1978).

[5] The Malabar hills of southwestern India (Karnataka state) are famed for fragrant sandalwood whose scent is said to travel northward on the winds.

[6] Sugandhi kusumagaṇa bikasae / phuṭi birahihṛdaye 'The sweet scented flowers bloom, bursting the hearts of separated lovers.' A pun is intended; phuṭ- can mean both 'blooming' and 'bursting'.

Your Krishna is greatly in turmoil
From the torment of your absence.
Leaving his home, Krishna dwells in deep forests.
The bed where he sleeps is the earth.
Day and night, upon your name
He reminisces with unabating fervor.
Now, Radha, hasten
And fulfill Krishna's longing!

Song 3

"Krishna is disturbed because he hasn't been seeing you, Radha.
It is he who has dispatched me now to come forward and find you.
Krishna is addressing you with words of polite supplication:
'She must come and show herself to me in Vṛndāvana gardens.'"
"Abhimanyu's mother is extremely severe with me, Granny.
She will not allow me to go out of the house for a minute.
How can I escape to his Vṛndāvana gardens, my Granny?
Think this over to yourself and tell me if there's a solution."
"On the pretext of collecting blooms for a sacred observance[7]
You can travel to Vṛndāvana gardens without any worry.
Radha, just supposing that you go there with all of your girlfriends;
Abhimanyu's mother won't be able to quibble about it."
"Abhimanyu's mother knows the point of your 'sacred observance';
I shall not be able to convince her with all those excuses.
Here inside my heart there is a strategy lurking, my Granny;
It's the only way that we can reach his Vṛndāvana gardens."
Granny placed a kiss on Radha's face and addressed her as follows:
"You must let me know yourself what strategy you have invented.
I shall carry out the plan and spare not an effort to help you.
Gladly I will take you and we'll go to Vṛndāvana gardens."
"Go and meet the mothers of the husbands of each of my girlfriends
And, somewhat reprovingly, convey to them all this suggestion:
'All because of Abhimanyu's mother, our sales are suspended.
If you were to chasten her, our daughters[8] could market their produce!'"
"Radha, what you've spoken is a sensible plan for our venture.

[7] Brata chala kari phula tulibāka tarě / bṛndābana yāsi '(You say that) you are going to Vṛndāvana for picking flowers, pretending it's for a religious observance (brata "vow").' The offering of flowers to a deity may be undertaken by a woman for various purposes: to secure a good husband, have a child, etc.

[8] Bahu jhi 'daughters-in-law and daughters.' Patrilocal residence being the rule, a traditional Indian household consists of a patriarch and matriarch, sons, sons' wives and unmarried daughters. Daughters shift to their husbands' residences after marriage.

Any sort of work like this requires immediate action.
I'll be off at once and handle matters the way you've suggested."

Song 4

Submitting to anger because of her goading words, the cowherd women,
Under the influence of Granny's prattering, addressed Abhimanyu's mother:

"You have caused ruin to cowherding households.
How much suspicion there is in your thinking!
Why do you see every woman as if she were
You? Not all daughters[9] these days are assertive![10]
Even when thousands of girls[11] go with Radha
There still is no driving the doubts from your thinking.
All of the women repeat your aspersions;
No one dares travel from home once she's heard them.
Buttermilk, ghee, milk and yogurt aren't selling
At market; the cowherds' employment is finished.
You are now greater than all of the herdsmen!
Because of this, we are resolved from this moment
That we shall each send our own daughters to market
And take neither beverage nor food from your household."[12]
The mother-in-law was alarmed when she heard this.
She bowed at the feet of them all and said, "Radha
Will travel to Mathurā town from tomorrow."

Song 5[13]

Finding this an opportune moment,
Granny eagerly scurried up to Radha and,
Reciting details of Hari's activities,
Zestfully brought her under love's sway.

Plighted your affection, he's departed for the assignation,
Charmingly adorning all his person.
Earnestly he plays a signal to you on his bamboo flute;[14]

[9] Bahu 'daughters-in-law.' See preceding note.

[10] E kālera bahu nahe satantarī 'All daughters-in-law these days are not independent (assertive).'

[11] Ṣola sahasra gopī, literally 'sixteen thousand dairymaids.' See Dānakhaṇḍa above, n. 9.

[12] Since Abhimanyu is the brother-in-law of the influential cowherd Nanda Ghosh, he and his family have superior status. Accordingly his mother enjoys some power over the neighbors. Hence their decision to neutralize her by mounting a social boycott.

[13] This song is modeled on *Gītagovinda* 5, song 11 (Miller 1978).

[14] Tohmāra śaṅketa beṇu (the Ray 1935 and 1973 editions read: śaṅketabeṇu) bājāe

Now move along, you mustn't dawdle, Radha.
Gentle winds are blowing on the Kālindī's[15] embankment; there
The son of Nanda sits. It's you he thinks of.
Krishna pays great homage to the dust which, having touched your limbs,
Is carried off to him upon the breezes.
When the nesting birds induce the leaves to flutter on the trees,
He spreads a bed, expecting your arrival.
Krishna casts his darting glances all about him as he ponders,
"How long will it be till Radha comes here?"
Cast aside your noisy bell-embellished anklets,[16] lovely Radha;
Hasten to that deep and dusky arbor.
Radha, you'll be radiant as lightning wreathed in clouds
When, in inverted love, you lie on Krishna's bosom.[17]
Loosening the waistband[18] from your hips, and with your clothes removed,
Bestow yourself upon his bed of tendrils.
Krishna grows increasingly despondent as the night continues.
Listen to my words: fulfill his wishes!
Radha, to delay departing now would be unseemly.

Song 6

Then Abhimanyu's mother instructed Radha to go to Mathurā;
Whereupon Radha set out, her heart dancing with elation.

When the morning hour had arrived, the girlfriends all together
Thoughtfully considered and agreed upon a program.
Readying her buttermilk, her milk and ghee and yogurt,
Radha went along. They headed toward the market in the city.
It was in a cheerful frame of mind that she departed . . .[19]

* * *

Sharing smiles and pleasantries, the dairymaids departed;
They had finally obtained consent from Abhimanyu's mother.

---

yatane 'He earnestly plays you a signal-flute.' See Janmakhaṇḍa above, n. 34.

[15] Kālinī (= Kālindī), a name of the Yamunā River, possibly derived from kālī nadī 'black river.' See Naukākhaṇḍa above, n. 19.

[16] Mukhara mañjīra 'noisy mañjīra (bell-anklets).' Similar to kiṅkinī (see Dānakhaṇḍa above, n. 269).

[17] Intercourse in which the woman is bestride the man is considered the height of sexual fulfillment in Indian erotics, since by adopting this position the woman demonstrates her eagerness. In Vaishnava lyric Radha is often depicted in this position. See Bāṇakhaṇḍa below, song 27, and *Gītagovinda* 12.10 (song 23) (Miller 1978).

[18] Rasana 'waistband'; refer to Naukākhaṇḍa above, n. 48.

[19] A full line of the song is missing at this point, probably omitted through scribal error.

Radha joined the company of all her many girlfriends; they
Embarked upon their journey. On their heads they bore their
produce . . .[20]

* * *

Calling out, they summoned Granny, asking her to join them.
Then the beaming Granny spoke to all the dairymaids as follows:
"You are all my grandnieces today. I feel delighted,
For, inside Vṛndāvana, all types of flower trees have blossomed.
We can put some on before we venture to the city."
When they heard what she suggested, all the girls became ecstatic.
Granny forged a pathway that would lead them to Vṛndāvana;
Then they proceeded there all in the most enthusiastic spirits.

Song 7

As they went along the path, the shrewd old lady told them:
"He's so well behaved these days, that handsome fellow Krishna.
Market taxes, river crossing tolls and tolls on highways—
He's renounced those charges and is living in the forest.
Nowadays, to everyone, he offers his assistance.
He's renounced adultery, observing moral standards.[21]
Krishna doesn't speak a word to anybody harshly.
I am well acquainted with the things he's doing lately.
Gladdening the merchants, he presents them fruits and flowers.
Leading them, he guides them to the Yamunā embankment.
Nowadays Dāmodara's a most impressive figure.
None of you should harbor any doubts at all about him.
You shall all be witness to my words when you behold him;
Seeing him is soothing to the vision—that's a bonus."[22]
All these things were said in heartfelt ecstasy by Granny.
Moving as a group, they reached the outskirts of his garden.
Eager for the flowers of Vṛndāvana, they gathered.

20 See preceding note.

21 Dharama dekhiā̃ 'observing dharma.' Refer to Naukākhaṇḍa above, n. 20, and Dānakhaṇḍa, n. 223.

22 Lābhe tāka dekhiā̃ juṛāyibe dui ākhī 'Seeing him, as a benefit it will soothe both eyes.'

Song 8[23]

At this point Madhusūdana emerged impulsively from
Vṛndāvana
And spoke beguilingly to Radha, who was surrounded by her
friends.

Oh Radha, the seasons of the year have dissipated themselves one by
one;[24] all the plants have come into bloom.
Nowhere in the universe could you see such a place as this; it is divinely
commissioned.[25]
Basil and single flowered jasmine are in blossom; Spanish jasmine,
creeping Roydsia, clove, garland flower, double flowered
jasmine,[26]
White rose, yellow jasmine, turmeric blossoms, yellow screwpine,
trumpet flower and garland flower.[27]
Oh Radha, be agreeable, step lively, come and see my Vṛndāvana!
Neither day nor night is known here; the sun's rays do not penetrate.
There's Pentaptera, June galangale, magnolia, fragrant rosebay,[28] wild
jasmine[29] and[30]
Rose chestnut blossoms,[31] as well as Dalbergia, parrot tree blossoms,
medlar, butter tree blossoms, night blooming jasmine,[32]

23 This song, in which Krishna reels off the names of the dozens of plants in his pleasure garden in rhymed verse, is a poetic tour de force. Moreover, the plant names are organized into these groups: lines 3–4 and 7–14 refer mainly to flowers and flowering plants; 15–20 refer largely to fruits and fruiting plants; 21–25, to ornamental trees; 26–28, to timber trees; and 29–30, vine plants.

24 Spring is the first season of the Bengali calendar year. Nearly all the listings in this song pertain to plants that flower in the spring. For confirmation, check individual entries in the Appendix.

25 Daiba niyojana hena thāne 'such a divinely appointed (commissioned) place as this.'

26 Phuṭila 'there have bloomed': gulāla 'basil'; māhlī 'single flowered Arabian jasmine'; mālatī 'Spanish jasmine'; mādhabī latā 'Roydsia vine, creeping Roydsia'; labaṅga 'clove'; dolaṅga 'garland flower'; neālī 'double flowered Arabian jasmine'. See Appendix.

27 Śebatī 'white rose'; kanakayūthī 'golden jasmine'; suthī 'turmeric'; kanakaketakī 'yellow screwpine'; pārali 'Bignonia (trumpet flower)'; dulālī 'garland flower.' See Appendix.

28 Gandhaṭagara, the reading given in Ray 1973, should be replaced by gandha ṭagara 'fragrant ṭagara.'

29 Bana māhlī 'wild māhlī' should replace the published reading banamāhlī.

30 Āsnai 'Pentaptera'; āsāṛhiā bhūmicampaka 'galangale (bhūmicampaka) of Āṣāṛha month (June–July; the start of the rainy season)'; campaka 'Michelia (a relative of magnolia)'; ṭagara 'rosebay'; māhlī 'single flowered Arabian jasmine.' See Appendix.

31 The actual reading, nāgeśara keśara, lists two names of the same plant. In the translation, the English version (rose chestnut) is given but once.

32 Nāgeśara 'rose chestnut'; keśara 'rose chestnut'; āra 'as well as' tiṇiśa 'Dalbergia'; śiriṣa 'parrot tree'; bahula 'Indian medlar'; mahula 'butter tree'; seālī 'night blooming jasmine'. See Appendix.

Safflower, red hibiscus, orange blossoms, tangerine blossoms,[33] Grislea, tamarind blossoms, oleander,[34]
Asoka, Bengal kino, mango blossoms, leadwort blossoms, cowitch, mountain ebony, flame of the forest, coral tree blossoms;[35]
Strychnine blossoms, Tellicherry bark blossoms, kadama, Malabar nut blossoms, ebony, star jasmine, thorn-apple, urn-fruit tree blossoms, chaste tree blossoms,[36]
Swallow-wort, sweet leaf, devil tree blossoms, glory tree blossoms, milk-plant,[37] Pterospermum blossoms, Indian dammer, Buchanania blossoms, horseradish[38] blossoms,[39]
Spanish jasmine, Eclipta blossoms, Sida blossoms, burweed, senna, Pentaptera blossoms,[40]
White teak, fragrant banyan blossoms,[41] glory tree blossoms, trumpet flower, banyan blossoms, cotton, Pentaptera blossoms;[42]
Citrus, tangerines, gooseberries, mangos, lemons, pomegranates, black plum, lemons, hog plum,[43]
– – –[44] Indian olives, thekara,[45] elephant apples, tamarinds, oranges,[46]

[33] The name of the tangerine plant, nāgaraṅga, is inverted (as rāṅganāgara) to preserve internal rhyme (with oṛa 'red hibiscus').

[34] Siali 'night blooming jasmine' (this reference is omitted in the translation because the same plant is mentioned at the end of the preceeding line); kusumbha 'safflower'; oṛa 'red hibiscus'; rebatī 'orange'; rāṅganāgara 'tangerine' (see n. 33); dhātakī 'Grislea'; āmulia 'tamarind'; karabīre 'oleander'. See Appendix.

[35] Āśoka 'asoka'; kiṃśuka 'Bengal kino'; cuā̃ 'mango'; citā 'leadwort'; khañcī 'cowitch'; kāñcana 'mountain ebony'; bandhulī 'flame of the forest'; mandāre 'coral tree'. See Appendix.

[36] Kujā 'strychnine'; kuṭuja 'Tellicherry bark tree'; kadamba 'kadamba (cadamba)'; bāsaka 'Malabar nut tree'; kendu 'ebony'; kunda 'star jasmine'; dhutura 'thorn-apple'; mathura 'urn-fruit tree'; sindhubāre 'chaste tree'. See Appendix.

[37] Dudhiākana kasāla, the reading in the text as published, should be replaced by: dudhiā kanaka sāla (as proposed by Mukherji 1976).

[38] Ḍagare, the reading in the text as published, should be replaced by ugare (per Mukherji 1976).

[39] Rabi 'swallow-wort'; lodha 'sweet leaf'; chātīana 'devil tree'; bhāṇṭi 'glory tree'; dudhiā 'milk-plant'; kanaka 'Pterospermum'; sāla 'Indian dammer'; piāla 'Buchanania'; ugare 'horseradish'. See Appendix.

[40] Mālatī 'Spanish jasmine'; madhukara 'Eclipta'; bāṛiāla 'Sida'; saināhula 'burweed'; kālakāsundā 'senna'; āsane 'Pentaptera'. See Appendix.

[41] The published reading, gandhapippalī, should be replaced by gandha pippalī 'fragrant pippalī.'

[42] Gambhārī 'white teak'; pippalī 'banyan'; bhā̃ṭi 'glory tree'; ghāṭā pāralī 'Bignonia (trumpet flower)'; pipalī 'banyan'; kāpāsi 'cotton plant'; āsane 'Pentaptera'. See Appendix.

[43] Cholaṅga 'citrus (this refers to no particular species)'; nāgaraṅga 'tangerine'; kāmaraṅga 'Coromandel gooseberry'; āmbu 'mango'; lembu 'lemon'; ḍālimba 'pomegranate'; jāmbu 'black plum'; jāmbīra 'lemon'; āmbaṛā 'hog plum'. See Appendix.

[44] Ceru beru sapheru. The line appears corrupt. For discussion, see Mukherji 1976.

[45] Thekara. The precise significance of this name is unclear. See Appendix.

[46] Ceru beru sapheru (see n. 44); jalapāyi 'Indian olive'; thekara (see n. 45); cālitā

Phyllanthus fruit, tangerines, plum, country gooseberries, jujubes, sepesten plum, beechnuts,[47] lemons,[48]
Mangos, pomegranates, lakoocha fruit, coriander, cālanī,[49] mangos, Hingtsha, Buchanania fruit, lemons;[50]
Betel nut, coconuts, jackfruit, palmyra fruits, bananas, date palms, quinces,[51]
Mimusops fruit, dates, wild ebony berries,[52] limes, as well as so many other delicious fruiting trees;[53]
Dense forests of fragrant sandal and red sandal,[54] agati trees, wood apples, looking-glass trees,[55]
Catechu, Madagascar plum, jujube trees, fir trees, aloewood, young button trees,[56] sugandhesarī;[57]
Butter trees, senna, pine trees, marking nut trees, sweet leaf, Spanish jasmine, star jasmine, globe thistle,[58]
Laurel, birch, magnolia, Hemionitis, custard apple, wild[59] olives,[60]
Fig trees,[61] wild Cassia,[62] winter cherries, bucephalon, angolan, arjuna, bedda nut trees;[63]

'elephant apple'; tentali 'tamarind'; sātakaṛā 'orange'. See Appendix.

47 The published reading, karañjakaraṇe, should be replaced by karañja karaṇe.

48 Ā̃olā 'Phyllanthus'; kamalā 'tangerine'; pāṇiāla 'Indian plum'; labalī 'country gooseberry'; badarī 'jujube'; bohārī 'sepesten plum'; karañja 'Indian beech'; karaṇe 'lemon'. See Appendix.

49 Cālanī. The significance of this name is undetermined.

50 Āmba 'mango'; ḍālimba 'pomegranate'; ḍauhāku 'lakoocha'; kuṛuma 'coriander'; cālanī (see n. 49); ā̃ba 'mango'; hiñcī 'Hingtsha'; piāla 'Buchanania'; ṭābhāgaṇe 'lemons'. See Appendix.

51 Guā 'betel nut'; nārikela 'coconut'; kaṇṭhoāla 'jackfruit'; tāla 'palmyra'; kadalaka 'banana'; piṇḍakhājura 'date palm'; śrīphale 'Bengal quince'. See Appendix.

52 The published reading, banakendu, should read instead: bana kendu 'wild kendu.'

53 Khirī 'Mimusops'; khājura 'date (palm)'; kendu 'ebony'; mahukuta 'lime' āra yata taru miṣṭa phale 'as well as miscellaneous trees with sweet fruits.' See Appendix.

54 Sugandha 'fragrant' candana 'sandal(wood)' ghana 'dense' rakata candana 'red sandal' bana 'forest'; i.e., 'dense forests of fragrant sandal and red sandal.' See Appendix.

55 Agatha 'agati tree'; kapitha 'wood apple'; sundarī 'looking-glass tree'. See Appendix.

56 The published reading, nabadhaba, should be replaced by naba dhaba 'young dhaba.'

57 Khadira 'catechu'; piṇḍāra 'Madagascar plum'; bara 'jujube'; debadāru 'fir'; āgaru 'aloewood'; dhaba 'button tree'; sugandhesarī (significance unclear). See Appendix.

58 Mahula 'butter tree'; kāsimala 'senna'; sarala 'pine'; bhālā 'marking nut tree'; bhilola 'sweet leaf'; cāmbhalī 'Spanish jasmine'; sukala 'star jasmine'; locane 'globe thistle'. See Appendix.

59 Jiāpūta baṇe, literally 'jiāpūta in the woods'; i.e., forest jiāpūta.

60 Tejapāta 'laurel'; bhojapāta 'birch'; cāmpātī 'Michelia' (a relative of magnolia); cākali 'Hemionitis'; ātabhaṛi 'custard apple'; jiāpūta 'wild olive'. See Appendix.

61 The actual reading pākaṛī nākaṛī lists two names of the same plant. In the translation, the English version (fig trees) is given but once.

62 The published reading, sonākaṛī, should be replaced by sonā kaṛī.

63 Pākaṛī 'fig tree'; nākaṛī 'fig tree'; bana sonā 'wild Cassia'; kaṛī 'winter cherry'; sāhaṛa 'bucephalon'; ā̃koṛa 'angolan'; kuhaya 'arjuna'; bahaṛā 'bedda nut tree'. See Appendix.

Timber from anatto,[64] Euphorbia, white siris, the regal pigeon-pea,[65]
arjuna, wood-oil trees, black myrobalan;[66]
Walnut, ridged gourd,[67] bead trees, Tinospora, large white waterlotus,[68]
milkwort,[69]
Aeschyomene, beech, mangosteen, clumps of Phoenix,[70] Himalayan
cherries and devil trees;[71]
There's mango and sugarcane and lush vines of ripe grapes;[72] all about
are splendid creepers of black plum,[73]
Muskmelon, winter melon, bursting melon, sweet melon, pĕhuṭī,[74]
sesame and cucumber.[75]
Swarms of bees, drunk with nectar after imbibing the ambrosia from
flower clusters, are humming deliciously.
Bouquets of various types are sprouting inside bowers of blossoming
creepers. Love is calling!
A pleasantly cool breeze is blowing. The cuckoo is warbling arpeggios;[76]
other varieties of birds are also singing.
The deer sit and listen!

Song 9

After they heard Krishna's talk of Vṛndāvana[77]
All of the dairymaid girls were excited.
Radha conferred with them all. They were of

64 Kāṭha lāṛikā 'timber of (from) lāṛikā.'

65 Āṛayi rāje, literally 'āṛayi royal,' i.e., regal āṛayi.

66 Lāṛikā 'anatto'; sāje 'Euphorbia'; kaṛayi 'white siris'; āṛayi 'pigeon-pea'; ārjūna 'arjuna'; garjjuna 'wood-oil tree'; hariṛā 'black myrobalan'. See Appendix.

67 Jiṅgālaru drākṣa, the reading in the text as published, should be replaced by: jiṅgaṇi rudrākṣa (as proposed by Mukherji 1976).

68 Māhāsundhī 'large sundhī'.

69 Ākorala 'walnut'; jiṅgaṇi 'ridged gourd'; rudrākṣa 'bead tree'; sudarśana 'Tinospora'; māhāsundhī 'large white waterlotus'; bājabāraṇe 'milkwort'. See Appendix.

70 Hentāla puñja 'clumps of hentāla.'

71 Jayantī 'Aeschynomene'; biṣakarañja 'beech'; tamāla 'mangosteen'; hentāla 'Phoenix'; padmakāṣṭha 'Himalayan cherry' āra 'and' chāñīyaṇe 'devil tree'. See Appendix.

72 Latā 'vine' āmba 'mango' kuśiāra 'sugarcane' pākila 'ripened' drākṣā 'grapes' āpāra 'in plenty'; i.e., 'There are mango and sugarcane and lush vines of ripe grapes.' See Appendix.

73 Latā 'vine' jāmbu 'black plum' śobhe cāri pāśe 'look resplendent on four (i.e., all) sides'; i.e., 'Vines of black plum look splendid all about.' See Appendix.

74 Pĕhuṭī. The significance of this name is unclear.

75 Kharamūjā 'muskmelon'; kāṅkaṛī 'winter melon'; bāṅgī 'bursting melon'; āmṛta kāṅkaṛī 'sweet melon'; pĕhuṭī (see n. 74); sāḍara 'sesame'; soāśe 'cucumber'. See Appendix.

76 Kokila pañcama gāe 'the cuckoos sing intervals of a major fifth.' See Tāmbūlakhaṇḍa above, n. 15.

77 Bṛndābana kathā śuṇī baṛāyira mukhe, the original reading, literally means 'Having heard talk of Vṛndāvana from Granny's mouth (i.e., lips). . . .' Baṛāyira seems to be in error and should be replaced by kāhnāñīra; hence kāhnāñīra mukhe 'from Krishna's lips.'

One accord as to seeing Vṛndāvana gardens.
Radha proceeded with all of her girlfriends.
Each one was smitten at once with desire;[78]
Extreme giddy feelings completely seized Radha.
Striking a course toward the gardens went Granny;
Candrāvalī followed behind the old lady.
Zestfully joking, the cowmaids all sang
Joyous songs. Radha entered Vṛndāvana gardens
With Krishna beside her. She cast her glance sidelong.[79]
Unbinding her hair, Radha once again bound it.
She heaved a great number of sighs very deeply.
Declaring her passion was due to their singing
So well, Radha kissed all her friends on their faces.
Thus she went into Vṛndāvana gardens.

Song 10

> Languid with desire, Mādhava[80] watched the women
> Submit to romantic passion. He told Radha earnestly of his feelings:

Look, here in the middle of Vṛndāvana, Candrāvalī,
The trees are all festooned with blossom clusters.
Emanating from them is the lilting drone of bumblebees.
The gods are charmed, what need I say of people?
Radha, now that you and I are meeting in Vṛndāvana,
Let's quickly use our youth to our advantage.
Let me tell you something: it's for you that I constructed
This Vṛndāvana; I'll swear upon it, Radha.
Put your wares down someplace; put some flowers on
And eat some fruits—the choicest in the universe await you.
No one but myself has any knowledge of the things of wonder
Lurking here and there within these gardens.
Give me your consent and I'll escort you and reveal them,
But take no one else along as your companion.
As you are the most desirable among all persons,
So this park of mine excels among all gardens.
That's why it's appropriate for you to take your pleasure here.

78 Takhaṇa sahmāra maṇe bedhila madane 'Thereupon love punctured them all in the heart.' Madana is a name of the god of love.

79 This gesture and the several that follow are conventional Indian gestures of flirting.

80 See Tāmbūlakhaṇḍa above, n. 41.

Song 11

How could I go with you into the forest,
Abandoning all my companions?
Say, Krishna, none of my girlfriends you see here
Is happy about your proposal.
You must devise such a plan on your own
That all my friends will consider attractive.
They are all covetous, seeing Vṛndāvana
Splendid with fruits and with flowers.
No one among them will let you escape;
They'll all stand in the way of your leaving.
Mother-in-law and my husband are strict,
And besides, the whole village is spiteful;
They are all searching for faults in myself
And in you. This is why I'm reluctant.
Sending away[81] all my girlfriends, whom you have been
Tempting with fruits and with flowers—
Do you believe it's the right thing to do?[82]

Song 12

"You yourself have stated what my heart is saying, Radha.
Hearing this, my worries all have vanished.
I'll endeavor to delight the hearts of your companions
—All those many dairymaids—together.[83]
Radha, I—the king of gods—will replicate my body and
Enjoy myself among the cowherd ladies.[84]
All the time, you're harboring suspicions in your thinking, but
Today itself, I'll banish them completely.

[81] Phula phalera diā̃ āśe / sakhigaṇa neha cāri pāśe 'Having given them hopes of flowers and fruits, you lead my girlfriends into four directions (i.e., all about).' A possible interpretation is 'you give them hopes of flowers and fruits and surround yourself with my girlfriends'; however, the more plausible interpretation seems to be '. . . you send away (drive to four sides) my girlfriends.'

[82] Tora mane hena parihāse 'Does this appeal to your mind?'

[83] Literally 'Your sixteen thousand girlfriends, I shall gratify the hearts of all.' See Dānakhaṇḍa above, nn. 9 and 10.

[84] Kariā̃ bibidha tanu āhme debarāje / bilasibõ gopī samāje 'Having made (my) body manifold I, the king of gods, will amuse myself in the company of the dairymaids.' Vaishnava purāṇas (*Harivaṃśa*, *Viṣṇupurāṇa*, *Bhāgavatapurāṇa*) mention Krishna's nocturnal sport in the forest with a large group of cowherd women. This episode, called rāsa, is usually construed as a kind of dance, though the poet of the present text imposes a rather more burlesque interpretation upon it (as will become clear in the text). *Bhāgavatapurāṇa* refers to Krishna's replicating his body upon the occasion in question. For descriptions of rāsa see Dutt 1897:315–18; Wilson 1972:423–26; and Tagare 1978:1431–64.

One by one, each dairymaid that I am now observing
I'll convert into your sympathizer, Radha.[85]
We shall do our entertaining here in such a fashion so that
No one will attempt to tease the others.
After I have won the heart of every one, you mustn't nourish
Feelings of resentment toward me, Radha."
Finishing this statement, Krishna went before the dairymaids'
Assembly in the happiest of spirits.
Krishna spoke to all of them in hopes of their affection.

Song 13

"Dairymaids, listen to my invitation. I give this assurance in person:
Going about as she likes, each of you may pluck blooms to her own satisfaction."
"Long life to Krishna, his family's treasure,[86] for offering us this assurance!
This is unwarranted, given the high sort of background and people you come from!"[87]
Krishna reflected a bit to himself after hearing the dairymaids' answer:
"Soon I'll achieve my objective, fulfilling the wishes I always have cherished."
All of those maidens, beholding the utterly radiant face of their Krishna,
Felt their emotions disabled by missiles of passion dispatched from the heavens.[88]
Krishna showed one of the girls, "Take a look over there, way up high is a flower."
Stretching her hand out, the dairymaid plucked it, while Krishna seized hold of her bosom.
One other dairymaid commented, "Krishna, that faraway branch holds a blossom.
How, Krishna, are we to reach to that flower? Explain the solution in detail."
Krishna held onto her, lifting her up so that she could herself pick the flower.

85 Ekẽ ekẽ rādhā yata gopīgaṇa dekhi / āji se karāyibŏ tora sakhī 'The dairymaids I see I shall, one by one, make into your friends today, Radha.' Since all are to share Krishna on an equal footing, there will be no cause of enmity among the dairymaids.

86 Kulera nandana 'the favored child of his lineage.'

87 Yena jātī tohme yehna loka tāhāra ucita hena na hae 'This is not appropriate (i.e., is unusually generous) (considering) your birth (ties) and the people thereof.'

88 Daiba niyojana madana bāṇe bikali bhaila parāṇe 'They became wounded in their souls with the divinely dispatched arrows of love.' See n. 78.

Raising her up and then letting her down, Krishna won her embrace without effort.
One other dairymaid in a Bignonia thicket[89] began to pluck blossoms.
No one was able to see her, since she was concealed by the leaves of the foliage.
He, Lord Dāmodara, just by coincidence, happened on her in the thicket.
When he discovered that dairymaid, he placed a kiss on her face with abandon.
The leaves of the bushes flew up in the wind; she put on a display then of terror.
Some of the cowmaids, with flickering glances, took hold of his neck and embraced him.
Telling them, "Look, here are excellent flowers; look, there are nice fruits," Lord Murāri
Guided the cowherding ladies afar and, in intimate fashion, embraced them.
Krishna proceeded to capture each dairymaid's heart in the woods in this manner.

Song 14

All the dairymaids dismissed their fears and inhibitions.
They approached Govinda[90] as a group and humbly told him:
"Lord, do not dismiss us over comments made by others.
We are all submitting to you from this moment onwards.
You are Nanda's son, Lord Vanamālī, and hereafter
You'll be like the sandal on the bosoms of us cowmaids.[91]
We have one additional request, do not ignore it.
After visiting Vṛndāvana this long, oh master,[92]
We are loath to leave the gardens even for an instant.
What were your intentions when you captured our affection?
We have not been able to perceive it, Jagannātha.
Why do you withhold the meal from those you've shown the dishes?[93]
Sorrow is unbearable when hopes are disappointed.

[89] Jhā̃ṭāla bane, literally 'in a Bignonia (trumpet flower) forest.' See Appendix.

[90] Miliā̃ buila giā̃ gobindacaraṇe 'Joining, they went and addressed Govinda at his feet (i.e., deferentially and respectfully).' See Dānakhaṇḍa above, n. 70.

[91] Āji haitẽ gopīra hṛdayacandana 'From today you are the cowmaids' hearts' sandalpaste.' Sandalpaste is traditionally applied to the body as a cosmetic. The dairymaids promise that Krishna will remain close to their hearts.

[92] Kato khana dekhi gosāñī tora bṛndābana 'Having seen your Vṛndāvana, Lord, for some time. . . .'

[93] Pāta pātiā̃ kehne nāhī deha bhāta 'Having tendered the dish, why don't you give the rice (i.e., meal)?'

You can read the thoughts of every being in the cosmos."[94]
Krishna felt delighted when he heard their supplication.
Both his ears were swimming in the sweetness of this nectar.
He resolved to satisfy the wishes of the cowmaids.

Song 15

Learning of the cowmaids' wishes,
For a moment, Krishna pondered:
"How will I appease so large a group of dairymaidens?"
Then, becoming manifold,[95]
He frolicked with the dairymaidens.
Each one that he dallied with saw Krishna in her presence.
All the dairymaids were thinking,
"In this forest, I alone have won Lord Madhusūdana."
Bees intoned seductively
In groves of blooming flowers. One by one,
Murāri led those maidens into different arbors;
Tasting pleasure in his heart,
He filled ambitions long denied, and,
In Vṛndāvana, enjoyed the savor of desire.
One by one, the dairymaids
All came to realize for themselves
That Krishna's heart was drawn to Radha more than to the others.
Krishna did not speak a word, although
He knew what they were thinking;
Cakrapāṇi thought of his Candrāvalī, his Radha.
Love for Radha made Govinda
Frantic. He, Murāri, left the
Cowmaids in their refuges,[96] withdrawing all his bodies.[97]
Hoping to enjoy her love,
He ventured close to Radha.

Song 16

Disturbed over Krishna, the cowherds' wives reproved one another,
Extolling the other one who was Dāmodara's favorite.

94 In other words, Krishna is invited to divine and satisfy the dairymaids' implicit longings.

95 Āneka hayiā̃ takhane 'Then, becoming many (in form). . . .' See n. 84.

96 Gopī eṛi kuñjagehe 'Leaving the dairymaids in the arbored enclosures. . . .'

97 Saṃharī sakala dehe / gopī eṛi kuñjagehe / bikala gobinda murārī rādhāra nehe 'Taking back in all his bodies, and leaving the dairymaids in the arbored enclosures, Govinda Murāri (was) frantic for Radha's love.'

"Whose austerities at sacred spots have made her favored?
Who is she, the woman who is making love with Krishna?
Where's Govinda gone?" Deprived of Krishna and disheartened,
All the dairymaidens started searching through the forest.
Clapping time and singing lovely songs, they looked for footprints.
"Where has he, our Vanamālī gone? He's missing, missing![98]
Who's conducted sacrificial rites in grassy meadows?[99]
Who has bathed in sacred Puṣkara to her advantage?[100]
Who has all at once attained perfection of the spirit?[101]
Whose may be the hands in which the fates have placed the treasure?
Who among us might have placed her hand upon Kedāra?[102]
At Vaṭeśvara and Badarī, who's practiced penance?[103]
Who has sacrificed herself where Ganges meets the ocean[104]
That, with her, Gadādhara is strolling through the arbors?"
In this manner they lamented, all those dairymaidens,
Failing to encounter him, their deity and master.
Meanwhile, he was being scolded angrily by Radha.

[98] Hari hari / sundara se gīta gāā̃ bāā̃ karatālī / dekha pāacihna kathā̃ gelā banamālī '"Alas, alas!" Singing lovely songs and keeping time by clapping, they watched for footprints. "Where has Vanamālī gone?"' On the expression 'hari hari' see Dānakhaṇḍa above, n. 78.

[99] Ke nā kuśakṣetre bidhibatē kaila dāna 'Who's made ritual offerings in a field of kuśa?' Kuśa, also called darbha, is a prickly-topped grass used in certain ancient rites. This and the actions mentioned subsequently are all thought to confer spiritual advantages upon the performer.

[100] Kāhāra phalila pukṣara punya sināna 'For whom has a sacred bath (in) Puṣkara attained results?' Puṣkara (Pokhara) is the name of a saltwater lake sacred to Brahmā near Ajmer, Rajasthan.

[101] Literally, 'Who has attained the eight great spiritual powers today?' According to Ray 1973:250, the traditional aṣṭa mahāsiddhi or eight spiritual powers are: aṇimā, the ability to disappear; laghimā, the ability to float or be light; prāpti, the ability to obtain whatever one desires; prākāmya, irresistible will; mahimā, greatness; īśitva, supremacy; vaśitva, domination; and kāmāvaśāyitva, freedom from desire.

[102] Ke nā kedāraśira parasila kare 'Who might have touched the crown of Kedāra with her hand?' Kedāreśvara is a sacred site in the Himalayas containing a chunk of stone said to embody Kedāranātha (Śiva). Pilgrims pour Ganges water on this shrine or touch the top of it.

[103] Near Kedāra (see n. 102) in Uttar Pradesh is Badarī or Badarika, site of a Viṣṇu temple and legendary setting of the hermitage of Vyāsa (see Dānakhaṇḍa above, n. 89). Ray 1973:250 identifies Vaṭeśvara as a pilgrimage site and setting of a Sivalinga in Kashmir.

[104] Ke gāa tejila gaṅgāsaṅgata sāgare 'Who gave up her body at the Ganges' confluence with the ocean?' Gaṅgāsāgara refers to the point where the Ganges enters the Bay of Bengal. Belief has it that one reaches heaven instantly if one drowns at this spot.

Song 17

"Hungry men do not relinquish a meal once they have it, nor poor men a treasure.[105]
You must have taken full leave of your senses then, Krishna, to give up the cowmaids.
Wanting is one thing; indulging an urge to one's own heart's content is another.
How you have flustered me,[106] chasing around after each of those cowherding women!
That was some worthy suggestion I offered you due to my own lack of judgment.
I am myself to be blamed now; I have to digest the results of my folly.
Now you are coming to me. You don't have any sense of propriety, Krishna.
You aren't of any good use to me; you should return once again to the cowmaids.
This is the outcome of offering love to a man who is not one's own husband.
When I submitted to you, Krishna, it was a sin; I betrayed my own husband.
You are the same both within and without. I'm aware of your true inclinations.
I had not realized before that your heart is a sea of duplicity, Krishna.
Now that I'm fully acquainted with you, I am taking control of my feelings.
Never does good come of being in love with a treacherous, lecherous person.[107]
Now I declare to you—I'll even swear on it!—I'll not go near you hereafter.
Who would not feel in contempt of you after observing your character, Krishna?"
Krishna was very upset, hearing Radha's remarks. He attempted to soothe her.

105 The last foot of this line is metrically defective; nidhane nidhī is to be replaced by nidhane pāiā̃ nidhī. Thus: rāṅke yena bhāta pāā̃ nā eṛe nidhane pāiā̃ nidhī 'As a famished person does not renounce rice (i.e., a meal) once he obtains it, nor a poor man a treasure when he finds it. . . .'

106 Ki rañjasi mora mukhe, literally 'How you redden my face!'

107 Ṭeṭana naṭaka loka same neha kohno kāle bhāla nahe 'Love for a crooked, rakish fellow is no good any time.'

Song 18[108]

Radha, the luster you cast from your glimmering teeth with each word that you utter
Serves to diminish the darkness of terrible dread I've been feeling, my darling.
You can observe[109] that my eyes, like a pair of cakoras,[110] have come to a standstill
—Greedy to drink, from the lips of your unstinted moon of a face, of the nectar.[111]
I am inflamed with the prickings of love on account of your groundless resentment.
Give me a drink of the mead from your lotus-like face and you'll spare my existence.
If you are truly enraged with me, then you should strike with the shafts of your glances;
Bite on my lips with your teeth, using both of your arms to restrain me securely.
You are as precious to me as a gem-laden ornament. You are my being.
Since you're aware of this, Radha, I ask you most earnestly, show me compassion.
Shadowy lily-pad blooms are your eyes; they are posing as red waterlotus.[112]
Krishna is being provoked by the prickings of love, reinforcing your proddings.[113]
Gemstones embellish your breasts. Let the waistband resound on your hips and your buttocks!
If you will give your consent, I shall place your hibiscus-like feet[114] on my bosom.
Radha, on top of my head you must lower your feet, which are like budding leaflets.

108 This song is modeled on *Gītagovinda* 10, song 19 (Miller 1978).

109 Paratekha 'manifestly'.

110 See Bhārakhaṇḍa above, n. 57.

111 Tohmāra badana saṃpuna cānda ādhara āmiā̃ lobhe / paratekha mora nayanacakora yugala niścala śobhe 'In greed for the nectar of the lips of the full moon (which is) your face, my pair of cakora-bird eyes is manifestly unflickering.'

112 Tohmāra nayana malina nalina dhare kokanada rūpe 'Your brooding lotus eyes take on the appearance of red waterlotuses.' On nalina (lotus) and kokanada (red waterlotus) see Appendix.

113 Madanabāṇe kṛṣṇaka rañjilē̃ hae tora ānurūpe 'The arrows of love have incited Krishna; they are your alter ego.' That is, love's arrows duplicate the inciting effect of Radha herself.

114 Thalakamala 'changeable hibiscus'. See Appendix.

They are my head's precious ornaments, Radha, attacking the toxins of passion.[115]
Quick, I must have some relief from this sickness of love. Let me have your prescription!

Song 19

Dismissing this as mere whining, the angry Radha made no reply.
Then, his heart laden with humiliation, Murajit[116] issued a harsh declaration:

Vṛndāvana's my highly valued[117] plant conservatory.
Granny, why did Radha raid the place without permission?
I was playing ball, with flute in hand, out in the pasture.
Let me see who's come and picked the flowers in my garden!
Using as accomplices those many dairymaidens,[118]
She shattered branches willfully, removing fruits and flowers.
Radha has extended hook-shaped poles[119] among the branches,
Plucked the flowers from my garden's trees, and broke their petals.
Wantonly she bound her hair with clove and garland flowers,[120]
While she entertained herself with basil blooms and jasmine.[121]
Radha doesn't realize things; her youth makes her disdainful.
After she had entered my Vṛndāvana, she snubbed me.
Inwardly I'm seething as I look about the garden;
Still, because of you, I shall avoid mistreating Radha.
Let her make repayment for the fruits and flowers taken.
Otherwise, I'll tie her up with ropes and not release her.
Even now, fair Radha may consider my proposal:
She can give her kisses and caress instead of payment.
Radha has no reason for responding to me harshly.

Song 20

Taking in Krishna's words, Granny was greatly annoyed.
Then she addressed the mortified Radha as follows:

115 Madana garala khaṇḍana rādhā māthāra maṇḍana more 'They are the ornaments for my head, the antidote to the venom of love, Radha.'

116 Murajit 'Defeater of Mura' (see Dānakhaṇḍa above, n. 77), an epithet of Krishna.

117 Lakṣakera bṛndābana mora phulabāṛī 'My flower house is Vṛndāvana, which is (worth) a hundred thousand.'

118 Ṣola sahasra gopījana karī saṅge 'Accompanying herself with the sixteen thousand dairymaids. . . .' Refer to n. 83.

119 Āṅkuṛī, a long-handled pole with a hooked end used for harvesting certain kinds of fruits, such as mangos.

120 Labaṅga dolaṅga 'clove and garland flower.' See Appendix.

121 Gulāla mālatīmāle 'with garlands of basil and Spanish jasmine.' See Appendix.

He, the son of Nanda, made great efforts to receive you,
Having me conduct you by the hand to this, his garden.
Gladdened in his heart upon observing your arrival,
Krishna went ahead to show the foliage to you, Radha.
Krishna now is telling me that all is in a shambles.
Radha, it appears to me that you've been misbehaving.
Time is passing quickly since our coming to his garden.
You've been tearing down the limbs to pluck the different flowers.
You yourself must realize how much damage you've been causing.
Since you've disobeyed his wishes, why should he excuse you?
Radha, I cannot make any sense of your behavior.
How long will you manage to go on beguiling Krishna?[122]
You cannot evade your obligations to him, Radha.
Understanding this, you should accept my helpful counsel.
He wants restitution for the fruits and flowers taken.
If you won't provide it, he has ropes prepared to bind you.
If he holds you bound by force, your house will be dishonored.

Song 21

Granny, I warned everyone: In the garden,
Don't use hook-shaped poles to break leaves, shoots or flowers.
Granny, I told them: If Krishna observes it,
He'll curse; taking hold of our clothes, he'll abuse us.
Granny, I told them that only while Krishna
Did not venture near, they could pluck the hibiscus.[123]
Take some magnolia, I said; take rose chestnut,[124]
But don't wreck the plants or take fruits in great numbers.
Seeing it, Krishna will ask us for payment;
Our in-laws won't let us go home when they hear this.
Granny, I warned them: Do not pick too much of the basil,
White roses, clove blossoms or jasmines.[125]
Krishna won't let anybody go home
If he looks, leaf by leaf, at the plants in the garden.
Now my prediction's come true;[126] on arriving,
He's hindered our leaving for Mathurā city.
This time we're helpless to deal with him, Granny.

122 Kāhnāñīke bhāṇḍitě pāribě kata kāla 'How long will you be able to deceive Krishna?' The line has a special sense following on the earlier Bhārakhaṇḍa and Chatrakhaṇḍa episodes in which Radha turns the tables on her wooer. Also, see Dānakhaṇḍa above, n. 33.
123 Bola 'hibiscus'; see Appendix.
124 Cāmpā nāgeśbara 'Michelia (a relative of magnolia) and rose chestnut.' See Appendix.
125 Gulāla mālatī / kanaka yūthikā māhlī labaṅga seyatī 'basil, Spanish jasmine, golden jasmine, single flowered Arabian jasmine, clove blossoms, white roses.' See Appendix.
126 Ebě phala dharileka āhmāra bacane, a pun: 'Now my words have taken fruit.'

Song 22

Promptly at this juncture the lovestricken Mādhava
Addressed Radha, partly harshly and partly soothingly:

Don't you have some sense of
How much effort I've invested? I
Designed Vṛndāvana all at my own expense, my lovely Radha!
Plundering my blooms, you've been
Consuming quite a lot of fruit;
Moreover, strewing branches all about, you have destroyed them, Radha.
Radha, you have vandalized Vṛndāvana,
Removing blooms whose scent is smelled afar:[127]
White roses, creeping Roydsia,
Jasmine and rose chestnut blossoms.[128]
Where have you been keeping all the flowers you've been taking, Radha?
Wife of Abhimanyu, I'm Lord
Vanamālī, forest gardener.[129]
Let us make a bed of all those flowers; you and I can romp there!
If you won't restore those blossoms,
You'll receive a fitting outcome:
How will you go home? I shall arrest you on a charge of stealing!
This time, heed my proposition:
Offer me your kiss and your
Embrace. I'm overwhelmed to see your unsurpassed fresh youthful beauty.
Why have you committed such an act?
You've taken all my fruits and
Flowers, Radha. Stripping all my trees, you've trespassed in my garden.
As I look around, my heart's in anguish.
I am nearly dying.
Who can I report it to? Would anyone believe my story?

Song 23

Listen to me, handsome Krishna, I didn't destroy your Vṛndāvana garden.
I'm not to blame if the people who come by the trail want to stop and enjoy it.

127 Se phula tuliā̃ nilẽ yāhāra yojana bāse 'You plucked off those flowers which give fragrance for yojanas.' See Tāmbūlakhaṇḍa, n. 10.
128 Yūthī keśara seathī / mādhabilatā mālatī 'Jasmine, rose chestnut, white roses / Roydsia-vine, Spanish jasmine.'
129 Deba banamālī is a pun; it means both 'the god Vanamālī' and 'divine forest gardener' (bana [Sanskrit vana] 'forest', mālī 'gardener').

Krishna, I usually take the main highway.[130] You mustn't accuse me for nothing.
If I had known you'd be acting like this, I would never have come by this pathway.
I wouldn't even have traveled for selling my produce at Mathurā market.
I can't imagine what rancor there is in your heart; that must be why you blame me.
It is improper for you to be speaking this way; you're the offspring of Nanda.
See, I won't venture your way any more for as long as there's life in my body!

Song 24

If you always travel by the public highway, Radha,[131]
Why did you come dashing to Vṛndāvana so madly?
Both my Spanish jasmine and white roses[132] have been ruined.
Whose idea was it for you to spoil so many flowers?
What variety of impulse, Radha, has possessed you?
What was the necessity to desecrate Vṛndāvana?
Radha, you've been mangling blooms of clove and Spanish jasmine,[133]
Crushing boughs of finger millet, garland blooms and and wormwood.[134]
Girl, what sort of temper do you have? I can't imagine.
Have you wrecked my garden on our messenger's suggestion?[135]
You've destroyed at least three different kinds of jasmine blossoms,[136]
Hacking up my trumpet blooms and also Roydsia creepers.[137]
You've destroyed Vṛndāvana and left me in distraction.
Now you must receive from me the punishment you merit.
If I didn't feel afraid of murdering a woman,
I would kill and send you to the house of Yama promptly![138]
I'm the only one who has a sense of what I suffer!

130 Mo jāõ rājapathe 'I go on the king's (i.e., public) road.'

131 See preceding note. Vṛndāvana gardens and the path thereto are private property.

132 Yāti . . . āara seyatī 'Spanish jasmine . . . as well as white roses.' See Appendix.

133 Labaṅga mālatī rādhā bhāṅgile āpāra 'Radha, you've broken clove and Spanish jasmine in quantity.' Cf. nn. 120 and 121 above, and see Appendix.

134 Danā maruā bhāṅgile dulālera ḍāla 'You've broken wormwood (danā), finger millet (maruā) and garland flower (dulāla) branches.' See Appendix.

135 Dūtāra bole bhāṅgasi bṛndābana 'Do you wreck Vṛndāvana on the word of the go-between (i.e., Granny)?'

136 Māhlī kunda . . . āyara neālī 'single flowered Arabian jasmine (māhlī), star jasmine (kunda) . . . as well as double flowered Arabian jasmine (neālī).' See Appendix.

137 Mādhabīlatā bhā̃gilẽ āara pāralī 'You broke my Roydsia-vine (mādhabī) as well as Bignonia (trumpet flower) (pāralī).' See Appendix.

138 Tabẽ āji māriā̃ pāṭhāõ yamaghara 'Then I would kill you today and sent you (to) the mansion of Yama (i.e., hell).' See Janmakhaṇḍa above, n. 13.

Song 25

Krishna, it was after we obtained your reassurance
That I entered your Vṛndāvana with all my girlfriends.
On your invitation, all of us were picking flowers.
How is it you're suddenly accusing me of stealing?
Cakrapāṇi, you're divine; you mustn't tell such falsehoods.
How can such remarks be on your lips? You mustn't say them.
Krishna, in my hands are neither fruits nor flower blossoms.
Jagannātha, where could I get flowers at this instant?
Oh, there are some three or four small blossoms that I'm holding;
If it's any consolation to you, you can take them.
I'm the wife and daughter of some fine distinguished persons.[139]
I can't bear your charging me with stealing flower blossoms.
No one else besides yourself is nearly this audacious.
You have witnessed nothing, yet you're making accusations.
Why are you indulging now in lies, Murāri darling?
What you say in insincere; withdraw it, shameless Krishna.
All the cowherd women have been plucking off your flowers.

Song 26

"Radha, I see your esteemed self before me
Trimmed in Vṛndāvana's efflorescence.
Flower-descended darling,[140] bestow
Your delightful person upon me!"

Mangosteen flowers in bloom are your tresses;[141]
Brooding, dark amaranth blooms are your eyes.[142]
A finely formed sesame bloom is your nose,[143] while
Your cheeks I would liken to butter tree flowers.[144]
Agati blooms[145] are your ears, and your colorful
Lips are like flowers of flame of the forest.[146]

139 Baṛāra bahuārī āhme baṛāra jhiārī 'I'm a big person's daughter-in-law (and) I'm a big person's daughter.'

140 Kusumānvavāye 'Oh flower-descended lady!' Radha is the daughter of a woman named Padmā, which means 'lotus'. See Janmakhaṇḍa above, song 7.

141 Tamāla kusuma 'mangosteen blossoms.' See Appendix.

142 Nila kurubaka tora nayane 'Your eyes are brooding amaranth (kurubaka).' See Appendix.

143 Tilaphule 'sesame (tila) blossom'. See Appendix.

144 Mahule 'butter tree'; see Appendix.

145 Bagahule (= baga phule) 'agati blossoms'; see Appendix.

146 Bāndhuli 'flame of the forest'; see Appendix.

Blossoming star jasmine serve you for teeth[147]
And your finery looks like the target hibiscus.[148]
Your arms are two garlands of gold colored jasmine;[149]
Each of your hands is a bunch of asoka.[150]
Your breasts are a pair of hibiscus in blossom;[151]
The hairline below them appears to be flaxen.[152]
Your navel is deep; it's a rose chestnut blossom.[153]
Your thighs look to me like a pair of gold screwpines.[154]
Your lotus-like feet are a pair of hibiscus;[155]
Your toes are magnolia buds placed in a series;[156] while
Blossoms of basil, in rows, are your toenails.[157]
Your body is soft, like the parrot tree flower.[158]
Your form, over all, has a beauty resembling
A column of golden magnolia flowers.[159]
Double and single and night blooming jasmine
—They all seem to bloom with your merest sweet laughter.[160]
You're the embodiment, Radha, of flowers![161]

147 Mukulita kunda 'blooming kunda (star jasmine)'; see Appendix.
148 Khastarī kusuma 'target-leaved hibiscus blossoms'; see Appendix.
149 Hemayūthikāmāle 'garlands (māle) of golden jasmine'. See Appendix.
150 Āśokatabaka karayugale 'Your two hands are clusters (tabaka) of asoka.' See Appendix.
151 Mukulita thalakamala 'blooming changeable hibiscus'; see Appendix.
152 Romarājī tāta ātayīgaṇe 'The line of hair there (i.e., below them) is ātayī.' Ātayīgaṇe consists of two combined words: ātayī plus the plural marker gaṇe. Neither Ray 1973 nor Mukherji 1976 provides a translation for ātayī. I surmise that the correct reading is ātaṣī (the Middle Bengali characters for 'y' and 'ṣ' are nearly written alike) derived from Sanskrit atasi (modern Bengali atasi) 'flax'. The flax plant has blooms which, like the line of hair on the abdomen, are dark in color (i.e., blue). Moreover, the general configuration of the plant is suggestive of the shape of the hairline under the navel. See ātaṣī in Appendix.
153 Nāgeśara phule 'rose chestnut blossom'; see Appendix.
154 Kanaka ketakī 'yellow screwpine'; see Appendix.
155 Caraṇakamala thalakamale 'Your lotus (kamala) feet are changeable hibiscus (thalakamale).' See Appendix.
156 Campaka kalikājāle 'Michelia (campaka) bud-series.' Michelia is a relative of magnolia. See Appendix.
157 Nakharanikara dekhi gulāle 'I view the array (nikara) of your (toe) nails (nakhara) as basil (gulāle).' See Appendix.
158 Śirīṣa kusuma tanu sakale 'Your entire body is a parrot tree (śirīṣa) blossom.' See Appendix.
159 Kanaka campaka kusumapāntī 'a column (pāntī) of golden (kanaka) Michelia (campaka; a relative of magnolia) blossoms (kusuma).' See Appendix.
160 Neālī seālī māhlī bikase / tohmāra madhura īṣata hāse 'With your small sweet smiles, there bloom double flowered Arabian jasmine (neālī), night blooming jasmine (seālī), and single flowered Arabian jasmine (māhlī).' See Appendix.
161 Dekhõ mo tora phulaśarīre 'I see you as having a flower-body!'

Song 27

You, among all people, are by far the most audacious, Krishna.
  No one can respond to your behavior.
Don't dispute with me; I have to reach the town of Mathurā.
  Remove yourself and don't continue fussing.
I have figured out the way you think; I'm well acquainted with it.
  Every girl you view like all the others.
What did I not do for you the first time you requested it?
  I said farewell to all my inhibitions.[162]
I disdained my husband and, for you, kept vigil; I endured
  abuse from both his sister and his mother.
Men have very callous hearts; by nature they're inconstant.
  There is nothing one can do about the matter.
Damn a woman's life! Her heart is fragile as the parrot blossom.[163]
  She regards small favors as enormous.[164]
All of your affection is but lotus-petal dew;[165] they're both
  impermanent. Go home. You mustn't seek me!

Song 28

Radha, my darling, see here: you must listen.
All my emotions are steeped in your being.
Why must you be so severe in responding?
Radha, see here: you must listen, my darling.
Just glance around my Vṛndāvana gardens;
Why aren't you putting the place to good purpose?[166]
Radha, my darling, see here; you must listen.
Though he may wander from blossom to blossom,
The bumblebee always remembers his jasmine.[167]
Daytime and nighttime, because of your blossoming
Youthful attractions, my soul never slumbers.
This is the reason my spirits are harrowed

[162] Lāje diā̃ tilāñjali 'saying farewell to my shame.' See Bhārakhaṇḍa above, n. 59.

[163] Chāra tirī yarama śirīṣa kusuma mana 'A woman's life (literally, birth) is dust, her heart is (soft as) a parrot tree (śirīṣa) blossom.' See Appendix.

[164] Baṛa māne tina upakāra 'She regards a blade (tina "grass")'s favor (i.e., a whit of a favor) as great.'

[165] Tohmāra neha sakala kamalinīdalajala 'All your affection is the moisture (dew) on the petals of a lotus-clump (kamalinī).'

[166] Niphala karaha 'you make it fruitless,' a pun (i.e., 'Why do you despoil it of fruits?' or 'Why do you fail to take advantage of it?').

[167] Nānā phule bule bhramare / . . . / tabhõ ki mālatī pāsare 'The bumblebee visits various flowers . . . Still, does he forget the Spanish jasmine (mālatī)?' See Appendix.

For want of a chance to make love with you, Radha.[168]
You are the one I prefer to all others;[169]
The sound of your name has me inwardly weeping.
Look, it was on your request that I gladdened
The cowmaids, then gave them a tactful dismissal.[170]
Radha, my thoughts never drift from your being.
Now speak to me. Let me be seated beside you.
We should be happy; away with misgivings!

Song 29

Touched by love, Radha was ardent.
She rapidly succumbed to Krishna's love talk.

Oh, dear Krishna,
It's a woman's nature to be jealous.
An experienced man isn't offended by it.
Oh, dear Krishna,
With these words of yours,
All my anger is now appeased.
Hey, look,
Oh, dear Krishna,
I pray you most humbly,
Don't make anyone my rival.
Love has knitted our two hearts,
Yours and mine, into one.
The confirmation[171] of this is in Vṛndāvana.
I shall no longer transgress your wishes.
Fate has made lovers of you and me;
We have but one soul, one body.
This love cannot tolerate a third party;
But that is no fault of mine.
Who can enumerate your virtues?
Each and every one abides in my heart.
Now come and sit by my side.

168 Tāhāta tohmā ramaṇe la / kheti kare āhmāra parāṇe 'That's why my soul is harrowed (literally, "it plows my soul") for making love with you.'

169 Saṃsārata tohmā kailõ sāre 'I chose you from the universe.'

170 Tora bolẽ gopīgaṇe la / tuṣiā̃ tejilõ parakāre 'On your advice, I gratified the dairymaids and abandoned them by (some) tactic (i.e., method).'

171 Ānurūpa 'confirmation, affirmation'; tāra ānurūpa bṛndābane 'its affirmation is in Vṛndāvana.'

Song 30

He fulfilled all his desires, embracing her in various ways.
Lord Madhusūdana pressed Radha's breasts. They were like pitchers of nectar; there he immersed himself.
His heart pulsating with zest,
Krishna sported in Vṛndāvana.
He put his mouth to her mouth; a rain of nectar struck the waiting soil.[172]
They looked into each other's eyes and, time and again, thanks to the force of his passion, the wagtail united with the lotus.[173]
Their tongues came together like a pair of young leaves; Dāmodara drank her ambrosia.
He kissed her all over, he joined his lips to hers; the balsam apple and the coral[174] became one.
He contacted Radha's hips again and again and sated his passion.
With excited hearts, the two of them made love in the woods.

[172] A portion of this line is missing: badane badana kaila . . . ucitě āmṛtě bṛṣṭi bhaila 'He put (his) face to (her) face . . . a rain of nectar occurred on the prepared field (ucitě).' The raining of nectar on a prepared (tilled) field is symbolic of the sex act. The symbolic identification of women, in their sexual capacity, with the earth has been a feature of Indian thought since very early times; see Eliade 1973:254.

[173] Kamale khañjana 'the wagtail bird (khañjana, see Dānakhaṇḍa above, n. 68) with the lotus.' These respectively symbolize the male and female organs.

[174] Bimba 'balsam apple' (see Appendix) poālě 'with the coral'. Radha's lips are assigned the bright red color of balsam apple, while Krishna's are assigned the duller scarlet hue of coral.

Kāliyadamanakhaṇḍa*

Song 1

Lord Cakrapāṇi had gladdened the hearts of the dairymaids.
He gave them leave to go to Mathurā town;
Then Dāmodara reflected to himself:
"That was a good time we had in the forest."
Krishna decided there were sports to be played in water as well.
Janārdana[1] considered for a moment[2] to himself:
"The Yamunā River flows through Vṛndāvana.
The deep Kāliya lagoon is there;
The serpent named Kāliya inhabits it.[3]
Because of his poison, the fish in the water and plants on the banks have perished.
No creature drinks the water there;
There is no place more desolate.
I shall trounce Kāliya, purify the water,
And engage in all kinds of water sports there."
So thinking to himself, Lord Dāmodara went
To the base of a kadamba tree on the brink of the Kāliya lagoon.
He climbed the kadamba and plunged into the lagoon
While the cowherds, looking on to their horror, sprang up with a shudder.
Accompanied by his kin, the angry serpent Kāliya
Bit Krishna all over with his fangs.
The serpentine family nipped Krishna inch by inch;
Binding him hand, foot and neck, they kept him there.

* *Kāliyadamanakhaṇḍa* 'The Vanquishing of Kāliya Episode', eighth episode of *Śrī-kṛṣṇakīrtana*; its actual name as given in the manuscript is Yamunāntargata Kāliyadamanakhaṇḍa 'The Vanquishing of Kāliya, a part of the Yamunā (River) Episode.' In this section of the text, Krishna banishes a serpentine monster named Kāliya from a whirlpool in the Yamunā River. This episode is strategically placed within the work so as to bring out the growing attachment Radha feels toward Krishna—an attachment which finds expression when Krishna appears to perish in the course of the adventure.

1 Refer to Bhārakhaṇḍa above, n. 42.

2 Khaṇi eka (= kṣaṇe eke) 'for a moment.'

3 Kālīdahe 'Kāliya lagoon', a pun (i.e., 'abyss of dissolution'). Vaishnava purāṇas recount the incident of Krishna's battle with the aquatic serpent; see, for instance, *Bhāgavata-purāṇa* 10.16–17 (Tagare 1978).

Then, his life withering in the fire of their poison,
Lord Krishna was stupefied.
At this very juncture all the young dairymaids
Were passing through Vṛndāvana on their way to Mathurā.
Observing there the frantic cowherds,
They asked, "Why are you troubled?"
The cowherds all told the dairymaids,
"Our lord, Krishna, has plunged into the Kāliya lagoon!"
All the dairymaids were horror stricken to hear this.

Song 2

Hearing from the cowherds that Mādhava had vanished inside the Kāliya lagoon,
Radha lamented unceasingly out of grief.

I was called back by some wretch of a woman[4]
As I was departing today on my journey;
This is why[5] Krishna, the lord of my spirit,
Has left me behind. God knows where he has vanished.
Come back, Murāri embodied as Krishna![6]
Your dairymaid, Radha, is frantic without you.
How can your form, which is dark and unhardened,
Withstand the affliction of withering venom?
Damn him to blazes, that Kāliya serpent,
That he did not bite me ahead of you, Krishna!
She whom you love more than anyone else
And with whom you partake of one body, beseeches you.
Krishna, why do you not answer Candrāvalī?
Krishna, I beg you in utter humility,[7]
Give up pretending and come to your Radha.
Why do you spurn your devoted attendant?

[4] Pāchẽ ḍāka dila kālinīmāe 'The wretched woman (kālinīmāe) called me from behind.' Elsewhere the expression kālinīmāe (literally, 'woeful mother') refers to Radha's actual mother (see Dānakhaṇḍa above, song 67, line 1). Here that interpretation is unlikely, since Radha lives in her husband's household and not with her mother.

[5] Tāra phalẽ 'as a fruit of that.' Being called back by name as one embarks on a journey is thought to suggest that one's mission will miscarry.

[6] Kāhnarūpa murārī 'Scourge of the demon Mura in the form of Krishna.' See Dānakhaṇḍa above, n. 77.

[7] Dā̃te tṛṇa kari, literally 'taking grass between the teeth'; i.e., humbly. See Naukākhaṇḍa above, n. 41.

Song 3

"Krishna, for whom I disregarded my own husband
And respected neither fear nor social standards,[8]
Has died by plunging into the Kāliya lagoon,
Depriving all the young dairymaids of their master."
The cowmaid, Radha, beat her breast
And, wailing,[9] beseeched Cakrapāṇi:
"I'll never disobey your bidding again.
Get up, scion of Nanda, get up out of the water!
What will I do with money, kin, life or home?
For me, Krishna, everything is pointless without you.
Oh, oh, why has cruel fate done such a thing?
Why was delicate Krishna made to perish in flaming poison?"
Looking on, all the dairymaids felt mortal anguish[10]
For Krishna, whose good looks and refinement had no peer in the
universe.[11]
Radha dispatched a cowherd without delay
And had the news conveyed to the house of Nanda and Yaśodā.
Nanda and Yaśodā were stunned upon hearing it.

Song 4

At once Nanda and Yaśodā
Came running to the spot with all the cowherd folk.
They saw that Nārāyaṇa had fallen into the Kāliya lagoon.
Nanda and Yaśodā mingled their sobs:
"Krishna, why have you brought such a calamity upon us?
Because of you, our surroundings are suddenly barren."[12]
The two of them writhed upon the ground and wept together.
"Why have you made our whole world empty?
Get up for just a moment, son, we want to see your face.
Son, what pleasure can you get out of making us miserable?"
All the cowherds held their heads in their hands and sobbed:
"Why, Lord Jagannātha, are you torturing us by disappearing?
Arise and tell us who has committed any slight!

[8] Loka dharama bhaya 'world's dharma and fear.' See Dānakhaṇḍa above, n. 223.

[9] Bināyiā̃, literally 'weavingly'; compare modern Bengali biniye-biniye kā̃ā̃daa 'to cry at length' (literally, 'to cry weavingly').

[10] Rāpāyila . . . parāṇe 'burned in their souls.' See Turner 1962–1966, entry 10621 (s.v. rappa 'burning').

[11] Tribhubane sundara nāgara bara kāhne 'for Krishna, the choicest (bara) of handsome (sundara), urbane (nāgara) people in the universe (tribhubane).'

[12] Tohme lāgi bhaila āji śuna daśa diśe 'On your account, today itself the ten directions (i.e., everything about) have become empty.'

Krishna, who were you annoyed with that you plunged into the lagoon?"
Balabhadra, brother of Krishna, quickly reflected:
"Krishna has lost awareness of himself and gone into a trance.
Let me bring him back to his senses by reminding him of the past."

Song 5

"You are forests, you are mountains; you are land and water.
You are Hari, God in hell, the mortal world and heaven.
You're the sun and moon, the sentinels of the horizons.[13]
Taking on a human form at will, you're now a cowherd.[14]
How is it you've lost your self awareness, Vanamālī?
What's a lowly snake to you, Disbander of the Cosmos?[15]
In the ocean, posing as a fish, you raised the scriptures.[16]
As a tortoise, you upheld the earth upon your body.[17]
As a mighty boar, you used your tusk to lift the planet.[18]
You destroyed Hiraṇyakaśipu as Narasiṃha.[19]
Taking on the figure of a dwarf, you cheated Bali.[20]
As Paraśurāma, you destroyed the ruling order.[21]
In the form of Rāma, you were Rāvaṇa's destroyer.[22]
Meditating on the truth sublime, you've posed as Buddha.[23]
In the form of Kalki, you've defeated the unrighteous.[24]
This time, you've been born to bring about the death of Kaṃsa."
Krishna, when he heard this, once again regained his senses.

13 Tohme dikapāla 'You are the guardians of the compass.' Dikpāla or lokapāla refers to sentinels thought to guard the four quadrants of the compass. Mani 1975:457 identifies them as Indra, Agni, Yama and Varuṇa.

14 Līlātanu dhari ebē hayilāhā goāla 'Taking on a whimsy-body (līlātanu), you have now become a cowherd.' The implication is that the god embodies himself at his pleasure.

15 Jagata saṃhara tohme koṇa chāra kālī 'You are the withdrawer of the world—what dust is Kāliyā!' Saṃhara 'withdrawer, destroyer, gatherer in' is cognate to the verb used in a passage of Vṛndāvanakhaṇḍa which describes Krishna withdrawing his manifold bodies. See Vṛndāvanakhaṇḍa above, n. 97.

16 See Dānakhaṇḍa above, n. 189.

17 According to puranic accounts Viṣṇu made his second descent as a fabulous tortoise; in this form he bore the earth on his back.

18 See Dānakhaṇḍa above, n. 192.

19 See Dānakhaṇḍa above, n. 193.

20 See Dānakhaṇḍa above, n. 41. The dwarf is Viṣṇu's fifth descent.

21 See Naukākhaṇḍa above, n. 38.

22 See Tāmbūlakhaṇḍa above, n. 21, and Dānakhaṇḍa, n. 97.

23 In the Vaishnava system, the Buddha is counted the ninth descent of Viṣṇu, following on the Krishna descent (see Janmakhaṇḍa above, n. 6).

24 The tenth and last descent of Viṣṇu, yet to come, is Kalki, who is to restore peace and purity following an age of decline.

Song 6

Nārāyaṇa arose at once,
Spreading his arms apart.[25]
As grass withers in a hot wind,
So did the serpents' bonds disintegrate.
Dāmodara attacked Kāliya
In the Yamunā's waters.
He climbed upon Kāliya's serpentine head
Like Viṣṇu upon his mount Garuṛa.[26]
Due to the tremendous pressure on his face,
The blood gushed out in streams.
Upon the serpent Kāliya's great hood
Dāmodara commenced to dance.
With each blow of his feet,
The life of the serpent was ebbing.
Realizing their husband was about to die,
The female serpents, frantic with love for him,
Paid reverential homage
At Krishna's feet.

Song 7

"You are in charge of the universe, Hari.
Being the Lord, you must not take these measures.
Even the world can't stand up to your prowess,
Much less this wretch of a Kāliya serpent!
You are the force which created the cosmos:
People and creatures, the land and the waters.
You have provided us serpents with venom;
Why do you now drive us out of existence?
You have conceded our husband permission
To be in this area. He is your servant.
He did not know who you were in the water;
Therefore he bit you, that serpentine moron.
Only this once, take some pity upon us;
Grant us our husband this one time, Dāmodara!"
Krishna was placated, hearing their pleading.

25 Spreading the arms represents a regal gesture.

26 Garuṛabāhana māhābire '(Like) Mahāvīra ('Mighty Hero'; here used as an epithet of Viṣṇu) (upon) his mount (vāhana) Garuṛa.' Viṣṇu is said to ride upon the king of birds, a fabulous eagle named Garuṛa. This bird is said to be both a kinsman of snakes and their enemy as well. Kāliya, according to legend, resorted to the lagoon because it was out of bounds for Garuṛa. On the origin of the enmity between Kāliya and Garuṛa, see *Bhāgavatapurāṇa* 10.17 (Tagare 1978) and *Harivaṃśa* 67–68 (Bose 1940).

Song 8

Dāmodara's heart was softened and he said:
"Move at once southward to the sea.
On my bidding you may go there and live happily,
Leaving your Yamunā dwelling without apprehension."
Kāliya's womenfolk made a great outcry
When they heard Krishna's merciful words.
Kāliya the serpent, hearing Krishna's decree,
Bowed before Krishna and said:
"It is my good fortune to be commanded to live in the sea,
But I am very fearful of Garuṛa over there."[27]
When Krishna heard this he said: "On your head,
Kāliya, there will remain the impressions of my footprints.
When he sees this, Garuṛa will not devour you.
You may live unmolested for all time in the sea."
Receiving Krishna's orders, the serpent Kāliya
Joined all of his kind and departed for the ocean.
Janārdana blithely arose from the water.

Song 9

When the cowherds and cowmaids saw Krishna,
Their eyes were moist with joy.
Some embraced him tightly in their arms;
Others kissed and rekissed his face.
All the young women were overjoyed
That the king of gods had survived the fangs of the serpent Kāliya.
Forthwith from the breasts of Yaśodā
There gushed a stream of milk for Lord Dāmodara.[28]
She cried: "All our surroundings had become desolate.
Long live our son Gadādhara!"
Thereupon Radha, momentarily deranged with love,
Gazed steadfastly upon Krishna's face;

[27] See preceding footnote.

[28] Here the poet depicts the regeneration of milk in Yaśodā's bosom upon the safe recovery of her grown son. Similarly, in *Bhāgavatapurāṇa* 10.46:28 (Tagare 1978), it is said that Yaśodā's breasts overflow with milk as she recalls Krishna following his coming of age and departure from the pasturelands. This motif (regeneration of milk) may be of South Indian origin. It occurs in Old Tamil Sangam poetry, according to Hart 1975:99, citing a poem in which a mother's breasts regenerate milk as she contemplates the valor of a son who has been slain in battle. *Bhāgavatapurāṇa*, for its part, appears to have a southern origin; for discussion see Hart, p. 279, and also Bhandarkar 1965:48–50. The use of the same motif by the poet of *Śrīkṛṣṇakīrtana* may be due to the influence of *Bhāgavatapurāṇa*.

She of sloe eyes moist and unblinking
Abandoned her shyness and apprehension before everyone.
The rest of the dairymaids, beholding Krishna,
All embraced one another;
They displayed their pleasure through their smiles.

Song 10

Madhusūdana honored Nanda and Yaśodā
By clasping their feet,[29]
And he looked with affectionate eyes
Upon the dairymaids all around him.
By showing graciousness after emerging upon dry land,
Lord Murāri gave satisfaction to all.
Observing Radha at his side,
Dāmodara flashed her a smile;
And he paid proper respect
To all the cowherd youths who were present.
Krishna folded his hands together and said:
"Please heed my one stipulation.
I vanquished Kāliya for this reason:
So that everyone might drink the water of this place."
Then, after eliciting everyone's approval,
Krishna built an embankment at the lagoon.
Everyone joined Krishna and they proceeded to their homes.

[29] See Dānakhaṇḍa above, n. 140.

Yamunākhaṇḍa*

Song 1

In his thirst to possess Radha, he haunted the Yamunā embankment.
As for Radha, after consideration she set out for water with her girlfriends.

"Come, friends, let's go to the Yamunā River together for drawing some water.
We shall return in great spirits from filling our pitchers with Yamunā water."
Saying this, Radha set out with her pitcher; her gait had an elephant's rhythm.[1]
Her face looked as bright with its ringlets of hair as the moon with its shadowy markings.[2]
Radha arrived at the brink of the Kāliya whirlpool with all of her girlfriends.
Abashed when they met Nanda's son on the landing, they ceased from discussing their business.
Reaching the banks of the river and seeing the lotus-like face of their Krishna,
None of the formerly laughing and capering cowmaids would fill up their pitchers.
None could reach out to take hold of the clothes which had grown disarrayed on their bodies.
Each of them glanced at the face of the next, and they all felt perturbed in their spirits.
During that time, as they stared, never blinking their eyes, at their dear Vanamālī,

* The name *Yamunākhaṇḍa* 'Episode of the Yamunā River' does not occur in the original manuscript; rather, this section, the ninth of *Śrīkṛṣṇakīrtana*, follows the Kāliyadamanakhaṇḍa section and is untitled. This episode depicts the water sports of Krishna and the dairymaids, culminating in his theft of their clothes and jewelry while they bathe.

[1] Jāe gajagaṛi chānde 'She went (along) with the tempo of an elephant's gait (gaṛi = gati),' i.e., swayingly.

[2] Ālakĕ śobhe badana tāhāra yehena kalaṅka cānde 'With its wisps of hair (ālakĕ), her face looked splendid, like the moon (with its) stigmata.' See Tāmbūlakhaṇḍa above, n. 10, and Dānakhaṇḍa, n. 93.

All of the dairymaid women, like dolls made of gold, simply stood in their places.[3]
Neither a foot could they budge, nor a single remark could the dairymaids utter.
All had their thoughts on the one who resembled a moon come to earth—by name, Krishna.
Radha exerted a powerful effort and managed to go before Krishna.
"Move for a moment," she told Krishna, "so that my friends may feel free to take water."
Since he was in an irreverent mood, Lord Dāmodara turned to his Radha,
Answering her in a manner as if he did not know to whom he was speaking.

Song 2

"Who are your in-laws and who is your husband?[4]
Why are you taking my Yamunā water?"
"I am the daughter of excellent people.[5]
What's it to you if I'm drawing some water?"
"Lower the jug from your hip for a moment.
There are some things I am anxious to tell you."
"Only a man with a head he can spare
On his shoulders should try to approach and address me!"[6]
"Here's betel quids, Abhimanyu's wife; take them.
Let Cakrapāṇi survive by consenting."
"Handing me betel-leaf quids to address me
Is using a crude sort of hook to go fishing!"[7]
"I'm in authority here at the river.
You should pay heed to my offer, my beauty."
"You and I have nothing further to talk about,
Krishna; I understand well your intentions."

[3] Sakala goāla yubatī rahilā yehna kanaka putalī 'All the cowherd girls remained (still), like golden dolls.'

[4] Literally, 'Whose daughter-in-law are you, whose wife?' Rāṇī means 'queen' or sometimes (as here) 'wife'; see Bhārakhaṇḍa above, n. 13, and cf. Bāṇakhaṇḍa below, n. 83.

[5] Literally, 'I am a big person's daughter-in-law, a big person's daughter.'

[6] Yāra kāndha base doṣara māthā / sesi āhmā same kahibe kathā 'Let him banter with me who has a second head on his shoulders!' Krishna risks decapitation for trifling with the wife of an important man.

[7] Tāmbula diā̃ more bolasī / khuda baṛasiẽ ruhī bāndhasī 'You speak to me giving me betel (as you might) catch a ruhī (fish) on a crude fishhook.' That is, you can as well get me to speak to you by offering betel as you can catch a ruhī fish on an inadequate hook. Ruhī (rohita) is the name of a freshwater fish popular on Bengali tables.

"Made of pure gold, I've a bell-girdle,[8] Radha.
You must accept it from me. Heed my wishes."
"I'm not a dancing girl, I am a cowmaid.
I have no use for your bell-girdle, Krishna."
"Look, my silk sari extends sixteen cubits.
Take it from me and fulfill my entreaties.
Genuine gold is this flute of mine, Radha;
Be pleased to sit at my side and accept it."
"I can't make use of your flute to mix cowdung.[9]
I can't stir milk with your flute in my clutches.
The sari of silk is just talk without substance
—The rags on my vessels of ghee[10] are no different!"
"I wear a crown on my head bright with baubles.
Radha, you must take it; do me the honor."
"Krishna, you're black on the outside and inside.
Your crown should be washed and the water discarded!"[11]
"Those pomegranate-like breasts you're possessed of
Are holding my thoughts in captivity, Radha!"
"My breasts resemble the fruit of the gooseberry gourd[12]
—Good to look at, but death if you taste them!"
He, Cakrapāṇi, became apprehensive
On hearing the harsh talk of Radha; she offered
No hope for their intimacy to continue.[13]

Song 3

You pretend, when lifting up your arms, to bind your hairdo.
The lotus of that face of yours is thoroughly in blossom.
Why do you display purportive gestures in my presence?
Now you must embrace me. Keep my life in your protection!
Radha, why have you allowed your muslin wrap[14] to tumble?

[8] Kiṅkinī, a belled ornament (see Dānakhaṇḍa above, n. 269); in this case it is a band or girdle strapped to the waist.

[9] It is common in villages for housewives to make patties of cowdung mixed with straw; these are allowed to dry in the sun and are used as a cooking fuel.

[10] Se mohora ghṛtabhāṇḍera nāthā 'It's the (same as the) rag on (one of) my vessels of ghee.' Radha uses cloths to cover her pots of dairy goods.

[11] Mukuṭa dhuyiā̃ āhukitẽ bhāla 'It is well that the crown be washed and the water sprinkled about (āhuka- from Sanskrit abhyukṣ- "sprinkle").' Wash water is scattered on the ground to dampen and reduce dust.

[12] Māhākāla phala 'fruit of māhākāla (gooseberry gourd),' a plant with an attractive but toxic fruit; see Appendix.

[13] Rasa rākhe rādhā nā dila āśe 'Radha did not give assurance for the preservation of their love affair.'

[14] Netera āñcala 'āñcala of muslin.' See Dānakhaṇḍa above, n. 21.

You've displayed the fullness of your breasts and made me frantic.
Under the kadamba at the Yamunā embankment,
Why have you been flickering your eyes at me, my Radha?
You've cloaked half your face in your diaphanous apparel;
Radha, that's the reason I can't manage my emotions.
In preparing, Radha, to draw water from the river,
Why'd you softly speak to me with words of flowing nectar?
I'm protecting Gokula because of you, my Radha.
You're aware, from start to end,[15] of all my undertakings.
It's your obligation to propitiate me, Radha—
You're the one whose fault it is that I've become enmaddened!
Longing for you keeps me at the Yamunā embankment.

Song 4

I was walking quickly and my hair became disheveled;
Therefore I put up my arms and once again secured it.
It was out of weariness that I was sighing deeply.
When I stretched myself, it was because of languor, Krishna.
If I were to see you and my heart became unsettled,
I should not deserve to go on living any longer!
In the breeze, the garment on my bosom slightly shifted.
It was a coincidence you happened to observe it.
It was out of modesty and fear my eyes were darting.
That was why I quickly hid my face with my apparel.
At the Yamunā, I was preparing to draw water;
It was no mistake for me to castigate you, Krishna.[16]
You have been patrolling Gokula to earn a living,
And, from start to end, I know you well, you scabby sinner![17]
One who lacks awareness of himself gets into danger.
Krishna, realize this, and give up trying to be clever.
It's your own delusion that has made you crazy, Krishna!

Song 5

Imbibing Radha's harsh reply, the crestfallen Madhusūdana
Mildly addressed this message to Granny:

You're acquainted with the fact that I am Radha's lover.

[15] Tohme jāṇa kājera āhmāra ādimūla 'you know the starts and ends of my doings' or 'you know the preconditions (ādi) and substance (mūla) of my activities.'

[16] Since onlookers may draw damaging conclusions about Radha's relationship to Krishna, he should understand her publicly snubbing him.

[17] Pāpa pāmara 'wicked pāmara.' See Dānakhaṇḍa above, n. 136. Pāmara is a masculine variant of pāmarī.

Why does Radha, then, speak so adversely in responding?
I have not committed any injury against her.
I don't know what rancor Radha feels that she rebukes me.
Granny, you're my very self; you must say this to Radha:
"Grant him your consent, restore your Krishna to existence!"
Granny, I've been thinking to myself of my great fortune:
All the dairymaids have joined to offer me devotion.
Since, in the event,[18] the foremost of them all is Radha,
Her responding disagreeably is my misfortune.[19]
I must say one thing to you, so listen with attention.
She may gather water from the river as she pleases;
Let the other matter drop. I won't insist upon it,
Since it is so difficult to come by her approval.
You yourself, my Granny, are aware of how my spirits
Suffer every time I hear the very name of Radha.
Longing for her keeps me at the Yamunā embankment.

Song 6

Hearing Krishna's message, the glib old lady
Addressed Radha, reminding her of his benign past behavior.

Krishna's never done a thing which goes against your interests.
Why are you displeased with him for no good reason, Radha?
Has there ever been a boon to you he failed to render?
Radha, why have you begun mistreating Krishna lately?
Radha, you must heed my words: by giving your approval,
You, Candrāvalī, can gratify your Vanamālī.
Not a single dairymaid has castigated Krishna;
How is it that you've become the first of them to do so?
Cakrapāṇi's happiness has vanished for this reason;
He's complained to me of his extreme humiliation.
Radha, you do not have any sense at all, I'm finding.
Such affairs as these[20] are golden treasure at one's fingers!
You should not refuse to hear what Krishna is proposing;
Just that much alone will furnish Krishna satisfaction.
Do not disregard what I'm suggesting to you, Radha;
Krishna is a raft for you in youthful passion's ocean!
Don't reject what Krishna is proposing to you, Radha.

[18] Henai sambhede rādhā haā̃ saba āge 'It being the case that, in this situation (sambhede), Radha is ahead of all. . . .'

[19] Bilasa buila rādhā āhmāra bhāge 'to my (bad) fortune, Radha has spoken disagreeably (bilasa = birasa).'

[20] Henai milana hāthe kanaka nidhī 'Just such a liaison is a trove of gold in the hand!'

Song 7

Only because you don't know Cakrapāṇi
Do you tell me these sorts of stories about him.
Granny, we cowmaids arrived at the shores
Of the Yamunā River; we'd come to take water.
But, at the outset itself, he restrained us
From that; he forbade us—we couldn't imagine!
Krishna is vile—when his purpose demands it
He fails to acknowledge his dearest companions.
Such an unprincipled person is Krishna
That uncles and aunts have no place in his feelings;
Nor does society hinder his doings.
There isn't a bit of reserve in his glances.
Any which way, he conducts his own business.
The king of the gods plays the fool in this fashion![21]
Krishna's intentions are very indecent;
Apart from myself, why, he thinks about nothing.
Please don't encourage his lustful ambitions.[22]

Song 8

Taking in Radha's reply as conveyed by Granny,
The eager though discouraged Krishna said this to Radha.

You and I, Radha, are intimate lovers.
We have but one soul between us, one body.
I have done nothing opposed to your interests;
Still you are angry—that's very perplexing.
Don't use such rigorous language, for I,
Cakrapāṇi, submit to your blossoming beauty.
I'm Vanamālī, the one you have given
Your love to, Candrāvalī; don't you remember?
Listen to me, listen, Radha Candrāvalī,
Destiny has me in thrall at this instant.
You must be able to realize my reasons
For ridding the river of all its pollution;
You can perceive it yourself, just consider.
Let's make immediate use of the water!
Radha, I've made you aware of my powers—
At heart, I don't have any rancor against you.
Tender some heed to my words, I beseech you!

21 Yehna tehna lae nija kāje / hena se ājala debarāje 'He takes his own affairs in this and that fashion; that's the sort of fool the king of gods is!'

22 Tāhāka nā diha rasa āśe 'Don't provide him with hopes of lovemaking.'

Song 9

"No one is taking the water because of the statements you've made to us, Krishna.
Realize yourself, Cakrapāṇi, the water's about to be properly wasted."
"You may take water, my beautiful Radha, as much as your own heart desires
—Still, though, by virtue of what[23] should the lot of those girls be allowed to take water?"
"Should I draw water while all of my girlfriends depart with their pitchers still empty?
I will be ridiculed, Krishna, by everyone, once they observe what has happened."
"I know quite perfectly well that the people are going to laugh at you, Radha.
After all, I don't relinquish one drop of this water unless someone begs me!"
"Krishna, we girlfriends together are many, while you are but one at the river.
After we girls beat you up with our fists, Krishna, we'll take your Yamunā water!"
"Radha, my darling, your friendly companions cannot do a thing whatsoever.
Only these upstanding youthful allurements of yours can subdue me, my Radha!"[24]
"Don't talk indecently. Look at me, I'm clasping hold of your feet, handsome Krishna.
Don't be contentious, young cowherd; allow these companions of mine to take water."
"Lend your attention, intelligent Radha, to one single thing I would tell you;
Then, with your friends, you may all take your fill of the water and head for the village."
"After my jug's filled with water, I'll climb up the steps and, with solid attention,
Honestly, darling Dāmodara, I'll listen, Lord, to whatever you tell me."
After he heard this proposal, the excellent Krishna was very delighted.
He gave permission for gathering water to all of the young cowherd maidens.
Radha had taken her water; she offered her ear as she paused next to Krishna.

23 Kamana guṇe 'by virtue of what?'

24 E tora yaubana unnata rādhā māritě pāre āhmāre 'Radha, (only) your advanced (upstanding) yaubana can smite me!' See Dānakhaṇḍa above, n. 228.

Krishna pretended that he was about to say something, then kissed her cheek smartly.
Then, at a furious pace, Radha strode from the spot in a huff from sheer anger.

Song 10

"Radha, in the pitcher on your hip you've taken water.
Speak to me a little with your words of liquid honey!
You've a splendid bodice on your breasts, your earrings glisten;
Brighter than the sun, they wear a halo's iridescence.
Dairymaid, slow down! You must pay heed to what I'm asking:
Banish my forlornesss now and then—let me embrace you![25]
Radha, you are spurning me, escaping with your water.
Why do you unsettle me this way by getting angry?
What's the reason you are not responding to me, Radha?
I'm burned up all over with the flames of your aloofness.
Listen to my counsel, Radha: cast aside your fury.
Think this over fully: it disfigures you, your anger.
I am in command here at the Yamunā embankment;
I will smash your pitcher on the path if you ignore me!
Radha, think this over to yourself from start to finish.
This time you must hear out my remarks, enticing Radha!"
Radha turned to stare him in the eye upon this outburst.

Song 11

"On this pathway, many people—good and bad—are going.
One should stand apart from them before discussing business.
But since you insist on making private matters public,
It is clear to me that there's no sense in your behavior.
On the path you ought to watch your feelings, son of Nanda.
Why is it you have to spend your time creating problems?
In my house my husband's mother stays, and she's malicious.
She is not afraid to cast unspeakable aspersions.
Since you are aware yourself of all your past adventures,
Why reveal them on the bank and pathway, Cakrapāṇi?
Krishna, you must promptly put a stop to your entreaties.
Don't you know my friends are not all friendly? Some are hostile.
If these things should be divulged by any one among them,
You will be disgraced, and I will be the butt of scandal."
Radha reached the door of her own house while she was speaking.

[25] Rahiā̃ rahiā̃ deha birahera kola, literally 'Stopping, stopping, give me the embrace for an estranged lover!'

Krishna did not answer; he was feeling apprehensive.
Meanwhile, each of Radha's friends departed for her household.

Song 12

Taking in Radha's words, the crafty Madhusūdana
Promptly went and lamented to Granny as follows:

Though I plunged into the Kāliya whirlpool,
Still I survived before all of the herdsmen.[26]
Also, I exercised various efforts,
And yet I don't have any place in her feelings.
Lost! Disappeared![27] So much time spent on Radha;
But still in her heart she's not satisfied, Granny.
Joining with all her companions, that dairymaid
Carried off Yamunā water and vanished
While failing to grant her consent to me, Granny.
This is the reason my heart is in anguish.
What might be lurking within Radha's thinking?
This much you have to explain to me, Granny.
I have committed no outrage against her;
Then why, over nothing, is Radha indignant?
You must convey my entreaties to Radha.
Let her be pleased to take Yamunā water;
I rendered it pure due to longing for Radha.

Song 13

After digesting the persuasive arguments of Madhuvidviṣ,[28]
Granny was very annoyed with Radha; she addressed these words
to her.

So much time you've spent in such an immature condition
—This is why you fail to see your own advantage, Radha.
Now that you're possessed of youthfulness in ample measure,
Why do you go on displaying obstinate behavior?
It's your greatest fortune that the handsome, worldly Krishna
Supplicates you, Radha; he's a sea of delectations.[29]

[26] Kālidahe dila āhme jhā̃pe la / āla hera baṛāyi / jilŏ monā̃ gokula āge la 'I gave a jump into the Kāliya whirlpool / hey, look here, Granny / I survived before Gokula.'

[27] Hari hari / eta kāle rādhāra kāraṇe la / āla hera baṛāyi / tabhŏ toṣa nāhī̃ tāra maṇe la 'Hari hari / so much time (spent) because of Radha / hey, look here, Granny / still there isn't satisfaction in her heart.' See Dānakhaṇḍa above, n. 78.

[28] Madhuvidviṣ 'Annihilator of (the demon) Madhu', an epithet of Viṣṇu-Krishna, equivalent in meaning to Madhusūdana (Tāmbūlakhaṇḍa, n. 29).

[29] Sāgara rasa nāgara sundara kāhnāñī / tora bhāgẽ kākuti karae tora ṭhāyi 'Handsome (sundara) urbane (nāgara) Krishna, who is a sea of pleasures (rasa sāgara "sea of pleasures"

Love that one engages in with someone young and handsome
Everywhere on earth is thought the pinnacle of rapture.
Krishna realized this and so he led you to submission.
On what imbecile's suggestion have you changed your thinking?
I would never talk you into anything improper.
None of the companions you observe here wants your welfare.
Each of them is just concerned about her own ambitions.
They want Vanamālī to be angry with you, Radha.
You should contemplate within your heart what I'm proposing.
Radha, let us take your friends and travel to the river.
After you arrive there, gladden Krishna by agreeing.

Song 14

At Granny's bidding, Radha headed for the Yamunā.
The crafty Krishna addressed glib assurances to her.

"It's a pleasure, Radha, that you've come to the embankment.
Right away the water will be put to good advantage.
Have a look about; the summer season is upon us.
It's delightful being in the deep, refreshing water.
Previously, in this very whirlpool there were serpents.
For that reason, people were afraid to come for bathing.
Your companions wished to do some swimming in this river;
But, afraid to bathe, they'd take their water here and vanish.
Now that I've sent Kāliya, the serpent, to the seacoast,
There's no longer any ground for you to fear this water.
You must have some faith in what I'm saying, dearest Radha;
Then I shall precede you all in entering the water."
"If you'll leave your schemes aside when entering the water,
Then I'll also take a dip with all of my companions."
While the girls observed him, Krishna stepped inside the water.
"Please don't mind my speaking of my unfulfilled affection."[30]
Offering permission to the dairymaids and Radha,
Krishna had them follow him in entering the water.
Krishna frolicked for his own amusement in the water;
Lovingly he gazed at all the dairymaidens' faces.
Radha's heart rebounded when she gazed upon her Krishna,
And the dairymaidens felt excited to observe him.
All became engrossed in making sport there in the water.

---

is inverted for the sake of meter as sāgara rasa), is agitating for you thanks to your (good) fortune.'

30 Unamata nahiha mora biraha bacane 'Don't be agitated by my expressions of longing in separation (biraha).'

Song 15

Under water went Janārdana;
He touched the hips of Radha.
Startled, Radha rose; she wrapped her clothes about her person tightly.
Noticing that it was Krishna,
Radha cast him sidelong glances
And, in doing so, she caused the love within his heart to waken.
In the Kāliya lagoon,
Fulfilling long-held aspirations,
Jagannātha started to engage himself in water pastimes.
Catching hold of someone's foot, he
Took her for some distance in the
Water; "Krishna! Krishna!" cried that dairymaid in utter panic.
Going underwater, Krishna
Covertly clutched someone's bosom.
Thereupon that dairymaid stood paralyzed from sheer emotion.
Spiritedly, Jagannātha
Laid his hand on someone's buttocks.
Whirling round, that dairymaiden grappled for the hand of Krishna.
Krishna brushed her off, submerged
And headed for a lotus clump.[31]
He long remained there; with his face exposed, he had the cowmaids baffled.[32]
Then he clambered out and, clasping
Granny's feet, he gave instructions.
Meanwhile, with the other
Dairymaidens in the water, Radha
Waited, disappointed. Krishna chuckled in his heart to see this.

Song 16

We were watching Krishna as he went inside the water.
How could he have vanished from our sight so quickly, Granny?
Has he plunged to Hades or ascended to the heavens?
In the Yamunā, could Krishna possibly have perished?
Offer us advice about a remedy sincerely—
How are we to find divine Dāmodara, dear Granny?
We are many dairymaids; Dāmodara is single.
Everyone may come to the unspeakable conclusion
That we've murdered Krishna, drowning him inside the water.
Inwardly we're withering to contemplate this, Granny.

[31] Padmabana, literally 'forest of lotus (padma)'; see Appendix.
[32] Their confusion is due to the similarity of Krishna's face to a lotus.

Though we cowmaids all combined to search for Vanamālī,
Nowhere have we found him; we're becoming apprehensive.
Are we really witness to the death of Krishna, Granny?
All us dairymaids have lost our wits about the matter!
If it were the case that Nanda's offspring hadn't perished,
Then, by now, we surely would have had a glimpse of Krishna.
You yourself must offer us some plan and means of action![33]

Song 17

Radha, on hearing the words that you uttered,
He, Cakrapāṇi, has drowned in the water.
Radha, I'm losing my hold on my senses.
Inwardly I feel enormous contrition.
Radha, before someone hears of what's happened,
Better for us if we make our way homeward.
You must take care to admonish your girlfriends
So no one will publicize word of his passing.
If this report should come out in the open,
Why, then everybody is going to perish!
He, the adorable son of a cowherd,
As well as the only small child of his mother,[34]
Has perished for you in the Yamunā River.
Now, in your heart, have you found satisfaction?
Let us all gather together tomorrow
In order to carry our search out completely.
Then we'll discover some trace of our Krishna.

Song 18

> Radha, in the company of her girlfriends,[35] was persuaded by Granny's proposal.
> Bearing grief in their hearts, each one departed for her home.

Krishna was watching as Radha went homeward.
Then he emerged once again from the water.
Hiding, he stayed in Vṛndāvana forest.

[33] Āpaṇeñī karaha se budhi parakāre 'On your own, make a plan (budhi) and means of execution (parakāre)!'

[34] Ekaiti māera chāoāla 'the one little boy of his mother.' Krishna is thought to be the son of Yaśodā, while his brother is thought to belong to a different mother (see again Janmakhaṇḍa above, songs 4 and 5).

[35] Sakhī sakhīvṛtā, which appears in the published text, is better treated in composition: sakhīsakhīvṛtā 'surrounded by girlfriends and girlfriends.' It is correlated with āgāramāgāraṃ 'to houses and houses' (i.e., 'each friend to each [respective] household') in the following line.

Nobody knew of the Lord's situation.[36]
Close to the Yamunā's banks, clever Krishna
Engaged in deception that he might taste pleasure.
When the first stage of the evening descended,[37]
That was when Krishna emerged to go homeward.
All night Govinda could not fall asleep
As he dwelt in his heart on the beauty of Radha.
Then, with a crow of the cock, it was morning.
Krishna set out for the river embankment.
Climbing the kadamba tree, Vanamālī
Remained in it, watching for Radha's arrival.
Prickings of love had his feelings impassioned.
Puckishly Krishna devised a procedure:[38]
"This time I'm going to devastate Radha!"

Song 19

> Deeply tormented by love's missiles, and encouraged by her
> girlfriends,
> Radha, whose thighs vied with exquisite plantain trees,[39]
> Duly embarked at daybreak upon a search for Mādhava
> Along the banks of the Yamunā River.

At that hour, Radha sent a summons to her girlfriends,
Heeding the proposal which her Granny had suggested.
With her pitcher on her hip, Candrāvalī roused Granny;
After that she went and reached the Yamunā embankment.
It was very early—not yet time to go for bathing;
That was why no dairymaid had brought a change of clothing.
All about her Radha cast her gaze, then spoke as follows:
"On the bank let's set our clothes and search the stream for Krishna."
"Nicely spoken, Radha," her companions all responded.
"There's no man here, after all, so why should we be bashful?"
Reasoning this way, with all the dairymaidens Radha
Took her clothing off and then descended in the water.
Radha splashed about[40] inside the water, seeking Krishna;
Failing to encounter him, her heart was agitated.
Notifying all of her companions, Radha asked them,

36 Keho nā jāṇila daiba ghaṭane 'no one knew the divine occurrence.'

37 Yabẽ gela rātī eka pahara 'when one prahara (three hours) (of the) night had gone by,' i.e., at about 9 PM.

38 Rasika kāhnāñī kaila yugatī 'Krishna the bon vivant (rasika) made a plan.'

39 Rāmarambhāripūrūr 'having thighs (uru) which were competitors (ripu) of splendid (rāma) (trunks of) banana trees (rambhā)'. See Appendix.

40 Āloṛiā̃ jale 'churning the water'; see āloṛa- in Sen 1971:60.

"Where has Cakrapāṇi gone? He's left us devastated!"[41]
Joining all her girlfriends, Radha supplicated Granny:
"What solution is there, Granny? How shall we find Krishna?"
At that point, Dāmodara descended from the treetop.

Song 20

Picking up the dairymaidens' necklaces and clothing,
Up the tree, the kadamba, Dāmodara ascended.
From his haven Vanamālī gave a call; he shouted:
"What do you exhaust yourselves to look for, all you cowmaids?
You should venture closer to me, all you dairymaidens.
You may witness right away if I am dead or living!"[42]
All the cowherd girls were overjoyed upon observing
Krishna, who, up in the tree, was in a wanton humor.
Having filched the dairymaidens' necklaces and clothing,
Krishna, chuckling heartily,[43] was in tremendous spirits.
Seeing that their clothes weren't on the bank, the cowherd women
Knew within their hearts that they'd been taken by Murāri.
Jagannātha then made this pronouncement very loudly:
"Have a look, those clothes of yours are here within my clutches!
Till you ladies venture out on shore and leave the water,
I, Dāmodara, am not returning your apparel.
Knowing this, come out upon dry land and claim your clothing!"

Song 21

Observing Krishna ensconced in the summit of the tree
With the stolen clothes and jewelry, Radha was abashed and said:

"All our clothes and necklaces we left on the embankment
Earlier, to seek the son of Nanda in the water.
All us girlfriends joined together, entering the water.
Krishna has removed by force our necklaces and clothing."
In the water totally unclothed, the cowmaid shouted,
"Oh! I'm so embarrassed! You are shameless, Vanamālī!"
With her right hand placed in front of both her breasts to shield them,
Radha raised herself halfway above the water's surface.
"You have got no sense of shame at all," she said to Krishna,

[41] Āhmāka māriā̃ kathā̃ gelā cakrapāṇi 'Killing us, where has Cakrapāṇi gone?'

[42] Āji kathā suṇa mora maraṇa jībane, literally 'Listen today itself (to the) story of my living or dying!'

[43] Hāse hāsi khali khali 'laughs, laughing khali khali' (from Sanskrit skhalitam skhalitam; i.e., 'laughs in a staccato manner').

"Treating an important person's wife in such a manner!"[44]
Speaking from the distance, Jagannātha said to Radha,
"Come out from the water, Radha; fold your hands together."
On dry land, with folded hands, Candrāvalī implored him:
"Offer us our necklaces and clothes, Lord Vanamālī."
Seeing Radha's attitude, divine Dāmodara
Draped her muslin clothing over Radha; he relinquished
Only her apparel, while her necklace he secreted.

Song 22

Making fun of Radha after having taken in her message,
Krishna addressed Granny as follows with unflagging zest in his heart:

Say, Granny, taking along some companions,
She made herself naked and entered the water.
Say, Granny, Radha does not mind her elders—
Can this be the wife Abhimanyu's supporting?
How is she able to do such things, Granny?
Radha goes swimming without any clothing!
You should accept the advice I'm proposing
And castigate Radha intensively, Granny!
Never again should she act in this manner,
Exposing her body to masculine glances![45]
I've given everyone back their apparel;
Why, then, is Radha still acting disgruntled?
That being so, there can be no solution,
Since I don't know anything else I can tell her.
Carefully go and inquire of Radha
Just why she's still here after getting her clothing.
Maybe her fancy for me hasn't faded!

44 Literally, 'you do such action to a big person's bahu ("daughter-in-law" or "wife").'
45 Puruṣera ākhi nibārihe 'she must ward off the eyes of men.'

Hārakhaṇḍa*

Song 1

Hearing Krishna's speech as conveyed by Granny,
The anguished Radha spoke to the old lady as follows:

There was a necklace of multiple strands[1]
On my sari of silk[2] when Gadādhara snatched it.
Scrupulously that young cowherd restored
My silk sari to me, but he's stolen my necklace.
Say, Granny, you must get going and tell my . . .[3]

* * *

This is the reason I'm coming before you.
Krishna repeatedly does certain actions
Which lead to dishonor for all of his kinsmen.
Just as I'm being molested by Krishna
These girlfriends of mine have been likewise molested.
You may look into the matter in person;
Now that you know of this, discipline Krishna.
You will be totally ruined, and we will be finished
If Kaṃsa should hear what has happened.
All of these things I am telling you humbly.[4]

* *Hārakhaṇḍa* 'Episode of the Necklace', name of the tenth section of *Śrīkṛṣṇakīrtana*. This portion of the text is abbreviated due to the loss of several leaves from the original manuscript. In this episode, Radha complains to Krishna's mother because, in returning her clothing at the end of the preceding Yamunā River episode, he has failed to return her necklace. In the original manuscript, this section is styled Yamunāntargata Hārakhaṇḍa 'The Necklace Portion of the Yamunā (River) Episode.'

[1] Sāteśarī hāre, see Tāmbūlakhaṇḍa above, n. 40.

[2] Pāṭola, silken material or a silk sari. This is the garment temporarily lost by Radha to Krishna's thievery in the preceding episode of the text.

[3] Seven numbered pages of the original manuscript are missing at this point. The text resumes as Radha addresses Yaśodā.

[4] Buyilõ tohmāra pāe 'I have spoken at your feet,' i.e., in deference; cf. Vṛndāvanakhaṇḍa above, n. 90.

Song 2

Taking in Radha's words, Yaśodā was badly frightened.
She conveyed the harshness of her anger to Keśava[5] in private.

All the cowherd folk are well acquainted with us, Krishna.
In this settlement of Gokula, we've lived since always.
As a son, you've been superb, the darling of our household.
You're about to bring about the death of us, my Krishna!
I am warning you that you must stop your wayward thinking.
How much must we suffer for your sake from everybody?
Time and time again you disregard my admonitions,
Doing just those things which I've forbidden you from doing.
Look, son Krishna, all the calves are roaming different places
While you are meandering about because of Radha.
Radha might protest before the king with all the cowmaids.
If they come for taking me away and hold me captive,
Then what explanation could I make to win my freedom?
Son, you must make clear to me what strategy to follow.
No one's more important than your mother and your father.
This, in just a word, is what I want to tell you, Krishna.
Son, on my request, you have to manage your emotions.

Song 3

Taking in his mother's admonitions, the tearful Acyuta[6]
Attributed the blame for the lost property to Radha and the other dairymaids.

Listen and I'll make it clear to you, Yaśodā mother.[7]
By my blessings, I survived; [8] if not, I would have perished.
I won't go to keep the calves from straying any longer.
That entire gang of girls[9] is picking on me, mother!
Some restrain my arms while some are tugging at my ringlets;[10]
On my head they lift and plunk their wares of dairy produce.
With the other cowmaids at the Yamunā embankment
Radha's been with other men, hilariously romping!

[5] Keśava 'Having Long Hair', a name of Viṣṇu-Krishna.

[6] Acyuta 'Impervious', an epithet of Viṣṇu-Krishna.

[7] Suṇa māya yaśodāa 'Listen, mother Yaśodā. . . .' Krishna may be in the habit of using Yaśodā's first name to distinguish her from other wives of Nanda.

[8] Bhāge puṇi jilāhõ 'I survived by fortune (bhāga) and (spiritual) merit (puṇi).' Personal merit that accrues from right action is thought to assist one through difficulties.

[9] Ṣola śata yubatīñā āhmāre bala kare 'Sixteen hundred girls intimidate me.' See Dānakhaṇḍa above, n. 9.

[10] Keho dhare ghoṛācule 'Some grasp at my cascading hair. . . .' See Dānakhaṇḍa above, n. 130.

Coming here, I wanted to inform of her misconduct;
Radha's come here first and, out of spite, it's me she's blaming.
Mother, I'm your child, the darling offspring of your Nanda.
I don't shirk my duty, and my thoughts are not on mischief.
Radha is disturbed with the delirium of passion.
Loading me with dairy goods, she's made my shoulders swollen.
I patrol the Yamunā embankment tending cattle.
When I tell her, "You're my aunt!" her badgering increases.
In complete humility, I've told you this sincerely.

Song 4

Granny came and intervened precisely at this juncture.
Trying to console her, she set out for home with Radha.
Showing agitation, she remarked to Abhimanyu:
"It's good luck I've managed to come home today with Radha."
Using sundry strategies on everybody, Granny
Cleverly succeeded in protecting Radha's secret.
"Krishna is a little boy, he can't control the cattle.
Springing with a lion's speed, a bullock charged at Radha.
Radha fell in terror in a clump of thorny bushes.
Seeing her disheveled form, she's come home with reluctance.
You yourself can verify the state of Radha's person;
In the bushes, all her giant pearls[11] were caught and scattered.
Radha's lips, because of her anxiety, are withered.
Giving her cold water, I restored her to her senses.
What can I report to you besides what I've reported?
It was by your blessings[12] Padmā's daughter didn't perish!"
Abhimanyu knelt at Granny's footsteps when he heard this.

[11] Gajamutī, refer to Dānakhaṇḍa above, nn. 233 and 157.

[12] Tohmāra pune 'by your merit.' (Pune and its variants, including puṇī, derive from Sanskrit puṇya.) See n. 8 above.

Bāṇakhaṇḍa*

Song 1

Reminiscing on Radha's transgression,[1] the infuriated
Madhusūdana
Told Granny that she should be suitably punished.

Radha has informed about my conduct to my mother.
This is why I'm feeling aggravated.
From this moment, Granny, I shall close my heart to Radha.
I'm advising you of this sincerely.
Granny, she has utterly destroyed my reputation.
Certainly I have to take my vengeance.
On my own, I'm going to devise just such a method
So that Radha kneels before me humbly.[2]
I shall strike her in the very heart with passion's missiles;[3]
I submit this, Granny, at your footsteps.
So that all will laugh at her and clap their hands together—
This is how I plan to trouble Radha.
Terrible resentment has awakened in my spirits;
This is why you mustn't blame me, Granny.
In my heart, I feel as if I'd like to murder Radha,
But, because of you, I shall not do it.
From this very day I've set aside my urge for Radha.

Song 2

Krishna, you should listen to my counsel. You're a cowherd;
Radha is a cowmaid. She is causing endless problems.

* *Bāṇakhaṇḍa* 'Episode of the Arrows', name of the eleventh section of *Śrīkṛṣṇakīrtana*. In this episode, Krishna takes revenge on Radha for her conduct in the preceding section. Masquerading as the love god, he shoots Radha with arrows made of flowers, thereby winning her total submission.

1 Radha has maligned Krishna in the preceding episode by complaining of his behavior to his mother.

2 Literally, 'so that Radha falls at my feet.'

3 Kāma or Madana, the love god, is the Indian Cupid; he is said to shoot people with long stemmed flowers, which constitute his arrows. Because of his physical beauty, Krishna is often compared to this god, whom he impersonates below in this episode. (See Dānakhaṇḍa above, n. 115, and Vṛndāvanakhaṇḍa, n. 78).

Shoot her with infatuation's shafts![4] Display no mercy.
Let there be an end to all the pretense of that cowmaid.[5]
Listen, won't you, Krishna, to the plan that I'm suggesting:
You must shoot at Radha with five arrows made of flowers![6]
Earlier I gave your quids of betel leaf to Radha;
Yet she would in no respect pay heed to my entreaties.
Was there any effort I withheld to win your interests?
I was struck for that; she called herself a faithful woman.
Krishna, you must listen to my counsel: do not dawdle.
Quickly nock the string upon your bow of flower blossoms![7]
You must take her life with shafts of longing and derangement,
Anguish and delirium, as well as stupefaction.[8]
You're the master of the universe, Lord Vanamālī;
Yet Candrāvalī is not in awe before you, Krishna.
Radha must reverse herself and supplicate you keenly!

Song 3

Having elicited Granny's approval, Krishna dressed himself up
And vowed to attack Radha with the five arrows of infatuation.

His topknot was bound with the feathers of peacocks; a garland of blooms was upon it.
His brow was embellished with sandalpaste markings which mimicked the moon at its fullest.
Putting a couple of wagtails[9] to scorn were his eyes, which were bright with mascara.
His merest of smiles lent enchantment to all of the world, like a lotus in blossom.
Raging inside with a spirit incensed by the withering censure of Radha,

[4] Hāṇa pā̃ca bāṇe, literally 'Strike with five arrows!' The love god's arrows are said to be five in number.

[5] Goālinī rādhāra khaṇḍuka saba māyā 'Let all the māyā of dairymaid Radha be broken!' Māyā broadly refers to illusion or sensory deception; it can also mean sorcery or attachment.

[6] According to Mani 1975:379, the five flowers of love's arrows (see n. 3 above) are aravinda (lotus), aśoka (asoka), cūta (mango), navamālikā (double flowered Arabian jasmine), and nīlotpala (waterlotus).

[7] According to Mani 1975:379, love's bow is made of sugarcane and its string is made up of beetles. The poet of the present text, however, describes love's bow, like his arrows, as being made of flowers.

[8] Stambhana mohana āra dahana śoṣane / ūchāṭiṇa bāṇe laa rādhāra parāṇe 'Take Radha's life with arrows (of) stupefaction (stambhana), delirium (mohana), as well as anguish (dahana), longing (śoṣane), (and) derangement (ūchāṭiṇa).' It is confirmed in Mani 1975:379 that love's arrows are stupefaction (stambhana), delirium (sammohana), anguish (tāpana), longing (śoṣana), and derangement (unmādana).

[9] See Dānakhaṇḍa above, n. 68.

Krishna set out for Vṛndāvana, clutching a bow in his hand made from flowers.
His cheeks were adorned with a couple of gem-studded earrings encrusted with diamonds.
His teeth were agleam like a series of pearls, dipped and rolled, as it were, in vermilion.[10]
Wearing a wonderful necklace and armlets, with both hands embellished by bracelets,
He, Jagannātha, put on most exquisitely ravishing gem-studded wristlets.
All of his body he coated with sandal; his dress was a loincloth of muslin.[11]
Over that, Krishna encircled himself in a bell-girdle[12] studded with gemstones.
Having his gold flute in hand and his mouth filled with betel quids scented with camphor,
Krishna sat down on some delicate leaves and remained at the base of the kadamba.
Warbling a song[13] was the cuckoo, enchanter of people. The breeze was refreshing.
All of the trees were ablossom with flowers. The bumblebees chanted a chorus.
Krishna remained there, extremely enraged, in his yearning to castigate Radha.

Song 4

Granny had Krishna remain by the pathway;
Then she returned once again and met Radha.
"Right now," she said, "is there something you're doing?
Look, Radha, why don't you travel to market?
Why do you hoard dairy goods in your household?
Has Abhimanyu turned royalty, Radha?
Quick as you can, get your merchandise ready.
Let's go and sell off those wares in the city.
This is the only career which sustains us;
Shirking it off would be out of the question.
Radha, there isn't a moment to squander.
Summon each one of your dairymaid girlfriends.
If we are quick in departing for market,
Then we can sell off our wares for a profit.

10 See Dānakhaṇḍa above, n. 75.

11 Sakala śarīra candane lepila neta dhaṛi paridhāne 'He anointed all his body with sandal, putting on fine muslin (neta) apparel.'

12 Kiṅkinī, refer to Yamunākhaṇḍa above, n. 8.

13 Kokila pañcama gāe 'the cuckoo sings pañcamas.' Cf. Vṛndāvanakhaṇḍa above, n. 76.

Realizing this, don't delay, but move quickly;
I'll go along with you happily, Radha.
Act in accord with my words; don't defy them."

Song 5

Radha Candrāvalī heard Granny's urgings
And set out for Mathurā, taking her produce.
Magnolia strings twined her frolicsome hairdo
As filigree gold twines the head of Lord Hara.[14]
The wagtail bird, seeing her eyes, disappeared, while
Her head wore a sunrise of brilliant vermilion.
Putting on various jewelry with care, Radha
Covered her produce with cloths of fine muslin.
Granny went first, Radha followed; they headed
For Mathurā. No one opposed their departure.
Going some distance, they forded the Yamunā,
Reaching the edge of Vṛndāvana forest.
There Krishna sat at the base of the kadamba tree.
Granny saw him and slowly approached him.
Radha stayed outside Vṛndāvana, waiting.

Song 6

Look, I've invested a great many efforts
In order to make Radha come here.
Act in accord with our earlier plan,
Krishna; salvage your honor this minute.
See, Krishna, I've had a vision of you
On this day; that is why it's auspicious.
What can I possibly say about Radha?
It pains me to even discuss her.
She has besmirched you to such an extent
That the shame you've received has no limit.
This is the truth I am telling you
And, in accord with it, you should act promptly.
Instantly fire the five shafts of passion[15]

[14] Lalita khõpāta śobhe campakera mālā / haraśire śobhe yehna kanakamekhalā (Sukumar Sen has suggested in personal consultations that kanakamekhalā, literally 'golden girdle', may be an error for kanakaśikhalā 'golden chain') 'A garland of campaka embellishes her frolicsome chignon as a golden chain embellishes the head of Hara (= Śiva).' Radha's hairdo encircled by golden blossoms is likened to the high-piled hair of the deity Śiva encircled by a chain of gold filigree.

[15] Literally, 'Today itself take Radha's life by discharging the five arrows of infatuation.' See n. 4 above.

And capture the spirits of Radha!
Once Radha searches for you in despair,
Vanamālī, because of your absence,
Then I shall feel a tremendous elation.

Song 7

"Granny, what you've said is precisely my thinking.
Now you must convey my message to Radha."

Granny, please discuss what I'm about to say with Radha.
For her sake, I've spent myself in various endeavors;
Still she hasn't given me her genuine compliance.
In her feelings, Radha is consistently inconstant.
Radha's brought enormous disrepute upon me, Granny.
I shall take her life without delay with these five arrows!
Earlier, I sent some quids of betel leaf to Radha.
Pitching them away, she made me feel humiliated.
I was the occasion for her giving you a slapping;
For this reason, I have felt great anguish due to Radha.
And, besides, how many different curses she has dealt me!
Though I am divine, I, Vanamālī, have endured them.
On my shoulders I have taken pains to bear the burden
Of her dairy produce; I complied with her instructions.
When I plunged in Kāliya's lagoon, and everybody
Trembled in their spirits, it was all because of Radha.
Still I don't have any standing, Granny, in her feelings.

Song 8

At Dāmodara's behest, Granny immediately
Approached Radha and informed her in private:

Krishna is unhappy from your actions. Having suffered
Great humiliation, he's dispatched me to you, Radha.
This is what he said: "I did so many things for Radha,
But, rejecting them, she's dropped a thunderbolt upon me.[16]
Now I am acquainted with her disposition fully.
Snitching to my mother, she's destroyed my reputation.
I have been enduring much abusive talk from Radha;
Furthermore, because of her alone, I bore a burden.
Granny, even now within her heart she's not contented.
What remains for me to do to satisfy this woman?"

[16] Tāka āna kari pāṛilẽ muṇḍe bāja '(But) by reacting adversely to that, she has caused a thunderbolt to descend on my head.'

Radha, this is what I've seen of Krishna's mental status.
It's because of you he's overwhelmed with great resentment.
He has got a bow of blooms, in fact, and with five arrows
He's about to load and take your life. He'll shoot you, Radha!
Grandniece, you are like my very self, so heed my counsel:
Venture on your own to him and clasp the feet of Krishna.
Then and only then is Krishna likely not to kill you.

Song 9

Hara, lord of deities, is witnessed in my hairdo, while my locks of hair
 are manifestly Nīla.[17]
Sun is the vermilion on my head and Moon, the marking on my brow;[18]
 my eyes are Passion's dwelling places.[19]
Listen, Granny, go and tell this message to Govinda:
What can Jagannātha do? The treasures of my youthfulness are guarded
 by the stalwarts of the cosmos.[20]
Karṇa[21] flanks my Pāṇḍu cheeks;[22] Vinatā's son makes up my nose;[23]
 with blossom teeth,[24] my lips are balsam apple.[25]
Yudhiṣṭhira are my breasts;[26] my arms are ornamental scepters;[27] on my
 body blithely sits Sugrīva.[28]

[17] Throughout this song Radha boasts in puns. Here she likens her hair to Nīla, a name of Śiva, whose manifestation is the linga or phallus, shaped not unlike a tall hairbun. Nīla also means 'dark color', such as that of a raincloud or lustrous hair; and, as Ray 1973:314 suggests, nīla also refers to nīlagaṅgā or the Ganges as it descends from the head of Śiva, suggesting an image of long, cascading hair. Radha brags that her hair is nīla bidyamāne or 'manifestly nīla.'

[18] Sisera sindūra sūra lalāṭe tilaka cā̃da 'The mark of vermilion in (the part of) my head is (like) the sun and the mark (sandalpaste dot) on my forehead is (like a) moon.'

[19] Nayanata basae madane 'Madana (a name of love or the love god) dwells in my eyes.'

[20] That is, sun, moon and the love god are three heroes (bīra) or potent forces of the cosmos (tīna bhubana).

[21] Karṇa (literally 'ear'), name of a hostile stepbrother of the Pāṇḍava princes in the epic *Mahābhārata*. See following note.

[22] Pāṇḍu (literally 'white'), name of the father of the Pāṇḍava princes in *Mahābhārata*; see preceding note and see again Dānakhaṇḍa above, n. 90.

[23] Vinatā, name of the legendary mother of Garuṛa, king of birds. See Kāliyadamana-khaṇḍa above, n. 26. The prominent or aquiline nose is an element of personal beauty; see Dānakhaṇḍa above, song 15, line 5, and song 23, line 15.

[24] Puṣpadanta 'Flower-Teeth', name of a mythological Gandharva king.

[25] Bimba oṣṭha 'lips which are bimba (balsam apple).'

[26] Yuddhiṣṭhira 'stout, valiant', name of the eldest of the Pāṇḍava brothers (see nn. 21 and 22 above).

[27] Daṇḍa manohara 'ornamental staves,' i.e., scepters.

[28] Sugrīva (literally 'fine neck'), name of a monkey ruler and ally of Rāma in the epic *Rāmāyaṇa* (see Dānakhaṇḍa above, n. 229).

Near my navel Bali sits;[29] my buttocks both are Pṛthu,[30] while my waistline is a manifested lion's.[31]
Regal Puru occupies my hips, well aged yet most attractive;[32] luminary clusters form my toenails.[33]
Messenger, tell Krishna: let him come in person clutching bow and arrow—even then I shall not fear him!

Song 10

Having imbibed Radha's boastful message from Granny's lips,
Hari personally went and spoke to her with his bow loaded and drawn.

"Most of your time you spend selling your produce.
How much intelligence you must have, Radha!"
"Krishna, although I was born among cowherds,
I have my senses, while you're addle-minded!"[34]
"One hundred thousand's the worth of your head
With its blossoms of basil. You haven't the money!"
"You may address me with flattering comments;
Still I am not taken in by them, Krishna."
"You are completely intractable, Radha,
Even though you are a dairyman's daughter."
"I'm not the one who's intractable, Krishna.
You are extremely audacious, Murāri."
"You are impulsive in temperament, Radha;
This is the reason I call you unworthy."
"Kaṃsa is very implacable, Krishna.
Since I'm afraid of him, I must resist you."
"I am about to assassinate Kaṃsa;
Then I'll be able to salvage my honor."
"Only a day ago, milk was your diet.

29 Bali, see Dānakhaṇḍa above, n. 41, and refer to Kāliyadamanakhaṇḍa, n. 20.
30 Pṛthu 'wide', name of a legendary king and father of Pṛthvī (see Janmakhaṇḍa above, n. 1).
31 Tautness of waist is an element of personal beauty; see Dānakhaṇḍa above, song 15, line 12.
32 Nūpuru, the original reading, appears to be an error for nṛpa puru 'King Puru.' Puru 'ample' is the name of a son of King Yayāti in *Mahābhārata*. Yayāti lost his youth due to a curse, and was obliged by his youngest son Puru with the loan of one thousand years' youthfulness. For this service Puru was rewarded with the succession to the throne. Since he regained his youth after a lapse of a millennium, he was, as Radha notes in this passage, quite attractive even at an advanced age. Guru 'aged' here also means 'heavy'; i.e., Radha's hips are heavy and attractive.
33 Padanakha nakṣatragaṇe 'my toenails are star-clusters.'
34 Mora budhī tora kheū (= kṣipta) matī 'I have sense, you are scatterbrained.'

Now you proclaim you're a hero, you midget!"
"While I imbibed Lady Pūtanā's milk,[35] I
Extracted the life from her body, my Radha."
"Did you destroy Lady Pūtanā, Krishna?
Why, you have murdered a woman, Murāri!"
"Forefathers don't accept votive oblations[36]
From those who avoid killing murderous people."
"I cannot look at your face any longer.
You are extremely unprincipled, Krishna."
"This very day, I'll discharge these five arrows
And snatch you away from the world of existence!"
"Don't take away my serenity, Krishna!"[37]

Song 11

Krishna, you must take to heart the plea which I am making.
Try, by every effort, to control what you are feeling.
Where will you find sanctuary after you have killed me?
Think this over to yourself and recognize it, Krishna.
Don't attack! You mustn't shoot me down with passion's missiles.
You will take my life when there's no reason for it, Krishna.
I am only fourteen years of age,[38] a dairymaiden.
It's not right to murder such a woman, Vanamālī.
On a kitchen cutter I'll impale myself and perish[39]
If you should attack with those five arrows and assault me.
Krishna, this is mindless of you. Listen to my counsel:
Don't string up that bow of yours on someone else's urging.
From the arrows of your bow, my death is sure to follow;
That will also be a weighty charge against you, Krishna.
He whose force is not withstood by demons, gods or mortals
Launches an attack upon a woman with five arrows!
I was not aware my words were callous to your honor.[40]

[35] See Janmakhaṇḍa above, n. 25.

[36] Mārantāka ye nā māre / tāra pāṇi nā lae pitare 'Forefathers don't take the water of one who fails to strike the murderous.' Here 'water' refers to funerary offerings made to departed ancestors.

[37] Tohme nā kara mora nirāse, literally 'Don't make me disappointed,' i.e., don't make me devoid of hope (nir + āsa), don't lead me to despair.

[38] See Dānakhaṇḍa above, song 12, line 1, and song 39, line 11. Radha seems to age slightly through the text. For discussion see Mukherji 1971:98–99.

[39] Kāṭārata bhara karī tejibŏ parāṇe, literally 'I'll give up my life by burdening the kitchen cutter (kāṭāra).' The kitchen cutter (modern Bengali bŏṭi) consists of a curved blade fixed to a wooden base, over which the user kneels to cut foodstuffs. To this day, harrassed Indian housewives threaten to commit suicide with the aid of the kitchen cutter.

[40] Nā jāṇiā̃ rukha builŏ tohmāra caraṇe, literally 'Unawares, I spoke harshly at your

I'll fulfill your wishes, Krishna; don't release those arrows.
On your side is Granny, that incompetent old woman;[41]
She's undoing all your sense of social duty,[42] Krishna.
If you kill me, for your crime there'll be no absolution!

Song 12

I dispatched my messenger to you with quids of betel.
She did not offend you in the least, but still you struck her.
For you, Radha, there's no task which I have not attempted;
Still, throughout the universe, you've soiled my reputation.[43]
I'll discharge infatuation's missiles and attack you;
Let the monarch, Kaṃsa, try to save you from extinction.
These are shafts whose force cannot be borne by gods or demons.
Radha, I'll extinguish your existence with these arrows.
In your spirit, if you feel the least bit apprehensive,
Then you must approach your Granny humbly for protection.
Radha, for your sake I issued many supplications.
Even then, again and yet again, you simply scorned me;
Therefore I've concluded that your judgment isn't stable.
Now I hold the certain death of you within my clutches!
I will kill both you as well as virile Abhimanyu;[44]
I've made up my mind, besides, to do away with Kaṃsa.
There's no more devices left to you for your survival!

Song 13

Taking in Krishna's message, Radha went to Granny
And pleaded with her for her own saftey as follows.

Granny, you must listen; I am speaking to you humbly.
Krishna mustn't shoot those shafts at me; you must restrain him.
You've been my deliverance in every situation;
Now it's on account of you that I'm about to perish!
Have some pity on me in your heart. Hey, Granny, listen:
Speak this once to Krishna; take my life in your protection.
You who are my Granny are the messenger of Krishna.
Just this once, prevail on him so Krishna treats me kindly.

---

feet.' Refer to Hārakhaṇḍa above, n. 4.

41 Garañjālī buṛhī āche tohmāra pāśe 'The doddering (garañjālī) old woman is beside you.'

42 Loka dharama, see Dānakhaṇḍa above, n. 223.

43 Saṃsāra bharāyili tõ āhmāra khā̃khāre, literally 'You've filled the world with my disrepute.'

44 Āihana bīra 'the heroic Abhimanyu,' possibly a sarcastic reference to the sexual impotence of Abhimanyu (see Janmakhaṇḍa above, song 7).

This time, Granny, offer me security from danger.
I shall hand my ring to you; it's worth a hundred thousand.
Krishna's wrath is just the first thing. You are also angry;
From this much I gather that, for me, there's no salvation.
Put your wrath aside and speak on my behalf to Krishna,
So that Lord Dāmodara will not destroy his Radha.
Never any longer will I go against your wishes;
You may do, then, anything at all your heart desires.
Granny, will his longings be fulfilled if Krishna kills me?

Song 14

Granny had a change of heart and tried to dissuade Hari.
Receiving her counsel, he again addressed Radha:

"After trouncing Kāliya, I purified the river.
I've made my descent here for assassinating Kaṃsa.
I'll destroy my uncle; it's my stated obligation.[45]
In a herdsman's household I was born for just this reason.[46]
These five missiles of infatuation will bombard you;
Who will put your life in his protection? Let him save you!
Look at these five flower-arrows, see this bow of blossoms.
I shall take your life in just an instant with these flowers.
You have sullied me in front of everybody, Radha.
That's why I am going to assault you with these missiles.
Someone else's wife—it's she I'll strike with these five arrows.[47]
In your impudence, you've been misjudging Krishna, Radha.
When you struck my messenger before, what was your reason?
See here, now I'm taking retribution with these arrows!"
Krishna's left hand held the bow; his right hand held the arrows.
Taking aim precisely at her heart, he wounded Radha.
Reeling with those flower-fashioned arrows, Radha toppled.

Song 15

A volley of arrows from that bow, drawn by Krishna's hand,
Pierced Radha's heart. Thereupon she addressed Granny as follows:

[45] Mo likhita karama 'it's my ordained (literally, "written") karma.'

[46] Sukumar Sen has pointed out in personal consultations that the higher one's birth, the more seriously one's crimes are evaluated; since Krishna is to perform the serious offense of killing an uncle, there is a special rationale for his having been born in humble circumstances.

[47] This is a statement of daring, since by Indian tradition a man is only entitled to physically castigate his own wife.

"Granny, I'll stay here preparing an enclosure.[48]
Here I shall summon the handsome son of Nanda.
Right on this spot I'll engage in love with Krishna,
Putting my fresh, ample youth to good advantage.
Granny, why, how much affliction must I suffer?
How long, why, must I be hurt by shafts of blossoms?
Here is Vṛndāvana, Granny; here's the river;
Here you must fetch me the darling son of Nanda.
Here's where I'll cling to the hem of Krishna's garment;[49]
Here, fast embracing, I'll press my breasts to Krishna.
Granny, my youth is an elephant enmaddened.
Even the goad of my shame cannot control it.[50]
I can't endure passion's unrelenting arrows;
Though they don't injure without, they blaze with me.
Struck by invisible shafts, I can't resist them.
Krishna's assailed someone's wife with five such missiles!"[51]
Saying this, Radha passed out from love's affliction.

Song 16

Seeing Radha fallen down in stupefaction, Granny
Started speaking somewhat reprimandingly to Krishna.
"I advised you jokingly to take the life of Radha.
Krishna, how come there were no restrictions on your temper?"
"On your urging, Granny, I annihilated Radha.
Why are you now saying that you spoke to me in humor?
In advance, both you and I devised a plan together;
On that basis, Granny, I've assassinated Radha."
"Radha had not heeded my advice. I spoke in anger.
Why are you still dwelling on the things I might have told you?
How come you did such a thing without reflecting, Krishna?
You've engulfed yourself in sin by murdering a woman!"
Granny's accusations made Dāmodara feel fearful.
At the feet of Granny,[52] Krishna muttered supplications.
"Granny," he lamented, "you must find a way to save me!"

48 Sajāibõ ghara 'I'll prepare a house,' i.e., an arboreal hut or enclosure. Cf. Vṛndāvana-khaṇḍa above, n. 96.

49 Ethāñī kāhnāñīra mõ dharibõ nicole 'Here I'll hold on to the hem of Krishna's garment,' i.e., in supplication and adoration.

50 Lāja āṅkuśẽ tāka nibāritẽ nārī 'I can't control it by the (elephant) goad (āṅkuśẽ) of modesty.'

51 See n. 47 above.

52 Cf. n. 40 above.

Song 17

If you'd killed a hundred Brahmans and a herd of cattle,[53]
Still that crime would not compare with murdering a woman.
Radha was so virtuous that all the world extolled her.
She's the one whom you have murdered, vicious[54] Cakrapāṇi!
Krishna, do not touch me.
You're the killer, Krishna, of a woman.
Don't you ever touch me, Krishna.
Make a journey, Krishna, to Benares.[55] Don't you touch me.
You've debased your person with the darkness of your mischief.[56]
Krishna, you have willfully wreaked death upon a woman!
Through the universe your notoriety is spreading
—Think of this yourself and you will recognize it, Krishna.
How had she, Candrāvalī, annoyed you that you killed her?
You have killed a woman and, what's more, the king's relentless.
Carry out some strategy to save yourself now, Krishna!
On whose counsel, Krishna, have you executed Radha?
Run away at once into Vṛndāvana, don't dawdle!
Krishna, find some method for restoring life to Radha.
Then and only then will you be free from condemnation.
In that case, then even I will take your side, my Krishna.

Song 18

If I'd known that Radha would abandon this existence,
Would I, then, have shot those shafts of flowers at her, Granny?
What I did was carried out at your suggestion, Granny.
Now that it's been done, what ground have you to reprimand me?
I have no devices for restoring life to Radha.
You must make some effort to have Krishna cleared of charges!
As the moon descends and disappears when day approaches,
Radha, who surpassed the world, has suddenly expired.
Her complexion, like magnolia, had a golden luster.[57]

[53] Māyilẽ gokula 'if one killed a group (herd) (kula) of cattle (go).' Cattle killing is a censured crime in the Hindu tradition. Killing a Brahman is also regarded as a serious crime; see Tāmbūlakhaṇḍa above, n. 8.

[54] Cāṇḍāla cakrapāṇi 'you cāṇḍāla, Cakrapāṇi.' See Dānakhaṇḍa above, n. 51.

[55] Benares, name of a city on the Ganges River in eastern India, a traditional holy spot for pilgrims and penitents.

[56] Āghora pāpẽ tora beāpila gā, literally, 'You've smeared your body with ghastly sin.' Refer to Dānakhaṇḍa above, n. 253. Granny seems to suggest that Krishna's physical darkness has its origins in his misconduct.

[57] Kanaka campaka (Ray 1973 has the reading kanakacampaka) sama tāra dehayutī 'The brilliance of her body equaled golden campaka.' See campaka in Appendix.

Where's she gone to, making me the killer of a woman?
Radha had committed endless outrages against me;
It's my luck[58] that no one is aware of those offenses.
How the cowherd people all will castigate you, Granny,[59]
When they hear of Radha's having died from blows of flowers!
Or, perhaps, displaying woman's wiles, is Radha sleeping?
Who has ever perished from the blows of flower blossoms?
I'll withdraw the river tolls and all my other jesting;
Just arrange for Radha to be resurrected, Granny!

Song 19

"Underneath the kadamba you squatted at your leisure,
Then used force relentlessly upon the pathway, Krishna.
Fatally you wounded Radha, using those five arrows.
Now what do you mean, you'll give up all the tolls and taxes?[60]
What, oh Krishna, what is this you've done in killing Radha?
I'd have made her mind you if you'd waited just a little.[61]
All her friends will weep, lamenting, 'You're the king of heaven;[62]
Was there any ground for you to shoot at Radha's bosom?'
Now your family, which bore no trace of moral error,
Bears a woman's death for seven generations, Krishna![63]
Why have you destroyed a woman? You're the child of Nanda.
People will not want to look you in the face hereafter.
Only by restoring Radha's life to her this minute
Can you make your way across this ocean of wrongdoing!
'It was at my messenger's behest that I killed Radha'—
Why do you indulge in these untruthful stories, Krishna?
Purely for your own enjoyment, you have murdered Radha,
Causing me to suffer most excruciating anguish.
Now I shall arrest you! I will hold you in confinement,

[58] Tāka keho nāhī̃ jāṇe karama āhmāra 'No one knows about that (because of) my karma,' i.e., due to my having earned an ill fate. Refer to Dānakhaṇḍa above, n. 25.

[59] Phulera ghāe haila rādhāra maraṇa / śuṇī toka ki bulibe saba gopagaṇa 'What will all the herdsmen say to you (who were responsible for her safety) when they hear of Radha's death (having occurred) from blows of flowers?'

[60] Ebē̃ ki bolaha mo chāṛilõ saba dāne 'Now what are you saying—"I've rescinded all (demands for) tributes"?!'

[61] Kathodina thākilē̃ mo ditõ ṣa mānāā̃, literally 'If you'd waited a few days I'd have given her to you submitting (i.e., obedient).'

[62] Literally, 'saying: you're the lord of the thirty (gods)'; see Dānakhaṇḍa above, n. 91.

[63] Tila eka pāpa kāhnāñī nāhīka ye baṃśe / ebē̃ tiribadha tora sapata puruṣe 'Krishna, on that lineage (of yours) which had not an iota (tila, literally "sesame seed") of moral error (pāpa) there is now (the onus of) a woman's murder to the seventh man,' i.e., for seven generations. It is a traditional belief that the effects of one's good or evil actions can devolve upon one's descendants for generations.

Krishna, till once more you resurrect the life of Radha.
Slaughtering a hundred Brahmans still would not be equal
To a woman's execution, Krishna; it will haunt you.[64]
What else is there left for me, my Krishna, to advise you?
If King Kaṃsa hears of this, you'll forfeit your existence!"
With this statement, Granny made a captive out of Krishna.

Song 20

Did I see the moon on Haritālī in September?[65]
Or, perhaps, I thrust my hand inside a brimming pitcher?[66]
Or, upon the ground, I might have written words with water.[67]
Consequently, I have been arrested on false charges.
Let alone my profits, my investment has been wasted;[68]
Granny, my essential compensation has been capture.
I've not won her love, much less her kisses or embraces,
And, because of Radha, I've been so humiliated.
What will all the people say to me if they should hear this?
How can I return this day to Gokula, my Granny?
You yourself were telling me that Radha had abused me;
I annihilated Radha only for that reason.
Of divinities I am the master, named Lord Krishna;
Yet, on your account, I suffer so much aggravation.
No one can object now to the plan that I'm suggesting:
I'll restore Candrāvalī once more to her existence.
Take away the bonds so that the gods will not observe them!

Song 21

I've removed those bonds from you; now listen, Vanamālī:
Right away you must revive Candrāvalī the cowmaid.
While this matter isn't known to fearsome Abhimanyu,

[64] Śateka brahmabadha nahe yāra tule / hena tiribadha kāhnāñī saṅge tora bule 'This killing of a woman, which the murder of a hundred Brahmans would not equal, (will) linger with you, Krishna.' Refer to n. 53 above.

[65] Haritālī, name of the fourth day of the bright fortnight of the lunar month Bhādra (August–September), when Candra ('Moon') is traditionally said to have abducted Tārā ('Star') (see Dānakhaṇḍa above, n. 93). Almanacs prescribe a prohibition on the viewing of the moon on this day; to gaze upon it is said to invite calumny upon oneself.

[66] To put one's hand into a filled pitcher is considered inauspicious. This may be due to the idea of pollution, since water is symbolic of purity.

[67] It is believed that one will become impoverished if one forms written symbols on the ground with water. In personal consultations, Sukumar Sen has suggested that this is due to a feeling that writing, being sacred, should be permanent.

[68] Āchuka lābha mora mūlata āphāra 'My initial capital (mūla) is wasted (āphāra; see Sen 1971:48), leave (alone) my (potential) profit.'

Figure some contrivance for restoring life to Radha.
Now it's close to noontime;[69] it was dawn at our arrival.
Use your efforts so that Radha lives and travels homeward.
It was in the heat of my emotions I addressed you;
Failing to consider that, you took the life of Radha.
Krishna, you're impervious! You've massacred a woman.
All the universe has been degraded by you, Krishna.
On our throne, the sovereign is unrelenting Kaṃsa.
Disregarding that, you've done such deeds upon the roadway.
Any acts against you that Candrāvalī committed
You must overlook now and revive her, Vanamālī.
Then, of course, Candrāvalī will be within your power.

Song 22

Krishna lamented ceaselessly, observing before him Radha,
The consummate seductress, smitten by his flower missiles.

Due to the incitement of my messenger, I struck you.
Why make me responsible for murdering a woman?
Earlier, you snitched on me before my mother, Radha.
Just this once return to life, for everything's forgiven.
Why go off to wakeless sleep?[70] Hey, listen, dairymaiden!
Radha, rouse yourself. Candrāvalī, respond to Krishna.
This one time, attend to my request, my darling Radha.
Earnestly I'm begging you to rouse your little body!
I've withdrawn the road tolls, I have set aside your taxes.
Get up, take your dairy goods and sell them in the market!
For your sake, is there a thing that I have not attempted?
You used every possible procedure to ignore me.
Anger overcame me, I attacked you with the arrows.
How could I have known that you'd forsake existence, Radha?
Raise your face and look at me; absolve me from this evil,
And let my distress, from your aloofness, be extinguished.
Only if you live can I go on with my existence.

Song 23

When you take your pitcher on your hip and gather water,
    Radha, on your feet the anklets jingle.
Both the conchshell bracelets on your arms are gem-encrusted;
    On your forehead's radiant vermilion.

[69] Duaja pahara 'it is the second prahara (prahara refers to a period of about three hours),' i.e., six hours have gone by and noon is approaching.
[70] Māhāninda yāsi kehne, literally 'Why are you going to the great sleep (i.e., death)?'

Lost! The girl is lost! She's vanished![71]
Dairymaiden, how did you expire?
Silk is your apparel, and your stole is made of muslin;[72]
Gemstone inlays show at both its edges.
Come to life one time; imbibe my love with pleasure, Radha.
Afterward I'll carry you to heaven.[73]
In my hands are discus, conch and mace; my mount's Garuṛa.[74]
I am the celestial Śārṅgadhara.[75]
How could I have known that you would perish? If I'd realized,
Would I have attacked you with five arrows?
Radha, rise! Get up and go for selling dairy produce.
I'll rescind the taxes which you owe me.

Song 24

Come back to life just once more, dairymaiden.
Look Radha, never again will I tease you.
Radha, for once clear your face of this darkness;
I, Vanamālī, am begging forgiveness.
Radha, which realm will you make your escape to,
Leaving your Krishna to blame for a murder?
I am consigning to blazes those flower-bloom arrows
Which made you take leave of your spirit.
Just this one time you must rescue my honor
Because, after all, I am Krishna, your darling.
Look, I implore you with hands clasped together.
Lift up your head now and look at me, Radha.
Rise and address me connectedly,[76] Radha.
Please do not make Jagannātha feel anxious.
In Gokula I'm a cowherding youngster,
While out in the world, I'm the greatest of heroes.
Rousing yourself, come be seated beside me.

71 Āla bālī hari hari ṣe. See Dānakhaṇḍa above, n. 78.

72 Pāṭa paridhāna tora netera ā̃cala 'Your garment is silken (pāṭa), your ā̃cala (see Dānakhaṇḍa above, n. 21, and cf. Yamunākhaṇḍa, n. 14) is of fine muslin (neta).'

73 According to a suggestion make by Sukumar Sen in personal consultations, the reading pāche toka nibõka bilāse which appears in Ray 1935 and Ray 1973 should be replaced by: pāche toka nibõ kabilāse 'Afterward I'll take you to heaven (kabilāse).' See Sen 1971:115.

74 See Kāliyadamanakhaṇḍa above, n. 26.

75 Śārṅgadhara 'Wielder (dhara) of the Bow Made of Horn (śārṅga)', an epithet of Viṣṇu.

76 Kara samaya bāta, literally 'make timely conversation.'

Song 25

People all over the world speak in praise of your face; it's the moon at its fullest.
Girl, you appeased your own vanity, treating the lord of the gods as a porter!
Hey, girl, wake up, my delectable Radha; arise with your face raised and see me.
I can't continue to live if you won't lift that face of yours up and behold me.
I will depart for Godāvarī or to Benares, forsaking this body.[77]
Radha, because of you, at Gaṅgāsāgara I shall take leave of my body.[78]
Looking upon your unfortunate state, I can't stand it,[79] adorable Radha.
If you refuse to respond to me, I shall take refuge in self-immolation.[80]

Song 26

Krishna laid his hand upon Radha's form
And the dissipated components of her being reassembled.[81]
Meditating, Vanamālī stroked Radha with his hand.
Little by little, Candrāvalī raised her body.
In Gokula's realms, Radha lived, having perished.
The king of gods was absolved of murdering a woman!
Krishna fanned Radha with the frond of a palmyra
And had her drink pure water of the Yamunā.
Reviving, Radha arose in perfect spirits.
Her girlfriends rained joyous cries in all directions.[82]
With Radha in his power, Krishna vanished into Vṛndāvana.
Radha went in pursuit of him, frantic with infatuation.
Bumblebees and cuckoos were singing in the forest;

[77] Godāvarī, name of a river which runs through the midsection of India, having its mouth on the eastern coast of Andhra Pradesh. Like the Ganges, it is held sacred; to bathe in it confers spiritual benefit, and to commit suicide by drowning in it is thought an act of supreme penance. Concerning Benares see n. 55 above.

[78] Sāgara saṅgame = gaṅgāsaṅgata sāgare, see Vṛndāvanakhaṇḍa above, n. 104.

[79] Dharitẽ nā pārõ parāṇe, literally 'I can't control my spirits.'

[80] Ānala śaraṇa kibā karibõ / yadi nā dibẽ bacane 'If you won't give me an answer, I shall take refuge in fire.'

[81] Bihaṛila āṣṭa dhātu āyila tāhāra 'There came (back) to her the scattered eight elements (āṣṭa dhātu).' The eight elements alluded to are highly valued and are used in the fabricating of sacred images; by implication, Radha's body is likened to such an image. The eight elements are gold (suvarṇa), silver (rūpa), copper (tāmra), iron (loha or lauha), lead (sīsa), tin (raṅga or vaṅga), mercury (pārala) or brass (pittala), and zinc (yaśada) (see Monier-Williams 1976:116; Biswas and Sengupta 1976:100; Apte 1976:67).

[82] Sakhijana hulāhulī pāṛe caudiśe '(Her) girlfriends cause (cries of) hulāhulī to descend upon all four directions (i.e., round about).'

Flowers were abloom; southerly breezes were blowing.
Fashioning a bed of tender leaflets, in a twinkling
Krishna concealed himself in Vṛndāvana forest.
Reposing in that place, Nārāyaṇa waited.

Song 27

After having slain her, Krishna resurrected Radha.
Then he lurked with eager expectations in the forest.
Radha spoke as follows in the company of Granny,
While she was examining Vṛndāvana for Krishna:
"Just this moment he was here! Now where can he have vanished?
Granny, answer truthfully; my life depends upon it."
After searching here and there inside the forest, Granny
Caught a glimpse of Krishna in the middle of the arbor.
Imperious Radha Candrāvalī, through Granny,[83]
Spoke a stream of honeyed supplications to her Krishna:
"Don't you have some pity in that heart of yours, my Krishna?
Why are you forsaking now the fascinating Radha?"
Granny put the pair together, Mādhava and Radha;
Then she headed quite a distance from the spot and waited.
Gazing at his Radha looking beautiful beside him,
Krishna felt the appetite within his heart awaken.
Like resplendent markings left by gold upon a touchstone
Was the form of Radha in the snug embrace of Hari.
Krishna gave her scratches on her ample hips and bosom,
Leaving here and there upon her form his tooth impressions.
After taking in the throaty, cooing cries of Radha
Krishna then made love to her, redoubling his momentum.
As the streaming nectar of the moon is drunk by Rāhu,[84]
Radha's sweet deliciousness was well imbibed by Krishna.[85]
Then, as Krishna's amorous insistence grew excessive,
Radha started supplicating Krishna very strongly:
"Stop it, Krishna, stop it! Why, be still for just a moment.

[83] Kāhnera thānata rādhā candrābalī rāṇī / baṛāyika buila hena madhurasa bāṇī 'Queen (rāṇī) Radha Candrāvalī told Granny these words of flowing honey for Krishna.' Rāṇī or 'queen' is a title that often accompanies women's first names, possibly used here to suggest Radha's effort to modify her customary haughtiness toward Krishna.

[84] Rāhu, name of a mythical demon thought to cause lunar eclipses by attempting to devour the nectar-filled moon. As Rāhu is said to have a head but no body, the moon escapes through his throat each time.

[85] Rādhāra madhu tārapala kāhne, the reading given in Ray 1935 and Ray 1973, should be replaced by the actual manuscript reading rādhāra madhu tāra pila kāhne 'Krishna drank the sweetness (tāra, modern Bengali taar "sweetness, taste, savoriness") of Radha's nectar.'

Otherwise, my bosom will burst open from your vigor!
My affection is to be experienced at leisure.
Let me have a chance, my lord Dāmodara, for breathing."[86]
Radha's build was slender, but her youth was well developed.
Krishna pressed her bosom and made love to her intently.
Then that wily dairymaiden Radha, feigning anger,
Rose on top by force and made her Hari lie beneath her.
Deftly Radha mounted Nanda's son; he lay below her,
Splendid as a cloud on which a crescent moon is mounted.[87]
Doubly as intensively as Krishna had been doing,
Radha then made love to him precisely in his fashion.
That attractive dairymaid looked radiant on Krishna;
Murky clouds were battered, as it were, by lightning flashes.
Radha, overcome by love, gave up her inhibitions.
Restless bells kept up a ceaseless pealing on her anklets.
Krishna's eyes were blooming in the blissfulness of passion.
Radha fully satiated Mādhava's desires.
Then Candrāvalī put on her colorful apparel;
Briefly, she reclined upon the bosom of her Krishna.
Motionless, she rested in the torpor of her passion,
Looking much like Indra's bow arisen in the heavens.[88]
Granny reappeared again precisely at that juncture,
Saying to them, "Krishna, you must give your leave to Radha.
I cannot delay in going home again with Radha."
Then, when he had given Radha leave to make her journey,
Cakrapāṇi vanished, singing songs and cutting capers.

[86] Literally, 'Give me opportunities to release my breath.'

[87] This passage is reminiscent of *Gītagovinda* 12.10 (song 23) (Miller 1978). See Vṛndāvanakhaṇḍa above, n. 17.

[88] Śakrera dhanu yehna ūyila ākāśe 'like Śakra's bow arisen in the sky.' The bow of Śakra (Indra, the king of gods) is the rainbow.

Vaṃśīkhaṇḍa*

Song 1

After meeting defeat in her encounter with love,
Doe-eyed, lithe-limbed Radha left the arena with Granny.

With her Granny, Radha was proceeding on her journey.[1]
All of her companions said, "Let's go for bathing, Radha!"
Many cowmaids[2] headed toward the Yamunā embankment;
Krishna saw them going and put on a dance performance.
For a time, he played mṛdaṅga;[3] then he played the cymbals.
Radha's many girlfriends were amused when they beheld this.
Krishna entertained them every day in that location;
Using different instruments, he played to many rhythms.
Abhimanyu's wife was not perturbed as she observed this;
Krishna then created an enchanting flute for playing.
It was built beyond compare. The finger holes were seven;[4]
Golden was its headjoint, while its shaft was worked with diamonds.[5]
When, most energetically, he filled the flute with music,[6]
By its singing he could have the cosmos in distraction.
Radha, at the riverside, perceived a flute was playing;
Abhimanyu's wife then headed homeward, taking water.
In the woods, a flute was being played by Nanda's darling.

* *Vaṃśīkhaṇḍa* 'Episode of the Flute', name of the twelfth section of *Śrīkṛṣṇakīrtana*, and one of the lightest episodes of the text. This episode foreshadows Krishna's waning fascination for Radha. In an effort to restore his interest, she plots with her Granny to steal a flute much played and treasured by him. Hilarity ensues as Krishna begs and badgers Radha and the other dairymaids for its whereabouts. Ultimately Radha does return the flute to Krishna, though she fails to win a renewal of his affection.

1 Baṛāyi laiā̃ rāhī gelī sei thāne 'With her Granny, Radha was going some place (literally, "to that place").'

2 Ṣola śata gopī, see Dānakhaṇḍa above, n. 9.

3 Mṛdaṅga, a kind of drum shaped like an elongated barrel.

4 The flute's seven finger holes permit the production of each note of the musical scale.

5 Subaṇṇera sāmbī hirāra bāndhila kāma 'Its headjoint (sāmbī, from Sanskrit śamba "headpiece") was of gold (and) the (overall) work was fixed (studded) with diamonds.'

6 Literally, 'On filling the sound oṃ into it with enthusiasm. . . .' Oṃ in Indian philosophy is associated with brahman, the sacred principle; it is the fundamental frequency of the universe. Reference to it in this passage seems to suggest Krishna's supreme godhood.

Song 2

Radha drank in the warbling of the flute; her fear of Kaṃsa notwithstanding,
She questioned Granny in order to find out who was playing.

Near the river Kālindī,[7] who plays the flute, oh Granny?
In these pasturelands of Gokula, who's playing, Granny?
In my body, I'm distressed. In spirit, I feel anxious.
Since I heard the music of that flute, I've spoiled my cooking!
Who's performing on the flute, my Granny? Who's that someone?
I'll become his slave and clean his feet upon my person.[8]
Granny, who is playing on the flute in rousing spirits?
What transgression might I have committed to his honor?[9]
From my eyes the tears are streaming, Granny, in a deluge.
From the music of his flute, oh Granny, I shall perish.
Could the one who plays that sweet-voiced flute be Nanda's darling?
Possibly his purpose is to trouble my emotions.
If I were a bird, then I would fly to his location.[10]
Let the earth split open, I shall hide myself within it![11]
Granny, when a blaze burns down a forest, people know it;
But my heart is like a potter's kiln, it burns discretely.[12]
I'm consumed inside because of longing over Krishna.

Song 3

Racked with lovesickness after she took in Krishna's playing,
Upon visiting the Yamunā, Radha said this to Granny:

Now I've arrived at the shores of the Yamunā, hearing the flute's dulcet music.
Now, with a grip on my well polished water container, I've forded the river.
Now I'm not hearing the sound of the flute, Granny. Krishna, perhaps, has departed.
How, on this day, can I make my way homeward? My spirits are growing uneasy.

[7] Kālinī naikule 'at the banks of the Kālindī River.' Refer to Vṛndāvanakhaṇḍa above, n. 15.

[8] Dāsī haā̃ tāra pāe niśibõ āpanā 'Becoming his slave, I'll wipe his feet with myself.'

[9] Literally, 'What fault have I done at his feet?'

[10] Pākhi nahõ tāra ṭhāi ūṛi paṛi jāõ 'I am not a bird, (otherwise) I would up and fly to his place.'

[11] Medanī bidāra deu pasiā̃ lukāõ 'Let the earth give a crack; entering it, I shall hide.'

[12] Bana poṛe āga baṛāyi jagajane jāṇī / mora mana poṛe yehna kumbhārera paṇī 'The world knows, Granny, (when) a forest burns, but my heart burns like a potter's oven,' i.e., imperceptibly.

Krishna is dark and his ringlets are wavy; his head is embellished with blossoms.
Have you observed him, my Granny? He might have been going along on the pathway.
I am aware, day and night, of no other; to whom can I speak of such anguish?
Though, in my shame, I've prevented from crying aloud, thoughts of Krishna assail me.
Under the kadamba tree on the shores of the Yamunā, Krishna embraced me.
Thinking of that, I grow anxious, but due to his carelessness, Krishna's lost interest.[13]
Trees all about are ablossom with flowers; the breezes of springtime are blowing.
Venomous shafts seem to strike from the mango tree branches as cuckoos sit chanting.
I can't distinguish the moon from the sun. Even sandalpaste withers my body.
Each instant is an eternity, Granny, for me, in the absence of Krishna.[14]
Now that he's plundered my heart with the sound of that flute of his, where's Krishna vanished?
I am completely in flames, as if tainted with poison inside from his absence.
Now you must summon the darling of Nanda and gratify all my desires!

Song 4

With these ancient[15] eyes of mine, I cannot see, my darling.
Where should I go wandering to find Lord Krishna Hari?
Tell me of some strategy, Candrāvalī, to follow:
Then I shall endeavor to deliver Vanamālī.
Hearing all the things that you have said, my darling grandniece,
In my spirits, there's an overwhelming sense of sorrow.
How am I to put the river Yamunā behind me?
It's the home of countless crocodiles and alligators.
Even if I cross, Candrāvalī, through sheer exertion,
How am I to find Lord Cakrapāṇi once I get there?
In the forest of Vṛndāvana, it's dark and fearsome.
Bears as well as tigers, Radha, dwell there in abundance.

[13] Kāhna birasila bhole 'Krishna, in his carelessness, has lost interest (bi- + rasa-).'

[14] Kāhna biṇi mora ebẽ eka khana eka kula yuga bhāe 'Without Krishna, one moment now seems to me a series of ages.'

[15] The original reading baṛa 'big' should be substituted by buṛha 'old'.

How would I be able to escape before them, Radha?[16]
If there's any suitable solution, you must tell me.
Krishna ferried you across the stream when it was swollen;
For your sake, he took a load of produce on his shoulders.
Even then he couldn't fully satisfy you wishes!

Song 5

Come now, Granny, it's your job to save my life from danger.
I've been overcome by those five arrows of attachment.
It's delicious springtime now; the cuckoo birds are warbling.
Flames of separation are devouring my spirits.
Tell me right away, what kind of plan should I be using
So that I can somehow carry on with my existence?
Who asserts that sandalpaste and moonlight are refreshing?[17]
Granny, to my thinking, they are similar to poison.
Tendrils have become, to me, like budding inflammations;
From his flute, the notes strike blows and blows upon my spirits.[18]
His Vṛndāvana is dark and dense with trees and creepers;
It's the choicest garden in the world. Let's go there, Granny.
I have youthful tendencies that can't be managed, Granny.
Save my life by summoning the darling son of Nanda.
For me, you're an elder mother.[19] Hear what I am saying:
What I'm going through is something you cannot imagine.
Lacking Krishna, Granny, I've no certainty of living.

Song 6

In the months from June until September,[20] just as clouds release their raindrops, so my eyes are moist with crying.
Though I've paid respect with folded hands and questioned all my friends, not one of them has tried to summon Krishna.

16 Sehi bṛndābana māhā ghora bhayaṅkara / bāgha bhāluka tāe base bithara / tāhāra āgata rādhā eṛāyi kemane 'Inside (māhā) that Vṛndāvana it's dark and fearsome; tigers and bears live in it numerously; before them, Radha, how can I escape?'

17 Ke bole candana cā̃da āti suśītala 'Who says sandalpaste and moon are very cooling?' Sandalpaste ointment is said to cool the body, and the moon is said to shine with a cool light.

18 Ghāata upare ghāa bā̃śīra sāna 'The flute's notes (strike) blow upon blow.'

19 Baṛi mā, literally 'grand mother.'

20 Āṣāṛha śrābaṇa māse 'In the months of Āṣāṛha (June–July) and Śrāvaṇa (July–August). . . .' These months of the Indian calendar year are associated with the monsoon rains.

Oh-oh, Granny, listen, listen.[21] Now he's playing on the flute;[22] from which direction is the music coming?
Where you see a lovely looking place stocked well with sundry fruits and flowers, that will be the realm of Krishna.
When I reminisce on him, my Krishna, darling son of Nanda, then I feel my life is ending, Granny.[23]
Everything has lost its essence due to Krishna's absence; the surroundings round about me have grown empty.[24]
Like a bit of gold, I had him knotted in my clothes;[25] which girl has snatched him, and what evil had I done her?
I shall do no other than your bidding, Granny; I sincerely promise this to you. Please summon Krishna.

Song 7

Grandniece, you must listen, for you haven't any judgment.
Where am I to go and try to find a trace of Krishna?
Since your birth occurred within the best of herdsmen's households,
All of this behavior is unworthy of you, Radha.
This is how a girl behaves whose mother was unfaithful;[26]
She's the type who craves for other men to make advances.
She who lets herself become involved in all these doings
Cloaks herself in mischief and does harm to moral standards.[27]
Think about this, wife of Abhimanyu, and sit tightly.
People mustn't hear all kinds of tales about you, Radha.
From her childhood, I have known your mother's good behavior.
How can you be having thoughts like these? Why, you're her daughter.

[21] Cāhā cāhā, literally 'look (out), look (out).'

[22] Mauhāri, a word of uncertain origin meaning 'flute'; sometimes seen in the sequence mauhārī bā̃śi 'mauhārī flute.'

[23] One foot of the line is missing: nāndera nandana kāhna . . . sõaritẽ pāñjara śeṣa 'Nanda's son Krishna . . . remembering him, I'm dead (literally, "I'm reduced to a rib-cage"; see again Dānakhaṇḍa above, n. 274).'

[24] The original reading sakala saṃsāra bhaila 'the whole world has occurred' may be an error for sakala āsāra bhaila 'all has become pithless (blank).' Thus: kāhnāñī bihāṇe mora sakala āsāra bhaila daśa diga lāge mora śūna 'In Krishna's absence all has become pithless for me; the ten directions (i.e., the surroundings) seem empty to me.'

[25] Women keep money and other small objects knotted in the ends of the saris they wear; Radha compares Krishna to a bit of gold which she once had tied to her sari.

[26] Ducāriṇi yāra mā tāra hena gati 'she has such inclinations whose mother is ducāriṇī.' Ducāriṇī = Sanskrit dvicāriṇī, literally 'a woman who serves more than one husband'—as opposed to ekacāriṇi 'a chaste woman'. Granny's assertion is that Radha's behavior would be explicable only had her mother been promiscuous; this being not the case, Radha's actions are incomprehensible.

[27] Pāpa beāpita se dharama kare khae 'besmirches (herself with) sin and destroys dharma.'

Earlier, the business that occurred was kept a secret;
Lately, though, you have an inclination to reveal it.
Pay attention, darling, you're the wife of Abhimanyu;
Why, accordingly, aren't you afraid of all this business?
If you act in such a way, I won't come near you, Radha.

Song 8

Gathering all my companions together,
Two kinds of jasmine we'll string into garlands.[28]
Taking you there as my spokesman, I'll go to see Krishna.
Having a canopied bedstead constructed,
Using gold trimmings, I'll get it embellished.
Till daybreak comes, in that bed I will make love with Krishna.[29]
Hearing the sound of his flute, any moment
I'll kindle a fire and be immolated.
Thus, on my own, I shall end all the lapses of Krishna.
Messenger, I can't release you from service.
You must urge Krishna: be gracious to Radha.
Gathering all my companions together,
Two kinds of jasmine we'll string into garlands.[30]
Taking you there as my spokesman, I'll go to see Krishna.
I shall eat musk; I shall also eat camphor.[31]
Making a bed out of tendrils and leaflets,
I shall refresh all my body, embracing my Krishna.
Granny, I'm losing my spirits[32] in brooding,
Hearing the sound of the flute Krishna's playing.
Messenger, hear what I say: you must fetch Cakrapāṇi!
If I were granted a favor from heaven,
Into a bird I'd at once be converted.
Flying away on my own, I would travel to Krishna.
As sandal ointment refreshes my bosom,
So does Govinda, that offspring of herdsmen.[33]
Taking along all my girlfriends, I'll offer him tributes.

[28] Mo je sakhi saba saṅge karibȍ / māhlī mālatī phula gāthibȍ 'I will get all what girlfriends (I have) together; we will string flowers of māhlī (single flowered Arabian jasmine) and mālatī (Spanish jasmine) (into garlands).' See Appendix.

[29] Kāhnāñī laiā̃ ratiñā pohāibȍ 'by (making) love with Krishna, I shall pass the night (literally, cause it to dawn).'

[30] See n. 28 above.

[31] Musk and camphor, which freshen the breath, are traditional accompaniments to romantic encounters.

[32] Parāṇa jāe mora, literally 'my soul goes.'

[33] Se gobinda gopanandane / mora kucayugera candane 'That Govinda, son of herdsmen, is my two breasts' sandal.' See Vṛndāvanakhaṇḍa, n. 91 and n. 17 above.

Summon him, Granny. Together with Krishna
Let me depart for Vṛndāvana gardens.

Song 9

"Why do you wish to expire, my Radha?
I'll seek him out and deliver your Krishna.
Talking to him, I'll cajole and convince him;
Then Cakrapāṇi will pay you a visit.
Summoning him to Vṛndāvana gardens,
I shall have Krishna make love with you, Radha.
All of the torment I've seen you enduring
I will describe to him little by little;[34]
Certainly, when he recalls your affection,
Krishna will come to your forest enclosure.[35]
If there are questions which lodge in your spirit,
Then, Radha, you can convey them to Krishna.
After that, Krishna will never forsake you—
This is the truth I am telling you, Radha."
Just at this point, from the depths of the forest,
Krishna played tones on his flute. As she listened,
Radha began to be greatly excited.

Song 10

Startled by the warbling of the flute, and with eyes darting from corner to corner,
Radha animatedly engaged in conversation with Granny.

"Holding his flute,[36] with his head crowned by feathers of peacocks[37] and limbs daubed with sandal,
Granny, who's playing the flute at the base of the tree by the shores of the river?"[38]
"Bracelets he wears on his arms; on his feet, snake-head anklets. His hair is cascading.[39]

[34] Literally, 'What sufferings I have seen in you I'll recount to Krishna one by one.'

[35] Kuñjagehe 'arbor house'; cf. Bāṇakhaṇḍa above, n. 48, and Vṛndāvanakhaṇḍa, n. 96.

[36] Hāthe bhāṇḍa 'with instrument in hand.'

[37] Māthe karī cānda 'placing the moon on his head. . . .' Cānda 'moon' refers to śikhicandraka 'peacock moon', i.e., the peacock's tailfeather, which is said to have the design of the full moon upon it. See Janmakhaṇḍa above, n. 28.

[38] Yamunāra tīre kadamera tale ke nā bāँśī bolāe 'At the Yamunā's banks under the kadamba tree, who's calling (on) the flute?'

[39] Pāe magara khāṛu hāthe balayā māthe ghoṛācūlā 'On his feet are magara anklets, on his hands are bracelets; on his head is manelike hair.' See Dānakhaṇḍa above, n. 130.

Powdery gray[40] is his shadowy form. Radha, such is the young son of Nanda."
"I go to Mathurā always with you, and each time I return with you, Granny.
He stays in Gokula, though, tending calves. Such a flute he has! Where could he get it?"
"You are a dim-witted dairymaid, Radha! Of Krishna you have no conception.
Radha, for you, there's no end to the schemes which that sharp-witted cowherd is trying!"
"He plays that sweet-sounding thing very charmingly. Listening to it, I might perish!
What sort of flute is it? How does he play on it? Tell me about it, my Granny."
"Krishna's the height of urbanity.[41] He, the adorable offspring of Nanda,
Plays seven tones[42] on his flute by attaching his lips to its aperture, Radha."

Song 11

Having heard details of the flute, Radha, who basked in beauty
As swans bask in a pond, now gently remarked to Granny:

Krishna, that intriguing man, is not inside his house. From which direction is the music emanating?
Granny, I must go in search of him, for with the playing of that flute of his, my thoughts have grown distracted.
Due to the intoning of that wretched flute, my Granny, I can't stay at home to churn the milk to butter.[43]
Entering the forest of Vṛndāvana, the handsome Krishna plays upon his flute to lilting rhythms.
Granny, I'll discard my wristlets, necklaces and all, for after hearing it, I can't contain my feelings.
Though I want to move, my feet refuse to budge at all; and so, my Granny, I've lost contact with my girlfriends.
Now it's up to you to track down Krishna by the playing of his flute. You'll have to fetch him for me, Granny.

40 Dhulāe dhusara 'grayish with dust,' i.e., from powder applied to the body.
41 Nāgara
42 Sapata sara 'seven tones,' i.e., the musical scale; see n. 4 above.
43 Ghole gharata māthāni nā bule, literally 'the churning stick doesn't move in the buttermilk at home.'

Song 12

Implored by Radha to search for Hari,
The exasperated Granny addressed this reply to Radha:

Sometimes Krishna's seated near the Yamunā embankment;
Other times, in Gokula, he's playing ball. My Radha,
Offer me advice and speak sincerely on the matter:
Where am I to go, Candrāvalī, and look for Krishna?
Sometimes, in Vṛndāvana, he takes his flute and plays it.
How can I be confident of finding him? Advise me.
How much chasing must I do in search of absent people?
I'm an older person, won't you show me any pity?
Please, you must excuse me; I entreat this of you, Radha.

Song 13

In the darkness of Vṛndāvana, dark cuckoos warble.
Darkness in the form of Nanda's son now overwhelms me.[44]
With the playing of his flute, the spirit in me trembles.
Krishna comes no longer to permit me to behold him.
Nanda's darling son has vanished, leaving me forsaken.
I cannot restrain these thoughts of mine, engrossed in Krishna.
As before, without delay, my Granny, you must take me
To that garden of Vṛndāvana which I frequented;
Having spread a paste of aloewood[45] upon my person,
With my lover Krishna, I'll engage in sundry pleasures.
I'm the daughter and the wife of most distinguished people;
What, though, is my lovely youth to me without my Krishna?
Where am I to venture with my youthful beauty, Granny?
Let the earth split open and I'll hide myself within it!
Near the river Kālindī,[46] the gentle breeze is blowing.
There my thoughts are restless as I brood upon my Krishna.
Lately it is Nanda's son who has me in distraction![47]

[44] Kāla kokila rae kāla bṛndābane / ebẽ kāla haila moke nāndera nandane 'Black cuckoos cry in dark Vṛndāvana; now Nanda's son has become disaster to me.' This passage is a series of puns: the cuckoos are kāla ('black'); Vṛndāvana is kāla ('dark'); Krishna is kāla ('disaster') to Radha.

[45] Āgara candane 'a paste (candane) of aloewood.' See āgara in Appendix.

[46] Refer to n. 7 above.

[47] Previously, by contrast, it was Krishna who claimed to be distracted, due to his love for Radha.

Song 14

At the time when Krishna had me take you quids of betel,
What did you imagine? Your reaction was offensive.
When he took your load of dairy goods upon his shoulder,
Why were you unwilling to comply with his entreaties?
In the autumn sunshine, as he carried the umbrella,
You proclaimed yourself to be a faithful woman, Radha!
Vanamālī thought of sharing pleasure with you, Radha;
In the waters of the Yamunā, he trounced the serpent.
Ornamenting it with many flowers, Nanda's darling
Built Vṛndāvana because of you, for your enjoyment.
For your sake, Dāmodara has made so many efforts;
Even then, again and yet again, you've judged him harshly.
Now what your propose will be the death of me, my Radha!
Where could I succeed this time in finding Nanda's darling?
Radha, give up hoping for him; heed my admonitions.

Song 15

Since I heard the music of the sweet-voiced flute, my Granny,
    listen to this tale of what I'm cooking.
Into sour dishes I've been mixing pungent spices;[48]
    to the brim I've drenched the greens in water.[49]
Ever since I listened to that flute resounding, Granny,
    I have lost my skillfulness in cooking.
When the transverse flute[50] is played by Krishna, Nanda's darling,
    songbirds[51] seem to warble in their cages.
Thinking it was snakegourd[52] as I listened to the music,
    in some ghee, I fried unripened betel.[53]
When I hear the playing of that flute of his, my Granny,
    I become distracted in my thinking.

[48] Āmbala byañjane mo beśoāra dilõ 'I put beśoāra (loosely, "pungent spices") into a sour (āmbala) liquidy dish (byañjane).' In personal consultations Sukumar Sen has advised that the pungent spices alluded to are not suitable additions to sour curries. They include ginger, cinnamon, cardamom, coriander and others.

[49] Sāke dilõ kānāsoā̃ pāṇi 'into greens (sāke) I put water to the brim level (kānāsoā̃ "brimful"; see Sen 1971:134).' By cooking greens in excessive water one renders them tasteless.

[50] Āṛabā̃śi 'transverse flute'; as opposed to a nontransverse flute such as a recorder.

[51] Yena rae pāñjarera śuā, literally 'it's as if caged parrots are calling.'

[52] Paralā buliā̃ 'calling it paralā.' Paralā (modern Bengali paṭol, English snakegourd) is a small edible vegetable with a green exterior. See Appendix.

[53] Bhājilõ e kā̃cā guā 'I fried unripened betel nut.' The betel nut (guā) fruit, when green, is roughly similar in appearance to snakegourd (see preceding footnote), but it is not a food item.

Into bitter curries I've been squeezing juice from citrus;[54]
setting rice to boil, I left out water.
Underneath the kadamba he squats beside the shoreline
when he plays the flute beside the river.
If you should be able to get Krishna to approach me,
Granny, you'll be saving my existence.

Song 16

What you have informed me of just now does not sound pleasant.
You yourself are boasting after ruining your cooking.
Krishna roams Vṛndāvana according to his pleasure.
Don't you feel ashamed to make confessions of this nature?
You've been squeezing sour citrus juice in bitter curries.[55]
Hoping he will come, you've let your cooking go unfinished.[56]
Radha, go and search around Vṛndāvana for Krishna!

Song 17

Bent on seeking Krishna, Radha set her pitcher on her hip
And journeyed with Granny to the Yamunā's shore.

Granny, with my pitcher on my hip, I'm walking slowly.
All around the Yamunā embankment I am looking.
Though I hear the music of the flute, I can't see Krishna.
Let the earth split open, I will hide myself within it!
Search and search, my Granny, at the Yamunā embankment.
How the singing of his flute is acting on my spirits!
Playing on that cool, enchanting flute—who is that person?
Like a cuckoo perched upon a branch, his flute is warbling.
Granny, as I listen to its music, I grow giddy.
If I fail to locate Krishna, Granny, I shall perish.
Underneath the kadamba beside the river, Granny,
I have sought auspicious blessings, offering my pitcher.[57]
If one gains a blessing, then one's worries are abated;
Then and then alone will my dear Jagannātha join me.
But just now, in seeking an auspicious omen, Granny,

[54] Cholaṅga cipiā̃ nimajhole khepilõ 'I squeezed citrus (cholaṅga; see Appendix) and tossed (the juice) into a bitter curry.' Bitter and sour in the same dish is an unpalatable combination.

[55] See preceding footnote.

[56] Tāhāka āṇitẽ tohme nāmbāyilẽ āmbale, literally 'In order to have him come you set down the sour curry (from the stove),' i.e., you interrupted your cooking.

[57] Pūrṇa ghaṭa pātī baṛāyi cāhita maṅgale 'Offering my full pot (of water), Granny, I have sought maṅgala ("auspiciousness, blessing").' Small water pots, called maṅgal ghaṭ, are used to this day in Bengali domestic rituals to ensure auspiciousness.

I have not observed one single sign of finding Krishna.[58]
Now you have to recommend some plan to me, oh Granny!

Song 18

"I have searched Vṛndāvana on various occasions.
Nowhere was I able to obtain a glimpse of Krishna.
Radha darling, we must travel home without delaying.
Try to keep your feelings in control. Accept my counsel.
There's no other strategy to follow at the moment.
In the morning, we'll return at dawn and look for Krishna.
Now it's afternoon,[59] while it was sunrise when we came here;
Abhimanyu presently will come home from the pasture.
He will be disgusted with me when he fails to see you;
What he'll do to me besides, I simply can't imagine.
Krishna tests your temperament pretending to be angry.
Now is not the time for you to make attempts to find him.
Krishna is your wooer; in your absence he'll grow anxious.
On his own, he'll venture forth once more to meet you, Radha.
Other than myself, who's most concerned about your welfare?
All the time, my mind remains alert to your best interests."
So advising Radha, Granny took her and went homeward.

Song 19

In the early evening, Radha's husband went for sleeping.[60]
Suddenly, upon his flute, Govinda started playing.
Radha, at the music of the flute, became uneasy.
Suffering from loneliness, that dairymaid lamented:
"Lord Govinda, you who are the cherished son of Nanda,
Take this unprotected woman; let her be your consort!"
Fast asleep was Abhimanyu later in the evening;[61]
To her doorway Radha went and searched for Nanda's darling.
All about her Radha looked; her heart was palpitating.
Nowhere was she able to detect a glimpse of Krishna.
In the middle of the night,[62] a cuckoo started warbling.[63]

[58] A sign might be, for instance, seeing an image of the desired object in water.

[59] Haila sā̃jha upasana 'the twilight has become imminent.'

[60] Prathama pahare goāla gelā ninda 'In the first prahara (of the night) the cowherd went to sleep.' A prahara is a period of three hours; hence the passage can be interpreted: 'between six and nine PM.' Goāla 'cowherd' in this context refers to Radha's cowherd (her husband).

[61] Duaja pahare 'in the second prahara,' i.e., between nine PM and midnight.

[62] Tiaja pahara rāti 'in the third prahara of the night,' i.e., between midnight and three AM.

[63] Kokila rae 'cuckoos call.' Cuckoos are said to begin singing before dawn but cease by

In her heart, the dairymaid disconsolately brooded:
"Even by this time, he hasn't come, that son of Nanda.
Cuckoos' calls, to me, are like the messengers of Yama."[64]
As the night was ending, Radha suffered from misgivings[65]
And, at dawn, because of Krishna's absence, she fell swooning.
On her face her Granny splashed some water and revived her.

Song 20

Then, observing the lovestricken Radha before her,
Granny in her cleverness suggested a trip to the Yamunā.

"Listen to the counsel I'm providing, darling Radha.
We'll approach the Yamunā pretending to take water."
"I can travel to the Yamunā as you're suggesting,
But, upon arrival, how shall we get hold of Krishna?"
"Let us make an effort there to steal the flute of Krishna!
He is always present at the Yamunā embankment."
"If we take his flute, then what advantage am I gaining?
Answer me sincerely, I request this of you humbly."[66]
"Nanda's darling son will come approaching you in person;
For that flute of his, my Radha, he'll make supplications!"
"How are we to steal the flute of Krishna, who is always
Present at the kadamba? He seats himself beneath it."
"With a sleep-inducing charm,[67] why, I shall make him drowsy;
At that juncture, you can take his flute and travel homeward."
"If some person should observe the flute within my clutches,
Then what can I offer him by way of explanation?"
"You can fit that little flute within your water pitcher!"

Song 21

Granny accompanied Radha to the brink of the Yamunā River.
She put Mādhava to sleep with incantations for the purpose of plundering his flute.

Next to the Yamunā under the kadamba cool, soothing breezes were blowing.

---

daybreak; they are also known to call at eveningtime and even during the night on moonlit nights.

64 See Dānakhaṇḍa above, n. 225. Cuckoos do have a certain association with the death's messenger or crow, as the Indian cuckoo lays its eggs in the abandoned nests of crows.

65 Cauṭha pahare guṇiā̃ pā̃ca sāte 'Thinking five and seven things (i.e., having misgivings; see Dānakhaṇḍa above, n. 250) in the fourth prahara (between three and six AM). . . .'

66 Literally, 'Tell me the truth, I clasp your feet.' See Dānakhaṇḍa above, n. 140.

67 Nindāulī mantre 'with a sleep-inducing mantra.'

Sitting there filling his flute up with sound was the king of the deities, Krishna.
Then sleep approached and descended on Krishna, and so he did not travel homeward;
Placing the flute by his head, he lay down on a cushioning bed of fresh leaflets.
Krishna unthinkingly drifted to sleep.
Due to his absence of mind, he would forfeit his flute; fate's designs can't be thwarted.[68]
All of the maidens set out for the Yamunā River for gathering water.
There Abhimanyu's wife Radha saw Krishna asleep at the base of the kadamba.
Stealthily edging up close to his side, Radha picked up his flute in a hurry.
Into the jug on her hip she inserted the instrument, then she went homeward.
Placing her jug on the ground after reaching her household, Candrāvalī Radha
Took out the flute; in exuberant spirits, she looked at it over and over.
Later, the flute was left hidden by Radha where no one was likely to venture.
Then she reflected and reached a decision: "I'll never return it to Krishna!"
Presently Krishna awakened again from his slumber and roused himself quickly.
Looking about, when he failed to discover his flute, he set up a loud wailing.
Noticing Granny, the very distressed Śrīnivāsa[69] addressed her, lamenting.

Song 22

"After taking many pains to study its construction,
I designed a flute right here in Gokula's dominions.
Being set with precious stones, that flute of mine looked splendid.
All the world, besides, became enchanted with its music.
Writhing on the ground in my despair, I can't help crying;
In this very Gokula, I've lost that flute, my Granny.

[68] Kāhna ninda gelā hele / daiba nibandhana khaṇḍana nā jāe bā̃śī hārāyila bhole 'Krishna carelessly went to sleep; the schemes of fate cannot be broken, he lost his flute for negligence.' Cf. Dānakhaṇḍa above, n. 19. Fate's decrees are violated neither by gods nor mortals.

[69] Śrīnivāsa 'Abode of Riches' or 'Refuge of the goddess Śrī', an epithet of Viṣṇu.

On its ends were streamers made of pearls with silken tassels;[70]
Gemstones were encrusted in its plating, which was golden.
Details of my flute were known to Indra, king of heaven—[71]
So enchanting was my instrument. Who might have snatched it?"
Grieving in his spirits for the flute which he was missing,
Krishna went, to no avail, from house to house to seek it.
In his hands he laid his head; Gadādhara sat weeping.
Radha heard his crying and felt very apprehensive.
Finally Lord Cakrapāṇi thought the matter over;
From his eyes, with both his hands, he wiped away the teardrops.
Afterwards, he told about the whole affair to Granny.

Song 23

"Don't you cry, don't cry. My Krishna, listen to my counsel.
Why become exasperated, you with eyes like lotus?
You set out for Gokula when it was inauspicious;[72]
This is why your flute, which lay below your head, has vanished.
Listen, Krishna, listen; you must not become unhappy.
I'll direct you to the flute; I'll tell you all about it.
Pay attention, please, to the suggestion I am making.
You have caused the cowmaids, as a group, to feel neglected.
Now my speculation is that this could be the reason
Why they might have robbed you of the flute you had, my Krishna.
That's the clue I offer you about the flute, Murāri—
Maybe it was taken by a girl among the cowmaids.
You must fold your hands before that group of many maidens;[73]
Listen, you will then obtain your flute, oh Jagannātha."
Folding both his hands together, Vanamālī pleaded.
Seeing this, Candrāvalī could not suppress a giggle.
Krishna, catching on, requested Radha for the flute.

[70] Mukutāra jhārā pāṭakhopa dui pāśe 'On its two ends were streamers (jhārā, modern Bengali jhaalar) of pearls (mukutā) with silken pompoms (pāṭa "silk", khopa [from Sanskrit kṣupa "bush"] "hairbun, pompom, etc.").'

[71] Surapatī jāṇe mora bā̃śira bāratā 'Surapati (a name of Indra) knows news of my flute.' Surapati derives either from sura 'gods' + pati 'master' (i.e., 'Lord of Gods') or from svara 'sound' + pati 'master' (i.e., 'Lord of Music').

[72] Āyātrāñā gokula kailẽ gamane 'You made your way to Gokula at a non-journeying (a- + yātrā "journey") (time).' It is believed that certain moments are unsuitable for the commencement of journeys.

[73] Ṣola śata yubatīka kara yoṛa hātha 'Do joined hands to the sixteen hundred girls.' See Tāmbūlakhaṇḍa above, n. 19, and Dānakhaṇḍa, n. 9.

Song 24

Say, look, my Radha, all dangers are vanquished
Thanks to the sound of my flute, whose vibrations
Carry as far as the threshold of heaven.[74]
Give me my flute, Radha; count it a present.
Say, just this once, Radha, care for my honor.
Thanks to the favor of Hara and Gaurī,[75]
I got that flute, so enchanting to look at,
And, by whose resonance, Gokula prospers.
With Abhimanyu as husband, you mustn't
Upset Vanamālī. Pay heed, dairymaiden:
Give me the flute and let's end the discussion;
Look, I've caught hold of the stole you are wearing!
What will my dad, Nanda, say to me, Radha,
Hearing that I lost the flute in my slumber?
Give me the flute and fulfill what I'm seeking!

Song 25

Radha's slender body trembled when she heard Krishna's
message.
She spoke in distress to her Granny as follows:

I prepared my wares of yogurt, ghee and milk in order to
proceed to Mathurā for selling, Granny.
Krishna holds the stole that I am wearing and detains me; I have
robbed him of his flute, that's what he's claiming.
Look here, I know nothing of that flute of Krishna's, Granny;
being childish, he is seeking to compel me.
I'll discard my armlets and my clothes; my anklets and my wristlets,[76]
Granny. I'll abandon all my baubles.
Time and time again I'm being criticized by Krishna, saying,
"Such-and-such a thing is due to Radha!"
I should immolate myself in flames or tie a boulder to my neck
and die by plunging in a whirlpool.
Otherwise, perhaps, I can escape from Krishna's bullying
by swallowing a devastating poison.[77]

[74] Jāra dhunī saragaduāre 'whose sound is at (i.e., goes to) the portals (duāra) of heaven (saraga).'

[75] Bā̃śi pāila hara gaurī bare 'I got the flute by the favor of Hara and Gaurī.' Hara and Gaurī are respectively names of the deity Śiva and his consort Pārvatī. They are said to be generous dispensers of boons.

[76] Tejilõ mo tāra cīra nūpura kaṅkana 'I'm abandoning my tāra (a kind of armlet; = modern Bengali taaṛ); cīra (fine cloth); nūpura (anklets) and kaṅkana (wristlets).'

[77] Kharala, from khara garala 'strong poison.'

Say to Krishna, Granny, on behalf of me: "Candrāvalī
requests to be released. Don't start a quarrel."

Song 26

After taking in Radha's reply as conveyed by Granny,
The aggravated Krishna spoke up with the aim of recovering his flute.

I'd been admonished at home by my mother:
"Krishna, my boy, never sleep in the pasture!"
I, Krishna, failed to pay heed to her warning;
Someone has stolen my flute for this reason.
Just look, oh Granny, it's lost! Oh, it's vanished![78]
Who is the one that's brought grief to my spirits,
Stealing the flute which relieved my forlornness?[79]
Studded with various gemstones and diamonds,[80]
I had a flute which was known through the cosmos.
Radha refuses to make a confession,
But, by deduction, I know that she stole it.
Father and mother will scold Vanamālī
If they should hear word of his flute being missing.
If someone brings back my flute and restores it,
I, Cakrapāṇi, will pay compensation.
Though I've committed no insult to Radha,
Taking my flute, she is killing me, Granny!
You must command her to hand my flute over!

Song 27

After hearing Krishna's message as conveyed by Granny,
The unperturbed Radha offered Gadādhara rejoinder:

"Everyone knows you; your mother's Yaśodā, your father is Nanda the cowherd.
Though you're their son, Lord Dāmodara, you are accusing me falsely of stealing!"
"I had positioned the flute at my head and, just here, I stretched out for relaxing.
Radha, you plundered my flute when you came by this way for collecting some water."

78 Hari hari, see Dānakhaṇḍa above, n. 78.

79 Birahabinoda bā̃śi 'the flute that gave relief (binoda) in (my bouts with) isolation (biraha "separation from one's beloved").'

80 Khiñcila māṇike hirā maṇī, the original reading, should be interpreted as: khiñcila hirā maṇīmāṇike 'it was studded with diamonds and all kinds of jewels.'

"I am the daughter and daughter-in-law of fine men. Abhimanyu's my husband.
Nevertheless, you've the nerve to accuse me[81] of stealing your flute from you, Krishna!"
"I am aware very well of your tendencies, Radha; I know you completely.
This is the reason I'm asking of you: in which place do you have my flute hidden?"
"Krishna, my dear, you should offer reliable evidence. Quit speaking falsely.
All my companions are fully aware of how terribly bad I am, Krishna!"[82]
"Radha, you're naughty! Don't talk like this. Don't make this kind of remark in my presence.
Everyone realizes perfectly well that my flute was right here and you stole it!"
"Krishna, give up your suspicions; you ought to have faith in the things that I tell you.
What would I gain if I'd stolen your flute and provoked your unhappiness, Krishna?"
"Radha, take all of my finery, take all my very expensive adornments;
Yet you must give me the flute, which is crafted of gold and encrusted with diamonds."
"I'm not replying deceitfully to you, Dāmodara; I tell you truly,
It was not I who made off with your flute. Don't go starting a fight with me, Krishna."
"You filched my flute, scabby slut![83] You unprincipled cowmaid,[84] your words are untruthful!"[85]

Song 28

When I started out, what was that inauspicious moment?
Neither lizards did I heed, nor sneezes, nor a stumble.[86]
Bearing empty water pots, my girlfriends went before me;[87]
From the left side to the right, a jackal crossed my pathway.[88]
Granny, for a flute, why, what disaster I am facing!

[81] Āhme bā̃śī tora corāyila kāhnāñī mukhe āna hena bāṇī, literally, 'Krishna, you bring such words into your mouth (as these, that) I stole your flute.'
[82] Radha makes this remark in sarcasm.
[83] Chinārī pāmarī, see Dānakhaṇḍa above, n. 136.
[84] Naṭakī goālī 'chorus-girl cowmaid.' Naṭakī literally means 'dancing girl'.
[85] Satya bhāṣa nāhī̃ tore 'There's no truthful talk (bhāṣa) in you.'
[86] Stumbling as one begins a journey is considered inauspicious. Also inauspicious are lizards and sneezes (see Dānakhaṇḍa above, n. 175).
[87] See Dānakhaṇḍa above, n. 226.
[88] It appears from this passage that the crossing of a jackal from the left side of one's path to the right has inauspicious implications.

Krishna's stoking wounds with flaming poison while they fester![89]
When I'd gone some distance on that path, I noticed vultures.[90]
Female mendicants with earthen bowls in hand were begging.[91]
Shouldering his pot of oil, an oilman went before me;[92]
Perching on a dessicated branch, a crow was cawing.[93]
I shall fling my yogurt, ghee and milk to blazes, Granny.
Posing as a mendicant,[94] I'll journey into exile.[95]
Otherwise, I'll sacrifice myself in some inferno;[96]
Or, instead, I'll die by taking poison, thanks to Krishna.
I address myself to you imploringly, dear Krishna;
Writhing on the ground, I clasp your feet in supplication.
Krishna, why are you accusing me in such a manner?

Song 29

"Why do you resort to shows of crying, clever Radha?
Using woman's wiles, you want to play a trick on Krishna.
'I don't know a thing about your flute,' you try to tell me.
You yourself have filched my flute worth seven hundred thousand!
If your life is not to be destroyed by Cakrapāṇi,
Think about yourself; return my flute and hand it over.
For that flute, I'll strip you of your ornaments completely.
I'll arrest you, Radha, and I'll hold you as my captive.
If, within you, there is some desire for survival,
Then you must restore the flute to me without delaying.
After getting back the flute, Gadādhara won't quarrel;
You may then go homeward if you so desire, Radha.
But if you will not return the flute—if you beguile me—
I shall take your life without delay or hesitation!
Give me back the flute; remember, it's to your advantage.
Otherwise I'm going to annihilate you, Radha!"
When she heard this, Granny could no longer keep from laughing.

89 Ākhāyila ghāata biṣa jālila kāhnāñī 'Krishna has stoked poison in festering wounds (ghāa)!' On ākhāyila ('bitten, festering') see Sen 1971:26.

90 Being suggestive of death, vultures are considered inauspicious omens.

91 Hāthe khāpara bhikha māṅgae yoginī 'Female ascetics (yoginī) were asking alms with khāpara in hand.' Khāpara refers to a broken piece of earthen pot or potsherd. A broken pot is considered an ill omen, while a female ascetic is suggestive of infecundity and therefore inauspicious.

92 See Dānakhaṇḍa above, n. 224.

93 See Dānakhaṇḍa above, n. 225.

94 Yoginīrūpě 'in the guise of a yoginī'; see n. 91 above.

95 Mo deśāntara laibŏ 'I will take exile (deśāntara).'

96 Ānalakuṇḍata kibā tanu teāgibŏ 'Perhaps, in a pit of fire (ānalakuṇḍa), I'll sacrifice my body.'

Song 30

It's because you've lost your flute that Granny's burst out laughing at you. Listen, Cakrapāṇi, to my message.
It would be like Granny's guilty outburst if a thief called out when sneaking in a house to rouse the master.
Go on, Krishna, it was Granny—she's the one who filched that flute away from you. So why are you complaining?
I cannot make sense of her intentions; that old lady's very impudent. She's used her wiles to cheat you!
Seek the flute from her, Murāri. Viewing others as it views itself, a wicked heart perceives things falsely;
How could I have robbed you of your flute? for, when I see that you're unhappy, in my heart I'm very saddened.
You are quite astute; just think it over, you will figure out that Granny is the bane of other people.
Don't do anything that's not in keeping with my words, for they're authentic. You had better go to Granny.
I reject your accusations; furthermore, the facts about the flute which I've conveyed to you are truthful.

Song 31

You are blaming Granny and your Granny puts the blame on you; it's all a retribution for my errors.[97]
Both of you are grinning insincerely after pilfering my flute; but you should not provoke me, Radha.
Why are you antagonizing me? I'm well aware that it is you who has the flute in her possession.
I am warning you, Candrāvalī, that I'm beside myself. It's you who stole the flute of Vanamālī!
Somewhere you have stashed the flute while, falsely, you're accusing an old woman. Aren't you feeling some compunction?
What has gotten into you? You have to tell me, Radha, what your reason is for putting me in anguish.
Just this once, restore the flute to me and I'll regard it as a favor. Don't dismiss what I'm requesting.
By coincidence, I fell asleep here and you stole my flute. Return that flute, don't leave me disappointed.

97 Saba mora karamera phala 'All (this) is a fruit of my karma.' Cf. Dānakhaṇḍa above, nn. 25 and 59.

Song 32

How aware I am of Krishna's accusations, Granny!
For the stealing of his flute, he's stained my reputation.
On the day of Haritālī, when the time was evening,
Might I have observed the moon in water by reflection?[98]
Or might I have plunged my hand inside a brimming pitcher?[99]
Jagannātha claims I stole his flute; is this the reason?
Maybe I plopped down upon the seat of someone older,[100]
Or, perhaps, I wrote some letters on the ground with water,[101]
Or I might have used a broken fan to cool my person.[102]
That must be why Krishna is accusing me of stealing.
Moon and sun, the wind and ocean deities be witness:[103]
May the one who stole that flute of yours go blind completely![104]
As an honest woman, if I've done an act of stealing,
Then, this very night, may I be bitten by a cobra!
Only just before the flute was here, right where you're standing.
Possibly a cowmaid went by earlier and took it.
I, Lord Madhusūdana, am not the one who stole it!

Song 33

> "Radha, I fully perceive the fraud you're perpetrating, being aware
> Of the deception practiced by your powerfully foolish Granny."

"With the flute below my head, I slept while tending cattle.
What location did you take that flute away to, Radha?"
"Krishna, darling son of Nanda, I declare before you,
Somewhere you have lost the flute, yet I'm the one you're blaming."
"Everybody knows the flute was right in this location.
What direction did you take that flute away to, Radha?"

98 Bhādara māsera tithi catutthīra rātī / jala mājhẽ dekhilõ mo ki niśāpatī 'On the fourth lunar day (tithi) of the month Bhādra, did I see the moon (niśāpatī "Lord of Night"; see Dānakhaṇḍa above, n. 156) in water?' See Bāṇakhaṇḍa above, n. 65. Radha ponders whether she might have performed the proscribed act indirectly.

99 See Bāṇakhaṇḍa above, n. 66.

100 As an act of insubordination, sitting on the seat of an elder (guru) is counted a moral offense.

101 See Bāṇakhaṇḍa above, n. 67. Radha wonders whether she performed this inauspicious act inadvertently, since she does not know writing (see Dānakhaṇḍa above, n. 29).

102 Winnowing instruments or hand fans are both considered inauspicious when broken. In personal consultations, Sukumar Sen has remarked that such broken objects are suggestive of domestic chaos.

103 Cānda suraja bāta baruṇa sākhī '(The gods of) moon, sun, wind and ocean are witness (to my declaration).'

104 Literally, 'Let the two eyes of whoever took your flute be eaten (i.e., destroyed)!'

"You can make a search for it through all my dairy produce.
You're the one who lost the flute someplace; it's me you're blaming."
"Shut up, Radha. Don't say such outrageous things before me.
You're the one who stole my flute. I know about it fully."
"I have sun and moon; they'll offer witness for me jointly.
Since you've blamed me falsely, you'll go blind completely, Krishna!"[105]
"You have robbed me of my flute worth seven hundred thousand;
What is more, you're giving me your curse, audacious Radha!"
"I had wares of milk and ghee and buttermilk; they're ruined.
I shall lodge a protest at the portals of King Kaṃsa."[106]
"I am not intimidated by your demon Kaṃsa.
Look, I seize by force the very stole which you are wearing!"
"Since you falsely raise a charge of stealing and detain me,
Certainly I, Radha, will bring ruin on you promptly!"
"If you fail to give me back my flute, you're going nowhere.
Be aware of this and hand my flute back as a present."
"Honestly, Gadādhara, I'm not the one who took it!"

Song 34

> Imbibing Radha's harshly worded message of denial,
> Kaṃsa's foe lamented unceasingly for his flute.

Rings were welded to my flute upon its outer surface;[107]
Purest gold was used to make it splendid.
Hearing that the flute which was below my head is missing,
What will brother Balabhadra tell me?
Who has snatched that charming flute? Oh dear, oh dear. Say, Radha,
Lovely one, I can't control my feelings.
Through the playing of that flute, I chant the fourfold Vedas—
Yajur and Atharva, Ṛg and Sāma.[108]
Hearing that the flute beneath my head was snatched by someone,
What will all the gods be saying, Radha?
I have necklaces and armlets. Take them all, oh Radha;
Only bring my flute to me, restore it.

105 Cānda suruja mora āche duyi sākhī / āhmā michā doṣa kāhna khāibi duī ākhī 'I have two witnesses (to my actions or words), (the gods of) moon and sun; you blame me falsely, Krishna. (Your) two eyes will be eaten (i.e., destroyed; see preceding footnote)!' There is a belief that lying results in diminished eyesight.

106 Such a protest is lodged at the palace gates, since a complainant does not dare to go uninvited beyond the king's threshold.

107 Nāla bāndhila tāra bāhire 'Rings were attached to its outsides.' Rings (nāla) might be put on the shaft of a flute to strengthen it.

108 Ṛga yaju sāma ātharbba / cārī beda gāð mo bā̃śira sare 'Ṛg, Yajur, Sāma and Atharva—I sing the four Vedas in the voice of my flute.' According to Vaishnava doctrine, the very foundations of Hindu belief originate with Krishna. See Dānakhaṇḍa above, n. 53.

Then I'll give you ornaments; I'll give you forest garlands.[109]
Anything you ask for, I will do it.
To my intuition, lovely Radha, it's apparent—
You're the one who's caused my flute to vanish.

Song 35

It was for gathering Yamunā water
That I approached; of your flute I've no knowledge.
Since, Krishna, you are divine Cakrapāṇi,
How can you utter these vile accusations?
Just by your head was the flute; having lost it,
Why do you blame me dishonestly, Krishna?
Krishna, as long as I've lived to the present,
No one has ever accused me of stealing.
Everyone's fully familiar with Radha;
Yet, in your view, I am merely a robber.
You must have grown simply frantic with passion;
Probably, then, you made good your own purpose by
Giving the flute which was yours to some woman!
Why, King of Gods, do you make me the culprit?
What I have told you, my Krishna, is honest.
Krishna, your flute isn't in my possession.
Go to the lady on whom you bestowed it!

Song 36

"Listen, wife of Abhimanyu, you're the one who robbed my flute; I'm after you for just this reason, Radha.
Giving me the flute will be entirely to your advantage; once I have it, I'll go home contented."
"Listen, I am not the one who took your flute; then why are you provoking me? You're just a prankster, Krishna.
I would use your flute for mixing cowdung if I found it;[110] or I'd break it into pieces,[111] then I'd burn it!"
"I have scanned the mortal world, the heavens and the underworld by introspection. You're the one who took it.
Wife of Abhimanyu, you should properly be sorry, yet you're smirking! Now you'd better hand it over!"

109 Banamālā 'garlands (or: necklaces) (mālā) of forest (bana) (flowers)'. Forest garlands are associated with Krishna (see Janmakhaṇḍa above, n. 10).
110 Ghasi ghāṭie 'I (would) turn (mix) cowdung.' See Yamunākhaṇḍa above, n. 9.
111 Cāri cīra kari 'I'd make four pieces of it and. . . .' Four is an arbitrarily chosen number; the intent is 'several pieces.'

"You demand the flute from me when you're the one who lost it in the bushes. Oh, my spirits can't endure it!
I'd cut off the nose and ears[112] of anybody else who said such things, but you I spare, since you're my nephew."
"All the gods are thoroughly acquainted with me. Devakī's my mother, while my father's Vasudeva.
What's the reason you presume to curse me, Radha? You, Candrāvalī, are just the daughter of a cowherd!"
"When he hears you're asking for the flute from me, the wife of Abhimanyu, then King Kaṃsa will be angry.
You're the one who, time and time again, has placed his curse on me; it's you yourself who'll suffer for your error!"
"Don't respond severely in this manner! Leave me hope to gain the flute; for I'm divine—I'm Cakrapāṇi."

Song 37

"Radha aggravates me with her refusals.[113]
Tell me directly, Granny, the way to recover the flute."

"Radha's companions are many in number.[114]
You have to go on your own to them, Krishna.
Pray to each one with your hands pressed together;
Then you'll be given your flute, Jagannātha.
Wipe off the tears from your eyes. How you're weeping!
Inwardly, Krishna, I burn with compassion!"
"Granny, the universe knows me as Hari.
I am discussed in the sacred traditions;[115]
Of the divinities, I am the master.
How can I pray with my hands pressed together?
I shall be humbled so very profoundly—
What will the gods say on hearing about it?"
"Listen to me, youthful scion of Nanda.
All are concerned, Krishna, with their own interests.
If you'll address her with hands pressed together,

112 See Tāmbūlakhaṇḍa above, n. 32.

113 The original reading in this Sanskrit verse, nirāśasavanena, is difficult to interpret; for translation purposes it is substituted by nirāśavacanena 'with disappointing words (i.e., refusals)'. However, for an attempt to interpret the original reading sensibly, see Ray 1973:269.

114 Ṣola śata rādhāra saṅgiṇī 'sixteen hundred are Radha's companions.' See Dānakhaṇḍa above, n. 9.

115 Āhmā laā̃ purāṇa bākhānī 'The purāṇas speak (or: speak praise) concerning me.' See Dānakhaṇḍa above, n. 53, and, concerning Vaishnava purāṇas, see Vṛndāvanakhaṇḍa above, n. 84.

Then Radha's heart will be satisfied, Krishna.
How can it be you're not grasping the matter?
Krishna, you can't get your flute by contrivance!"[116]
"Even if I hold my hands pressed together,
Will Radha give back the flute to me, Granny?
What if I'm ridiculed later by people?
Watch, then, as Krishna the lord, at your urging,
Ventures to Radha with hands pressed together."

Song 38

Seeing before her Mādhava uttering words of entreaty
With folded palms, Granny said this to Radha:

Out of his eyes run the teardrops in torrents,
Pouring as clouds do from June till September.[117]
Due to his crying, his face is distorted.
How much distress on his part must I witness?
Over his flute, Cakrapāṇi's in mourning.
Bring back that flute now, restore it, my Radha.
Krishna, the lord, has his hands pressed together;
Now you should give him his flute as a present.
Krishna's neglecting his handsome appearance;
Physically, he is in fragile condition.
Listen attentively to my suggestion:
Radha, you ought to be gracious to Krishna.
Just place the flute in the hands of your Krishna;
Let the divine Jagannātha be happy.
Then, Radha, what there may lurk in your feelings
You can recount on your own to your Krishna.
Krishna will cheerfully act on your bidding!

Song 39

Heeding Granny's pleas, the infatuated Radha
Addressed Gadādhara with contrived solicitude.

Your inclinations defy all description.
You have a different idea every minute.
But, since you've realized the need, Jagannātha,
You, who are lord, hold your palms pressed together.
Offer this oath in the presence of Granny—

[116] Taṇḍī kayilĕ 'by doing taṇḍi.' Taṇḍī is related to Sanskrit taṇḍaka 'juggler'. See Sen 1971:388.
[117] Megha yehna āṣāṛha śrābaṇe / jhare tāra pāṇī nayane 'Like clouds in Āṣāṛha and Śrāvaṇa, water pours from his eyes.' See n. 20 above.

Swear that you'll never dismiss my instructions.
Krishna, you went to Vṛndāvana forest;
Playing your flute here and there, you ignored me.
Each time I listened, my dear Vanamālī,
I grew distracted because of your absence.
Now you must firmly decide on it, Krishna—
Never are you to refuse my entreaties.
You'll gain your flute once again on complying;
This much I tell you, Dāmodara, truly.
With your own lips, you will have to assure me
That you will never cause grief to me, Krishna.
Then I'll explain where the flute is positioned.

Song 40

Though slackened by the enormity of his delight on taking in Radha's assurances,
Krishna addressed Granny as follows with some urgency for the flute's recovery.

Granny, you must listen with attention to my message.
I shall be sincere in what I tell you.
I'll do nothing, Granny, which in any way opposes
That which Radha's stated in your presence.
Radha must return my flute and let me go on living.
Granny, dear, convey my words to Radha.
Through my own mistakes, I've had to take the consequences
Of whatever grief I've caused to Radha.
Now I've thought it over and I've made a resolution
Not to disregard what she's requesting.
You are well acquainted with my disposition, Granny;
I do not go back on what I promise.
Since you are aware that this is true, persuade her, Granny;
Radha must return the flute to Krishna!
No one is acquainted with the character of Krishna
As you are acquainted with it, Granny.
I'll comply unfailingly with Radha's stipulation.

Song 41

Hearing Krishna's message as conveyed by Granny,
The anguished Radha gently addressed Mādhava:

"I cannot describe to you how greatly I feel saddened
Listening to your message from the lips of Granny, Krishna.
I was in perplexity because of your aloofness;

That was why I took away your flute, my Vanamālī."
"You yourself are guilty if my absence caused you anguish.
It was vengefulness which made you take the flute, my Radha.
If you had refrained from bringing down my reputation,
Would I, then, have made you feel the pain of separation?"
"It was due precisely to the fact that I maligned you
That my life was withering in fires of estrangement.
Nevermore are you to be inconstant in your feelings;
Please don't be annoyed with me on anybody's urging."
"In my heart, I'm not at all annoyed with you, my Radha.
Realize this sincerely and return the flute to Krishna.
If you offer back the flute, my spirits will take comfort;
Then you'll easily be in good grace with Jagannātha."
"If I search for you when I'm insane from separation,
You must come to me without the slightest hesitation.
Look, survey your flute with care, and then accept it, Krishna.
From now onwards I, Candrāvalī, will be your servant."
"All of your mistakes, Candrāvalī, have been forgiven;
Furthermore, your Vanamālī wishes you no evil."
After having thus obtained his flute, in happy spirits
Krishna traveled home from the embankment of the river.[118]
Radha, later on, was taken home again by Granny.

118 Kālī naitīre haitẽ 'from the edge (tīre) of the Black (kālī) River.' Cf. n. 7 above and refer to Vṛndāvanakhaṇḍa, n. 15.

Rādhāviraha*

Song 1

Though her heart was lost to Krishna,
Somehow Radha carried on as usual for a time with her
household labors.
Being lovesick, however, in Hari's absence,
Radha with eyes surpassing a doe's eventually spoke to Granny:

Messenger, it's been forever.
Vanamālī's still not coming.
How long will it be until I find him?
In my dreams, I'm seeing Krishna;
In my thoughts there is no other.
Isn't there some way for me to find him?
March is here; it's nearing April.[1]
What remains for me to hope for?
My abundant youth has proven fruitless.
When I lie beneath the kadamba,
The flames which sear my soul
Consume my spirits even more severely.
Into space he's vanished,[2]
With his charming flute in hand,
And with his garb of finest muslin—such was Krishna.
On my friends' advice, I lay
On moistened lotus petals.[3] Still,
Compared to them, why, even flames are cooler.
Krishna sent me basketfuls
Of flower blooms and betel quids,

* *Rādhāviraha* 'Radha's Isolation', name of the thirteenth and final episode of *Śrīkṛṣṇa-kīrtana*. Having at last submitted both in love and devotion to Krishna, Radha struggles desperately to evoke his response. Krishna will have none of it, however, as he explains (song 29) that yogic discipline has made him immune to her appeals. Though he later relents—to the extent of permitting a final meeting—ultimately the story concludes with Krishna's departure toward Mathurā for the fulfillment of his divine mission upon earth.

1 Āila caita māsa 'The month of Caita (= Caitra, i.e., March–April in the Indian calendar) has come.' Caitra occurs in the hot season preceeding the monsoon.

2 Gelā ākāśe 'has gone (vanished) into air.'

3 Waterlotus petals, like moonlight and sandalpaste (see Vaṃśīkhaṇḍa above, n. 17), are regarded as cooling.

But I refused to lay a hand upon them;
Krishna is dismayed with me
Because, although I slapped you,
I would not accept his quids of betel, Granny.
Messenger, look here, I clasp
Your feet; my very life is ending!
Tell me of some method for survival!
In the morning, from the Malabars
There blow refreshing breezes;[4]
In Vṛndāvana, the cuckoos warble.
Going to the river's mouth,[5]
I'll trim my person of its flesh
And use myself to feast the ocean creatures![6]
I've no luck in life, it seems—
I'm out of touch with Krishna.
Having lost him, I might not regain him ever.[7]
Or, perhaps, I left a vow
Undone in some preceding life;[8]
In consequence, I might be missing Krishna.
You must summon Vanamālī!

Song 2

Seat yourself and listen to the dream I had in early evening—[9]
        let me tell you everything about it.
Underneath the kadamba, embracing me, sat Krishna in my dream—
        upon my face he kissed me, Granny.
My existence, Granny, is in vain.
You have to fetch me Krishna!
Then he spoke to me; he sweetly played upon his transverse flute,[10]
        with sandal ointment spread upon his person.

[4] See Vṛndāvanakhaṇḍa above, n. 5.

[5] Sāgarasaṅgama giā̃ 'Going to sāgarasaṅgama . . . ,' i.e., going to the union (saṅgama) of the river with the ocean (sāgara). Refer to Bāṇakhaṇḍa above, n. 78.

[6] Gāera mā̃sa kāṭiā̃ / āpaṇā magara bhoja diā̃ 'I myself, with flesh cut from my body, will be a feast for the magaras.' On magara (a kind of aquatic creature) see Dānakhaṇḍa above, n. 130.

[7] E janme bā nā kayilõ bhāga / hārāyilõ kāhnera lāga / āra tāra nā pāyibõ lāga 'In this life, perhaps I haven't had (literally, "done") luck; I've lost contact with Krishna; no more will I gain his contact.'

[8] Kibā puruba jarame / khaṇḍabrata kaila āhme 'or, perhaps, I did a vow-breaking in an earlier life.' See Dānakhaṇḍa above, n. 18.

[9] Literally, 'in the first night,' i.e., the first three hours of the night or first prahara (see Vaṃśīkhaṇḍa above, n. 60).

[10] Āṛabā̃śī, see Vaṃśīkhaṇḍa above, n. 50.

Later on,[11] I had a dream that Krishna had requested me for love,
but I refused to give permission.
Later in the night,[12] though, I was dreaming that I sat on Krishna's lap
and, toward his face, I cast my glances.
With the smiling[13] look upon his face, he stole my heart away. The love
that he inspired made me giddy.
Toward the dawn,[14] as Krishna drank my lips, my taste for love was
roused—then callous cuckoos' warbling broke my slumber!

Song 3

Granny, why, even in dreams, I see Krishna.
Lost am I, lost![15] I can think of no other.
Granny, my spirits are burning with passion.
Lost am I, lost! I've been struck by its missiles.[16]
Blossoms of jasmine[17] are blooming in arbors.
Summon me, Granny, the warden of forests![18]
Southerly Malabar breezes are blowing.
How they affect me! I can't comprehend it.
Let me call Krishna at once; till the morning
We'll while away night in the pleasures of passion.
Always the armlet I wear slithers down
And descends on my arm; I'm becoming so wasted.[19]
Keeping a watch, never blinking my eyes,
On the path of his coming, I'm growing distracted.
Why is it now, in my fullness of season,
That Krishna's becoming annoyed with me, Granny?[20]
You must make Krishna approach me this instant!

11 Duaja pahare 'in the second prahara.' See Vaṃśīkhaṇḍa above, n. 61.

12 Tiaja pahara niśi '(in) the third prahara (of) the night'; see Vaṃśīkhaṇḍa, n. 62.

13 Īsata badana karī 'making a little (īsata) face,' the original reading, seems to be in error and should be substituted by: hasita badana karī 'making a smiling (hasita) face.'

14 Caūṭha pahare 'in the fourth prahara'; see Vaṃśīkhaṇḍa above, n. 65.

15 Ki hari hari 'why, hari hari.' Refer to Vaṃśīkhaṇḍa above, n. 78.

16 Literally, 'by love's five arrows'; see Bāṇakhaṇḍa above, n. 4.

17 Neālī 'double flowered Arabian jasmine'; see Appendix.

18 Āṇiāra banamālī 'You must bring Vanamālī!' See Vṛndāvanakhaṇḍa above, n. 129.

19 E mora bāhura balae / saba khana khasiā̃ paṛae 'This armlet of my arm slips and falls all the time.' The slipping down of one's armlet, symptomatic of a lovesick person's wasted condition, is alluded to by the poet Kālīdāsa in Act Three of the play *Abhijñānaśākuntalam* and in the opening lines of his narrative poem *Meghadūta*.

20 Ebẽ mora saṃpuna baese / kike kāhna kare āmariṣe 'Now, on my completion of (coming of) age, why is Krishna annoyed?'

Song 4

Radha, in your hands I placed the betel quids of Krishna.
At my head you flung those very quids of betel, Radha!
Lately, though, that heart of yours is smoldering in fire.
Bundle up your youthfulness and try to save its freshness![21]
Radha, why, your mind's become deranged, you dairymaiden.
Where am I to find the son of Nanda and Yaśodā?
On your person, Radha, I put fragrant sandal ointment,
But, with your left foot,[22] you wiped away that fragrant sandal.
Now what further message will you tell me, dairymaiden?
Krishna's gone beyond Vṛndāvana; he's vanished, Radha.
There were countless things I tried to say to you for Krishna;
But, with your left hand,[23] you dealt a slapping to me, Radha!
Now, because of Krishna, your survival is in peril—[24]
What am I to do about it? Is there some solution?
After making many supplications of you, cowmaid,
Cakrapāṇi, lord sublime, is absolutely seething.
Now you must sit tight; assume control of your emotions.

Song 5

Youthfulness, possessions—all is worthless to me, Granny.
Breaking up my strand of giant pearls, I shall disperse them;
From my head, I'll wipe away the traces of vermilion;
Into dust I'll pulverize the conchshell of my bracelets.
As a gift, restore my life to me, you heartless Granny!
Thanks to mortal errors on my part, I'm missing Krishna.
Going to the sea, I'll shave my head and throw my hair in;
Posing as a mendicant,[25] I'll journey into exile.
If, in retribution for my errors, Krishna shuns me,
I'll procure some poison; by my very hand I'll take it.
In romance with Krishna, I had not achieved fulfillment;
Fate has snatched the treasure which was knotted in my clothing.[26]
Be that as it may, my Granny, you can still assist me;

[21] Poṭali bāndhiā̃ rākha nahulī yaubana 'Tying a bundle (poṭali), keep your blossomed youth (therein)!'

[22] This suggests an act of extreme ingratitude. See Dānakhaṇḍa above, n. 66. The foot, being the lowest part of the body and that least likely to be kept clean, is held in low regard.

[23] The implication is that insult has been added to injury. See preceding footnote.

[24] Literally, 'Now, for Krishna, your life (or: soul) is going.' Cf. Vaṃśīkhaṇḍa above, n. 32.

[25] Yoginīrūpa dharī 'taking the form of a yoginī'; see Vaṃśīkhaṇḍa above, nn. 91 and 94.

[26] See Vaṃśīkhaṇḍa above, n. 25.

Just this once, you simply have to summon me my Krishna!
On my head I've hair like Śambhu's;[27] on my crown's vermilion.
After he observed this, how could Krishna go so distant?
By withdrawing, Krishna has deprived me of my master.

Song 6

Krishna is the darkness;[28] he's unyielding in his feelings. Not in gestures nor in words will he approach you.
Krishna has departed for Vṛndāvana because he's suffered anguish more than once for your affection.
Discipline your feelings, for you must sit tightly, Radha.
Krishna has gone someplace of his own these days in order to protect himself; now how am I to trace him?
Smoldering inside as he reflects on your behavior, and ignoring both what's righteous and unrighteous,
Krishna's sworn a vow and disappeared into the middle of Vṛndāvana, dismissing your affection.[29]
Fairfaced girl, what clues am I to go on? Where am I to find a trace of Krishna? You yourself must tell me.
Must I use no end of schemes to summon Lord Murāri for you? Only then can I persuade him, cowmaid.
What distinctive marks can I detect him by? Gadādhara's an actor; he adopts no end of poses.[30]

Song 7

"Granny, come on! You must spare my existence.
Arrows of love are beyond my endurance!"[31]
"Where is this love of yours? Where are the arrows?
How can those shafts take away your existence?"
"Cuckoos are calling, for spring is the season.
Those are the arrows, the love's in my feelings!"
"Lend your attention to what I'm suggesting:

27 Māthe śambhu sama khõpā 'on my head is a topknot like Śambhu's.' Refer to Dānakhaṇḍa above, n. 146.

28 Kāla kāhnāñī 'Krishna is kāla.' Kāla has multiple senses, including 'dark', 'sinister', 'disaster'. See Vaṃśīkhaṇḍa above, n. 44.

29 Pratijñā kariā̃ kāhne gela mājha bṛndābane tora nehe tilāñjali diā̃ 'Krishna has made a promise (to himself) and gone into the midst of Vṛndāvana, giving tilāñjali to your love.' See Bhārakhaṇḍa above, n. 59.

30 Naṭaka se gadādhare aśeṣa muruti dhare koṇa cihne pāibõ uddeśe 'That Gadādhara is an actor (naṭaka, literally "dancer, performer"); he takes no end of forms. By what characteristic can I trace him?'

31 Sahitẽ nārõ manamathabāṇa 'I cannot endure infatuation's shafts.'

Sleep out of doors in the rays of the moonbeams."[32]
"What, should I sleep in the rays of the moonbeams?
Then, Granny, passion becomes more tormenting!"
"Here's my advice; in your heart, think about it.
Spread cooling sandalpaste over your person."
"That very sandal is roasting my person!
Take me and go to Vṛndāvana, Granny!"
"Tigers and bears throng Vṛndāvana densely.
How are you going to travel there, Radha?"
"Let me be eaten by bears or by tigers!
Let my life end while I'm searching for Krishna!"
"How will you get past the Yamunā River?
Radha, it surges with powerful currents."
"If I should drown in the waves of the river,
Then I shall go and gain union with Krishna!"
"Radha, relinquish your longing for Krishna!"

Song 8

Take a hundred golden pieces,[33] Granny, and get moving.
Go for me in search of Krishna, master of my spirit.
Krishna's hair is like a mane;[34] he's shadowy in color.
By these clues, my Granny, search in Gokula for Krishna.
Granny, he spreads fragrant sandalpaste upon his person,
And he plays a dulcet flute, with cymbals on his fingers.
Krishna's form is dark; the clothes he drapes it in are yellow.
As he goes along, he's flanked by many dairymaidens.[35]
Front and back a muslin garment trails him; that's his costume.[36]
Anklets on his feet resound with pleasant pealing jingles.
Take some camphor-scented quids of betel with you, Granny;
Rigorously search for him. You have to fetch my Krishna!
Search at first within the house of Vasudeva, Granny;
Krishna's childlike character is thoroughly beguiling.[37]
Look within Yaśodā's lap, if there you fail to find him;

[32] Bāhira candrakiraṇe soa 'Sleep in the moon's rays outside.' Refer to n. 3 above.

[33] Literally, 'Take a hundred palas of gold and begone. . . .' A pala is a traditional measure equivalent to about one and one-half ounces; thus one hundred palas of gold is a valuable amount.

[34] Māthāte ghoṛācule 'with manelike hair on his head'; see Dānakhaṇḍa above, n. 130.

[35] Literally, 'sixteen hundred dairymaids go at his side.' See Dānakhaṇḍa above, n. 9.

[36] Neta dhaṛī pindhi āgu pāchu lāmbāe 'He puts on a muslin dhoti (dhaṛī "lower garment") and lets it extend front and back.'

[37] Ābāla caritra kāhna māyā baṛa kare 'Krishna, in his portrayal of a child, makes great māyā.' See Bāṇakhaṇḍa above, n. 5.

That's where Krishna makes a show[38] of being lost in slumber.
If you fail to find him there, then search along the river;
That's where Krishna goes for tending cattle in the pasture.
If you do not find him there, then search the river crossing.
Near the river Yamunā, he roams with other youngsters.
Strenuously search within Vṛndāvana for Krishna;
Up the different kinds of trees, to eat the fruits, he clambers.
Bearing staff in hand, he plays a flute with keen enjoyment.
Look for him to be with Nārada[39] in that location.
Once you've sought him there, if you do not discover Krishna,
Then you'll have to look for him among the cowherds, Granny.
Seek him there as well as in the places of our meetings;
There, perhaps, he may be dallying with other cowmaids.
If you've sought him there and you have still not found that cowherd,
Go, then, to the banks of the Bhāgīrathī[40] and seek him.
Search the house of Sāgara,[41] if there you still don't find him;
Urgently seek news of him from Sāgara, the cowherd.
After going there, if you do not discover Krishna,
Then you must make inquiries of everybody, Granny.
You may then gain clues about where Jagannātha's staying.
There, I've told you everything from start to finish, Granny.
Krishna will approach my presence only on your bidding.

Song 9

Radha, I'm so utterly decrepit that, my darling, I do not possess the stamina to travel.
You yourself must search for Krishna; this is my advice to you. Accept it, Radha; don't reject my counsel.
Travel on your own upon the path where you obtain some clue; and then you'll be united with your Krishna.
After you succeed, through constant searching, in detecting Krishna's whereabouts, then speak to him politely.
Here's another tactic I'm suggesting: you should clasp him by the feet, for when you do, he'll treat you kindly.

[38] Māya pāte kāhnāñī tathā̃ nindabhole 'There Krishna makes a māyā of being lost in sleep.' Cf. preceding footnote.

[39] Tathā̃ cāiha nārada muni saṅge 'Seek him together with the sage Nārada there.' See Janmakhaṇḍa above, n. 12.

[40] Bhāgīrathī is a synonym of the Ganges, usually applied to the portion of the river eastward from its confluence with the Yamunā at Allahabad.

[41] See Janmakhaṇḍa above, song 7, line 6. Since Radha and Krishna are acquainted from childhood as playmates, the household of Radha's father, the cowherd Sāgara, is a haunt of the youthful Krishna.

Travel to the town of Mathurā, traversing sundry mountains, forestlands and caverns, tracking Krishna.
After you have striven to the utmost while observing Caṇḍī's worship,[42] then you'll get a glimpse of Krishna.
Go along to Mathurā and Hari may receive you there. You mustn't leave his side thereafter, Radha!

Song 10

Readying buttermilk, milk goods and yogurt,
Off we'll go selling in Mathurā market.
Granny, although we may not sell our produce,
Still I'll have managed to speak there with Krishna.
Mathurā's name has my heart weeping, Granny.
Listen, look here, I've an urge to see Krishna.
Wearing a garland with blossoms of medlar,[43]
And, on my ears, fixing earrings with diamonds,[44]
Costliest silken apparel I'll dress in,
Only to swoon on beholding my Krishna!
Right from the moment of meeting my Krishna,
I shall forsake him no longer, oh Granny.
Like an ascetic intent upon yoga,
I am aware of no other than Krishna.
Granny, I failed to pay heed to your counsel,
Shunning the betel-leaf quids sent by Krishna.
All that I did was because of misjudgment.

Song 11

Isn't springtime known about there, Granny,
In the realm where Cakrapāṇi's dwelling?
Nowadays my spirit is in torment—
Burning like the oven of a potter.[45]
Granny, which direction must I travel—
Where am I to find my cherished Krishna?

[42] Baṛa yatana kariā̃ caṇḍīre pūjā māniā̃ 'Making great effort while observing Caṇḍī's worship. . . .' Sukumar Sen has advised in personal consultations that Caṇḍī is typically the goddess appealed to when a person or animal is missing. Her name figures in the poet's sobriquet, Caṇḍīdāsa 'Slave of Caṇḍī.'

[43] Baūla 'Indian medlar'. See Appendix.

[44] The original reading, kaṇṇata kuṇḍala hirāra dhāra, may be substituted by: kaṇṇata kuṇḍala hirādhāra '(with) diamond-bearing (hirā "diamond", dhāra "holding, bearing") earrings on the ears. . . .'

[45] Ebẽ mora maṇera poṛanī / yena ūye kumbhārera paṇī 'Now my heart is aflame, smoldering like a potter's kiln.' See Vaṃśikhaṇḍa above, n. 12.

Greedy for the honey, bees are buzzing,
Granny, in the blossomed trees of mango.
Cuckoos perched on branches there are warbling—
Devastating me like bolts of lightning.[46]
Demons, human beings and celestials
All are subject to the shafts of passion;
Does there not, then, dwell infatuation
There, where my Nārāyaṇa is staying?
When I find him, I'll embrace my Krishna
To my upraised, firm and fulsome bosom.
If Dāmodara should still refuse me,
Then I'll simply gaze at him and perish.
I declined to listen to his pleadings,
Nor would I accept his quids of betel.
What I did was all for lack of judgment.

Song 12

I'll give the facts to you: your Vanamālī
Is very offended, Candrāvalī, having
Been made to approach you with hands pressed together;[47]
This is why Krishna has spurned you and vanished.
Ah, now you're anguished because of his absence!
Where will you venture to find Cakrapāṇi?
This is the thing which your girlfriends are seeking;
They want for Krishna to spurn your affection.
Then in the woods of Vṛndāvana, Radha,
Those very cowmaids will frolic with Krishna!
Your Vanamālī, Candrāvalī Radha,
Abides in Vṛndāvana forest, indulging
His whims in a gamut of savory pleasures
With hundreds[48] of cowmaids. He cheats on you, Radha!
Come, let us go to Vṛndāvana, Radha;
There we may garner a glimpse of your Krishna.
Maybe then Krishna will even address you.

[46] Yehna lāge kuliśera ghāe 'That affects (me) like a volley of lightning.'

[47] Yoṛahātha karī banamālī / tāta baṛa pāila āpamāna 'Vanamālī folded his hands together (before you); from that he has received great humiliation.' See Tāmbūlakhaṇḍa above, n. 19, and Vaṃśīkhaṇḍa above, songs 37 and 38 and n. 73.

[48] Literally, 'with sixteen thousand dairymaids'; see Dānakhaṇḍa above, n. 9, and cf. n. 35 above.

Song 13

Abhimanyu's wife was physically racked with love's missiles.
Anxiety overtook her; her every pleasure was gone.
Brooding constantly upon Hari's actions,
She addressed herself to Granny as follows:

For his sake, I cared for no one else; I disregarded other people, both superior and lowly.[49]
Now it seems to me that Krishna's spurning me in anger; in Vṛndāvana, he cheats with other women.
Granny, just how many sorry stories shall I tell you?
In a way of speaking, I have plunged into a wellspring that's gone dry on me;[50] I'm such a wretched woman!
Krishna is the darling child of Nanda; he's Yaśodā's son, the one to whom I offered my affection.
Seeking to conceal what's taken place, I've aired the secret—in return for this, I'm getting proper justice:
I've a stringent husband who's a celebrated herdsman; and his sister carps at every word I utter.
Furthermore, the dairymaids have all maligned my reputation, saying, "Radha's spending time with Krishna!"
I have been enduring all this torment for the sake of Krishna's love. Oh Granny, take me to my Krishna!

Song 14

Oh, she's lost! She's lost![51] Don't fret, but listen, dairymaiden.
Presently your cherished Vanamālī will be coming.
Lost, she's lost! Don't let your moonlike face be gloomy, Radha!
Looking at your physical condition, I feel saddened.
Stick with me and, Radha, let your spirits take assurance;
Krishna, on his own, will come from Gokula and meet you.
Come along, we'll travel to Vṛndāvana together,
Searching through the arbors[52] for Nārāyaṇa, your lover.
We must ask of everyone for information, Radha;
Certainly Lord Madhusūdana's been seen by someone.
One by one, you have to tell me all the details, Radha—
How your Krishna moves about, the forms he's been assuming.
Surely someone's bound to know where Krishna may be staying;

49 Literally, 'I did not mind people light (laghu) or weighty (guru).'

50 Daha 'wellspring, whirlpool'; here a metaphor for Radha's love affair with Krishna.

51 Hari hari, cf. n. 15 above.

52 Cāhi kuñje kuñje tora priya nārāyaṇe '. . . looking in arbors and arbors for your dear Nārāyaṇa.'

Let's continue asking till we gain a glimpse of Krishna.
Whether Nanda's son be tending cows or in the forest,
Whether in Vṛndāvana, on land or in the water,
We shall seek him everywhere and summon Śrīnivāsa.[53]

Song 15

Messenger, the son of Nanda—laughing, singing, playing flute—makes journeys on this path. Have you seen Krishna?
Twisted in a circle is his hair; his topknot's bound with peacock feathers; golden blooms adorn his headdress.
Mounted like a full moon in the heavens, fragrant sandal dots the dark and cloudlike sheen of his complexion.
Flawless as a lotus is his face; dark waterlotus are his eyes. His ears are bright with jeweled earrings.
Gems in series form his teeth; his throat's adorned with giant pearls. The sight of him rejuvenates his Radha![54]
Sandalpaste anoints his form; his feet wear anklets, belled and serpent-headed.[55] That's his costume and appearance.
Into space he's vanished[56] with his flute in hand and finery of muslin for apparel—such was Krishna.
Wretched Radha that I am, I've been deprived of him. Now, Granny, let us search the forestlands for Krishna.
There, perhaps, we might succeed, by means of your intelligence, my Granny, in obtaining information.

Song 16

You are like my very self to me, for you're a grandniece.
I shall not advise you anything which might mislead you.
Krishna always comes to where the kadamba is standing;[57]
Taking staff in hand, he keeps the pasturelands protected.
Cowmaid, go. Proceed to the embankment of the river;
That is where you certainly will find the youthful cowherd.
In Vṛndāvana, be it at night or in the daytime,
Your Nārāyaṇa enjoys the many fruits and flowers.
There he takes his pleasure with the youthful dairymaidens.
Radha, if you travel there, you'll get a glimpse of Krishna.

[53] Śrīnivāsa, see Vaṃśīkhaṇḍa above, n. 69.
[54] Jīe rāhi tāra daraśane 'I, Radha, survive by the vision of him.'
[55] Ghāghara magara pāe '. . . (and) with serpentine-headed (magara) bell-anklets (ghāghara) on his feet. . . .' Refer to n. 6 above.
[56] Se kṛṣṇa gelānta gagane 'That's the Krishna who's gone into the sky.' Cf. n. 2 above.
[57] Ābasi āise kāhna kadamera tale 'Krishna habitually comes to the base of the kadamba.'

Start your trip auspiciously;[58] be stout of spirit, Radha.
Once you're there, the longings of your heart will find fulfillment.
I'm acquainted thoroughly with all of Krishna's conduct;
He can't stay away from where the kadamba is standing.
Rest assured, my Radha, of the counsel I have given;
Nothing am I telling you apart from what's authentic.
Let's go cheerfully to where the kadamba is standing!

Song 17

Binding her hair with some flowers she'd gathered
And, having dressed in apparel of muslin,
Into a tin she put betel with camphor,
Carrying with her a flask filled with water.[59]
Such was her love that, on Granny's instructions,
Radha set out in exuberant spirits.
When to the kadamba's base she'd proceeded,
Radha constructed a bed from fresh leaflets;
Rubbing her person with aloewood ointment,
Both of her eyes she adorned with mascara.
Leaves on the trees were disturbed with the breezes;
Radha imagined that Krishna was coming.
Heaving a sigh when she failed to detect him,
Radha requested assurance from Granny.
Under the kadamba, elegant[60] Radha
Remained for a good deal of time in this manner,
But still, through ill fortune,[61] she failed to find Krishna.

Song 18

Hot with the fire of love after long remaining
Under the kadamba, Radha lamented without ceasing:

Daytimes I'm roasted to death by the sun; by that wretch of a moon in the evenings.
Sleep is eluding me, Granny.[62] Oh, how are my spirits to suffer this torment?

[58] Literally, 'making an auspicious journey (śubhayātrā)'; i.e., starting out with the right preliminaries and at an auspicious moment (see Vaṃśīkhaṇḍa above, n. 72).

[59] Bhṛṅgāra bhariā̃ naila jale / bāṭā bhari karpūra tāmbule 'Filling a flask, she took water, having stuffed a tin with camphored betel.' The flask of water is for drinking, while the betel-leaf quids are for refreshing and scenting the mouth.

[60] Rādhā rāhī 'queenly Radha' or 'beautiful Radha.' See Ray 1973:273.

[61] Nā pāila kāhnāñī daibadoṣe 'She did not find Krishna, owing to her defective fortunes.'

[62] Literally, 'my eyes are not approached by sleep.'

Comforting sandal I rub on my limbs, but my sense of forlornness still lingers.
Granny, the earth should split open, I feel like concealing myself in its belly![63]
Damn her to blazes, that sinister messenger!
She roused me, urged me, and got me to come, but I've wasted the night here for nothing.[64]
Granny, I asked you before what I'd gain if I tendered affection to Krishna.
Now I'm approached by and nearly in reach of the imminent death of me, Granny!
Misery doubly afflicts me on having devoted so few days to pleasure.[65]
Being no longer allowed to observe Krishna's face is reward for my errors.[66]
Always my cheeks were receiving the kisses of Nanda's adorable offspring.
Due to my wretched neglect, who has snatched such a treasure right out of my fingers?
What was the need to blow air on that well-nourished fire? It blazed to begin with.[67]
Being unable to closely embrace him, for me, is a thorn in the bosom.
What good, to me, are possessions or youth? What is hearth, what is home to me, Granny?[68]
Eating and drinking aren't one bit appealing;[69] what hope do I have for survival?
Shaving my head, I shall wander through various lands as a female ascetic!

Song 19

Very terrifying is the night; it's dark and cloudy.
All alone beneath the kadamba, I'm seated, weeping.

63 Lukāŏ tāhāra peṭe '(May) I hide in its belly!'

64 Dahe paisu kāla dūtī / uthāā̃ pāthāā̃ āhmā āṇila niphale pohāila rātī 'Let the sinister (kāla) messenger enter a whirlpool! Rousing and goading me, she brought me (here, but) I've fruitlessly spent the night.'

65 Dina pā̃ca sāta rasata lāgiā̃ duguṇa poṛani sāre 'In my marrow the torment is double due to the amorous enjoyment of (only) a few (literally, five–seven) days.'

66 Āra tāra mukha dekhitē̃ nā pāilŏ karamaphala āhmāre 'I did not get to see his face further; that's the fruit of my misdeeds.'

67 Ekē̃ dahadaha ghasira āguṇa āre ke nā jāle phuke 'At the outset (ekē̃ "at once") the cowdung (fueled) fire was burning intensely (dahadaha); who stoked it on top of that by blowing?' The fire here is a metaphor for Radha's passion; the stoker was Granny.

68 Ki mora basatī bāśe 'What, to me, is my settlement (basatī) and home (bāśe = vāsa)?'

69 Āna pāṇī moke eko nā bhāe 'Food and drink don't appeal to me one bit.'

All about[70] I'm looking, but I fail to notice Krishna.
Let the earth split open and I'll hide myself within it.
Granny, I'm unable to suppress my youthful feelings.
All the time this heart of mine is crying to see Krishna.
Bumblebees together, male and female, make a hubbub;
Cuckoos perch on branches of the mango trees and warble.
Granny, I regard them as the messengers of Yama![71]
When will he, the offspring of Yaśodā, end this sorrow?
In the forest I arrived in great anticipation,
But the handsome son of Nanda still has not approached me.
Day by day my well developed youthfulness is lapsing;
Krishna fails to understand this fact; that's my misfortune.[72]
It's the spring, and breezes of the Malabars are blowing.
Wafted from the distance is the scent of blossomed flowers.
Don't delay, but quickly fetch me Nanda's darling, Granny!

Song 20

Underneath the kadamba upon the path to Mathurā, the springtime breeze is gently blowing, Granny.
Having just prepared a bed, my Granny, out of different kinds of flowers, I am calling, "Krishna! Krishna!"
Say, dear Granny, summon Krishna; Granny, look, you must bring Krishna.
How am I to be transported over isolation's ocean?[73] It's profound, oh Granny, and enormous!
I shall be delivered if and only if my Krishna, using both my breasts as rafts,[74] conveys me over.
Granny, in this forest of Vṛndāvana I'm anguished unto death. When I recall the love of Krishna,
Then my thoughts are not to be appeased by any means; for want of Krishna, I shall imminently perish.
Though I've searched each inch of this Vṛndāvana, oh Granny, I have not discovered any trace of Krishna.

70 Literally, 'in the four directions.'

71 See Janmakhaṇḍa above, n. 13, and Vaṃśīkhaṇḍa above, n. 64.

72 Kāhnāñī nā bujhe daibẽ e biśeṣa 'Krishna does not understand this fact because of (my) fate (ill fortune).'

73 Biraha sāgara mora gahīna gambhira baṛāyi ehāta kemane hayiba pāra 'For me, Granny, the ocean which is separation (from him) is enormous and profound; how am I to cross it?'

74 Yadi kāhnāñī kara pāra e mora kucakumbha bhelā karī hae mora tabẽsi nistāra 'If Krishna, using these jug-breasts of mine as flotation devices, conveys me, then and then only shall I be safe.'

Song 21

Seeking Mādhava in the forest, Radha became exhausted.
Then, feverish with love, she spoke to Granny.

Wretch that I am, I did not pay attention
To that which my lord, Jagannātha, requested.
Lost! I'm forsaken! It seems to me lately
That this must be why I am dealt such affliction.
See, Granny, this is my earnest entreaty:
Tell him that Radha requests his affection.
She from whom Krishna was seeking affection
Was only an immature infant, my Granny;
Now that my youth has become well developed,
My Krishna's deserted me; where has he vanished?
Vanquishing sin with his lotus-like glances,
Krishna, whose face is the moon at its fullest,
Relishes love with some other young woman,
Placing me in the extremes of affliction.
What have the fates preordained for me, Granny?[75]
That youthful cowtender shows me no pity.
I have discovered no trace of my Krishna.

Song 22

"Just recently Govinda was eager to make love with me!
Granny, I submit to you;[76] tell me how to approach him."

Recently, Granny, I saw in a dream,
Coming to me, Nanda's darling.
Capturing him in my tendril-like arms,
Intimately I embraced him.
Playing his flute, he's arrested my soul.
Lost! Oh, I'm lost! Ah, Govinda!
Various ornaments gleam on his throat;
Dark like a cloud is his person.
Anxious in spirit because of his love,
I brood and I brood in his absence.
Various blooms I laid out for a bed;
Then, in his arms, I was lying.
That was the instant at which I awoke—

[75] Literally, 'What has fate written on my forehead?' See Dānakhaṇḍa above, nn. 17 and 19.

[76] Praṇāme 'I bow (to you)', in the Sanskrit verse preceding the song, is an error for praṇame, the proper inflected form of praṇam- 'bow, submit'.

Dawn was at hand; night was wasted.[77]
Gladdened by Krishna with gestures of love,
A woman's existence is fruitful.

Song 23

"Radha, as my grandniece, you should listen to my counsel.
Playing on his flute at dawn, Gadādhara departed.
Krishna has set out to reach the forest, so I gather;
Going there, I'll look for him. No need for you to worry."
"You're a silly Granny; why, you haven't any judgment.
How'd you let that trove of virtues slip between your fingers?
Come, we'll have to travel to Vṛndāvana together;
Once we're there, we'll surely find the darling son of Nanda."
When they reached Vṛndāvana as Radha had suggested,
Then, to Radha, Granny gave the following instructions:
"Go ahead now by yourself to search for Krishna, Radha.
Then and only then Lord Cakrapāṇi will approach you."
Radha's heart rebounded when she heard her Granny's counsel.
On her own, Candrāvalī proceeded through the forest.
Spotting Vanamālī as he wandered tending cattle,
Radha fell unconscious due to sheer infatuation.
Splashing water right away upon the face of Radha,
Granny, acting urgently, restored her to her senses.
Radha, on recovering awareness, started speaking:

Song 24

You're my master, Vanamālī. Due to my aloofness
While I was a youngster, you were made to feel distracted;
I refused your betel quids and blooms, I struck your spokesman.
Being love incarnate, please absolve me of that error.[78]
Thoughtlessly, because of foolishness, I caused you sorrow
Underneath the kadamba; for that sin, too, forgive me.
Lord Gadādhara, excuse as well the lapse committed
Time and time again when I disdainfully addressed you.
And, whatever hurt I caused when crossing in the dinghy—
Pardon me that error too; I clasp your feet, oh Krishna.
For the sin of any further anguish which I caused you,
Loading you with burdens, please excuse me, Jagannātha.
I ignored your urgings as I went for fetching water;

[77] Niphale pohāila rātī 'I had spent (literally, made to dawn) the night fruitlessly.'

[78] Seho doṣa khaṇḍa mora madanamurutī 'Dispel as well that sin for me, you who are the image of love!'

Pardon me for that mistake as well, Lord Cakrapāṇi.
You're the cherished son of Nanda; do not disregard me.
Spare my life, oh Krishna, by bestowing your embraces!
How long will you bear a grudge against a helpless woman?

Song 25

Dairymaid, each time you went for selling dairy produce,
I paid great devotion to you; why did you ignore me?
Taking you across the Yamunā, I bore your burdens;
Even after that I couldn't satisfy your wishes.
In your youthful arrogance, you gave me great affliction.
Radha, I don't care to see that face of yours hereafter!
You're a big man's daughter[79] and the wife of Abhimanyu.
How have you the nerve now to pursue Lord Cakrapāṇi![80]
Radha, I'm ashamed to mention acts that you committed.
Tricking me, the king of gods, you made me carry burdens.
Go along, you dairymaid; be off! Restrain your feelings.
Head for home, attend upon your husband Abhimanyu.
What's the point of making these entreaties of me, Radha?
I'm proceeding through Vṛndāvana; now, don't annoy me.
Nowadays I look upon your youthfulness as rubbish!
That is how I've overcome my feelings for you, Radha.
Recognizing this to be the case, be off; go homeward!

Song 26

Krishna, you're the son of Nanda; you are Vanamālī;
You're the overlord and ruling master of the cosmos.
In the form of Narasiṃha, you destroyed the demon;[81]
You've descended into Gokula for slaying Kaṃsa.
You who are Govinda, Madhusūdana and Hari—
Take me with you, Lord, when you return to your dominion!
Now that you have claimed my soul with varied acts of passion,
Krishna, you are going elsewhere, leaving me distracted!
Having had to search for you, my life is all but finished.[82]
Only now have I caught up with you, Lord Hṛṣīkeśa.

79 Baṛāra bahuārī tohme āihanera rāṇī 'You are the daughter-in-law of a big person, wife of Abhimanyu.' Cf. Yamunākhaṇḍa above, nn. 4 and 5.

80 Koṇa lājẽ bhaja ebẽ deba cakrapāṇī 'How dare you (literally, "by what shame do you") now adhere to Lord Cakrapāṇi?'

81 Narasiṃharūpẽ tohme hiraṇya bidārī 'In the form of Narasiṃha (Man-Lion), you tore apart Hiraṇya (Hiraṇyakaśipu).' See Dānakhaṇḍa above, n. 193.

82 Tohmāka cāhiā̃ bhaila pāñjara śeṣa 'Seeking you, my life is ending (literally, "I'm reduced to a ribcage").' Refer to Vaṃśīkhaṇḍa above, n. 23.

My enticing youthfulness is pointless in your absence;
Knowing this, I went to where the kadamba is standing.
There, because of you, I wasted all the night for nothing—
Even then you wouldn't let me witness your appearance.
Once you were intoxicated with my youthful beauty;
Through your messenger, you sent me camphorated betel.
In a state of mindlessness, I struck your spokesman, Krishna;
Now my heart is anguished in the flames of your aloofness.
Oh, my lord, I fold my hands before you and entreat you:
Banish to the distance all the grievances I've caused you![83]
Offer me permission to be seated in your presence.

Song 27

Don't approach me! People will say ugly things about us.
Stand apart when speaking, Radha. Listen to my message.
Now I recognize that there's an age of doom upon us—[84]
Over others, women have a preference for nephews!
What is this dispute that you are starting with me, Radha?
I don't covet women who belong to other herdsmen!
You received your breeding in the very best of households;
I should be the same as God to you, for I'm your nephew.
Radha, to amuse myself with you would not be proper.
You must not continue, Radha, trying to incite me.
Giant pearls to grace your throat I sent you through my spokesman;
In response, you called yourself a faithful little maiden!
Why is it that, nowadays, your heart's on fire, cowmaid?
Bundle up your youthfulness and try to save its freshness!
Dad is Nanda Ghosh; my uncle's stalwart Abhimanyu.
She who reared and fed me milk was mother—that's Yaśodā.
You're an aunt to Vanamālī; that's why I avoid you.

[83] Āhmāra sakala doṣa khaṇḍaha bidūre 'Banish afar all my errors (against you)!'

[84] Ebesi jāṇila bhaila kali ābatāra 'I have just realized that the descent of kali has occurred.' In Indian philosophy, time is divided into ages of unequal length called yugas, of which there are four; in order, the kṛta or satya yuga, the tretā, the dvāpara, and the kali or age of doom. The four ages are associated with progressive moral degeneration and are said to be concluded with the arrival of Kalki, the last descent of Viṣṇu. (See again Kāliyadamana-khaṇḍa above, n. 24.) Further details about the four yugas are available in *Viṣṇupurāṇa*, bk. 1, chap. 3 (Wilson 1972:19ff.) and *Mārkaṇḍeyapurāṇa*, canto 46 (Pargiter 1969:224ff.).

Song 28

Count yourself a bumblebee; forsake the forest, Krishna.[85]
Come to me, a lotus flower blooming in the wasteland.[86]
Why are you adopting this decision to forsake me?
This is not becoming to a man of your refinement.
Passion's missiles strike at me whenever I behold you.
Exercise some pity on me, callous-hearted Krishna!
Not at all[87] are you a close relation to me, Krishna;
Rather, you're my one salvation—check on this with Granny.[88]
Nourishing great hopes, I filled my hair with flower blossoms;
In pursuit of you, to this Vṛndāvana I wandered.
Krishna, be appeased with me in body and in spirit;
You who are divine, just once display consideration.
I, Candrāvalī, am fully worthy of you, Krishna;
Yield your love to Radha. You're her cherished Vanamālī.
Don't allow my youthfulness, oh Krishna, to be wasted.
Krishna, you must gratify a person who entreats you.
Offer your embraces, you'll be sparing my existence!

Song 29

"By day and by night I practice yogic meditation.[89]
I've arrested the currents of the mind in the plexus of the sky.[90]
I have consumed the nectar in the lotus of the lowest plexus,[91]

85 Guṇa bujhi madhukara parihara bana 'Understanding (yourself to be) a bumblebee, leave the forest.'

86 Āisa bana mājhẽ bikaca nalīna 'Come (to) the blossomed lotus in the wilderness.'

87 Kāhna mora kuṭumba sahodara nāhi matī 'Krishna, you are not at all (matī) my family relation.'

88 Eka tohmā gatī puchiñā̃ cāhā dūtī 'You are the one salvation; ask the messenger and see!'

89 Yoga dheāi 'I meditate (in) yoga.' Details of the yogic regimen (sādhana) which Krishna has undertaken are given through the balance of this song. It is a significant portion of the text in two ways: first, in that it shows the poet was not only familiar with the tenets of yoga, but also expected the same awareness in a contemporary audience; second, in that it links *Śrīkṛṣṇakīrtana* as a work of Middle Bengali literature to the much older *Caryāpadas* or Buddhist tantric songs, which comprise the sole extant corpus of the Old Bengali language. A critical edition of these songs is available in (Nilratan) Sen 1977.

90 Mana pabana gagane rahāi 'I arrest the mind-wind in the sky.' The expression mana pabana 'mind-wind' also occurs in *Caryāpada* 19.2 as a code word for mental restlessness. To arrest the 'mind-wind' in the 'sky' (gagana) is to cause one's thoughts to be concentrated on the highest truth. This is an aim of sādhana or yogic regimen.

91 Mūla kamale kayile madhupāna 'I have drunk the nectar in the fundamental lotus.' In yogic physiology the body is said to contain several plexuses, called lotuses in Hindu tantra, which extend along an imaginary line from the lower trunk to the head. The process of attaining enlightenment is said to involve the symbolic 'drinking' (raising) of a

And now I have attained spiritual understanding.[92]
Be off with you, exquisite Radha!
You lust in vain to possess Krishna.
At the conjunction of the Iṛā, Piṅgalā and Suṣumnā channels,[93]
I have arrested the currents of the mind.[94]
I've barred the tenth door;[95]
I've taken now to the yogic path.[96]
I have broken the spikes of love by the missiles of enlightenment,[97]
And therefore I am no longer fascinated by your youthfulness.
Now there is no discord in my person;
I look upon the entire world as hollow."
Divine Cakrapāṇi, that most urbane of men,
Answered Radha without sympathy;
He continued to meditate, his heart unmoved.

---

vital fluid from the lowest plexus to the highest. This fluid is widely termed nectar and the lowest plexus (or lotus), said to be situated between penis and anus, is the mūla or fundamental.

92 Ebẽ pāiñā̃ āhme brahmageāna 'I have now attained the wisdom of brahman.' Perfect enlightenment is said to be attained when the vital fluid reaches its maximum ascendancy (see preceding note) and is consumed by the heat of the energies generated in sādhana. At this point—the stage of awareness in which existence and sentience merge—the sādhaka or practitioner is said to be absorbed into brahman, the ultimate principle of the universe.

93 Iṛā piṅgalā susamanā sandhī 'At the conjunction of Iṛā, Piṅgalā and Suṣumnā. . . .' Yogic physiology postulates a number of channels within the body, of which three are the most important: the Iṛā, said to be feminine, on the left side; the Piṅgalā, said to be masculine, on the right side; and the Suṣumnā, which rises through the middle of the body. The point of merger of these three, in the lowest plexus, is the point of origination for the body's vital fluid.

94 Mana pabana tāta kaila bandī '. . . there I have captured the mind-wind.' The vital fluid (see n. 91) must be roused, controlled, and made to ascend the central channel, avoiding the right and left channels, so as to reach each of the physiological plexuses in turn. Controlling the vital fluid in the lowest plexus in preparation for its ascent is said to involve a process of steadying the mind (here, the mind-wind; see n. 90). *Caryāpada* 3.10 enjoins the sādhaka: 'Steady it (the mind-wind) and cause it (the nectar or vital fluid) to move!'

95 Daśamī duyāre dilõ kapāṭa 'I have put a bar on the tenth door.' Tantric physiology adds to the nine bodily apertures (mouth, nostrils, ears, eyes, anus, and penis) a tenth aperture or 'tenth door.' It is said to be situated in the rear of the oral cavity, at the opening of the throat. Unless blocked, it is believed that the vital fluid or nectar, on approaching the highest plexus, will escape and be wasted. The yogic practice referred to as stopping the tenth door involves severing the frenum of the tongue so as to allow the tongue to be turned back and inserted like a stopper into the throat. *Caryāpada* 3.5 refers to this practice. For details, see Dasgupta 1969:242 and Eliade 1973:247.

96 Ebe caṛilõ mo se yogabāṭa 'Now I have embarked on that yogic path.' The process of enlighenment is typically described as a way or path with many intermediary stages. For a complete study see Eliade 1973.

97 Geānabāne chedilõ madanabāṇa 'I have broken love's arrows by enlightenment's arrows.'

Song 30

When, ultimately, she had imbibed the unpalatable reply of
Madhu's foe,[98]
The seductress of the world[99] beseechingly addressed him:

Stung to the soul by love's missiles,
I'm the most wretched of maidens,
Tender as gooseberry blossoms.[100]
Clasping your feet, I entreat you:
Don't make me die of estrangement!
Aren't you afraid of the sin of destroying a woman?
Why, Krishna, do you refuse me?
Lift up your face and observe for yourself my condition!
While this existence yet lingers,
Let me obtain your approval.
This meditation of yours will be death for me, Krishna.
Why did you fail to reject me
Right from the first time you met me?
Now you are making me utterly miserable, Krishna.
All through the night I kept vigil
Due to my love for you, Krishna;
Being unable to find you, I felt very wretched.
Now that I've managed to meet you
Thanks to whatever my blessings,[101]
Please, Lord Dāmodara, try to regard me with favor!
You see the state of my being,
Yet, in your heart, you're unyielding.
It's not for me, as a woman, to understand menfolk.
Joined with you, I'll go on living
If, even now, you'll show mercy.

Song 31

Listen to my history, for I'm the lord named Rāma—
foremost in the lineage of Raghu.[102]

[98] Madhuripu 'Madhu's foe', an epithet of Viṣṇu-Krishna; cf. Yamunākhaṇḍa above, n. 28.

[99] Jagatāṃ ramyā 'the (most) desired woman (ramyā) of the world (jagat).'

[100] Labalīdalakoalī 'tender (as) petals (of blossoms) of country gooseberry (labalī)'. See Appendix.

[101] Ebe pāyilõ daraśane la / āra jaramera pune 'Now I have obtained a sight (of you) due to whatever merit (I have accrued) in other (earlier) lives.'

[102] Raghubaṃśa paradhāna 'principal member of Raghu's lineage.' Raghu is the name of the founder of the lineage in which Rāma (see Tāmbūlakhaṇḍa above, n. 21) was born.

I cut off the tenfold heads of Rāvaṇa of Laṅkā—
Rāvaṇa, who thrived with sons and allies.[103]
Vasudeva is my father, Devakī's my mother.
Radha, I've dismissed you from my thinking.
I was born, my Radha, in a household of distinction;
I don't get involved with other women.[104]
In the universe, I am the quintessential master.[105]
I'm Nārāyaṇa, Mukunda,[106] Hari and Murāri;
through the ages, I take incarnation.
I have made the earth secure by devastating demons,
thwarting all their evil machinations.
Radha, while the herdsmen have no knowledge of your longing,
banish it; go home, you shameless woman.

Song 32

You are destiny's reward to me for acts of penance.[107]
Why do you command me to go home, oh trove of virtues?
If, forsaking everything, you turn into a yogi,
I'll become a yogi, too,[108] attending on you, Krishna!
Anguished in your absence, I have suffered very greatly.
Nevermore shall I go home, for you'd be left forsaken.
Lord Gadādhara, you mustn't shatter my existence;
How can you be unafraid of murdering a woman?
Dreaming and awake as well, it's you of whom I'm thinking;
I've received a fine reward from you for that, my Krishna.
Think this over to yourself, oh ruler of the cosmos:
What advantage will there be for you in having killed me?
I'm a helpless woman, your obedient attendant.
Why do you continue to disdain me now, Murāri?
For a lengthy period, because of your attachment,
You possessed no will to even leave me for a moment.
Now how dare you say to me that I should travel homeward!

103 Saputra bāndhabe bāṛhe laṅkāra rābaṇe la tāhāra kāṭilõ daśa māthā 'Rāvaṇa of Laṅkā thrived with sons and adherents; I cut off his ten heads.' See Dānakhaṇḍa above, n. 97. Rāvaṇa is characterized as a ten-headed demon.

104 Uttama kulata mora jarama bhaila la āhmā lañā nāhi paradāre 'My birth was in a fine household; with me, there's no adultery.'

105 The first two-thirds of this line are missing, leaving only the concluding foot.

106 Mukunda, a name of Viṣṇu-Krishna.

107 Nānā tapaphale tohmā mora dila bidhī 'Fate gave you to me as the outcome of many (acts of) asceticism.' It is believed that austerities result in the accrual of merit, through which, in turn, one receives the good things of life.

108 Thākiba yoginī hañā tohā̃ka sebiñā 'I shall become a yoginī (female ascetic) and remain serving you.'

Song 33

I couldn't eat—so intense, in your earliest youth, was my sense of your absence.
In the extremes of my rage, on my spokesman's suggestion, I struck you with arrows.
But, by avoiding you carefully, I've cleansed my wrongs and subdued my emotions.
Now you are pleading in order to win me, but dairymaid, it's to no purpose.
Beautiful Radha, you mustn't belabor it; don't try your witchcraft upon me.[109]
Through Kali, Dvāpara, Tretā and Satya, my spiritual form has no blemish.[110]
For you, I wore myself out; I remained, days and nights, at the shores of the river.
How can it be that you now seek me out, overcome with the prickings of passion?
Radha, I made my requests with a smile, but you wouldn't concede your approval.
Now, Abhimanyu's wife Radha, attend to my words: let your youth go to blazes!
You are the daughter of Sāgara; I'm the descendant of Kaśyapa rishi.[111]
Listen to me: in the pride of your youth, scabby fool,[112] you would not recognize me!
It was for you that I personally went into combat with armies of demons.[113]
Joining together, the gods all created a plan; using you, they condemned me.
Go from my presence. To make love with you isn't tempting to me any longer.
Having me carry all Gokula's burdens, you've utterly sullied my honor.

[109] Āhmāta nā pāta māyā 'don't apply your māyā on me.' Refer to nn. 37 and 38 above.

[110] Satya tretā dbāpara kalī āhme nirañjana kāyā 'I am without qualities in my body through the satya, tretā, dvāpara and kali (ages).' See n. 84 above. In Hinduism, the supreme being is considered nirañjana, devoid of qualities or unmarked by them.

[111] On Sāgara, refer to n. 41 above. Kaśyapa is the name of a legendary rishi or sage referred to in the *Mahābhārata* and *Devī Bhāgavata*; owing to a curse, he is said to be reborn as Vasudeva, father of Krishna (Mani 1975:397). Krishna's intent in pointing out his and Radha's respective parentage is to emphasize his relative status over hers.

[112] Suṇa mugadhī pāmarī 'listen, foolish pāmarī.' See Dānakhaṇḍa above, n. 136, and cf. Vaṃśīkhaṇḍa, n. 83.

[113] Saba daityagaṇa āpaṇe mārilo moñe tohmāra āntare 'For you, I myself attacked all demon hosts.'

Now you should leave me; go back where you live and abandon your hopes for me, Radha.

Song 34

"I was just a youngster; I knew nothing of flirtation or romance. I'm growing wasted now from fretting.
Krishna, day and night I've but one thought—that, lacking you, I have no destiny. Now offer me instructions!"
"Cowherd people know me well, for Gokula is where my dwelling is, and Vasudeva is my father.
I've no business with you; if they hear of this, I'll be dishonored. You've no reason, Radha, to approach me."
"Wayward and contemptible are womenfolk,[114] born base in many ways. How long can we remain indignant?[115]
In your absence, Krishna, I'm distressed in spirit! Why are you refusing me in such a callous manner?"
"I'm aware you're chaste by disposition! Listen, gorgeous, hear me tell how good and evil are distinguished.
If one does what's right, one goes to heaven; one gains various rewards. There's hell to pay for doing evil!"[116]
"You are Vasudeva's scion, you're the son of Devakī. My lord, you are the enemy of Kaṃsa.
Hari, you're a crescent moon that cowmaids can't attain;[117] while I, a woman languishing, can't live without you."
"Look, Candrāvalī, I tell you, I'm celestial Vanamālī. Why do you make wicked propositions?
You're a natural aunt to me, for Abhimanyu's my maternal uncle, since my mother is Yaśodā."
"Don't say disappointing things, but take me to your side for once. To me, you are a husband, Śrīnivāsa.[118]
Thanks to merit I've accrued in more than one existence,[119] at your feet I have the honor of attending."[120]

[114] Chāra tirī bāmā jāti nānā doṣẽ ūtapatī 'Women are dirt, a sinister (literally, "left-side") race, conceived in varied faults. . . .' Cf. Dānakhaṇḍa above, n. 256.

[115] Tāka kopa rahe kata khane '. . . how long does anger remain in them?'

[116] Suṇa la sundarī satī bujhilõ tohmāra matī suṇa pāpa puṇyera ūttara / puṇya kailẽ sbagga jāie nānā upabhoga pāie pāpẽ hae narakera phala 'Listen, lovely chaste woman, I've figured out your disposition; hear (my) reply on sin and virtue. If one does right, one goes to heaven; one obtains various enjoyments—by sin, the outcome is hell!'

[117] Gopīra bālendu harī 'Hari, you who are the crescent moon (bālendu) (i.e., unattainable) to a dairymaid. . . .'

[118] Tohme mora pati śrīnibāsa 'You are my master, Śrīnivāsa'; refer to n. 53 above.

[119] Āneka jarama pune 'by the merits of many lives. . . .'

[120] Bhajilõ tora caraṇe '. . . I have (been able to) adhere at your feet,' i.e., to be a humble devotee.

Song 35

Radha, look, I crossed you when the Yamunā as swollen,
Turned my back upon my shame, and bore your load of produce.
Through this kingdom, Radha, my dishonor has been spreading.
You, though, in your prideful immaturity, ignored me.
Now you, too, have learned the sting of separation, Radha!
Mighty anguish I endured from love's relentless prickings;
Due to you, my Radha, I received extreme affliction.
Now I wouldn't like to see your face; that's my decision.
Radha, on account of you, I left my home abandoned;
Still you wouldn't offer some response to my entreaties.
It was for your sake that I became a tax official,
But you bragged that you were Abhimanyu's faithful missus!
How come now you're having such desires, dairymaiden?
Your mentality is warped with lust—I'm moral-minded![121]
Better keep your distance from your close relations, Radha,
Lest our demon ruler, Kaṃsa, get this information.
Now this heart of mine no longer dwells upon you, Radha.

Song 36

What is my offense that you're relinquishing me, Krishna?
Master, think this over to yourself and contemplate it:
Krishna, since my youth's developed fully, it befits you.
It's not proper, king of gods, for you to disregard it.
No one leaves a woman and avoids incurring error;[122]
Listen, Cakrapāṇi, Rāma suffered, as did Sītā![123]
Through the day as well as through the night, awake and dreaming,
Underneath the kadamba I sit alone, repining.
If my life is ended on account of you, my Krishna,
You will have to face the charge of murdering a woman!
Hari, spare my life, for I'm distracted due to passion!
Free yourself from anger! Take a look at my condition.
Let's go to Vṛndāvana this once, just you and Radha!

121 Tohme ratīñā kumatī āhme dharmmamatī 'You have a mentality defiled with lust, I am dharma-minded (or: my mind is on my duties)!'

122 Biṇi doṣe keho nāhĩ teje ramaṇī 'Without moral fault (doṣa), no one abandons a woman.'

123 According to the *Rāmāyaṇa* (refer to Dānakhaṇḍa above, n. 229), after Rāma recovered his wife Sītā from Rāvaṇa, doubts about her chastity obliged him to expel her from his kingdom. At that time she was pregnant with Rāma's twin sons, to whom she gave birth in exile. Rāma lost sons together with wife, and Sītā lost husband and royal status.

Song 37

I sent my spokesman to you at that time; you sent her back with derision.
Now my affection for you is destroyed; yet your attachment continues.
Oh, go away from me, Radha, begone; I have renounced you, my beauty.
Mother's Yaśodā and dad's Nanda Ghosh; you are the wife of my uncle.
If gold is shattered, then there is a cure; it can be molded by fire.
If, though, there shatters the love of a man, who in the hell[124] can remold it?
When I frequented the Yamunā's shores, longing to win your affection,
You gave your promise, then made me bear loads; people were laughing to see it.
Beautiful lady, considering this, I have withdrawn my affection.
Radha, relinquish your longing for me!

Song 38

It is spring, the luscious time
Of cuckoos' raucous caroling.
In its youthful freshness, can my life endure, dear Krishna?[125]
Now, because of your withdrawal,
Physically I've grown unsettled.
Krishna, it's not right for you to leave me isolated.
No, I'm not your aunt! I'm not your uncle's wife. Oh, Krishna,
All the gods are well aware that you and I are lovers!
Lacking any sense of passion,
I had been a childish youngster;
That is why I didn't give approval to your pleadings.
Now that I am well developed,
Lacking you, I've no salvation.
Realize this and offer your consent to my entreaties.
I shall sacrifice my person
Where the river meets the ocean;[126]
Or, perhaps, it's here that I may die by taking poison.
Since, Gadādhara, you know this,
Just this once, why, show compassion.

[124] Literally, 'by whose father can it be remolded?' Refer to Naukākhaṇḍa above, n. 29.
[125] In personal consultations, Sukumar Sen has suggested that the original reading in this line, prāṇa re, be substituted by prāṇa rahe; this is both to give better sense and to preserve rhyme (with nahe, which ends the next verse). Hence: e naā yaubana kāhnāñī prāṇa rahe '(How) can my life endure, Krishna, (in) its fresh youthfulness?'
[126] Sāgara saṅgama jale / tejibõ mo kalebare 'In the water of the confluence (of the river) with the ocean, I will sacrifice my body.' Cf. n. 5 above.

Otherwise I'll have you charged with murdering a woman!
Lost to me, my Krishna, is
The cumulative moral credit[127]
Of whatever self-denying acts or vows I practiced.[128]
I assume this oath before you:
Nevermore will I betray you.[129]

Song 39

My Candrāvalī, when I was laboring to please you,
You were placing curses on my father and my mother.
Why are you attracted now to making love with Krishna,
Showing disregard to Abhimanyu, your own husband?
Why do you display your wiles to fascinate me, Radha?
They do not entrance the son of Nanda any longer.
In the Vedas, providence[130] has taken care to mention
That, if one does wrong, there's no success in one's endeavors.
I'm to lift a burden from the earth by killing demons;
If I act unrighteously, then I shall not achieve that.
Do not importune me, Radha, wife of Abhimanyu;
You have been forsaken by celestial Cakrapāṇi!
Through my meditation,[131] I have purified my person,
And my heart no longer is attracted when I see you.
Daytime and at night, I practice yogic meditation.
Nevermore by you will I, Lord Krishna, be distracted!
Knowing of this, dairymaid, dismiss your urge to win me!

Song 40

What great end's accomplished if you torture someone dying?[132]
In your heart, oh Krishna, why, you ought to think this over.
In this universe, you are the highest of the powers;
Krishna, in your presence, what's a lowly dairymaiden?
In misjudgment, I did not pay heed to your entreaties;
Therefore love has fittingly delivered retribution.

[127] Naṭha hae kāhna mora se saba dharama 'Krishna, destroyed is all that dharma of mine. . . .'

[128] Yata kailõ saṃyama / karilõ brata niyama '. . . (from) whatever self-abnegation (saṃyama) I practiced or (from) observance (niyama) of vows (brata). . . .'

[129] Kabhõ yabẽ tohmā harõ, literally 'if ever I betray you!'

[130] Yatana kariā̃ beda kahilenta bidhi 'Fate (bidhi) carefully declares (in) the Vedas. . . .'

[131] Brahmaṇe cintane kailõ nirmmala kāe 'I have purified my body by contemplation on brahman.' See n. 92 above.

[132] Maināka mārilẽ 'if one kills a corpse'; cf. modern Bengali mayanaa, e.g., mayanaa tadanta 'post-mortem examination', mayanaa ghar 'mortuary.'

Due to your affection, I esteemed myself too greatly,
Being unaware that this would stimulate your anger.
If I had known earlier that you'd become offended,
Than I'd have avoided telling stories to Yaśodā.
Krishna, at your footsteps I entreat you for asylum.
Treat me as you will without the merest hesitation.
Krishna, I am capable of bearing any anguish,
Only I cannot endure the torture of your absence.
Just this once, my Jagannātha, offer your assistance;
By your grace, my sense of isolation can be banished.
Use your sidelong glances to provide me with assurance!

Song 41

Nowadays, cuckoos and bees are love's missiles—
Passion assails me whenever I listen.[133]
Have you no fear of destroying a woman?
Why call me falsely the wife of your uncle?
How come you don't take some pity upon me?
Give up your hard-hearted attitude, Krishna!
Speaking the anguishing truth, I inform you:
You are my life. Cross my heart,[134] Jagannātha!
Glance at me sidelong and you can revive me;
I, Radha, die in the flames of your absence!
My youth is not in the slightest diminished.[135]
Lacking you, Krishna, my bosom is bursting.
Realizing this, show some pity upon me;
Take me with you to a forested arbor.
Thinking of you, day and night, I've been weeping.
Why do you still not respond with compassion?
Please, Śrinivāsa, you mustn't destroy me!

Song 42

"As we were going to Mathurā, taking your goods by the Yamunā pathway,
I tried and tried, but you gave me no hope; disappearing, you left me in anguish.

133 Literally, 'Passion strikes me lately with arrows—the bees and cuckoos I am hearing.'
134 Literally, 'I put my hand on my head,' a gesture of oath-taking.
135 Tileka yaubana nāhī̃ ṭuṭe 'My youth is not diminished (literally: broken) a whit (literally: a sesame-seed)!' The implication is that Krishna has no substantive justification for spurning Radha.

Radha, you smart, scabby slut,[136] why attempt to cast spells of delusion upon me?
Why did you not treat me kindly, if you were considering me as your lover?
Putting some betel-leaf quids in the hands of my spokesman, to you I dispatched them;
Flouting my urgings, you threw down the betel quids, using your left foot to shove them![137]
I was the one they'd have blamed for the murder of Granny, so badly you struck her!
Only because of the fact that I'm Hari Nārāyaṇa, Granny survived it.
I'll go to you when your Granny directs me to!" Saying this, Krishna fell silent.

Song 43

Taking in Krishna's reply, Radha returned to Granny
And asked her to save her life.

When the darkness comes with evening, how can any woman
Stay alive who doesn't have a man beside her, Granny?
What can this thing be which is occurring to me, Granny?
Maddened by his absence, I must seek the son of Nanda.
In the night, I dreamed that I reclined in Krishna's lap; but I could not detect that cowherd youth on waking.
Utterly devoid of value is my ample youthfulness; my refuge, messenger, is immolation![138]
On a branch I placed my burden, so to speak. That branch has broken; now no branch remains for me to rest on.
Granny, if you summon Krishna, I will press him to my bosom; nevermore in life will I forsake him!
You who are my messenger, I clasp you by the feet; see here, this life of mine is terminating, Granny.
Take away my priceless jewels, but carry out my supplications. Just this once, my Granny, fetch me Krishna.

Song 44

When those quids of betel leaf were sent to you by Krishna,
You would not address a gracious answer to him, Radha.

[136] Chinārī pāmarī nāgarī rādhā 'wayward (chinārī), scabby (pāmarī; refer to n. 112 above), cunning (nāgarī) Radha.'
[137] Refer to n. 22 above.
[138] E mora yaubana bhāra sakala bhaila āsāra ānala saraṇa haibe dūtā re 'This burden of my youth is entirely sapless; messenger, (my) refuge will be fire (i.e., self-immolation).'

Now you are directing me to go and fetch you Krishna.
Even as I'm growing old in age, you give me problems.
Nowadays I can't meander here and there; I'm feeble.
What would be the means by which I might deliver Hari?
Leave me be, I'm going home. Don't put me under pressure!
If Gadādhara's unwilling, where am I to find him?[139]
Krishna has grown ill disposed to you, I well imagine;
While he lives, your Krishna won't approach you any longer!
Men and bumblebees are both alike in disposition;
They meander many, many places tasting nectar.
Krishna is engaged in sundry thrills with other women!

Song 45

Due to my juvenile absence of judgment,
Granny, I spurned Krishna's betel-leaf quids.
Now, though, my attentions are engrossed in that cowherding youngster.
Start at a time that's auspicious for travel.[140]
Granny, make haste to the place Krishna stays;
Summon me my Krishna, having pleased him with affable greetings.
Tell Krishna, messenger, when you approach him,
He should have compassion this one time and allow me to see him.
Thinking about my Murāri each moment,
I am unable to tame my emotions.
While my youth remains, why, how am I to inhibit my feelings?
I am a woman of withering fortunes,[141]
Cursed with the name of Candrāvalī.[142] Granny,
Other than my darling Vanamālī, I have no salvation.
When I was gathering Yamunā water,
He, Cakrapāṇi, was teasing me, Granny.
Being not composed of mind, I told all those tales to Yaśodā.
It was myself I destroyed snubbing Krishna.[143]
Let sun and moon serve me jointly as witness:
Only for my Krishna I'm reserving my youthful attractions!

139 Kathā̃ ginā̃ pāyibō̃ niṭhura gadādhara 'Where shall I go and find the unrelenting Gadādhara?'

140 Yātrā kara śubhakṣaṇe 'travel at an auspicious time'; cf. n. 58.

141 Moñā̃ se dagadhakapālī 'I am that woman of burnt forehead . . . ,' i.e., an ill fated woman. Refer to n. 75.

142 Nāma mora candrābalī '. . . (but) my name is Candrāvalī.' Radha has begun reviling her namesake, i.e., the moonlight (candrāvalī); in a sense, then, she is the very thing she reviles.

143 Kāhna nā cihnilō̃ khāilō̃ ākhī, literally 'I did not recognize Krishna; I ate (i.e., destroyed) my eyes!' In other words, by snubbing Krishna, Radha has condemned herself to going without a glimpse of him.

Cuckoos would offer response by their singing[144]
When Krishna used to perform on his flute;
Then the breezes from the south would wither my person like fire.
Now I have flung inhibition aside.
I seek Śrīnivāsa's sanctuary; so now, summon Krishna.

Song 46

Scorning the outcome, you impudent woman,
Due to your pride, you offended your Hari.
Roused in his heart is such rage, I'll be lucky
If he doesn't strike me on hearing this, Radha![145]
Now it is you who must make some suggestion—
I have no competence left in these matters.[146]
Krishna attempted to plead with you, Radha;
Time and again, he dispatched me to see you.
Still you neglected to treat him with honor;
This is the reason why Krishna's indignant.
Once any friend has been alienated,
How can your ballads or verses appease him?[147]
Krishna is very intelligent, Radha;
Is there a soul by whom he can be thwarted?[148]
Radha, my spirits can't cope with your torment;
Being a grandniece, you're dear to me, Radha.
Where might I locate some trace of your Krishna?

Song 47

In her longing to find Mādhava, the lovestricken maiden
Listened to Granny's words and then conferred with her girlfriends.

Radha then made this reply to her Granny: "Is it my counsel you're seeking?

144 Kokila kaila pāli gāne 'Cuckoos would give the refrain (pāli) with their songs.' That is, cuckoos would give their musical response.

145 Ehā śuṇī nā māre moke baṛa bhāge 'On hearing this, (only by) great fortune will he not strike me!'

146 Moñā bhailõ ehāta mugadhi 'I have become a dunce in this.'

147 Chande bande toṣibe kamane 'How can you please (him) with (laudatory) verses (chande) and hymns (bande)?'

148 Tāka bhāṇḍī kāhāra parāṇe, literally 'Whose soul deceives him?' Cf. Vṛndāvanakhaṇḍa above, n. 122.

Krishna's like sandal; he's close to my heart.[149] You must yourself find the answer!"
Hearing the message of Radha, her Granny thought to herself and advised her:
"You and I, Radha, will go search the forest; then we may find Cakrapāṇi."
Joining, they looked for, but couldn't find Krishna; both of them mingled their sobbing.
Just at that juncture, the sage Nārada came there, revealing his presence.[150]
Radha fell prostrate at Nārada's feet; folding her hands, she inquired:
"Where's Jagannātha residing, oh sage? Where's Nanda's hard-hearted darling?
Nārada, what is my youth? What is life? What are my home and possessions?
As an ascetic, I'll roam every land if I'm deprived of my Krishna!"
Listening to Radha's request, that great seer, sitting in yogic reflection,
Made divination that, under a tree, debonair Krishna was sitting.[151]
"Go to the base of the kadamba tree in Vṛndāvana," Nārada answered.
"There you will find him, the kind of divinities, seated on cushioning blossoms!"
Holding the counsel of Nārada equal to scripture,[152] Candrāvali Radha
Searched through Vṛndāvana and, all at once, happened upon Vanamālī.
When Radha saw Krishna's face from afar, instantly she fell unconscious.
Trying to bring her around, on her face Granny splashed jugfuls of water.
Radha revived; then she clasped Granny's feet, telling her greatly in earnest,
"Granny, my feet are refusing to budge. I can't say anything, Granny."
"Now, my dear grandniece, don't fret in your heart. What shall I do? You should tell me.
I shall take pains to accomplish your ends, even if life must be yielded!"
"Think it all through, have compassion on me; go on your own to him, Granny.
Show that impenitent Krishna respect; tell him in full my sad story."[153]
Granny departed; to Krishna she went after she heard this entreaty.

[149] Ki puchaha more budhī / āhmāra hṛdaya candana kāhnāñī 'What, do you ask advice of me? Krishna is my heart's sandalpaste!' Cf. Vṛndāvanakhaṇḍa above, n. 91.

[150] Nārada muni āsiā̃ dila daraśane 'The sage Nārada, coming, gave (them) a sight (of himself).' Refer to n. 39 above.

[151] Rādhāra bacana śuṇi māhāmunī basilī yoga dheāne / jāṇila kadama talāta basiā̃ āchenta nāgara kāhne 'Hearing Radha's words, the great sage sat in yogic contemplation; he found out that the urbane Krishna was sitting at the base of the kadamba.'

[152] Beda samatula 'equivalent to Veda.'

[153] Bhālamatē mora dukhakathā kaha nidukha kāhnacaraṇe 'tell my tale of woe well at the feet of Krishna, who is devoid of woe (i.e., who is not sorry).'

Song 48[154]

She regards as burdensome
The necklaces upon her breasts.
Radha cannot travel, for her heart is badly wasted.
She severely rues the moistened
Sandalpaste upon her skin;
She regards the moon as an inferno in the evenings.
Only by a glimpse of you can Radha go on living;
She's consumed by anguish from your absence.
Seated and withdrawn, repeated
Sighs does Radha heave—sighs heated
In the conflagration of the flower-shafts of passion.[155]
Radha's eyes resemble brooding lotus
With their stems truncated—[156]
Welling up with moisture, they are cast in all directions.
Equal to a heap of cinders
She regards her bed of tendrils;
Though her eyes are often closed, her heart is very restless.
Radha puts her head in hand[157]
And keeps her eyes upon the sky;
Constantly she thinks of you with undisturbed attention.
Sometimes laughing, sometimes raging—
Sometimes in her agitation
Radha shakes; she weeps sometimes; at times she's animated.
Owing to the fury of her love,
Your Radha can't approach you.

Song 49

Radha constantly reviles the moon and sandal ointment.
She regards the breezes of the Malabars like venom.
She constructs her bed from blooms, the blooms of passion's missiles,
And she is adopting vows to capture your embraces.
Owing to the reveries she's having of you, Krishna,
Radha has been seething with the torment of bereavement.

154 This song is reminiscent of Jayadeva's *Gītagovinda* 4, song 9 (Miller 1978).

155 Kusumaśara hutāśe / tapata dīrgha niśāse / saghana chāṛae rādhā basi eka pāśe 'Seated to one side, Radha releases at length intense sighs heated in the conflagration of the flower arrows (of love).'

156 Radha's eyes are here compared to lotuses, which drip when their stems are removed.

157 Bāma karate badane 'with head in left hand. . . .'

Day and night, infatuation strikes her with its missiles;
Using lotus petals, she's been armoring her bosom.[158]
You are dwelling all the time within her spirit, Krishna;
She attempts all strategies to keep you for this reason.
Down her face, which replicates the moon, there ooze in currents
Streams of nectar, as it were, expressed by Rāhu's pressing.[159]
Krishna, she depicts you with infatuation's features;[160]
Truthfully I tell you, she pays homage to those pictures.[161]
When she broods to excess and imagines you before her,
Then she laughs, she rages, cries, she trembles or she panics.[162]
Friends, for her, have turned to snares, and home has turned a jungle.
Love's unyielding agony intensifies her sighing.
Radha looks about with darting eyes in all directions;
Like a forest doe, within her heart, she's agitated.
Have compassion on her now and offer your embraces!

Song 50

"Why are you yet inclined
To have other women?
Your lust may be slaked, Krishna, but in your absence,
Passion wreaks havoc on that shapely lady!"

Using gentle words to coax him, Granny spoke to Krishna:
"In your absence, Krishna, your Candrāvalī is dying.
Radha's form resembles cream atop a sea of passion.[163]
You should taste her love, Dāmodara; her youth's unstinted.
Lend your ear, adorable Murāri. Don't be tardy;
Even when I stroke her head and kiss her face, oh Krishna,
Radha's life cannot withstand this agonizing torment!"
Granny clasped his hands and uttered words of supplication.
Time and time again, from start to end, she remonstrated:
"Krishna, do not disobey my urging; gladden Radha!"
When, to his delight, he heard the arguments of Granny,

[158] Hṛdaye nalinīdala saṃnāhā kare 'She armors lotus petals on her heart.' A similar line occurs in *Gītagovinda* 4.3 (song 8) (Miller 1978).

[159] Nayanaśalila paṛe badane tāhāra / rāhuñā gālila yena cā̃da sudhādhāra '(Down) her face descends eye-water (tears), like streams of moon's nectar made to ooze by Rāhu.' See Bāṇakhaṇḍa above, n. 84.

[160] Tohmāka likhiā̃ kāhna madanarūpa 'Krishna, having drawn you (in) the image of love (madana). . . .' On Madana (or Kāma), the love god, see Bāṇakhaṇḍa above, n. 3.

[161] Praṇāmagaṇa kare kahilõ sarūpa '. . . she pays obeisances to it; I tell you this truthfully.' A similar passage occurs in *Gītagovinda* 4.6 (song 8) (Miller 1978).

[162] Compare *Gītagovinda* 4.19 (song 9) (Miller 1978).

[163] Luṇī sama deha tāra rasera sāgare 'Her body is like cream on the sea of passion.' The implication is that the survival of Radha's delectable physical being is precarious.

Krishna contemplated to himself; then, with a chuckle,
Made reply: "The dairymaid should come in charming costume;
I shall tell her words of nectar. She may sit beside me."
Granny went away elatedly on Krishna's orders;
Hastening to Radha's side, she gave a full accounting.
Thereupon, to Radha, every moment seemed like ages.

Song 51

Granny was overjoyed at Mādhava's instructions and prepared
A heart-capturing costume for the exhilarated Radha.

"You have Śiva's topknot."[164] She encircled it with blooms. Upon her head, like dawning sun, was streaked vermilion.
On her throat and both her upraised breasts a necklace gleamed; its giant pearls were interspersed with brilliant gemstones;
On the highest point of Sumeru[165] it seemed to fall, like double courses on Sureśvarī descending.[166]
Eagerly she had her drape her throat with many ornaments until it looked most ravishingly splendid;[167]
It appeared that goldsmiths had assembled and, with endless care, prepared a conchshell set with layers of gemstones.
In great ecstasy, she had her cover both her arms with armlets, shimmeringly bright with jeweled haloes.
Golden bangles set with pearls and precious stones were on her forearms; on her wrists were gem-encrusted wristlets.
Strung and fastened at her waist, a girdle trimmed with bells[168] was pealing victory's report in love's arena.[169]

164 Literally, 'You have a topknot (khompā) like Śambhu (said by Granny to Radha).' Refer to n. 27 above.

165 Paṛe yena sumeruśikhare 'It seemed to fall on Sumeru's pinnacle . . . ,' the pinnacle being Radha's bosom. On Meru or Sumeru see Dānakhaṇḍa above, n. 48.

166 Haā̃ samāna ākāre sureśarī duī dhāre 'being comparable in appearance to double courses of the Sureśvarī.' The Ganges River is called Sureśvarī in heaven. According to *Viṣṇupurāṇa*, bk. 2, chap. 2 (Wilson 1972:134ff.), the river descends from heaven upon the crest of Sumeru or Mount Meru, from which it flows down through the country of Bhārata or greater India, dividing into seven tributaries as it moves to the sea. The poet suggests that Radha's gleaming pearl necklace is like a doubled image of the cascading Sureśvarī.

167 Pahrāila hariṣamaṇe kaṇṭhata bhūṣaṇagaṇe dekhi ābhisāra suśobhane 'Eagerly she caused her to wear ornaments on her throat; it looked ravishingly splendid. . . .' Ābhisāra 'ravishing' derives from abhisāra 'assignation'.

168 Kiṅkiṇī, refer to Yamunākhaṇḍa above, n. 8.

169 Ratiraṇe jayadhunī karae kiṅkiṇī tāka gānthi bāndhila mājhe 'The bell-girdle made peals of victory (jayadhunī) in the warfare of love (ratiraṇe); it was strung and fastened on her waist.'

Anklets made of gold and trimmed with bells adorned her legs; her feet and toes were trimmed with toe-rings in abundance.[170]

Scented colors beautified her face—a mix of musk as well as camphor and the scarlet hue of betel.[171]

Quite alluring even in her natural state, and now ornately dressed and in an attitude of passion,

Radha reached the side of Krishna. As he looked upon her, undulations of emotion stirred within him.

Song 52

Seeing Radha feverish with love
And groomed more ravishingly than ever before,
Hari was charged with passion.
He approached her by degrees in this way:

Krishna held her in his arms
And embraced her.
Radha, too, clasped Krishna with great fervor.
Krishna kissed her
First on her cheeks, then on both her eyes,
On her forehead, her lips, and again on her jewel-like eyes.
Krishna began to make love to Radha,
Satisfying her ardent desires.
Joining his tongue to hers,
He drank the nectar of her mouth;
Radha abandoned herself to union with him.
Upon Radha's lips
Krishna impressed his teeth.
Radha gestured her surrender to his wishes;
Then he grazed both her breasts
With his nails.
Krishna moistened Radha's organ with his nectar.[172]
Radha cooed.
The exultant Krishna savored her sweetness;
Waves of it engulfed him, as it were, during that act of passion.
Their union was exquisitely extended.
They made love in various positions.

170 Kanaka mallatora āra pāsalinikara jaṃgha pada āṅgulita sāje 'Her legs, feet and toes were dressed with golden mallatoras and with multitudes of pāsalīs.' Mallatora refers to a belled anklet. For pāsali, see Dānakhaṇḍa above, n. 271.

171 The first line of this couplet seems to be missing in the original manuscript owing to scribal error.

172 In the original reading of this line, the word maraṇe 'in death' seems to occur mistakenly for ramaṇe 'on the female organ'.

No one had ever performed such feats of passion![173]
Their eyes blossomed;
Both became happy.

Song 53

After Radha tasted bliss in love, the dairymaiden
Clasped him by the feet and murmured, "Listen, Cakrapāṇi,
There's no other destiny for me if I forsake you;
Now it's you to whom my thoughts are dedicated, Krishna.
Make your lap available to me this time, Govinda;
Lying down, I'll go to sleep, for I am quite exhausted."
Hearing this proposal, Krishna gave her his approval.
Using young and tender leaves, he made a bed for Radha.
He himself then placed her on his thigh, inert, for resting.
After that, within his heart, he started to consider.
At that juncture, cooling winds were blowing, Krishna noticed.
Bumblebees and cuckoos had combined their dulcet singing.
All about, the fragrances of flower blooms were wafted;
And the eyes of Radha had retreated into slumber.[174]
Krishna made his mind up to be gone, forsaking Radha.
Thereupon he traveled till he came to Granny's presence;
Then, addressing Granny, he admonished her as follows.

Song 54

"Granny, I have given my compliance to your urging.
Now you'll have to give me leave. I'm going.
Here within the wilderness the evening is approaching;
Hasten home discretely, taking Radha.[175]
Granny, I've allowed myself to be involved with Radha—
You and you alone have been the reason.
Granny, look, I clasp your hands, so give me your attention.
There is one thing more which I must tell you.
You must keep this to yourself—make use of your discretion—
Granny, I'm departing for the city.[176]

[173] Kabho keha nā kaila yena rasa prabandhe 'No one had ever used such techniques of lovemaking!'

[174] Rādhāra nayane giñā̃ ninda kaila bāsa 'Sleep had gone and made dwelling in Radha's eyes.'

[175] Sā̃jha upasanna bhaila banera bhitare / rādhā lañā̃ jhā̃ṭa binae yāhā ghare 'Twilight has become present in the forest; quickly take Radha and go home with discretion (binae = binaye).'

[176] Tāka rākhiha yatane āpaṇa āntare jāiba āhme mathurā nagare 'Keep that with care within yourself. I shall go to Mathurā city.'

You remain with Radha and pretend that you've been sleeping."
Earnestly he made this plea of Granny.
Stealthily from Radha's head he'd drawn his thigh; now Krishna
Started off for Mathurā, the city.
At her side, Candrāvalī did not see Krishna later
When she woke. She roused and spoke to Granny:

Song 55

Here beneath the kadamba was where that youthful cowherd was;
my head was on his thigh as I relaxed here.
Being utterly fatigued from love, I had been overcome with drowsiness.
He's vanished in my slumber!
In Lord Madhusūdana's oppressive absence, Granny,
I shall die alive. You have to fetch him!
Day and night, I wonder every moment singlemindedly,
how long must pass until I find my Krishna?
He and I must see each other. Messenger, I kneel before you!
Fetch him, he's the master of my spirit.[177]
Would I have departed to infernal slumber if I'd known
that Krishna would abandon me and vanish?
I shall swallow poison, for there isn't any substance in
my ample youthful charms in Krishna's absence.
Oh my messenger, see here; I clasp your feet, beseeching you:
this time you must accomplish my desires.
Make your way, my messenger, to where Lord Madhusūdana
is staying; then persuade him to approach me.

Song 56

Just a little earlier your Krishna was right here beneath the kadamba,
engrossed in your affection.
Radha, you're a fool, for you yourself let Vanamālī go! Now where am I
to come across that cowherd?
How shall I discover Krishna's whereabouts? I wouldn't have a clue in
which direction he'd be headed.
Using, oh, how many coaxing words, I had persuaded him and
summoned him, uniting you with Krishna.[178]
But, just now, you've been so very careless in your slumber that, from
underneath that head of yours, he's missing.

177 Caraṇe paṛõ dutī āṇi deha prāṇapati tāra mora hau daraśane 'I fall at your feet, messenger. Deliver the master of my soul! Let there be a meeting of him and me!'
178 Prabodhabacana kata bujhāñā tāhāre āṇiñā melāilo tora thane 'How many persuasive words I explained to him! I brought him and had him reach your proximity.'

Men tell women different things in order to seduce them. They're a horrid race; their heads are full of mischief.
In this very way, your Krishna must be tasting love, or so it seems, with other girls in sundry arbors!
Now you should stay here and I shall go away and search for him. I'll summon him for you when I detect him.

Song 57

"Radha, I've been burdened with fatigue from wandering the forest alone.
Now I'm depressed, for I have failed to find Madhusūdana."
"Granny, because of what you say, my heart is devastated.
The world appears blank to me. Hear my account!"

Granny, in the early part of evening I was dreaming[179]
That my cherished Krishna was approaching me that moment.
It was for this reason that I didn't go to seek him;
For my own ineptness, I've been suitably rewarded.
How am I to carry on alone now in the arbor?
Where is Krishna, and with whom does he enjoy love's pleasures?
Later in the evening,[180] in my solitude, I fretted:
"Where has Hari gone this time, abandoning his Radha?
With which woman blessed by having bathed at sacred places[181]
Is Murāri savoring the ecstasies of passion?"
Toward the middle of the night, a cuckoo warbled loudly.[182]
Due to Krishna's absence, I was restless in my spirits.
Worrying, I searched my mind; but there was no solution.
"Krishna!" I was crying out continuously, "Krishna!"
As the hours slipped away, the night completely ended;[183]
To the kadamba I came once more,[184] bereft of Krishna.
How shall I continue to survive this any longer?

179 Prathama pahare, refer to n. 9 above.
180 Duyaja pahare, cf. n. 11 above.
181 Ke nā sutītthe snāna kailā dhanya nārī / yā lañā 'Who is the blessed woman who has bathed at sacred spots that, with her. . . ?' Bathing in a spot designated sacred is considered one means of earning spiritual merit. See Vṛndāvanakhaṇḍa above, n. 100, for a more specific example.
182 Tiyaja pahare, cf. n. 12 above; see also Vaṃśīkhaṇḍa, n. 63.
183 Cāri pahara dina purila sakala '(With) the fourth prahara, an entire day (day and night cycle) was completed.' Refer to n. 14 above.
184 Āyilāhõ āhme kadambera tala 'I came to the base of the kadamba.' Apparently between the time of the previous song and the present one, a night has passed which Radha has spent in her own house, returning to her vigil by the kadamba tree in the morning. Granny's search for Krishna may have continued till the late evening of the previous day, possibly with a resumption of searching in the morning.

Song 58

"It's been an auspicious day for her, that favored lady—
She with whom your Krishna has been tasting passion's savor!
Radha, the conjecture you have made is very valid!
Now I'll search exhaustively to find your darling Krishna.
Sometimes he's beneath the kadamba or by the river.
Or, with other boys, he gaily roams the roads and market.
When I do encounter him, then how shall I address him?
You should give me suitable instructions, dairymaiden."
Radha animately replied to Granny's question:

Song 59

Search and search and search beside the Yamunā; and, Granny,
Search with concentration. Look for him beneath the medlars.[185]
Seek him at the Yamunā embankment and in arbors;
Also make a search for him in all the highest treetops.
After you encounter him, imploringly inform him,
"In the forest, she's alone. Your dairymaid is frantic!"
Seek him also where the other youths are congregating,
Since, on some occasions, Krishna poses as a youngster—
No one's comprehended his endeavors through the ages![186]
Search for him with care in such a way that you may find him.
This time, Granny, if you can detect my darling Krishna,
Then he'll be my life; I won't forsake him for a minute.
When the time arrives that you deliver me my Krishna,
Never more, my Granny, shall I give you any trouble.
Hara, bearing Ganges on his head, is partly Gaurī;[187]
Woman, then, is bodily a part of man, it follows.[188]
If you so convince him, you can summon me my Krishna.[189]

185 Bakulatalāta cāhā cāhā ekacite 'search, search for him singlemindedly beneath the medlar (or: medlars; see bakula in Appendix).' See n. 190 below.

186 Carita nā bujhe keho tāra cāri yuge 'No one in the four ages understands his nature!' See n. 84 above. Also see Dānakhaṇḍa above, n. 33.

187 Hara ārddha āṅge gaurī śire gaṅgā dhare 'Hara, half of whose body is Gaurī, holds the Ganges on his head.' Hara is a name of Śiva, Gaurī of his consort (see Vaṃśīkhaṇḍa above, n. 75). Often this god is depicted as androgynous. Bhandarkar 1965:87, citing the *Brahmavaivartapurāṇa*, mentions that Krishna is said to be Radha in the left side of his spiritual body. The Ganges, according to legend, was cursed by Brahmā to descend from heaven to earth, where Śiva obliged her by receiving her on his head.

188 Yeteke yāṇila nārī yehena śarīre '. . . from which it is discovered that his woman is like (part of a man's) body.'

189 Hena bujhāyiñā kāhna āṇa mora pāśe 'Explaining it in this way, you (can) bring Krishna to my side.'

Song 60

Toward Vṛndāvana, the forest, Granny
Made her way on Radha's supplication.
Heeding Radha's earnest wishes, Granny
Took with her no person as companion.
Taking Radha's pleas to heart, her Granny
Searched the forest through and through for Krishna.
Not detecting him beside the river,
She continued onward to the medlars.[190]
There Gadādhara was not discovered;
So she looked for him among the treetops.
Searching, she could not find Vanamālī.
Granny grew fatigued from the exertion.
Being all alone there in the forest,
Inwardly she shook with apprehension.
Granny traced her footsteps back to Radha.
Ultimately, reaching her, she told her:
"I could not discover his location."

Song 61

Lost, I'm lost! Fatigued, I put
My head upon his lap, reclining.
Horrid sleep possessed my eyes,[191] dear Granny;
When I woke, I saw Govinda
Wasn't there. His image has
Become a dreamlike thing for me, dear Granny.
Which direction has he vanished?
Tell me his location, Granny;
When I go there, you'll be my companion.
I have suffered many kinds of
Sorrows. Krishna's absence pains me;
Why does he refuse to let me meet him?
What unlucky day is this,
Or what transgression have I done,
That Krishna is annoyed with me, dear Granny?
As I reminisce on Krishna's words,
My life is all but finished.
Now I am forsaken by my senses.[192]

[190] See n. 185 above. The text is not specific as to whether one particular medlar tree or a cluster of medlar trees is intended.
[191] Dāruṇa nayane bhaila ninde, literally 'sleep occurred in my awful eyes.'
[192] Cetana nāhika mora dehe 'There is no cognition (left) in my body.'

I've abandoned every comfort;
Day by day, I grow emaciated,
Brooding on the love of Krishna.
Providence has turned against me;
Leaving me, my Krishna's vanished.
How long can I live in isolation?
Granny, you must give me guidance:
Which direction has he gone in?

Song 62

"It's been quite a while since our arrival in the forest.
I'm too apprehensive to delay here any further.
Radha, don't be flustered over this; compose your feelings.
We must travel home as long as no one is the wiser.[193]
I shall have your Krishna pay a visit to you later;
No one will find out, for I myself will handle matters.
One must not give notice when one does important business;
Through one's circumspection, one enjoys prolonged contentment.[194]
Pacify your sentiments. Give heed to my proposal—
If we hurry homeward, Abhimanyu won't rebuke us.
Heed my plan; I kiss your face and urge this of you, Radha.
If we're prompt, then no one can say anything against us.
Do not be distressed, although your heart be torn with sorrow;
On his own, divine Gadādhara will come and meet you."
Once she had devised this plan, no time was lost by Granny,
But, persuading Radha, she accompanied her homeward,
Having all her girlfriends go along as her companions.

Song 63

> Radha carried on somehow for a time despite her desire for Krishna;
> Then, anguish-laden,[195] she addressed Granny as follows:

Branches of the kadamba are bowed with blooming flowers;
Still that cowherd youth is not returning to the pastures.
Callous-hearted Krishna, saying nothing, has departed.
How long must I keep this muslin wrapper on my bosom?[196]

193 Yā yānāhi, the original reading, should be substituted by yā nāhi 'as long as.'

194 Cirakāla sukha bhuñje sesi siāṇī 'She who is wise in just this way experiences prolonged contentment.'

195 Ādhibhavato, the original reading in this Sanskrit verse, should be replaced by ādhibharato 'due to the pressure of anguish (ādhi).'

196 Kata nā rākhiba kuca nete ohāṛiā̃ 'How long am I to keep my bosom covered with fine muslin?' In other words: how long till I can unbosom myself (of the anguish of separation)?

Granny, who has meddled in the passion of our childhood?[197]
Krishna, master of my soul, is still not coming homeward.
From my head I'll wipe away the traces of vermilion;
Into dust I'll pulverize my conchshell bangles, Granny!
Lacking Krishna, I am always seething in my spirits
Like the doe who's been attacked by arrows tipped with poison.[198]
All the other dairymaids are fortunate; they're happy.
What is my mistake that fate is dealing me these sorrows?
Day and night, as I recall the virtues of my Krishna,
Only by its stoutness has my heart resisted bursting.[199]
Now the month of May is past; the time of rains approaches;[200]
Somber clouds are casting shadows on the southern regions.[201]
Even now that heartless son of Nanda isn't coming!

Song 64

> "You must get through these four cloud-shadowed months by
> your wits,
> For, Radha, I am now without stamina to wander about."

In the fullness of my youth, I've been betrayed by Krishna.
Four long months of rain are coming; how shall I survive them?[202]
During June, the newly forming clouds begin to rumble;[203]
Tears well up to brimming in my eyes from love's affliction.
Were I born a bird, then I would fly away where Krishna,
Master of my spirit, oh my Granny, may be dwelling.
With the waxing of July,[204] as heavy rains are falling,
On my bed in solitude I'll lie, deprived of slumber.[205]

197 Śaiśabera nehā baṛāyi ke nā bihaṛāila 'Granny, who might have disrupted the love of (our) childhood?'

198 Literally, 'like a doe at the blows of poisoned arrows.'

199 According to a suggestion made by Sukumar Sen in personal consultations, the original reading gaṭila is a mistake for gaṛhila, which appears in some editions of the published text. Hence: bajare gaṛhila buka nā jāe phuṭiā̃ 'my chest, made of adamantine stuff (bajare), does not go bursting.'

200 Jeṭha māsa gela āsāṛha parabeśa 'Jyestha month is gone, Āṣāṛha is entered.' The former, May–June, is the month immediately preceding the monsoon and the latter, June–July, is the first of the monsoon.

201 Sāmala meghẽ chāila dakṣiṇa pradeśa 'The southern regions are shadowed with dark clouds.' The monsoon begins earliest in southern India and gradually arrives in the northern areas.

202 Kemane bañcibō re bāriṣā cāri māṣa 'Oh, how will I survive monsoon's four months?' See Naukākhaṇḍa above, n. 2.

203 Āṣāṛha māse 'in the month of Āṣāṛha.' See n. 200 above.

204 Śrābaṇa māse ghana ghana bariṣe 'With the month of Śrāvaṇa, it rains heavily.' See Vaṃśīkhaṇḍa above, n. 20.

205 Literally, 'Lying alone in bed, sleep doesn't come.'

Oh, how long must I endure the sting of passion's missiles?[206]
In this season, Granny, reunite me with my Krishna!
During August,[207] Granny, in the days and nights of darkness,
Peacocks, frogs and partridges will make a real commotion.[208]
That is why my heart will burst from worrying and brooding
If I am not able to behold the face of Krishna.
As September wanes,[209] the rainy season will be ended.
Clouds will float away and thatch grass blossoms will be blooming.[210]
Then, bereft of Krishna, my existence will be barren!

Song 65

"Radha, my good lady, don't mope, but take heart;
Krishna will come soon and contact you!"

Promising the moon in easy reach,[211] you've made me crazy.
Kissing off my shame, I turned my back on Abhimanyu.[212]
Always at the sidelines you've been there to give assurance;
Now I'm in a state of agitation over Krishna.
I've been learning, Granny, I've been learning. I know Krishna.
He won't let me see him, let alone come into contact!
Granny, on your counsel I extended my affection,
But I've managed only to taste partial bliss with Krishna.
Maybe in a life gone by I left a vow unfinished;[213]
That may be the reason my desires aren't accomplished.
I could not explain my joys, my griefs and other matters;[214]
Instantly, like water in a strainer,[215] he escaped me.
Day by day, because of love's disease, I'm growing wasted.
Eagerly I proffered love, but that was my undoing.
Furthermore, because of what you say, my heart is shaken.
How am I to find Lord Madhusūdana, my Granny?

206 Kata nā sahiba re kusumaśarajālā 'Oh, how much shall I endure the burning of the flower arrows (of love)?'

207 Bhādara mā̃se 'in the month of Bhādra (August–September),' the height of the rainy season.

208 Śikhi bheka ḍāhuka kare kolāhale 'Peacocks (śikhi), frogs (bheka) and partridges (ḍāhuka) make a racket.' All three creatures are sexually active during the monsoon.

209 Āśina māsera śeṣe 'at the end of Āśvina month (September–October).'

210 Kāśī, the thatch grass plant or its blossom; see Appendix.

211 Hāthe cānda mānī 'promising the moon in hand.'

212 Āihanaka pīṭha dilõ lāje tilāñjalī 'I gave (my) back to Abhimanyu and tilāñjalī to my modesty.' Refer to n. 29 above.

213 Puruba jarame kibā khaṇḍabrata kaila, cf. n. 8 above.

214 Dukha sukha pā̃ca kathā kahitē̃ nā pāila 'I did not get to tell (him) (of my) distress, happiness, five matters (pā̃ca kathā, i.e., this and that, mundane affairs).'

215 Jhāliāra jala yena takhane pālāila 'He vanished (just) then, like water from a sieve.'

This is what I wish: that you depart in search of Krishna.

Song 66

"Radha, it doesn't matter whether or not I know the particulars
of Hari,
Inasmuch as I am unable any longer to pursue him."

"Look, come on now, Granny! Take to heart what I'm requesting of you.
Put my jeweled ring upon your finger.
See, I'm paying homage at your feet and I'm entreating of you:
summon and deliver Jagannātha!"
"Oh, be still, immodest Radha! Where am I to go and find him?
Don't you feel ashamed, you wayward woman?
I had asked him: gladden Radha's heart for once. The king of gods
complied with my request before departing!"
"Oh, don't say such utterly unsympathetic things to me;
your age has caused this defect in you, Granny.
Blessed with lack of enterprise,[216] you've never known the face of
hardship; that's the thing about you which annoys me!"
"Stop your sassing! Who can tell you anything? That insolence
of yours is just stupendous for a cowmaid.
Where will I discover Krishna? Those are the directions you must give
me; I will seek him out and fetch him."
"These are words in which I take delight; I kiss your face. Today's
a day which is auspicious for me, Granny.
Carry out your search in those locations he frequents and, Granny,
you will then obtain a glimpse of Krishna."
"Listen, Radha, I've no strength for wandering around; precisely
where should I go searching for him, Grandniece?
It's my intuition that the distant town of Mathurā
is where your Krishna headed when he left you."
"In my sleep, my spirit's master left me, you old woman, and
escaped to Mathurā by your connivance!
Summon Krishna back this once. I clasp your feet, my Granny!
Otherwise, you shall be guilty of my murder!"
"I shall travel to the town of Mathurā for you, but
swear before me that you'll never vex me further.
Truthfully I tell you, it is fortunate I haven't perished;
time and time again I've had to suffer."
"See, I cross my heart[217] and take a solemn pledge before you
that hereafter I shall give you no vexation.

216 Ālisera parasādĕ 'by grace of indolence.'

217 Hera śira kara yoge 'See here, with hand joined to head. . . .' See n. 134 above.

In its season, that will come to pass which has been fated for me;
meanwhile, this time only, go to Krishna!"
"Look, as you've requested, I am setting out for Mathurā,
my grandniece, with the aim of tracing Krishna.
If I should be able to discover his location, then
I'll exercise my efforts to the utmost."

Song 67

Going to the city of Mathurā, Granny told Krishna:
"Radha is overcome in your absence, she seeks sustenance in you."
When the dashing Hari heard this, he conveyed to Granny
His ultimate message to conclude Radha's anguish.

Radha's quite flirtatious;[218] with a look, she steals one's spirits.
I'm too much afraid to pay a visit to her, Granny.
All of them are base at heart; no dairymaid is wholesome.
You yourself must tell me: why should I approach her, Granny?[219]
What is this you're asking? I should pay her further visits?
What has Krishna failed to undertake because of Radha!
You yourself had held her hands on my behalf and, Granny,
Told her of the anguish which had cauterized my spirits;
Even then, since Radha wouldn't give me her approval,
Handsome Krishna doesn't care to see her face hereafter.
Plenty has been said, but there's no purpose in it, Granny;
You're aware of how much Radha's previously babbled.
I'm requesting you; I clasp your feet and say, go homeward.

Song 68

Krishna, your behavior is beyond my comprehension—
You reject ambrosia when its coaxingly presented![220]
She, Candrāvalī, will not abuse you any further;
Trust in my assurances and come, oh Vanamālī.
Poor Candrāvalī is overtaken by bereavement;
It's not right for you to leave her stranded at the moment.
If you don't approach her in the way that I'm suggesting,
Later you shall surely suffer, Krishna, in her absence.
Once, because of Radha, you refused to eat a morsel;[221]

218 Naṭhī baṛa rādhā 'Radha's a very wicked (literally, "ruined") woman.'
219 Literally, 'why should I extend my foot?'
220 Yācitẽ ūpekhaha tohme se āmṛta 'You reject that ambrosia when with pleading (it is presented)!'
221 Literally, 'You would not eat (your) rice (i.e., meals) then because of her.'

How is it that lately you are keen to relish gravel?[222]
If a pitcher made of gold should break, then one can mend it;
So it is, Murāri, with the love of worthy persons.[223]
On the other hand, the love of one who is unworthy
And whose heart is insincere, is like an earthen pitcher.
Radha has remained behind; she's waiting at her dwelling.
You have come to Mathurā; you've settled in the city.
I'm the one who frantically goes back and forth between you!

Song 69

Don't behave insistently with me. I tell you, Granny,
When I hear her name, I've no desire to approach her.
You have some awareness of the misery she's caused me;
Now I have my mind made up; no more will I behold her.
Granny, go along with you; go back to where you've come from.
Don't attempt to put me under pressure over Radha.
How much acid will you put in open wounds that fester?[224]
You're aware of how I have been spoken to by Radha.
Home, possessions, everything can I, Murāri, forfeit;
But the crushing sting of her remarks I won't put up with.
I have come to Mathurā and left my pasture homeland
With my heart resolved upon assassinating Kaṃsa.
Out of separation—[225]

* * *

222 Śākara khāitẽ tohme ādarāha kehne 'Why do you show enthusiasm (ādara) for eating śākara?' Śākara (from Sanskrit śakara 'particle, grain') refers in some modern Indian languages to sugar, which has only recently come into common household use. In the present passage, this word refers to grains or gravel. It is implied that, compared to Radha, other women are undesirable.

223 Bhā̃gila sonāra ghaṭa yuṛībāka pārī / uttama janera nehā tehena murārī 'A broken golden pot can be remolded; the love of superior persons is like that, Murāri.'

224 Kāṭila ghāata lemburasa deha kata 'How much lemon juice (lemburasa) you put into open (literally "cut") wounds!' Cf. Vaṃśīkhaṇḍa above, n. 89.

225 At this point an unknown number of concluding pages from the manuscript are lost. According to *Bhāgavatapurāṇa*, once Krishna leaves his home in Gokula for Mathurā, he never returns. Whether the poet of *Śrīkṛṣṇakīrtana* concludes the text by stipulating that Radha never again meets Krishna is a matter for speculation, until and unless a second SKK manuscript is discovered. There is, however, a possible clue to the poet's intentions in the opening section, Janmakhaṇḍa, song 7. There it is stated that Radha is an incarnation of the god's divine consort. In all probability the lost ending of the text recurs to this statement, bringing about a reunification at some supramundane level of the divine personality and his beloved.

Appendix

Sources:

Kirtikar and Basu 1975 (KB)
Monier-Williams 1976 (MW)
Mukherji 1976 (M)
Roxburgh 1832, 1971 (R)
Sukumar Sen, personal communication (SS)
Turner 1962–1966 (T)
Usher 1974 (U)
Van Wijk 1962 (VW)

ā̃ba: mango. *Mangifera indica* (R)

āgara: aloewood, an immense tree flowering in April, having fragrant wood, native to the mountainous areas east of Sylhet. *Aquilaria Agallocha* (R)

āgaru: see āgara

agatha: agati tree, a small delicate tree 20′–30′ high of a few years' duration; has edible pods and large flowers which occur in both red and white varieties; both pods and flowers appear most of the year. *Aeschynomene grandiflora* (R), *Sesbania grandiflora* (U)

ākorala: walnut. *Aleurites triloba* (R)

ā̃koṛa: angolan, Sanskrit aṅkoṭa; a small tree with beautiful wood, producing 5–10 petaled flowers in the hot season, and a fruit purplish red when ripe. *Alangium hexapetalum* (R), *Alangium Lamarkii* (VW)

āmba: see ā̃ba

āmbaṛā: hog plum, a large tree producing very numerous, small, white flowers at the beginning of the hot season, and an astringent fruit which ripens in the cold season. *Spondias mangifera* (R)

āmbu: see ā̃ba

āmṛta kāṅkaṛī: sweet melon, probably a sweet variety of kāṅkaṛī

āmulia: tamarind, Sanskrit āmlikā, modern Bengali aamla 'sour, acid'; a tree producing very small, pale yellow flowers; its crescent-shaped greenish-brown pods contain an edible, sour pulp. *Tamarindus indica* (R) ā̃olā: Phyllanthus, Sanskrit āmalaka; a large tree producing minute, greenish yellow blossoms at the beginning of the hot season; its roundish fruit has a sharp acrid taste. A relative of labalī. *Phyllanthus Emblica* (R), emblic myrobalan (KB)

āṛayi: pigeon-pea, also called tuvar; a shrub producing large yellow flowers and edible, pea-sized seeds. *Cytisus Cajan* (R), *Cajanus indicus* (KB)

ārjjuna: white murdah, Sanskrit kakubha; a stout, quick growing timber tree, flowers April–May. Related to āsane. *Pentaptera Arjuna* (R), *Terminalia Arjuna* (KB)

ārjuna: see ārjjuna

ārjūna: see ārjjuna

āsane: Pentaptera, a large timber tree flowering in April and May. A relative of ārjjuna. *Pentaptera tomentosa* (R), *Terminalia tomentosa* (U)

āsāṛhiā bhūmicampaka: a larger and later blooming variety of bhūmicampaka which flowers in June during the rains (SS)

āsnai: see āsane

āśoka: asoka, a beautiful flowering tree whose blossoms, appearing at the beginning of the hot season, are a lovely orange when they first expand, changing later to red, and fragrant during the night. *Jonesia Asoca* (R), *Saraca indica* (KB)

ātabhaṛi: custard apple, also called atamarum (R); a tree about 20′ tall, producing solitary flowers at the beginning of the rainy season; the globose fruit, 2″–4″ in diameter, is yellowish green when ripe and contains smooth, brownish black seeds. *Anona squamosa* (R)

ātaṣi: flax, a small plant producing blue flowers; *Linum usitatissimum* (R) (see Vṛndāvanakhaṇḍa, n. 152)

badarī: jujube, a small tree flowering in the rainy season; the globular, smooth fruits are yellow when ripe and the size of a large cherry, ripening after the rains. *Ziziphus Jujuba* (R)

baga: modern Bengali bak; see agatha

bahaṛā: bedda nut tree, a large tree producing edible kernels; grows in mountainous areas; produces small flowers of a dirty gray color with a strong offensive smell at the beginning of the hot season. A relative of haṛirā. *Terminalia Bellerica* (R), belleric myrobalan (KB)

bahula: Indian medlar, a large tree (trunk extends 8′–12′ to the lowest branches) with drooping, white, fragrant flowers. *Mimusops Elengi* (R)

bājabāraṇe: milkwort, Sanskrit vajrakaṇṭaka (KB); a large shrub or small tree (4.5′–9′ high) having a stout trunk; flowers in the cold season, produces a juice used medicinally. *Euphorbia antiquorum* (R)

bakula: see bahula

bana sonā: see sonā

bandhulī: flame of the forest, an elegant bush with numerous flowers, scarlet when they first open, changing to crimson; in bloom the whole year, especially during the rains. *Ixora Bandhuca* (R), *Ixora coccinea* (VW)

bāndhulī: see bandhulī

bāṅgī: bursting melon, Hindu ṭūṭī (R); a vine whose smooth and cylindrical fruit, weighing 4–8 lbs., bursts spontaneously when ripe. *Cucumis Momordica* (R)

bara: see badarī

bāṛiāla: Sida, a plant producing red blossoms during the rainy and cold seasons. *Sida cordifolia* (R)

bāsaka: Malabar nut tree; a small tree or large shrub whose flowers, the lower part of both lips of which are streaked with purple, appear in the cold season. *Justicia Adhatoda* (R), *Adhatoda vasica* (KB)

baula: see bahula

baūla: see bahula

bela: Bengal quince, a large tree producing a large smooth fruit with a hard shell. *Aegle Marmelos* (R)

bhālā: marking nut tree, grows in mountainous areas, flowers May–August, bears nuts; its wood yields a black juice used to mark cotton cloth, hence its English name. *Semecarpus Anacardium* (R)

bhāṇṭi: glory tree, a shrub producing numerous, large, white flowers with a small tinge of red, appearing in February–March; the fruit is bright red when unripe; black, shiny and smooth when ripe, the size of a black cherry. *Volkameria infortunata* (R), *Clerodendron infortunatum* (KB)

bhā̃ṭi: see bhāṇṭi

bhilola: sweet leaf, a small tree (12′–20′) native to Burdwan and Midnapore districts of West Bengal; produces small, lively yellow flowers; its bark is used to make red dye and powder, the latter being used during the Holī festival. *Symplocos racemosa* (R) bhojapāta: birch, a small deciduous tree or shrub with white bark. *Betula utilis* (KB)

bhūmicampaka: galangale, an elegant plant blossoming in March and April; produces large fragrant flowers in various shades of purple with white. *Kaempferia rotunda* (R)

bimba: balsam apple, a plant with edible berries, red when ripe. *Momordica monadelpha* (R)

biṣakarañja: Indian beech, a large timber tree in whose shade grass grows well; flowers in the hot season; its name may derive from one of its Sanskrit names, viṣaṇi (KB), or may be explained by the fact that its seed is bitter (biṣa 'poison'). *Galedupa indica* (R), *Pongamia glabra* (KB)

bohārī: sebesten plum, a large but low tree producing numerous, small, white flowers at the end of the cold season; its edible fruit is globular, smooth, cherry-sized, yellow when ripe, with a nearly transparent, tough, viscid pulp. *Cordia Myxa* (R)

bola: hibiscus, producing drooping, large, campanulate flowers of a bright yellow, with the bottom of the bell crimson. *Hibiscus tortuosus* (R), *Hibiscus tiliaceus* (KB)

cākali: Hemionitis, a plant growing in rich wet soil. *Hemionitis cordifolia* (R)

cālanī: unknown

cālitā: elephant apple, a tree very beautiful when in flower during the hot season and at the beginning of the rains; produces large flowers (9″ in diameter), five-petaled, white, which look to earth, delightfuly fragrant; produces an acid fruit. *Dillenia speciosa* (R), *Dillenia indica* (U)

cāmbhalī: Spanish jasmine. *Jasminum grandiflorum* (R)

campā: Michelia, a large evergreen tree with large, yellow, delightfully fragrant flowers, said to be related to magnolia (*Webster's New Twentieth Century Dictionary of the English Language*, 2d ed., s.v. "Michelia"). *Michelia Champaca* (R)

cāmpā: see campā

campaka: see campā

cāmpātī: possibly from cāmpā + pāti 'small'; see campā

candana: sandalwood or sandal. *Santalum album* (R)

cā̃pā: see campā

chāñīyaṇe: devil tree, Sanskrit chattraparṇa; a tall (12′–18′) tree with greenish white flowers, producing a bitter milky juice. *Alstonia scholaris* (KB)

chātiana: see chāñīyaṇe

cholaṅga: citrus, a term that seems to apply to no specific variety but to the genus Citrus in general

citā: leadwort, a perennial, stubby plant with pure white flowers. *Plumbago zeylanica* (R)

cuā̃: see ā̃ba

ḍahu: lakoocha, Sanskrit lakuca, modern Bengali ḍeo; a tree containing much milky juice, blooming at the beginning of the hot season; its lobulate, velvety yellow fruit, 2″–3″ in diameter, has an acid, astringent taste; related to the jackfruit, kaṇṭhoāla. *Artocarpus Lakoocha* (R)

ḍālima: pomegranate. *Punica Granatum* (R)

ḍālimba: see ḍālima

danā: wormwood, a plant with floral leaves and small, globular, numerous flowers which blossom in the cold season. *Artemisia indica* (R)

dāṛima: see ḍālima

ḍauhāku: see ḍahu

debadāru: fir tree, very full of resin, achieves a great size. *Pinus Deodora* (R)

dhaba: button tree, a fruiting and flowering tree 55′–65′ high which yields a usable gum. *Anogeissus latifolia* (VW)

dhātakī: Grislea, a very beautiful flowering shrub or small tree which produces large red flowers during the cold and beginning of the hot seasons; its bright, red, permanent calyx makes for a gaudy appearance. *Grislea tomentosa* (R), *Woodfordia fruticosa* (KB)

dhutura: thorn-apple, a plant producing a round, spinous fruit; the flowers, which appear all year, are sacred to Śiva and are white with violet; shaped like large medicine phials (SS). *Datura Metel* (R)

dolaṅga: garland flower, a plant producing large, white fragrant flowers, which blossom profusely during the rainy season; there are also yellow varieties. *Hedychium coronarium* (R)

drākṣā: grape. *Vitis vinifera* (R)

dudhiā: milk-plant, grows in hedges, yielding flowers and foliage in the rainy season; blossoms large and white with a small tinge of rose-color, striated with purple veins, inodorous; all parts of the plant yield a milky juice. *Asclepias rosea* (R)

dulāla: see dolaṅga

dulālī: see dolaṅga

gambhārī: white teak, a moderate sized tree growing up to 55′ high, having drooping, large flowers colored yellow and tinged with brown; produces an astringent drupe, orange-yellow when ripe; the oil of the tree is used for waterproofing boats (SS). *Gmelina arborea* (R), *Premna arborea* (U)

garjjuna: wood-oil tree, an immense tree 110′–135′ high whose flowers, solitary, large, white with a faint tinge of red, appear at the beginning of the hot season; the tree yields wood oil. *Dipterocarpus turbinatus* (R)

ghāṭā pāralī: Bignonia or trumpet flower, produces exquisitely fragrant blossoms of a dark, dull crimson. *Bignonia suaveolens* (R)

guā: betel nut, also called areca; a flowering and fruiting tree whose trunk extends 40′–50′ high; the most beautiful palm in India. *Areca Catechu* (R)

gulāla: basil, a plant 2′–6′ tall with large white blossoms that bloom most of the year, especially in the rainy and cold seasons. *Ocymum caryophyllatum* (R)

gulāle: see gulāla

haladi: turmeric, a plant yielding beautiful yellow flowers in April. *Curcuma Zerumbet* (R)

hariṛā: black myrobalan, a large tree with numerous small, dull white, offensive smelling flowers appearing in the hot season. A relative of bahaṛā. *Terminalia Chebula* (R)

hemayūthikā: golden or yellow jasmine, Sanskrit svarṇayūthī. *Jasminum chrysanthemum* (R), *Jasminum bignoniaceum* (KB)

hentāla: Phoenix, a tree whose trunk extends 6′–16′ high, producing oval, smooth, shiny black berries; native to the Sunderbans. *Phoenix paludosa* (R)

hiñcī: Hingtsha, Sanskrit hilamoci; a marsh herb growing in a moist rich soil, sometimes extending itself over the surface of pools of water; flowers in hot and cold seasons, has edible leaves and stalks. *Hingtsha repens* (R), *Enhydra fluctuans* (KB)

jalapāyi: Indian olive (not a true olive); a small tree native to northern Bengal and nearby mountainous areas, producing numerous small white flowers pointing toward earth in the hot season; fruit resembles the olive. *Elaeocarpus serratus* (R)

jāmbarī: lemon. *Citrus acida* (R)

jāmbīra: see jāmbarī

jāmbu: black plum, a plant producing a smooth, roundish, succulent fruit the size of a large cherry, black when it ripens in July and August, with an astringent flavor; related to clove, labaṅga. *Eugenia Jambolana* (R)

jayantī: Aeschynomene, a small beautiful tree of a few years' duration, flowering in the wet and cold seasons; blooms are large, dark purple with yellow spots (a red with yellow variety also occurs); related to agatha. *Aeschynomene Sesban* (R)

jhā̃ṭāla: see ghāṭā pāralī

jiāpūta: wild olive (not a true olive), Sanskrit putrañjīva, jīvanaputra, etc. (KB); a tall evergreen timber tree with shiny green leaves and a large spreading shady head; flowers March–April, blossoms green; parents have their children wear necklaces strung with the nuts to protect health (R). *Nageia Putranjiva* (R), *Putranjiva Roxburghii* (KB)

jiṅgaṇi: ridged gourd, a vine producing an edible fruit. *Luffa acutangula* (R)

kadalaka: banana. *Musa sapientum* (R)

kadalī: see kadalaka

kadama: kadamba, an ornamental, large tree whose flowers form a beautiful large orange-colored globular head with white clubbed stigmas projecting; useful for shade. *Nauclea Cadamba* (R), *Anthocephalus Cadamba* (KB)

kadamba: see kadama

kala: see kadalaka

kālakāsundā: senna, Sanskrit kāsamarda(ka); produces yellow flowers in the cooler months; specified in Ayurvedic and Yunani pharmacopoeia as a cough suppressant (KB). *Cassia Sophora* (R)

kamala: lotus, beautiful sacred plants with flowers 9″–10″ in diameter, tending to grow in sweet water lakes; there are two varieties, one whitish with a greenish cast, the other rose colored. *Nelumbium speciosum* (R)

kamalā: tangerine, modern Bengali kamlaa lebu; widely called orange in India, but closer to the Western tangerine in being less difficult to peel, less sweet in taste and smaller in size than the orange. *Citrus Aurantium* (R)

kamale: see kamala

kāmaraṅga: Coromandel gooseberry, produces blossoms in the rainy season and ripened fruit in the cold season; both sweet and sour fruiting varieties occur. *Averrhoa Carambola* (R) kanaka: Pterospermum, a plant producing large, pure white, fragrant flowers at the start of the hot season. *Pterospermum acerifolium* (R)

kanakaketakī: yellow screwpine, Sanskrit svarṇa ketakī. See ketakī

kanaka ketakī: see kanakaketakī

kanakayūthī: see hemayūthikā

kanakayūthikā: see hemayūthikā

kanaka yūthikā: see hemayūthikā

kāñcana: mountain ebony, a small ramous tree or large shrub 8′–10′ high, in bloom most of the year, producing large, inodorous, pure white flowers. *Bauhinia acuminata* (R)

kāṅkaṛī: winter melon or field cucumber, a vine whose fleshy fruit is a perfect oval, downy when young, when ripe smooth and variegated with deeper and lighter yellow; used ripe or unripe as a food item. *Cucumis utilissimus* (R)

kaṇṭhoāla: jackfruit, a tree 30′–40′ high with a shady head, producing an edible fruit; flowers in the cold season. *Artocarpus integrifolia* (R)

kāpāsi: cotton, a plant cultivated all over Bengal, with white and yellow blossoming varieties (SS). *Gossypium herbaceum* (R)

kapitha: wood apple, a large tree with hard durable timber, flowering at the beginning of the hot season; its edible fruit, very sweet and pleasantly fragrant, is hard shelled, in size about the same as a tennis ball. *Feronia elephantum* (R)

karabīre: oleander, a year round flowering plant with red, white and double flowered varieties. *Nerium odorum* (R)

karaṇe: lemon (see jāmbarī). T (listing 2810) gives various species of Citrus under this heading. KB lists it (as karnānebu) under *Citrus Medica* var. *Limonum*

karañja: see biṣakarañja

kaṛayi: Albizzia, also called white siris (see śiriṣa); an unarmed flowering tree 18′–24′ in height. *Albizzia procera* (R)

kaṛī: winter cherry, Sanskrit kaṭabhī; a vine producing white flowers and globose, smooth, black seeds, both appearing year round. *Cardiospermum Halicacabum* (R)

kāśī: thatch grass, Sanskrit kāśa; a tall erect grass which grows in moist areas, used to make mats. *Saccharum spontaneum* (R)

kāsimala: see kālakāsundā

kendu: ebony, a tree with black, hard, heavy wood; produces a berry with a soft, yellow, edible pulp. *Diospyros tomentosa* (R) keśara: rose chestnut, Sanskrit nāgakeśara; an elegant tree with large, delightfully fragrant white-petaled flowers having a globe of bright golden anthers in the center. *Mesua ferrea* (R)

ketakī: screwpine, a tree growing up to 15′ in height, used to make hedges; has white-petaled flowers with a powerful, delightful perfume. *Pandanus odoratissimus* (R)

khadira: catechu, a flowering plant. Related to śiriṣa. *Mimosa Catechu* (R)

khājura: date palm, a tree with yellowish or reddish fruit which flowers at the beginning of the hot season; tapped for its juice, which is made into date sugar and toddy. *Phoenix sylvestris* (R)

khañcī: cowitch, a plant with twining, ramous stems and large, fleshy, tender edible legumes; produces very large, pendulous white flowers. *Carpopogon niveum* (R), *Mucuna prurita* (KB), *Mucuna pruriens* (U)

kharamūjā: muskmelon, a vine having many varieties, including cantaloupe; related to kāṅkaṛī, bāṅgī. *Cucumis Melo* (R)

khastarī: target-leaved hibiscus, a plant 10′–12′ high flowering in the cold and wet seasons; the flowers are large and bright yellow, the bottom covered with deep purple, very ornamental. *Hibiscus Abelmoschus* (R)

khirī: Mimusops, a large spreading tree flowering in the hot season and producing an oval, drooping, orange-red fruit (T listing 3703). *Mimusops Kauki* (R)

kiṃśuka: Bengal kino, a large flowering tree whose large blossoms, appearing in March–April, are deep red, shaded with orange and silver colored down; the bark gives a red juice through fissures. *Butea frondosa* (R)

koka: red waterlotus, an aquatic plant related to utapala. *Nymphaea rubra* (R)

kokanada: see koka

kuhaya: see ārjjuna

kujā: strychnine, a middle-sized tree with small, greenish white flowers appearing in the cold season; produces an attractive, smooth, round, orange berry the size of a large apple. *Strychnos Nux-vomica* (R)

kumuda: white water lily, a night blooming aquatic waterlotus of a dazzling white, related to utapala, koka, and sundhi. *Nymphaea Lotus* (R)

kunda: star jasmine, Sanskrit śuklapuṣpa, sadāpuṣpa (KB); a ramous shrub with large, pure white, fragrant flowers which open in succession. *Jasminum pubescens* (R) kurubaka: amaranth, also called coxcomb and love lies bleeding, etc.; a plant 1′–2′ tall which grows year round if watered; the leaves are emarginate, with a bristle, usually red. *Amaranthus tristis* (R)

kuṛuma: coriander, Sanskrit kustumbarī; an herb 13″–16″ high. *Coriandrum sativum* (R)

kuśa: also known as darbha; a prickly topped grass. *Poa cynosuroides* (MW)

kuśiāra: sugarcane. *Saccharum officinarum* (R)

kusumbha: safflower, a plant whose seeds yield a useful oil. *Carthamus tinctorius* (R)

kuṭuja: Tellicherry bark tree, a shrub or small tree with white inodorous flowers whose bark, in Hindu pharmacopoeia, is the principal medicine for dysentery (KB). *Holarrhena antidysenterica* (KB)

labalī: country gooseberry, an elegant small tree about 14′–18′ high bearing very numerous, small, reddish flowers at the beginning of the hot season; produces a yellow-green sour fruit 1″ long. *Phyllanthus longifolius* (R), *Phyllanthus distichus* (KB)

labaṅga: clove. *Eugenia caryophyllata* (R)

laṅga: see labaṅga

lāṛikā: possibly anatto, modern Bengali laaṭkaan; a small evergreen tree with white flowering and pink flowering varieties. *Bixa Orellana* (R)

lāu: gourd, more specifically bottle gourd or calabash. *Lagenaria vulgaris* or *Lagenaria siceraria* (U)

lembu: see jāmbarī

locane: globe thistle, Sanskrit mahāśrāvaṇikā; a purple-flowered herb about 9″ high, inodorous; flowers in cool season. *Sphaeranthus indicus* (R)

lodha: see bhilola

mādhabī: Roydsia, a vine indigenous to Sylhet, having numerous, rather large, fragrant pale yellow flowers which bloom in March. *Roydsia suaveolens* (R)

madhuka: butter tree, a middling sized tree with numerous crimson flowers that bow toward the ground. *Bassia latifolia* (R)

madhukara: Eclipta, Sanskrit bhṛṅgarāja, keśarāja; modern Bengali kesuriyaa; blossoms year round; the juice of the leaves is used in tattooing and for dyeing hair black. *Eclipta prostrata* (R), *Eclipta alba* (KB) māhākāla: gooseberry gourd, a relative of cucumber, soāśe; has an attractive, globular, smooth, but offensive smelling fruit whose pulp can be fatal if consumed. *Cucumis Colocynthis* (R), *Cucumis myriocarpus* (U)

māhāsundhī: probably the same as sundhi

māhlī: single flowered Arabian jasmine. *Jasminum Zambac* (R) (one variety; see neālī)

mahukuta: lime, Sanskrit madhukukkuṭī; the sweet lime or limetta (KB). *Citrus acida* (R)

mahula: see madhuka

mahule: see madhuka

mālatī: see cāmbhalī

mallikā: see māhlī

mandāre: coral tree, a large tree with dazzling, numerous, large scarlet flowers; very useful for shade owing to its numerous large leaves. *Erythrina indica* (R)

maruā: finger millet, a plant 18″–36″ high which produces flowers as well as a medicinal seed that is round, globular, dark brown, a little wrinkled. *Eleusine coracana* (R)

mathura: urn-fruit tree, a shrub whose tender parts, and the undersides of whose leaves, are covered with a soft, white, stellate pubescence; flowers all year. *Callicarpa incana* (R), *Callicarpa macrophylla* (KB)

nāgaraṅga: see kamalā

nāgeśara: see keśara

nāgeśbara: see keśara

nākaṛī: fig tree, a large beautiful tree with a dense head, native to Bengal; related to the banyan, pipalī. *Ficus infectoria* (R)

nālicā: jute. *Corchorus olitorius* (R)

nalina: see kamala

nalīna: see kamala

naline: see kamala

nalinī: see kamala

nārīkala: coconut. *Cocos nucifera* (R)

nārikela: see nārīkala

neālī: double flowered Arabian jasmine. *Jasminum Zambac* (R) (one variety; see māhlī)

oṛa: red hibiscus, yellow and white varieties also occur; the flowers are sacred to the goddess Kālī. *Hibiscus Rosa-sinensis* (R)

padma: see kamala

padmā: see kamala

padmakāṣṭha: Himalayan cherry, a middling to large tree found in the outer Himalaya at high altitudes; produces glossy leaves and flowers of white, pink, or crimson, as well as a roundish yellow-red fruit with an acid taste. *Prunus cerasoides* (R), *Prunus Puddum* (VW)

pākaṛī: see nākaṛī

pāṇiāla: Indian plum, a large tree with globular, smooth, purple, succulent berries. Related to piṇḍāra. *Flacourtia cataphracta* (R)

paralā: snakegourd, a plant producing an edible fruit which somewhat resembles a small cucumber, being cylinder-shaped with tapering ends and a green exterior. *Trichosanthes dioica* (R)

pārali: see ghāṭā pāralī

pāralī: see ghāṭā pāralī

pārijāta: see mandāre

pȇhuṭī: unknown

piāla: Buchanania, a large tree native to mountainous areas of the Coromandel coast, bearing kernels rather similar to almonds, and numerous small, whitish-green flowers which appear January–February. *Buchanania latifolia* (R), *Buchanania Lanzan* (KB)

piṇḍakhājura: see khājura

piṇḍāra: Madagascar plum, a shrub or small tree with greenish yellow flowers producing a fruit 5/16″–1/2″ in diameter, globose, red or dark brown or dark purple; a relative of pāṇiāla. *Flacourtia sapida* (R), *Flacourtia Ramontchi* (KB)

pipalī: banyan, a large, sacred tree which flowers in the hot season. *Ficus religiosa* (R)

pippalī: see pipalī

rabi: swallow-wort, a large, ramous shrub common throughout India that flowers year round and grows everywhere, especially near ruinous places; the large, beautiful flowers are a mixture of rose colored and purple. A relative of dudhiā. *Asclepias gigantea* (R)

rakata candana: red sandalwood (not a true relative of sandalwood); flowers in the hot season. *Pterocarpus santalinus* (R)

rambhā: see kadalaka

rāṅganāgara: see kamalā

rātā utapala: see koka

rātā utapalā: see koka

rebatī: orange. The name seems to derive from irāvat (irā 'juice')—cf. Sanskrit airāvata 'elephant' or 'snake'; elephants and oranges are associated with a single part of India, the Assam foothills (SS). *Citrus Aurantium* (R)

rudrākṣa: bead tree, a tree which blossoms February–March, producing white, drooping, middle-sized flowers, and a purplish drupe the size of a large cherry; the seeds are strung and worn by Śaivas. Related to jalapāyi. *Elaeocarpus ganitrus* (R)

sāḍara: sesame, Sanskrit sārāla (Ray 1973:248); produces red flowers. *Sesamum orientale* (R)

sahakāra: see ā̃ba

sāhaṛa: bucephalon, Sanskrit śākhoṭa; a shrubby plant producing pea-sized berries; its minute, greenish-yellow flowers appear in the cold season. *Trophis aspera* (R)

sāhāre: see ā̃ba

saināhula: burweed. *Xanthium Strumarium* (R)

sāje: Euphorbia, Sanskrit sehuṇḍa (T listing 13599); a tree 9″–27″ high with leaves appearing usually only in the rainy season; flowers in the hot season; prefers barren soil. Related to bājabāraṇe. *Euphorbia nereifolia* (R), *Euphorbia Nivulia* (KB)

sāla: Indian dammer, an immense timber tree which flowers in the hot season. *Shorea robusta* (R)

sarala: pine tree, a relative of debadāru; produces numerous flowers at beginning of hot season. *Pinus longifolia* (R)

sātakaṛā: equivalent to Kannada satagadi, Tamil sadagadi, Telugu satghadi (KB) and Persian sangtara (Sen 1971:870, 856); see rebatī

seālī: night blooming jasmine (not a true jasmine), a large shrub or small tree whose numerous middle sized, honey-scented flowers open at sunset and fall off at sunrise; the tube is orange colored and the border, white. *Nyctanthes Arbor-tristis* (R)

seathī: white rose, surprisingly the only true rose mentioned in *Śrīkṛṣṇakīrtana*. *Rosa glandulifera* (R)

śebatī: see seathī

seyatī: see seathī

siali: see seālī

sihāla: eel-grass, a grasslike plant growing in shallow standing waters. *Vallisneria octandra* (R) sindhubāre: chaste tree, an elegant small tree with small, numerous flowers of a lovely bluish purple which appear year round. *Vitex Negundo* (R)

śiriphala: see bela

śiriṣa: parrot tree, a deciduous tree 35′–65′ high with pale bark, producing white, fragrant flowers during the hot and rainy seasons. In *Gāthāsaptaśatī* 1.55 (Basak 1971:13), the limbs of a woman exhausted from lovemaking are compared to this plant's withered flowers. Related to khadira. *Mimosa Sirissa* (R), *Albizzia Lebbek* (KB)

śirīṣa: see śiriṣa

soāśe: cucumber, Sanskrit sudhāvāsa. *Cucumis sativus* (R)

sonā: Cassia, also called pudding pipe, Sanskrit svarṇaka, svarṇāṅga, svarṇavṛkṣa, modern Bengali sonaali (KB); a beautiful tree 6′–9′ high whose flowers, five-petaled, large, yellow, fragrant, appear in April. A relative of kālakāsundā. *Cassia Fistula* (R)

śrīphala: see bela

śrīphale: see bela

sudarśana: Tinospora, a climbing plant. *Tinospora malabarica* (U, KB)

sugandhesarī: unknown

sukala: see kunda

sundarī: looking-glass tree, a large timber tree native to the Ganges delta, producing numerous dull orange flowers in the hot season. It lends its name to the Sunderbans region. *Heritiera minor* (R)

sundhi: white waterlotus, an aquatic plant; related to utapala. *Nymphaea esculenta* (R)

suthī: see haladi

ṭābhāgaṇe: from ṭābā (modern Bengali 'lime, lemon') + gaṇa (a pluralizer). See jāmbarī

ṭagara: rosebay, a shrub producing pure white flowers most of the year, with shining green leaves and with both single and double flowered varieties; delightfully fragrant during the night. *Tabernaemontana coronaria* (R)

tāla: palmyra, a tree with a long slender trunk having a head of fronds at the top, which shadow the fruits; these are large, perfectly round, about 8″ in diameter, blackish, brown at the base. *Borassus flabelliformis* (R), *Borassus flabellifer* (VW)

tamāla: mangosteen, a beautiful tree; large, dark-barked, straight-trunked, producing large (3/4″ in diameter) white flowers in spring, and having a lovely yellow, very sour fruit similar in appearance to an orange; native of mountainous areas. *Xanthochymus pictorius* (R), *Garcinia Xanthochymus* (KB)

tejapāta: laurel, also called bay tree; an elegant tree growing in mountainous areas, producing whitish flowers at the beginning of the warm season. *Laurus Cassia* (R)

tentali: see āmulia

thalakamala: changeable hibiscus, flowers nearly white when they first open in the morning, deep red by night. *Hibiscus mutabilis* (R)

thalakamale: see thalakamala

thekara: possibly teak, Malayalam tekka, Tamil tekku, etc. (KB). *Tectona grandis* (R)

tila: see sāḍara

tiṇiśa: Dalbergia, Sanskrit syandana; a timber tree with numerous small blossoms of a pale rose color, nearly white, which blossoms in March–April. *Dalbergia Oojeinensis* (R)

ugare: horseradish tree, a small to middle sized tree cultivated throughout India, having corky bark and white flowers; flowers, leaves and seeds are edible. *Hyperanthera Moringa* (R), *Moringa oleifera* (KB)

utapala: waterlotus, an aquatic plant with leaves pale green on upper side and deep purple on lower; the flowers are azure, pale blue, or pale violet. *Nymphaea cyanea* (R), *Nymphaea stellata* (KB)

utapalā: see utapala

ūtapala: see utapala

utapale: see utapala

yāti: see cāmbhalī

yūthī: jasmine, produces small, white, sweet-smelling flowers. *Jasminum auriculatum* (R)

yūthikā: see yūthī

Bibliography

Apte, Vaman Shivram. *The Student's Sanskrit-English Dictionary*. Reprint. Delhi: Motilal Banarsidass, 1976.

Archer, W. G. *The Loves of Krishna in Indian Painting and Poetry*. London: Allen & Unwin, 1957.

Bandyopadhyay, Asit Kumar. *Bāṃlā sāhityera itibṛtta* [History of Bengali literature]. Vol. 1. 3d ed. Calcutta: Modern Book Agency, 1970– [in Bengali].

Bandyopadhyay, Brajendranath, and Das, Sajanikanta, eds. *Bhāratcandra-granthābalī*. 3d ed. Calcutta: Bangiya Sahitya Parisat, 1962 [in Bengali].

Bandyopadhyay, Haricaran. *Baṅgīya śabdakoṣa*. 2 vols. Delhi: Sahitya Akademi, 1978 [in Bengali].

Bandyopadhyay, Sekhar. "Caste and Politics in Eastern Bengal: The Namasudras and the Anti-Partition Agitation, 1905–1911." Occasional paper, Centre for Southeast Asian Studies. Calcutta: University of Calcutta, 1981.

Basak, Radhagovinda, ed. and trans. *The Prākrit Gāthā-Saptaśatī*. Calcutta: Asiatic Society, 1971.

Bhandarkar, Sir R. G. *Vaiṣṇavism Śaivism and Minor Religious Systems*. Benares: Indological Book House, 1965.

Bhattacarya, Amitrasudan. *Baṛu caṇḍīdāsera śrīkṛṣṇakīrtana*. 3d ed. Calcutta: Jijnasa, 1975 [in Bengali].

Biswas, Sailendra, and Sengupta, Subodhcandra. *Samsad Bengali-English Dictionary*. Calcutta: Sahitya Samsad, 1976.

Bose, D. N. *Harivaṃśa*. Pt. 1. Dum Dum, India: Datta Bose and Co., 1940–.

Bühler, G., ed. *The Laws of Manu*. The Sacred Books of the East, edited by Max Müller, vol. 25. Oxford: Clarendon Press, 1886.

Chatterji, Suniti Kumar. *The Origin and Development of the Bengali Language*. 3 vols. London: Allen & Unwin, 1970.

Clark, T. W. "Evolution of Hinduism in Medieval Bengali Literature: Śiva, Caṇḍī, Manasā." *Bulletin of the School of Oriental and African Studies*, University of London, 17 (1955), pt. 3, pp. 503–18.

Coomaraswamy, Ananda K. *History of Indian and Indonesian Art*. 1927. Reprint. Delhi: Munshiram Manoharlal, 1972.

Das, Jnanendra Mohan. *Bāṅgālābhāṣāra abhidāna* [Dictionary of the

Bengali language]. 2 vols. 2d ed. Calcutta: Indian Publishing House, 1937 [in Bengali]. Reprint. Calcutta: Sahitya Samsad, 1979.

Dasgupta, Sasibhusan. *Obscure Religious Cults*. 3d ed. Calcutta: Firma K. L. Mukhopadhyay, 1969.

———. *Śrīrādhāra kramabikāśa—darśane o sāhitye* [The evolution of Radha—in philosophy and history]. 4th ed. Calcutta: E. Mukherji, 1974 [in Bengali].

Dutt, Manmatha Nath. *A Prose English Translation of Harivamsha*. Calcutta: Elysium Press, 1897.

Eliade, Mircea. *Yoga: Immortality and Freedom*. Translated by Willard R. Trask. Bollingen Series, no. 56. Princeton: Princeton University Press, 3d Princeton/Bollingen Paperback printing, 1973.

Hart, George L. III. *The Poems of Ancient Tamil: Their Milieu and Their Sanskrit Counterparts*. Berkeley: University of California Press, 1975.

Jaiswal, Suvira. *The Origin and Development of Vaiṣṇavism*. Delhi: Munshiram Manoharlal, 1967.

Kirtikar, K. R., and Basu, B. D. *Indian Medicinal Plants*. 8 vols. Reprint, 2d ed. Dehra Dun: M/S Bishan Singh Mahendra Pal Singh and Delhi: M/S Periodical Experts, 1975.

Macdonell, Arthur. *Vedic Mythology*. Reprint. Delhi: Motilal Banarsidass, 1974.

Majumdar, Bimanbehari. *Kṛṣṇa in History and Legend*. Calcutta: University of Calcutta, 1969.

Mani, Vettam, *Purāṇic Encyclopaedia*. 1st English ed. Delhi: Motilal Banarsidass, 1975.

Miller, Barbara Stoler, ed. and trans. *Jayadeva's* Gītagovinda: *Love Song of the Dark Lord*. NY: Columbia University Press, 1977, and Delhi: Oxford University Press, 1978.

Monier-Williams, Sir Monier. *A Sanskṛit-English Dictionary*. Reprint. Delhi: Motilal Banarsidass, 1976.

Mukherji, Tarapada. *Śrīkṛṣṇakīrtana*. Calcutta: Mitra o Ghos, 1971 [in Bengali].

———. "Śrīkṛṣṇakīrtanera bṛkkhanāmera tālikā" [Glossary of plant names in *Śrīkṛṣṇakīrtana*]. *Visvabharati Patrika* 29 (1976), no. 1, pp. 20–32 [in Bengali].

Pargiter, F. Eden, trans. *The Mārkaṇḍeya Purāṇa*. 1904. Reprint. Delhi: Indological Book House, 1969.

Randhawa, M. S. *Kangra Paintings on Love*. Delhi: National Museum, 1962.

———. *Kangra Rāgamālā Paintings*. Delhi: National Museum, 1971.

Ray, Basanta Ranjan, ed. *Śrīkṛṣṇakīrtana*. 2d ed. Calcutta: Bangiya Sahitya Parisat, 1935 [in Bengali].

__________, ed. *Śrīkṛṣṇakīrtana*. 9th ed. Calcutta: Bangiya Sahitya Parisat, 1973 [in Bengali].

Roxburgh, William. *Flora Indica; or, Descriptions of Indian Plants*. 3 vols. Calcutta: W. Thacker & Co., and London: Parbury, Allen & Co., 1832.

__________. *Flora Indica; or, Descriptions of Indian Plants*. Revised ed. in one vol. Delhi: Today and Tomorrow's Printers and Publishers, 1971.

Roy, Manisha. *Bengali Women*. Chicago: University of Chicago Press, 1975.

Sarkar, Sudhirendra. *Paurāṇic abhidāna*. 2d ed. Calcutta: M. C. Sarkar & Sons, 1963 [in Bengali].

Sen, Nilratan, ed. *Caryāgītikoṣa*. Simla: Indian Institute of Advanced Study, 1977.

Sen, Sukumar. "Śrīkṛṣṇakīrttanera byākaraṇa" [The grammar of *Śrīkṛṣṇakīrtana*]. *Sahitya Parisat Patrika* 2 (1935): 123–47 [in Bengali].

__________. *Bipradāsera manasā-bijaya*. Calcutta: Asiatic Society, 1953.

__________. *An Etymological Dictionary of Bengali: c. 1000–1800* A.D. 2 vols. Calcutta: Eastern Publishers, 1971.

__________. *Chandidas*. Delhi: Sahitya Akademi, 1971a.

__________. *Bāṅgālā sāhityera itihāsa*. Vol. 1, pt. 1. 6th ed. Calcutta: Eastern Publishers, 1978 [in Bengali].

__________. *Women's Dialect in Bengali*. Calcutta: Jijnasa, 1979.

Siegel, Lee. *Sacred and Profane Dimensions of Love in Indian Traditions as Exemplified in the* Gītagovinda *of Jayadeva*. London: Oxford University Press, 1978.

Tagare, Ganesh Vasudeo, trans. *The Bhāgavata Purāṇa*. Pt. 4 (10th skandha). Ancient Indian Tradition & Mythology Series, vol. 10. Delhi: Motilal Banarsidass, 1978.

Turner, Sir Ralph. *A Comparative Dictionary of the Indo-Aryan Languages*. London: Oxford University Press, 1962–1966.

Usher, George. *A Dictionary of Plants Used by Man*. London: Constable, 1974.

Van Wijk, H. L. Gerth. *A Dictionary of Plant Names*. 2 vols. Amsterdam: A. Asher & Co., 1962.

Wilson, H. H., trans. *The Vishṇu Purāṇa: A System of Hindu Mythology and Tradition*. 3d ed. Calcutta: Punthi Pustak, 1972.